Environmental
Protest and
Citizen Politics
in Japan

Published under the auspices of
The Center for Japanese Studies
University of California, Berkeley

Environmental Protest and Citizen Politics in Japan

Margaret A. McKean

University of California Press

Berkeley · Los Angeles · London

University of California Press
Berkeley and Los Angeles, California
University of California Press, Ltd.
London, England
© 1981 by
The Regents of the University of California
Printed in the United States of America

1 2 3 4 5 6 7 8 9

Library of Congress Cataloging in Publication Data

McKean, Margaret A
    Environmental protest and citizen politics in Japan.

    Bibliography: p.
    Includes index.
    1. Environmental policy—Japan—Citizen participation.   I. Title.
HC465.E5M3   363.7'0523'0951   80-12991
ISBN 0-520-04115-1

To my husband and parents
and to J.V., in memory

Contents

Tables and Figures

Figure

Abbreviations

Political Parties

Clean Government Party	CGP
Democratic Socialist Party	DSP
Japan Communist Party	JCP
Japan Socialist Party	JSP
Liberal Democratic Party	LDP
New Liberal Club	NLC
Socialist Citizens' League (later the Social Democratic League)	SCL
United Progressive Liberals	UPL

Government Agencies

Legal Training and Research Institute	LTRI
Ministry of Health and Welfare	MHW
Ministry of International Trade and Industry	MITI
Ministry of Finance	MOF
Tokyo Metropolitan Assembly	TMA
Tokyo Metropolitan Government	TMG

Periodicals

Asahi Shimbun	AS
Japan Times	JT
Japan Times Weekly	JTW

Miscellaneous

Nitrogen oxides	NOx
Organization for Economic Cooperation and Development	OECD
Polybrominated biphenyl	PBB
Polychlorinated biphenyl	PCB
Polluter Pays Principle	PPP
Subacute-myelo-optico-neuropathy	SMON
Sulfur oxides	SOx

Japanese names are presented in Japanese order (surname first) except in footnotes that refer to Japanese authors of publications in English.

Preface

WHEN I BEGAN this work in 1972 I had no idea of the size of citizens' movements (the clearest evidence that they encompassed millions rather than thousands would only come in later) or of the fact that citizens' movements would grow rather than fade in significance in the eyes of scholars and politicians. In fact, I undertook the research solely because of my interest in political behavior and participation, believing that citizens' movements would be an enlightening focal point for the study of communal modes of participation, but doubting very much the enthusiastic claims of journalists and scholar-activists that they were different in nature or consequence from other organizations. I expected to learn quickly that citizens' movements resembled either other protest groups of the late 1960s or leader-dominated organizations in which individual commitments are to the group itself rather than to a political objective (such as neighborhood organizations and many candidate support groups). It did not occur to me then that citizens' movements might turn out to be something quite new, which combined the traits of protest groups and more conventional community organizations. Similarly, although I already knew that many citizens' movements were successful in achieving their immediate goals, I did not expect to find political socialization occurring to any significant degree, nor did I anticipate any impact on politics beyond the substance of the dispute that was resolved in each instance.

Not only did citizens' movements defy my prejudices and expectations, but in retrospect 1972 turns out to have been an ideal time to conduct the empirical survey on which much of the ensuing study is based. Citizens' movements proliferated rapidly from 1970 until the oil crisis of 1973–1974 (they resumed again after recovery from the 1974–1975 recession), and the 1972 survey was able to tap the phenomenon at what was probably its richest and most varied. The year 1972 was also early enough in the evolution of citizens' movements so that the survey helps us to understand the emergence of the phenomenon itself. A similar survey a few years later could have yielded equally valid information about individual activists, but these more recent participants may only be going along with what has already become a well-established trend, and they are certainly not creating a new social movement in the face of great resistance anymore. The motives and beliefs of these recent activists would be unlikely to explain why citizens' movements evolved as a vehicle of participation in the first place.

Enough time has passed since 1972 to permit us to observe the political accomplishments of the citizens' movements surveyed here and to temper our evaluation of what citizens' movements have and (more important) have not done to alter the nature of conflict and political processes in Japan. For example, in 1972 one might reasonably have interpreted citizens' movements as a force contributing to the end of rule by the Liberal Democratic Party, but conservative resilience shown in elections since then up through 1980 requires a different and more modest interpretation of the significance of citizens' movements for electoral change. Wherever possible the manuscript is current through March 1980 though I have undoubtedly missed relevant material that would have crossed my path had I been in Japan during the writing.

I owe debts of gratitude to those who encouraged me in the pursuit of Japanese politics: to Hans Baerwald who introduced me to the world of Japanese politics, to Jack Citrin who sparked my interest in political behavior and socialization, to Herbert McClosky under whom I studied attitude and belief change, to Robert Bellah who interested me in social and cultural change in Japan, and to Robert Scalapino who supervised the dissertation research from which this book evolved. Ide Yoshinori, Masumi Junnosuke, and Tanaka Yasumasa provided invaluable help with the research design and the construction of the questionnaire. Nishihira Shigeki, Nagai Yōnosuke, and Takane Masa'aki extended their friendship and offered helpful advice throughout the period of research. Chikushi Tatehiko, Tanaka Ki, Kihara Keikichi, Matsui Yayori, Nomura Katsuko, and Okuzawa Kikue very kindly gave me access to a wealth of information about citizens' movements and made connections for me with the groups interviewed. The respondents and other informants in the study, who must remain anonymous, freely gave of their time to share their experiences; I am very grateful for their enthusiastic cooperation. Machiko Tadokoro Hollifield, Rick Johnson, and Brenda Kurz provided cheerful and thorough research assistance.

A long list of colleagues have read portions of the work, provided helpful comments and criticisms along the way, or acted as sounding boards: Gary Allinson, John Campbell, Harold Clarke, Cynthia Enloe, Peter Fish, Miles Fletcher, Jerry Hough, Allan Kornberg, Ellis Krauss, Jack Lewis, Terry MacDougall, Bill Mishler, Muramatsu Michio, T. J. Pempel, Susan Pharr, Kathleen Price, Michael Reich, Ron Rogowski, Marianne Stewart, Ken Stunkel, Arturo Valenzuela, and Jim White deserve special mention. Naturally, I take all responsibility for interpretations or errors. Finally, Meri-li Douglas, Cathy Eason, and Patsy McFarland devoted tedious hours to turning the manuscript into neatly typed copy.

I also owe very special thanks to the family of Mimori Shigeyoshi for having accepted me as a family member and given me the emotional comforts of a home, in addition to an immense amount of practical advice, while I conducted my research in Japan. My parents, Anne and Roland McKean, provided warm support and encouragement during the toughest of times. Finally, my husband, John Peraza, endured with me all the travails involved in producing this work, including the two years I had to spend without him, and supplied the incentive, coaxing, and sense of discipline (not to mention the submarine sandwiches and soda pop late at night) which I needed to complete it.

Musashino, Tokyo
March 1980

These protest groups are created on the spur of the moment without developing concrete goals or principles, and they have incompetent leaders. . . . Japanese join them without serious concern for any objectives, primarily out of social pressure or out of the desire to appear to be part of the leftist intelligentsia. . . . There is really no need to take these leftist-sponsored protests very seriously.

Special Committee on Pollution Countermeasures, Policy Affairs Research Council, Liberal Democratic Party. Interview, October 6, 1972

Citizens' movements . . . represent a new political trend that seeks genuine popular sovereignty and democracy, with full citizen participation in government. . . . We are seeing the onset of a genuine "citizen revolution [*shimin kakumei*]," a revolution marked by a steady deepening of political maturity rather than by any dramatic upheaval.

Matsushita Keiichi, "Politics of Citizen Participation," *Japan Interpreter* 9:4 (Spring 1975), 451–464, originally published in *Shimin Sanka* (Tokyo: Tōyō Keizai Shimpōsha, 1971)

i

Participation and Environmental Protest

PEOPLE AROUND the world realize that Japan has serious pollution problems because the mercury scare originating there affected lives elsewhere: the United States government began to monitor mercury content in swordfish and actually recalled canned tuna from grocery shelves for fear of mercury contamination. Paradoxically, what is much less well known outside of Japan but far more important is that pollution stimulated a tremendous wave of political protest, almost certainly the largest and most significant social movement in Japan's modern history. These "citizens' movements" against environmental pollution were discredited at first by the institutions they criticized—industry and the ruling conservative Liberal Democratic Party (LDP). But sympathetic observers hailed them as much more than environmental protests: as both cause and manifestation of a new interest in political participation, citizen consciousness, and enhanced local autonomy; as forces that could convert political parties and government bureaucracies into responsive institutions; and therefore as the foundation for an indigenous democratic revolution.[1]

The wave of participation embodied in citizens' movements merits investigation for its own sake:

1. References to specific items in the literature on citizens' movements are given in footnotes where necessary; for a comprehensive list of general works on citizens' movements, see the Bibliographic Note.

History, it seems, is a winding tale of frustration for all but a few members of the human race. Records of the past indicate that in most times and places the ordinary human being has been dominated by traditions and elites. The inclination for self-determination has been largely stymied. And especially in public affairs: that is, those matters that go beyond individuals and families to affect many members of a community. Consequently, an outbreak of participation in any age becomes a significant event.[2]

But beyond this there are compelling reasons to monitor citizen participation in Japan, which today still serves as a living experiment in the transplantation of democratic institutions to an apparently hostile environment. Because the 1947 Constitution and other legal reforms that accompanied it were imposed on the Japanese through military occupation after World War II, rather than being the product of the people's own demand for a role in decision-making, we cannot assume that political attitudes supportive of democratic institutions were already widespread within the population. Since 1945, scholars and others have nervously awaited definitive evidence as to whether democratic political norms and attitudes would take root in the population or whether the Japanese would continue to opt for democratic institutions or eventually revise them in the direction of a return to the authoritarianism and enforced conformity of the past.[3]

One view holds that Japan's political heritage was far more likely to produce authoritarian forms than democratic ones, and that the Popular Rights movement of the late nineteenth century and the relative liberalization of "Taishō Democracy" during the interwar years were easily

2. James V. Cunningham, "Citizen Participation in Public Affairs," *Public Administration Review* 32 (special issue, October 1972), 589.

3. For general studies of political opinion in postwar Japan, see Bradley Richardson, *The Political Culture of Japan* (Berkeley and Los Angeles: University of California Press, 1974); and Jōji Watanuki, *Politics in Postwar Japanese Society* (Tokyo: University of Tokyo Press, 1977). In Japanese see Tōkei sūri kenkyūjo [Institute of Statistical Mathematics], *Kokuminsei no kenkyū* [A Study of Japanese National Character] (Tokyo: Taiseidō, 1961); Nishihira Shigeki, *Nihonjin no iken* [The Opinions of the Japanese] (Tokyo: Seishin Shobō, 1963); Hayashi Chikio et al., for Tōkei sūri kenkyūjo, *Nihonjin no kokuminsei* [The National Character of the Japanese] (Tokyo: Shiseidō, 1965); and also the two sequels to the last volume, *Daini Nihonjin no kokuminsei* (Tokyo: Shiseidō, 1970), and *Daisan Nihonjin no kokuminsei* (Tokyo: Shiseidō, 1975). See also Kyōgoku Jun'ichi, *Seiji ishiki no bunseki* [The Analysis of Political Consciousness] (Tokyo: University of Tokyo Press, 1968); Ishida Takeshi, *Nihon no seiji bunka: dōchō to kyōsō* [The Political Culture of Japan: Conformity and Competition] (Tokyo: University of Tokyo Press, 1970); Ikeuchi Hajime, ed., *Shimin ishiki no kenkyū* [A Study of Citizen Consciousness] (Tokyo: Tōkyō Daigaku Shuppankai, 1974). A comprehensive bibliography of work by Japanese scholars on Japanese political behavior is now available in Scott C. Flanagan and Bradley M. Richardson, *Mass Political Behavior Research in Japan: A Report on the State of the Field and Bibliography* (New York: Social Science Research Council, July 1979).

overcome by these traditions.[4] Although the specialists' appreciation of Japanese modernization, prewar democracy, and militarism has undergone considerable revision owing to new scholarship since Barrington Moore produced his mammoth study of dictatorship and democracy, Moore's neo-Marxist classification of Japan as a conservative (fascist) modernizer is still widely accepted.[5] Moore based his analysis of the Japanese case on prewar developments to the exclusion of any consideration of the postwar period, presumably because he regarded defeat and occupation as external interventions which took Japanese society away from its "natural" course.

In contrast, perhaps the most charitable view of the democratic potential in Japan's past is that of Edwin Reischauer, who argues that the experience of war and defeat "would in any case have forced Japan to move in the directions it took during the occupation," in political, social, and economic terms, and suggests that the occupation reforms were well received because of this natural coincidence between external forces and internal impulses.[6] Reischauer notes that on graphs of many quantitative indicators over time, the war period appears as a temporary departure from a steady continuous trend uniting prewar with postwar eras, rather than as a force that permanently deflected the indicator from its original trajectory. Unfortunately, these provocative observations cannot yield definitive evidence, and we shall never be able to control for the effect of occupation reforms in order to gauge what Japan's political evolution might have looked like in other circumstances.

4. For works examining the strengths and weaknesses of the democratic party movement, see Robert A. Scalapino, *Democracy and the Party Movement in Japan: The Failure of the First Attempt* (Berkeley and Los Angeles: University of California Press, 1953, 1968); George O. Totten, III, *The Social Democratic Movement in Prewar Japan* (New Haven: Yale University Press, 1966); Peter Duus, *Party Rivalry and Political Change in Taishō Japan* (Cambridge: Harvard University Press, 1968); and Gordon M. Berger, *Parties out of Power in Japan, 1931–1941* (Princeton: Princeton University Press, 1977).

5. Barrington Moore, Jr., *Social Origins of Dictatorship and Democracy* (Boston: Beacon Press, 1966), pp. 228–313, 413–452. Recent research, far too voluminous to cite here, challenging Moore's argument would indicate that the samurai who conducted the Meiji Restoration may have possessed a coherent revolutionary ideology, that the samurai should be regarded as salaried bureaucrats rather than landed aristocrats in any class analysis of the Tokugawa and Meiji periods, that rich peasants favored economic modernization, that tenant militancy and tenancy disputes increased steadily during the prewar period until a peak in 1935–1937, that it was the vitality rather than the weakness of prewar parliamentarism which stimulated an antidemocratic response, that the *zaibatsu* opposed militarism during the 1930s and finally succumbed under protest to the militarists' demands for economic mobilization for war, that the peasantry and important segments of the intelligentsia were sources rather than victims of militaristic extremism, and finally that wartime Japan simply was not fascist.

6. Edwin O. Reischauer, *The Japanese* (Cambridge: Harvard University Press, 1978), p. 109.

However, the rise of citizens' movements can provide crucial evidence on this question. If this expansion of participation proves to be a spontaneous result of demands from below, without artificial manipulation by external forces, then we can no longer think of Japan as an intrinsically authoritarian or antidemocratic society, and research on modernization and development will have to consider Japan's present as well as its past. Similarly, comparative research and democratic theory will have to accommodate this unique reversal of evolutionary sequence in which change in political culture follows, rather than causes, institutional change. Obviously, then, its unusual political history makes Japan a particularly important *site* for the study of participation.

In addition, citizens' movements are a particularly important *form* of participation to study because research on the subject—in all countries—is conventionally confined to the study either of attitudes (rather than behavior) or of voting (the one behavior most easily studied). The prevailing assumption that participation was a unidimensional phenomenon for which voting and attitudes were convenient and adequate measures disturbed Verba, Nie, and Kim when they began their cross-national studies (including Japan) in 1966.[7] They discovered that among democracies with competitive party systems participation falls into four distinct "modes"—voting, campaigning, communal activity, and particularized contacting—each involving different participants, different recruitment processes, and different implications for the results achieved and the long-term distribution of power in society. Therefore, voting and attitudes are not suitable surrogates for the other modes of participation.

Indeed, the most seriously neglected form of participation—communal activity, defined as collective action by groups of citizens and citizen-initiated contacts with public officials to obtain a collective benefit—may, along with election campaign activity, be the most important in ensuring that a polity is democratic. After all, attitudes are no guarantee of behavior, and voting occurs (by compulsion) in totalitarian countries. Even where voting involves a choice among several options, it requires decidedly little initiative and communicates almost nothing to governments about the preferences of the governed. Communal activity

7. Sidney Verba, Norman H. Nie, and Jae-on Kim, *The Modes of Democratic Participation: A Cross-National Comparison* (Beverly Hills: Sage, 1971); Verba, Nie, et al., "The Modes of Participation: Continuities in Research," *Comparative Political Studies* 6:2 (July 1973), 235–250; Nie, Verba, and Kim, "Political Participation and the Life Cycle," *Comparative Politics* 6:3 (April 1974), 319–340; and Verba, Nie, and Kim, *Participation and Political Equality: A Seven-Nation Comparison* (Cambridge: At The University Press, 1978). Preliminary but detailed analysis of the Japanese survey is available in Ikeuchi Hajime, ed., *Shimin ishiki no kenkyū* [Research on Citizen Consciousness] (Tokyo: Tōkyō Daigaku Shuppankai, 1974).

that takes place between elections probably does much more than the other modes to transmit popular concerns to officials, thus to influence rather than merely support politicians, and also to compensate for the otherwise great access to government which professional lobbyists hired by "special interests" have. Because they fall into this long-neglected category of communal activity, citizens' movements clearly deserve close attention.

What follows is an attempt to resolve this question by providing a comprehensive assessment of citizens' antipollution movements in Japan, with emphasis on the formative period in the early 1970s, when the rapid proliferation of citizens' movements contributed most conspicuously to the expansion of political participation. The investigation must deal with both environmental pollution and citizen participation because these are inextricably interwoven in the Japanese context: environmental protest occurs entirely through the vehicle of citizens' movements, and almost all citizens' movements are concerned with some sort of environmental issue. Nonetheless, the primary concern will be to evaluate the significance of citizens' movements as a new avenue of citizen participation and as a new political force in Japan.

The inquiry will be built around two sequential questions. First, why did citizens' movements arise (or what caused citizens' movements)? Are they a result of the same forces that have been found to stimulate participation elsewhere? Or, as protests, do they bear similarities to the wave of protests that rocked most of the other democracies in the late 1960s and early 1970s? Why did pollution rather than some other issue become the central concern of most citizens' movements? Has this preoccupation with environmental problems affected the nature or function of citizens' movements? Who are the participants? Can their characteristics or motives tell us why they abandoned existing patterns and channels of participation and instead chose to marshal their energies to create this "new" form, the citizens' movement, to resolve their grievances?

Second, once they exist, what effect do citizens' movements have on Japanese politics (what do citizens' movements cause)? Do they succeed in their objectives? What socialization effects do they have on their own members? How do they affect the communities where they emerge? Have citizens' movements had any influence on electoral politics since their heyday? Can we discern any long-term effects of citizens' movements on patterns of participation, the articulation of demands, or the resolution of conflicting demands by policy makers? If citizens' movements complicate the decision-making process by increasing the number of participants in it, do they also polarize—or paralyze—Japanese politics?

A Definition of Citizens' Movements

Before we can begin to study citizens' movements, we must develop a working definition that distinguishes them from similar phenomena. First there is the question of terminology. The Japanese refer to any protest movement consisting of residents of a particular locality "residents' movements" (*jūmin undō*), but sometimes reserve the term "citizens' movements" (*shimin undō*) for the most experienced groups, those which use the most sophisticated political tools and which become principally concerned with the issue of citizen participation. For the sake of uniformity the latter term will be used except in literal translations from the Japanese.

According to the flood of accounts published in the early 1970s, citizens' movements differ from earlier political movements and interest groups in both the prewar and postwar periods in their recruitment patterns, internal structure, relations with other groups, tactics, and (most important) in the fact that in addition to the goal of eliminating pollution, they often become concerned with the larger question of citizens' rights to participate in decisions.

Sociological and anthropological studies invariably comment on the great extent to which Japanese carry out their activities within the context of a group, both in traditional society and in contemporary Japan.[8] However, interest-group activity in politics was traditionally intended only to procure particular benefits for the group concerned and did not evolve into successful efforts to increase popular participation in decision-making. Generally speaking, ordinary citizens did not become involved in politics on their own initiative. Ishida Takeshi, Japan's foremost specialist on interest groups and associational activity, argues that truly voluntary associations were simply not part of the Japanese tradition and are very rarely seen.[9]

Although prewar groups interested in widening political participation—those aimed at organizing labor unions, universal manhood suffrage, equality for Japan's outcaste community, and the like—did achieve some success, these reform movements were always weak. In spite of the postwar proliferation of small societies committed to political programs, and the eruption of groups of all varieties in Japan, most restricted their attention to issues left over from World War II and the Allied occupation, and neglected the question of political participation itself. Because these issues involve Japan's position vis-à-vis other nations (or vis-à-vis symbols of foreign domination left behind after the occupation), they could

8. See Chie Nakane, *Japanese Society* (Berkeley and Los Angeles: University of California Press, 1970); Takeshi Ishida, *Japanese Society* (New York: Random House, 1971), pp. 37–39; and Reischauer, *The Japanese*, pp. 123-233.

9. Ishida, *Japanese Society*, pp. 61–64.

all be viewed in terms of national pride. We cannot legitimately conclude that these postwar disputes provoked many people into thinking about the fundamental issues of political opposition or citizen participation. Furthermore, prewar and postwar protests were both the province of "regular" activists among intellectuals, the labor movement, the political left, and students.[10] Only the 1960 controversy over the Security Treaty appeared to mobilize more ordinary citizens than usual, or touched on the question of parliamentary democracy.[11]

Ishida considers Beheiren (the League for Peace in Vietnam), which emerged in the late 1960s, to be the most important forerunner of today's citizens' movements. Although it was concerned about foreign policy and its participants were motivated by nationalism (hostility to the American use of Japanese bases for the prosecution of the war, and fear that Japan's cooperation with the war effort might endanger Japanese security), Beheiren was structurally similar to the citizens' movements of the 1970s.[12] It had no official leaders, no official structure, and no formal members. Any group could call itself Beheiren, and at least 250 such separate groups eventually formed, attracting many ordinary citizens beyond the usual population of students and labor union activists. Although considered a leftist movement because of its opposition to militarism and the American war effort, Beheiren's spokesmen stressed the importance of individual spontaneity in participation and tried to keep the antiwar issue itself, not any ideology, paramount.[13] The fundamental difference between Beheiren and the much larger number of citizens' movements later is that the latter are concerned not with a foreign policy issue but with local problems affecting the daily existence of ordinary citizens.

Finally, another trait that causes great excitement in Japan is the size of citizens' movements as a whole, which have mobilized such large numbers of ordinarily apolitical Japanese. Using figures from a combination of sources it is possible to estimate that at any given moment from 60,000 to 135,000 adults are intimately involved in the core of these movements, and that up to 6 million more participate on the periphery as rank-and-file members of citizens' movements. Although we can derive approximate figures only by rather crude methods, it is also fair

10. Herbert Passin, "The Sources of Protest in Japan," *American Political Science Review* 61:2 (June 1962), 391–403.

11. George Packard, *Protest in Tokyo: The Security Treaty Crisis of 1960* (Princeton: Princeton University Press, 1966), especially pp. 105–122 on popular mobilization.

12. Takeshi Ishida, "Emerging or Eclipsing Citizenship? A Study of Changes in Political Attitudes in Postwar Japan," *Developing Economies* 6:4 (December 1968), 420.

13. Yoshiyuki Tsurumi, "Beheiren," *Japan Quarterly* 16:4 (October–December 1964), 444–448; Makoto Oda, "Making Democracy Our Own," *Japan Interpreter* 6:3 (Autumn 1970), 234–254.

to assume that as individual movements come and go, the number of people who have been involved in citizens' movements is increasing all the time.[14]

This brief and necessarily simplified description permits us to construct an operational definition of citizens' movements according to three criteria and thus to distinguish between citizens' movements and more familiar forms of protest or of conventional interest-group activity.

Composition: Citizens' movements are grass-roots movements, independently organized by the members themselves (or founded by local opinion leaders acting in a private capacity), not by external forces and particularly not by established authority.

Style: Citizens' movements are engaged in protest over grievances against established authority, as distinguished from "cooperative" groups, often sponsored by neighborhood associations whose very raison d'être is to work with local government, and as distinguished from such things as politicians' local support groups (*kōenkai*).

Goals: Citizens' movements are concerned about a local problem (such as pollution) that affects the livelihood or well-being of ordinary people, as opposed, for example, to foreign policy issues.

Obviously, arriving at a well-rounded understanding of a phenomenon so diffuse and unstructured poses special difficulties. Even though citizens' movements taken collectively make up a huge social movement that is recognized by observers of the Japanese scene as having considerable longevity as an abstract political force, each individual movement exists for only a brief period, during which it keeps no register of members and is only informally organized. Coalitions are only as stable as their components, and therefore change in character along with the movements composing them. It is impossible to revive citizens' movements that have dissolved, and very difficult even to identify a large num-

14. On May 21, 1973, *Asahi Shimbun* reported that citizens' movements had proliferated all over Japan and already numbered at least 3,000. According to conservative estimates made in articles drawing on this Asahi data, the average group has about 20 to 30 core members and perhaps 300 to 500 rank-and-file members. This would permit us to conclude that at any particular moment there are from 60,000 to 90,000 active adults and from 900,000 to 1,500,000 rank-and-file participants in citizens' movements. An earlier but equally detailed survey of movements conducted in November 1970 indicated that the average group, excluding coalitions, contained 45 core members and 2,000 rank-and-file participants. These figures would lead us to the even more generous conclusion that about 135,000 adults had already been very active in citizens' movements by 1973, along with 6 million more peripheral participants. Articles using the Asahi data are "Citizens' Movements," *Japan Quarterly* 20:4 (October–December 1973), 368–373; and Nakamura Kiichi, "Jūmin undō no soshiki to kōzō" [The Organization and Structure of Residents' Movements], *Chiiki kaihatsu* 154 (July 1977), 22–32. The November 1970 survey is reported in "Zenkoku no shimin undō" [Citizens' Movements Across the Nation], *Shimin* 1 (March 1971), supplement 1–82.

ber of the citizens' movements functioning at any moment in order to subject a representative assortment of them to careful scrutiny.

The same physical obstacles similarly constrain the study of important social movements elsewhere, movements that are also based on countless individual groups—voluntary associations of all types, neighborhood organizations, environmental protest, and so on. Even where research funds are readily available, it is a formidable task (very nearly impossible in a larger and more decentralized country like the United States) to hold such amorphous phenomena still in order to delineate their general contours, let alone to survey individual participants.[15] Understandably, these constraints have limited serious scholarly work on Japanese citizens' movements largely to case studies of a single movement at a time and thus have impeded the processes of learning about individual participants or developing firm generalizations about citizens' movements as a whole.

The bulk of the early writing on citizens' movements consists of testimonials by a self-selected subset of articulate activists recounting their own experiences, case studies of well-known movements written by journalists and free-lance writers, and abstruse theoretical writings by scholar-publicists whose purpose seems to be to build morale and to create a favorable climate for citizens' movements. As a result, the literature, though voluminous, consists largely of subjective description and speculative analysis and prediction. The authors of these works were not objective observers using a carefully constructed research design with built-in safeguards to compensate for bias. There is still only a small, though growing, body of scholarly analysis intended first and foremost to analyze the political implications of citizens' movements and thereby to enlarge our understanding of political behavior, voluntary associations, interest-group activity, and the nature of informal political processes in Japan.

It is my purpose here to add to our broader knowledge of citizens'

15. As a result, the only attempt to study individuals in a variety of American voluntary associations is Murray Hausknecht, *The Joiners: A Sociological Description of Voluntary Association Membership in the United States* (New York: Bedminster Press, 1962). Work on citizen participation through environmental protest in America is also limited to the case study approach. See William Burch, Jr., Neil H. Cheek, Jr., and Lee Taylor, eds., *Social Behavior, Natural Resources, and the Environment* (New York: Harper and Row, 1972); Lynton K. Caldwell, Lynton R. Hayes, and Isabel M. MacWhirter, *Citizens and the Environment: Case Studies in Popular Action* (Bloomington: Indiana University Press, 1976); Citizens' Advisory Committee on Environmental Quality (CACEQ), *Citizens Make a Difference: Case Studies of Environmental Action* (Washington, D.C.: Government Printing Office, 1973); CACEQ, *Community Action for Environmental Quality* (Washington, D.C.: Government Printing Office, 1970); Odom Fanning, *Man and His Environment: Citizen Action* (New York: Harper & Row, 1975). The literature on neighborhood organization is similarly composed of an accretion of case studies.

movements by going beyond the secondary literature and the single-case approach to assemble a comprehensive picture of citizens' movements, both their emergence and their consequences. Although the very real physical obstacles recounted above could not be wished away, the limited means at my disposal made it possible to ground the investigation in case studies of fourteen different movements, carefully selected to represent the full range of variety that would have been impossible to capture with a narrow focus on just one or two cases. In addition to analysis of each sample movement taken as a unit, this study draws upon intensive interviews with sixty-four participants in the fourteen movements and less formal interviews with other informants associated with each of the movements. The interviewing took place in the fall of 1972—during the formative period before citizens' movements were fully accepted as a legitimate or permanent political force by the institutions they challenged—and each movement has been followed as closely since then as newspaper coverage and personal correspondence allowed. (For a discussion of sampling procedures and statistical techniques used to analyze the interview data, see the Appendix.)

We shall proceed in the following sequence. The body of this chapter assesses the state of popular participation in Japan in the 1960s—the context out of which citizens' movements arose—and then provides an account of the prototype movements, the first wave of citizens' movements to earn the name. Chapter II analyzes the major pollution-disease lawsuits and their verdicts, which made a crucial contribution to the politicization of the pollution issue, to the proliferation of citizens' movements, and to citizens' increased use of the courts as a channel of participation. Chapter III recounts the case histories and achievements of each of the fourteen movements in the survey, along with discussions of pollution problems and policy outcomes where they are relevant to the understanding of a particular movement. Data from interviews with participants are used to analyze the mobilization and strategy of citizens' movements (in chapter IV), the attitudes and beliefs of environmental activists (in chapter V), and their partisanship and voting behavior (in chapter VI). The final section (chapter VII) incorporates our findings with recent research by others to compare Japanese citizens' movements with environmental protest and social movements elsewhere, and to evaluate their causes and significant consequences.

Mass Participation before Citizens' Movements

The first step in assessing citizens' movements as a form of participation is to understand the context from which they arose. The ample literature on voting and attitudes in Japan, along with the cross-national effort led by Verba, Nie, and Kim to examine the infrequently studied modes of participation, can be used to assemble a comprehensive picture of participation in the 1960s, consisting of five themes.[16]

• Community-based Participation

Researchers have long been troubled by Japan, where political participation followed unexpected patterns. Almost all theories of political and economic change stipulate that increased participation is likely to result from economic progress, industrialization, and urbanization. This "mobilization model" of participation predicts that as people migrate from the farm to the city they are simultaneously liberated from the authoritarian constraints of traditional rural society and politicized through intense exposure to new ideas, information, and educational opportunity in the cities. Participation supposedly increases as people are "mobilized" by their move from the periphery to the center.

However, in Japan participation is higher in the rural "periphery" than in urban centers. In the 1960s rural residents had higher rates of voting and affiliation with social organizations. Moreover, even though rural residents displayed lower rates of psychological involvement and political information about politics in general, with respect to *local* politics (which was of greater concern than national politics to Japanese people), rural residents were even more involved and informed than city dwellers. Rural voters also had relatively benign images of politicians, whereas urban voters measuring politicians against more idealistic standards came away with negative images of politicians. Thus Japanese

16. This discussion of mass behavior in the 1960s draws on Richardson, *Political Culture of Japan*; Watanuki, *Politics in Postwar Japanese Society*; Kyōgoku, *Seiji ishiki no bunseki*; and Ikeuchi, *Shimin ishiki no kenkyū*; as well as Naoki Komuro, "Social Change and Voting Behavior in Postwar Japan," *Developing Economies* 6:4 (December 1968), 510–533; Bradley Richardson, "Japanese Local Politics: Support Mobilization and Leadership Styles," *Asian Survey* 7:12 (December 1967), 860–875; Richardson, "Urbanization and Political Participation: The Case of Japan," *American Political Science Review* 67:2 (June 1973), 433–452; Richardson, "Party Loyalties and Party Saliency in Japan," *Comparative Political Studies* 8:1 (April 1975), 32–57; Richardson, "Stability and Change in Japanese Voting Behavior, 1958–1972," *Journal of Asian Studies* 36:4 (August 1977), 675–694; Scott C. Flanagan, "Voting Behavior in Japan: The Persistence of Traditional Patterns," *Comparative Political Studies* 1:3 (October 1968), 391–412; Flanagan and Richardson, *Japanese Electoral Behavior: Social Cleavages, Social Networks and Partisanship* (London: Sage, 1977); Akira Kubota, "Party Identification and Social Cleavage in Japan," paper presented at the annual meeting of the American Political Science Association, Chicago, 1974; Flanagan, "The Genesis of Variant Political Cultures: Contemporary Citizen Orientations in Japan, America, Britain, and Italy," in Sidney Verba and Lucian W. Pye, eds., *The Citizen and Politics: A Comparative Perspective* (Stamford, Conn.: Greylock Publishers, 1978), pp. 129–163; Flanagan, Value Change and Partisan Change in Japan: The Silent Revolution Revisited, *Comparative Politics* 12:1 (April 1979), 253–278; and Flanagan, "Value Cleavages, Economic Cleavages, and the Japanese Voter," *American Journal of Political Science* 24:2 (May 1980), 177–206.

rural voters were highly participant in spite of low interest, whereas urban voters were highly interested and concerned but relatively inactive, a
state labeled "inhibition" or even "alienation." Watanuki suggests as an
explanation that rural areas were simply not as "peripheral" as the mobilization model assumes, because of the early spread of mass education in
the nineteenth century, followed by the gradual extension of the suffrage
by a prewar government consciously trying to use rather than destroy the
traditional group structures of the village in the process.[17] In addition,
researchers argue that the survival of a strong sense of community in
rural Japan provided a stimulus to participation which was absent for
the lonely crowd in Japanese cities, an explanation known as the decline-
of-community model.

Ironically, Verba, Nie, and Kim learned from their cross-national
analysis of the various modes of participation that what was once considered the Japanese exception was in fact the rule elsewhere also: except
for psychological involvement, political participation by all other indicators and especially in the form of communal activity was higher in rural
populations than urban ones. Moreover, when levels of socioeconomic
resources were held constant to eliminate any "spurious" edge which the
wealthier, more educated urbanites might have, the gap grew. Although
the mobilization model may well be appropriate for predicting changes
in participation during early phases of nation-building or in the salience
to individuals of politics as an intellectual topic, it does not hold in well-
established systems. In Japan as in other democracies, the stability and
intimacy of a closely knit community was a more important basis of political participation than the cosmopolitan atmosphere of the big city.

· Apolitical Groupism

One feature of Japanese society on which there was universal agreement in the 1960s was the tremendous importance to the Japanese of be-
longing to a group. Cross-national evidence demonstrates that Japan was
indeed a nation of joiners (72% of the population had some sort of affiliation, more than in any other nation in the study by Verba, Nie, and
Kim). However, the majority of these groups were local organizations
based on workplace, neighborhood, or personal interests—agricultural
and fishing cooperatives, enterprise unions, merchants' associations,
neighborhood associations, hobby groups, and service clubs—rather
than political groups. The major political parties had no mass base, and
only 13 percent of the population belonged to political groups, less than
in any other nation studied except India. Although the survival of strong
communities in rural areas contributed to unusually high voting rates in

17. Watanuki, *Politics in Postwar Japanese Society*, pp. 74–76.

Japan, "groupism" as a whole was apolitical and produced only middling rates of communal activity and overall participation. What communal activity there was in Japan did require high psychological involvement in politics, but in contrast to communal activity elsewhere, it was not associated with strong partisan feeling. Additional research indicates that Japanese voters had very diffuse, undifferentiated images of the political parties, even of the party they supported, consisting of vague affect with almost no substantive content.[18]

• Dominance of Affiliation over Resources

Socioeconomic resources had the expected effect of raising political discussion and interest, but resources had almost no bearing on any kind of participatory behavior. Verba, Nie, and Kim concluded that participation in Japan was more egalitarian than in any other nation they studied. (Austria and the Netherlands came close to Japan, but the United States was quite inegalitarian.) They found that participation in Japan was dominated by institutional affiliations rather than resources, so that low-status persons were able to participate in politics if they were affiliated with some organization—a neighborhood group, a service club, an economic cooperative, not just political parties—whereas high-status persons without such affiliations were effectively "locked out" of the political process in spite of their resources. Lockout was particularly noticeable in communal participation because formal institutions dominated the scene in Japan, unlike the Netherlands where numerous informal citizen-action groups created additional avenues to communal participation. In effect, institutional affiliation served to compensate for inegalitarian distribution of resources to equalize participation in Japanese politics.

• Cohesion within Segments Rather Than Conflict between Segments

The Japanese political scene in the 1960s appeared on the surface to have its fair share of conflict. Student protest closed down major universities for a year in 1968–1969, and the 1960s saw several bitter confrontations over foreign policy issues between the majority party and the opposition (in ascending order of radicalism in official platforms, the Democratic Socialist Party, or DSP, the Clean Government Party, or CGP, the Japan Communist Party, or JCP, and the Japan Socialist Party, or JSP). But looking at individuals in the general population, Verba, Nie, and Kim, as well as Flanagan and Richardson, concluded that in comparative terms Japanese society was relatively free of both horizontal and

18. Richardson, "Party Loyalties and Party Saliency in Japan"; Kubota, "Party Identification and Social Cleavage in Japan."

vertical cleavages of the sort so important in the classical sociological paradigm used to explain political groupings in other societies. Japanese society was too homogeneous for any political party to appeal to a narrow ethnic division, and class identification was too weak for any party to succeed in appealing to particular economic strata, however radical the official platforms might have seemed. The DSP, JSP, and JCP all made explicit appeals to "the working class" and won their strongest support from labor unions, but apparently the factor important to their voters was affiliation with the union rather than identification with the working class. The only distinctive source of social cleavage reflected in political affiliation was the Clean Government Party (CGP), whose adherents were devout members of the Sōka Gakkai, a Buddhist sect. The strength of religious and partisan feeling among this 5–10 percent of the population only served to highlight the absence of similar intensity as a potential basis for conflict in the other 90–95 percent of the population. Despite the popularity of Marxist rhetoric and the party elites' predilection for casting issues in ideological terms, class and ideological conflict were not significant elements of mass belief systems. Watanuki and Flanagan both suggest that the only dimension of disagreement which resonated in the Japanese population was cultural—the conflict between "traditional" and "modern" (or "libertarian") values.[19] Thus the disputes that occupied political elites during the 1960s would appear to be either artifacts of these cultural conflicts or concerns limited to the party elites themselves.

Further, Flanagan and Richardson argue that political affiliation in Japan was based on social networks rather than on social cleavages, in that preexisting affiliation with an intimate face-to-face group (not with an abstraction like social class) was more significant than disagreement or conflict with some other group in determining an individual's political allegiance.[20] Thus the blue-collar worker who voted Socialist was expressing collegiality with co-workers in his own company, whose enterprise union happened to be distantly affiliated with the JSP, rather than identifying with blue-collar workers as a whole or viewing management as his class enemy. Similarly, the cohesion of Sōka Gakkai members behind the CGP was an expression of organizational strength rather than doctrinal cleavage. Though each network might be separated from the others, thus dividing Japanese society into separate, non-overlapping segments, cohesion outweighed conflict as the chief organizing dimension of political affiliation in Japan.

19. Watanuki, *Politics in Postwar Japanese Society*, pp. 92–98; Flanagan, "Value Cleavages, Economic Cleavages, and the Japanese Voter"; Flanagan, "Value Change and Partisan Change in Japan."
20. Flanagan, "Voting Behavior in Japan"; Flanagan and Richardson, *Japanese Electoral Behavior.*

• Passive Formalism

Richardson concluded from his study of attitude surveys conducted from 1958 to 1967 that political culture in Japan was as participant as that in most democracies (data from Verba, Nie, and Kim confirm this conclusion), but that the quality of this participation was passive and formalist. Most Japanese were willing to rely on their political leaders and the vote (formal channels) for results; only a tiny minority saw any need for more energetic forms of participation, and those who did considered such activity more appropriate in the local than the national political arena. Japanese had a keen sense of citizen duty but less of a sense that they possessed the right to initiate, influence, or demand. Flanagan, using Almond and Verba's scheme of citizen orientations and political culture types, described Japan in the 1960s as a spectator culture because of the prevalence of passive "parochials" and especially deferent "subjects" as opposed to active "participants" in the Japanese public. Richardson attributed this passive orientation to the disparity "between learned and experiential components of political attitudes" and argued that Japan in the 1960s still possessed considerable carry-over from the prewar period of a "subject" political culture (widespread attitudes of dependency and deference), causing a greater gap between high political involvement learned as an ideal and low concrete experience with activism than is the case in most other democracies.[21] In essence, most Japanese had learned democratic norms as ideals but had not yet internalized these norms through personal experience.

Thus in the 1960s Japan had relatively high participation when citizen duty or commitments to group and community functioned as important stimuli to action, but rather low participation of the sort where citizen initiative or the wish to influence decisions was required. Japan's cultural heritage—a carry-over from the "subject" culture of the past—discouraged the open expression of conflict and resistance to authority. The contradiction between these "traditional" values and more "modern" ones provided a potential for conflict which surfaced occasionally during the decade, but most political disputes concerned ideological questions that mattered only to the elites involved. Otherwise there were no issues of great importance around which conflict might emerge. Economic issues were simply not fertile ground for political mobilization or conflict. As a whole, the Japanese people felt themselves to be quite prosperous, and patterns of institutional affiliation neutralized inequalities in the distribution of socioeconomic resources as a basis for participation. Even the status differences so important in personal relationships provided no basis for political organization or conflict. Japanese partici-

21. Flanagan, "The Genesis of Variant Political Cultures"; Richardson, *The Political Culture of Japan*, pp. 91–101, 230–231.

pated in politics out of a sense of duty to citizenship, group, and local community, rather than out of any embittered sense of hostility or competition with other groups. As a result, partisan feelings were low in intensity, and politics itself was not a particularly salient aspect of life for the Japanese. Finding their involvement in segmented apolitical groups satisfactory for their needs, and having no pressing reasons to become involved in the more demanding forms of political participation, Japanese people had not acquired concrete experience in political activism to accompany their abstract learning of participatory norms, so their orientation to politics remained passive.

Then, in the late 1960s, citizens' movements somehow arose out of this setting. They blended into it in some ways: they had a strong foundation in local communities as grass-roots organizations, they were concerned principally with local issues, and they were yet another *group* vehicle of participation. But citizens' movements contrasted with the 1960s setting in other ways. They were, first and foremost, the communal type of participation which researchers found mysteriously lacking in Japan up to the late 1960s. Formal institutions had monopolized what communal activity had existed, but citizens' movements were an informal channel (resembling action groups in the Netherlands). Citizens' movements required far more energy, initiative, and aggressive consciousness of citizens' rights (as opposed to duties) than the average complacent passive citizen had displayed thus far. Second, they were involved in conflicts that existing political patterns and organizations could not resolve, and thus added a conflictual aspect to the otherwise segmented but cohesive nature of organization in Japanese politics. The traits of Japanese participation just mentioned suggest questions we might ask in trying to understand how citizens' movements came into being and how they changed the nature of political participation in Japan.

Given the importance of a sense of community in participation, what is the relationship between citizens' movements and the local community? Most earlier protests consisted of one national organization centered in big cities where there existed a visible core of perennial opposition activists, but these protests never spread into Japan's less industrialized, more conservative and traditional areas. What is the significance of the emergence of citizens' movements in local areas all over Japan in the complete absence of any central group? How do citizens' movements fit into the local political scene? Do they draw upon—or in turn affect—the local sense of community?

What is the relationship of citizens' movements to other political and apolitical groups? Do they build upon the structures and personal networks of preexisting groups? Do they politicize such groups? Or do citizens' movements function independently as if to challenge, rearrange, or displace these other groups? What place do citizens' movements occupy in local partisan politics? If citizens' movements emerge to oppose the policies of a conservative local government, what is their relationship to the local leftist opposition? How do citizens' movements function in cities where leftist coalitions have been elected to power?

What does the rise of citizens' movements signify for the dominance of institutional affiliations over socioeconomic resources in participation? Who participates in citizens' movements, and what resources and group affiliations do they have? Are these people flocking to citizens' movements because they are "locked out" of other groups, or are they experienced political activists in search of a new cause?

As mobilizers of conflict around an issue, what do citizens' movements do to social cohesion as an organizing force? Do citizens' movements reinforce the segmentation of society into many separate networks, or do they erode this pattern by bringing different cross sections of people together? Does the concern for pollution signify the increasing importance of issues, as opposed to cultural politics at the mass level or ideological politics among elites?

Finally, what is the relationship between citizens' movements and the passive, formalist qualities of Japanese political culture? How did citizens' movements come out of such a political culture, and what have they done to it? Do citizens' movements provide the "missing" experience Japanese needed to internalize participatory values? Do citizens' movements educate democratic citizens?

These are all important questions, but unfortunately in some cases the evidence to establish crisp definitive answers is either unavailable at present or even theoretically impossible to extract. Nonetheless, these questions serve as a guide to the ensuing investigation of causes and consequences of citizens' movements, and we shall exploit the evidence that is available to the fullest extent possible.

The Emergence of Environmental Protest
• The Pollution Crisis

The preceding discussion indicated that economic issues were not likely to become the focal point of political controversy around which Japanese citizens might mobilize or protest. Obviously the issue that did have this capacity was pollution, which reached critical levels in the late 1960s. We can begin to understand why Japan was literally the most polluted nation on earth by regarding the concentrations of energy consumption and economic activity in Japan as reasonable predictors of potential pollution. As table 1 shows, from the late 1960s through the mid 1970s, Japanese energy consumption per capita was only one-fourth to

TABLE 1 / *Indicators of Potential Pollution in the United States and Japan*

	United States	Japan	Ratio of Japan to U.S.
Area (km²)	9,363,123	372,313	0.0398
Level Area (km²)	4,356,130	67,010	0.01538
Population density (per km²)			
1970	22	280	12.73
1975	23	298	12.96
Population density per level area			
1970	47	1,557	33.13
1975	49	1,657	33.82
Energy			
Energy per capita (kilograms of coal equivalent)			
1969	10,773	2,828	0.2625
1972	11,624	3,568	0.3070
1975	10,999	3,622	0.3293
Energy per area (kilotons)			
1969	234	782	3.34
1972	259	1,016	3.92
1975	251	1,079	4.30
Energy per level area			
1969	503	4,348	8.64
1972	557	5,649	10.14
1975	540	5,999	11.11
Gross Domestic Product			
GDP per area (U.S. $)			
1973	$139,060	$1,100,148	7.91
1975	$161,590	$1,316,902	8.15
GDP per level area			
1973	$298,979	$6,116,823	20.46
1975	$347,419	$7,321,975	21.08
Manufacturing Output			
Manufacturing per area (U.S. $)			
1970	$ 67,975	$ 521,950	7.68
1973	$ 93,908	$1,036,937	11.04
Manufacturing per level area			
1970	$146,146	$2,902,042	19.86
1973	$201,902	$5,765,370	28.56

Sources: Ministry of International Trade and Industry, *Energy Statistics*; Oriental Economist, *Japan Economic Handbook*, 1971–1977; *United Nations Statistical Yearbook 1976*; *United Nations Yearbook of Industrial Statistics 1975*. Yen exchange rates from the *Federal Reserve Bulletin*.

one-third that of the United States. However, Japanese population density, thirteen times that of the U.S., meant that energy consumption per unit of area in Japan and thus potential pollution grew to over four times that of the U.S. (or over sixty times the world average).[22] Taking into ac-

22. Norie Huddle and Michael Reich, "The Octopus That Eats Its Own Legs," *Ecologist* 3:8 (August 1973), 293.

TABLE 2 / *Reported Damage from Pollution in National Surveys*

	July 1970[a]	November 1971[b]	October 1973[c]
Are you presently suffering from pollution in some form? (% of total sample replying yes)	55[d]	36[e]	45[e]
(Asked of those who reported not being troubled by pollution at present) Do you worry that you may eventually be affected by pollution? (% of total sample replying yes)	26	36	39
Cumulative total: (% of total sample affected by pollution now *or* worried about future effects)	81	72	84

[a] Mainichi Shimbun, "Kōgai Mondai," *(Gekkan) Seron chōsa* 2 : 11 (November 1970), 52–60.
[b] Sōrifu, "Kōgai Mondai," *(Gekkan) Seron chōsa* 4 : 6 (June 1972), 2–28.
[c] Sōrifu, "Kōgai Mondai," *(Gekkan) Seron chōsa* 6 : 2 (February 1974), 2–50.
[d] "Are you receiving damage from pollution?"
[e] "Have you received damage from pollution in the last five years?"

count the fact that industry was heavily concentrated on the scarce amount of level land in Japan, we can see from the Gross Domestic Product and manufacturing output per unit of level land in the table that Japan would be between twenty and thirty times as likely as the United States to have serious pollution problems in certain areas. Even compared with the more congested industrial nations of Western Europe, Japan faced a much higher risk of pollution per unit area and pollution per capita.[23]

The types of pollution that troubled Japanese citizens most often show how population density and concentration of economic activity exacerbated the problem. Noise, vibrations, ground subsidence (due to lowering of the water table), interference with sunlight and electric-wave transmission, and foul odors frequently out-ranked air and water pollution in terms of the formal complaints registered and replies to opinion polls.[24] These forms of pollution were unusually prevalent and offensive in Japan because of the rapid, relatively haphazard nature of urbanization and the resulting high population densities and inadequate housing in Japanese cities.

Public alarm over pollution paralleled its growth as an objective problem, and by the late 1960s pollution was a paramount concern with

23. Kankyōchō [Environment Agency], *Kankyō hakusho 1978* [White Paper on the Environment 1978] (Tokyo: Ōkurashō Insatsukyoku, June 1978), pp. 17, 55.
24. Formal complaints filed from 1971 to 1977 all reflect this tendency. See *Kankyō hakusho 1979*, pp. 382–384. For opinion polls, see sources cited in table 2.

the Japanese public. Table 2 indicates that by the early 1970s about half of the Japanese public claimed to be suffering directly from pollution damage, and over 80 percent of the entire population worried about becoming pollution victims in the future. By far the single most visible symptom of the crisis, and therefore the most important catalyst in stimulating the public outcry, was pollution disease. All of the world's major pollution-caused diseases appeared first in Japan and resulted either from air pollution or from the ingestion of polluted food and water over a long period of time. The government was finally forced to launch a relief program to provide medical aid and unemployment compensation to the victims in 1969. By January 1979 this system extended official recognition as pollution victims to over 73,000 persons, and hundreds had died directly from these diseases. Needless to say, many people who were not officially certified were nonetheless affected by pollution, and the contamination responsible for these readily detectable levels of illness undoubtedly acted in many yet-undiscovered ways as well. The number of victims is likely to increase still further as diagnostic techniques become more refined.

Public concern about the pollution crisis led quickly to environmental protest. From 1967 to 1969, victims of the "Big Four" pollution diseases filed lawsuits that won wide publicity and eventually resulted in verdicts, handed down from 1971 to 1973, awarding them victory in every case. The publicity given to the major court cases as they went to trial, along with the severity of local pollution problems everywhere, stimulated the formation of at least three thousand citizen movements by 1973. These lawsuits and citizens' movements caused the government to respond by creating increasingly stringent environmental legislation. The government did not experience direct pressure from any national lobbying campaign—citizen movements never coalesced into such an effort. Rather, it was indirect pressure from the highly charged atmosphere of crisis which the lawsuits and citizen movements created that was responsible for the legislation, as the government acknowledged in its own white paper on the environment in 1974.[25]

The first official act of the national government to acknowledge the crisis was the creation of the Basic Law for Environmental Pollution Control in 1967. This modest statement of intent stipulated that the government would aim at environmental protection as long as that goal was "in harmony with" the health of the economy. However, the law had no enforceable provisions to control pollution, which continued to grow worse. In 1969 the national government began assisting victims of pollution disease. Finally, the 1970 extraordinary session of the legislature

25. Kankyōchō, *Kankyō hakusho 1974* (Tokyo: Ōkurasho Insatsukyoku, May 1974), pp. 76–80.

(called the Pollution Diet) passed fourteen laws to regulate specific types of pollution, including the first law in any nation to designate as a crime an act of pollution that damaged human health.[26] This battery of new laws was expected to nip the problem in the bud.

However, during the next three years pollution continued to grow worse, citizen movements literally exploded onto the Japanese political scene, and the Big Four verdicts surpassed existing legislation in their impact on the behavior of polluting industries. As a result, pollution remained an important issue with the general public, even after the oil crisis of 1973, which shook the Japanese economy severely. In national surveys conducted between 1972 and 1975 asking whether environmental protection measures should be undertaken even at the cost of an increased burden on taxpayers, the most frequent response was that a cleaner environment was worth the increased expense. This group (from 35% to 45% of the sample, depending on the survey) was from three to five times larger than the number of respondents who preferred to allow environmental deterioration in order to save money.[27] This concern is noteworthy in view of the fact that pollution takes a back seat to inflation, unemployment, taxation, and other such pocketbook issues even in other industrial nations where environmental issues are taken seriously.

This continued public concern kept the environmental issue alive at a time when pressing economic worries might have submerged it. Responding to this concern and also to the Big Four pollution verdicts, which highlighted the inadequacies of existing environmental legislation, the government proceeded to revise and strengthen environmental laws and regulations. The associated ambient and effluent standards were progressively tightened, to the point where Japan now has the strictest pollution standards in the world, most of them more stringent than the levels recommended by the OECD and the United Nations.[28] The willingness of citizens to foot the bill for this effort is reflected in the fact that Japan now spends more of its gross national product on antipollution measures than any of the other affluent democracies.[29] By 1978 these regulatory

26. On the early evolution of this legislation, see Margaret McKean, "Pollution and Policymaking," in T. J. Pempel, ed., *Policymaking in Contemporary Japan* (Ithaca, N.Y.: Cornell University Press, 1977), pp. 201–238.

27. Environment Agency, *Quality of the Environment in Japan 1976* (Tokyo: Ministry of Finance Printing Bureau, November 1976), pp. 33–40.

28. Current standards are listed in the "Sankō shiryō" [Reference Materials], supplements to each white paper on the environment. For 1978, see *Kankyō hakusho 1978*, pp. 456–473. A comparison with other countries is available in Organization for Economic Cooperation and Development (OECD), *Environmental Policies in Japan* (Paris, 1977), pp. 24–36; and Hashimoto Michio, "Kankyō hozen seisaku no shinkyokumen" [New Directions in Environmental Protection Policies], *Jichi kenkyū* 51:9 or 619 (September 1975), 3–16.

29. OECD, *Environmental Policies in Japan*, pp. 68–73.

policies and increased expenditures had already yielded significant results in the form of a decrease in many measurable indicators of air and
water pollution.[30] Japan's nearly total recovery from aftershocks of the
oil crisis as severe as those experienced by Italy, while simultaneously
making more progress toward environmental cleanup than was once
thought possible and dealing with the political tumult caused by citizen
movements and other powerful forces of change, deserves admiration
and careful analysis, although we shall be able to devote time and space
only to the third element in this picture, the role of citizens' movements.

• Regional Development and Local Government

The story of citizens' environmental protest begins at the local level
because in most instances pollution can be attributed not simply to industrial activity but particularly to the prevalent practice among local
governments of encouraging regional industrial development as a solution to financial distress. Japan has a unitary rather than a federal structure, in which the forty-seven prefectural governments and hundreds of
cities, towns, and villages are regarded as branches of the central administration rather than as self-contained or autonomous units of government.[31] The prefectural and municipal layers of government are financially weak, in that they spend 72 percent of the total government
budget, yet collect only 30 percent of total tax revenues themselves. Local taxes are an assortment of property, sales, entertainment, and activities taxes, along with charges and fees for certain local services and
the inhabitants' tax based partly on income. Although local governments
have the authority to generate revenues independently through certain
restricted methods, even the floating of bonds requires permission from

30. *Kankyō hakusho 1978*, pp. 1–18.

31. Kurt Steiner, *Local Government in Japan* (Stanford: Stanford University Press,
1965), pp. 231–299; Hideo Wada, "Aspects of Local Self-Government: Subordination and
Resistance to the Central Government," *Journal of Social and Political Ideas in Japan
(Japan Interpreter)* 2:3 (December 1964), 74–78; Ken'ichi Miyamoto, "Local Self-Government and Local Finance," *Developing Economies* 6:4 (December 1968), 587–615. For
sources on the weakness of local government with respect to pollution problems and citizens' movements, see Miyamoto Ken'ichi, "Jūmin undō no riron to rekishi" [The Theory
and History of Residents' Movements], in Miyamoto Ken'ichi and Endō Akira, eds., *Toshi
mondai to jūmin undō* [Urban Problems and Residents' Movements], vol. 8 in the series
Gendai Nihon no toshi mondai [Urban Problems in Contemporary Japan] (Kyoto: Sekibunsha, July 1971), pp. 2–69; Miyamoto Ken'ichi, "Jichi seido wo ikasu undō e" [Toward a
Movement to Bring Life to the System of Self-Government], *Shimin* 3 (July 1971), 157–164;
Matsubara Haruo, *Kōgai to chiiki shakai: seikatsu to jūmin undō no shakaigaku* [Pollution
and Regional Society: The Sociology of Livelihood and Residents' Movements] (Tokyo: Nihon Keizai Shimbunsha, October 1971), pp. 178–253; Kaji Kōji, *Kōgai gyōsei no sōtenken:
kaiketsu no michi wa?* [A General Examination of Pollution Administration: A Road to
Solutions?] (Tokyo: Gōdō Shuppan, May 1971), pp. 78–141; Yoshirō Kunimoto, "Pollution
and Local Government," *Japan Quarterly* 18:2 (April–June 1971), 162–167.

the Ministry of Home Affairs. As a result, local governments depend on the redistribution of revenues from the central government for well over half of their funds.[32] Because the national government controls not only the amounts transferred but also the purposes for which transfer funds may be used, this financial dependence of local government is often labeled "30 percent autonomy."

The financial dependence of local government on the central treasury grew increasingly serious during the 1950s. Although economic growth permitted an absolute increase in total tax revenues without increases in tax rates, local governments did not share in this prosperity. The national government gradually assigned more obligations to local governments without surrendering more authority to the local level to collect revenue. Governments in rural areas faced a net outflow of skilled, youthful labor and therefore a declining tax base. Governments in areas of net in-migration found themselves forced to expand public services—roads, sewers, schools—faster than revenues increased. Local governments in both situations responded by attempting to increase their independent sources of revenue with the limited means open to them. Just as in the United States, where local governments find it more palatable to increase the tax base (by attracting industry and thus new population) rather than to increase the rate of taxation, prefectures and municipalities in Japan competed to attract industry as a revenue-generating device. The national government, seeing this strategy as a way of handling the insolvency of local governments and stimulating economic growth at the same time, encouraged this approach with special legislation, such as the New Industrial Cities Law designating certain areas for major development. Thus industrial development increased rapidly, not only in fast-growing urban areas, but also in areas trying desperately to maintain population by becoming industrial havens, a pattern of urbanization which Shōji Kōkichi calls a two-way Japanese style "enclosure movement."[33] Not only did the people leave the countryside to migrate to the cities, but new cities popped up all over the countryside.

The prevailing political pattern in local governments that hoped industrial development would alleviate their financial problems was conservative. Although progressive or leftist parties had a strong foothold in the largest cities of Japan and in the several prefectures containing these cities, conservatives predominated at the prefectural and municipal levels elsewhere (see table 3). Typically, conservative local governments argued

32. Material on the financial dilemma of local governments is drawn from Steiner, *Local Government in Japan*, pp. 267–299, and Terry Edward MacDougall, "Political Opposition and Local Leadership," (Ph.D. diss. in Political Science, Yale University, 1975), pp. 79–97.

33. Kōkichi Shōji, "Sociological Factors in Japan's Economic Structure," (unpublished manuscript, August 1978 draft).

TABLE 3 / *Conservative Strength in Local Government*
(after the April 1975 local elections)

Level of Government	Executive Offices	Legislative Offices
National Level		
House of Representatives (December 1976)	—	$\dfrac{258}{511} = 50.49\%$
House of Councillors (July 1977)	—	$\dfrac{124}{252} = 49.21\%$
Prefectural Level (to-dō-fu-ken)		
(includes Tokyo-to, Osaka-fu, and Kyoto-fu)	$\dfrac{34}{47} = 72.34\%$	$\dfrac{1,808}{2,864} = 63.13\%$
Municipal Level (shi-chō-son)		
(excluding 9 designated cities)	$\dfrac{452}{634} = 71.29\%$	$\dfrac{14,505}{20,086} = 72.21\%$
Designated Cities		
(Kita-Kyushu, Sapporo, Kobe, Yokohama, Kawasaki, Nagoya, Kyoto-shi, Osaka-shi, Fukuoka)	$\dfrac{3}{9} = 33.33\%$	$\dfrac{263}{650} = 40.46\%$

Sources: Terry Edward MacDougall, "Political Opposition and Big City Elections in Japan, 1947–1975," in Scott Flanagan, Ellis Krauss, and Kurt Steiner, eds., *Political Opposition and Local Politics in Japan: Electoral Trends, Citizens' Movements, and Progressive Administrations* (Princeton University Press, 1979), Statistical Appendix. *JTW*, 16 July 1976. Richard J. Brynildsen, "A Decade of Japanese Diet Elections," *Asian Survey* 17:10 (October 1977), 970.

Note: Conservative strength: the number and percentage of seats held by LDP members and those independents who can clearly be identified as conservatives (i.e., not neutral or reformist). Owing to uncertainty about the course of coalition politics at the national level, conservative independents and New Liberal Club members have been excluded from our definition of "conservative."

that with the conservative LDP controlling the national government and thus the distribution of revenues downward to local government, they could offer a "pipeline to the center" to procure benefits for their constituents. Even though many local governments complained that they received less in transfer funds than they were actually promised and that they were expected to comply with bureaucratic directives that exceeded the intents and limits of the law, they were reluctant to use the legal recourse available to them to protest violations of local autonomy.

The timidity of local governments vis-à-vis the center was based not just on the practical fear of retaliation by ministries with discretion over funds, but also on political attitudes and practices of long standing.[34] Local elites, especially conservatives, believed that deference toward the center and avoidance of conflict were both proper and practical behav-

34. MacDougall, "Political Opposition and Local Government," pp. 98–112; Michio Muramatsu, "Central-Local Relationships in a Changing Political Context," paper given at the Conference on Urban Choice and State Power, Cornell University, June 1977.

ior, in the best interests of the community. Their constituents shared the same political tradition and accepted these arguments on the wisdom of cultivating a smooth working relationship based on consensus between local elites and the national government. Since local governments received pressure mainly from above and rarely from below, it is not surprising that they usually did the bidding of the central government and ignored their veto powers over the zoning and sale of land for industrial development, over sewerage, utilities, road construction, and other public services required by industry.[35]

The foundation of conservative control at the local level was usually an old boys' network of *yūryokusha* ("the powerful people") of local bosses, neighborhood leaders, heads of merchants' associations, and other civic groups bearing some resemblance to fraternal associations in the United States. Although Japanese and Western observers alike usually refer to this phenomenon as a uniquely Japanese carry-over from feudal times, it is actually quite similar to the patriarchal politics of deference, patron-client relations, and personal political machines in the old Democratic South in the United States.[36] Just as in the American South, this system worked smoothly as long as there were no serious conflicts in the community and those who were placed at a disadvantage by the system either failed to recognize their plight or were effectively disenfranchised.

However, the consequences of rapid and haphazard industrial development produced conflicts that this informal system of friendly consensus within a like-minded elite could not absorb. Many projects failed to live up to expectations that they would provide financial relief to local governments and bring pollution-free jobs to the area. Local governments sometimes erred in their calculations, and in their eagerness to offer attractive circumstances to industry simultaneously promised deferred taxation and committed themselves to lavish spending programs to provide facilities. Moreover, this strategy peppered the Japanese landscape with pollution, no longer concentrated primarily in major cities or large industrial zones as in other countries. Those who disapproved of the results—in this case, pollution victims—began to make demands on local governments that could not be handled within the framework of conservative consensus politics, so they formed citizens' movements instead.

35. Tomita Eijirō, "Jūmin no kōgai ishiki no kōyō to hantai undō no shinten" [The Rise in Residents' Pollution Consciousness and the Development of Opposition Movements], *Jūrisuto* 458 (10 August 1970), 101–105.
36. Compare the political machines described in V. O. Key, Jr., *Southern Politics in State and Nation* (New York: Vintage Books, 1949), with the support organizations in Steiner, *Local Government in Japan*, pp. 409–475; Nathaniel B. Thayer, *How the Conservatives Rule Japan* (Princeton: Princeton University Press, 1969), pp. 82–110; and Gerald L. Curtis, *Election Campaigning Japanese Style* (New York: Columbia University Press, 1971), pp. 33–178.

• Stages in the Evolution of Citizens' Movements

Although the number of citizens' movements seems to have increased exponentially since the late 1960s, no individual citizens' movement was really born overnight. An evolutionary process occurred within individual movements and among citizens' movements as a whole, as they gained practical experience. Almost all early groups took shape in the same way. Victims and other residents opposed to pollution would first approach their local *jichikai*, *chōnaikai*, or *burakukai*, traditional neighborhood associations.[37] Although these associations were not legally recognized as units of local government, they were tacitly recognized by the municipal level of government and, until the rise of citizens' movements, were the most important "pressure groups" vis-à-vis the local administration to deal with issues of zoning, taxation, municipal services, and the like.[38]

Almost invariably these appeals to local neighborhood associations were petitions (*seigan* or *chinjō*), phrased as humble requests directed toward *okami* (political or social superiors) rather than as forthright demands. However, because of the pattern of personal ties among the local elite just described, neighborhood leaders tended to soften the already humble tone of petitions as they sent them upward in the local political hierarchy. These leaders usually had a strong commitment to support the industry or development plan in question, based on personal acquaintance, political and factional ties, campaign contributions, and what may truly have been sincere and honest beliefs in the value of heavy industrial development and in the possibility that a nonvocal majority still favored the plan. Instead of transmitting the intense concern about pollution that lay behind the complaints of neighborhood residents, these leaders were quick to accept mild reassurances and weak compromises, and according to some sources they were very easily "bought off" by the vested interests which sought to protect the "pro" pollution interests in the area.[39] None-

37. Opinion polls show that neighborhood associations are the conventional channel for voicing complaints. More people who want to do something about pollution go first to their neighborhood association than to any other place (such as the public health bureau, the police, or even the pollution source). See national polls, taken in August 1966, reported in Naikaku sōri daijin kambō kōhōshitsu, *Kōgai ni kansuru seron chōsa* [Opinion Poll on Pollution] (March 1968), pp. 9–10; a November 1971 poll reported in Naikaku sōri daijin kambō kōhōshitsu, *Kōgai mondai ni kansuru seron chōsa* [Opinion Poll on Pollution Problems] (March 1972), p. 11, which is also in Sōrifu, "Kōgai mondai" [Pollution Problems], *(Gekkan) Seron chōsa* 4:6 (June 1972), 2–28; and an October 1973 poll reported in Sōrifu kōhōshitsu, "Kōgai mondai" [Pollution Problems], *(Gekkan) Seron Chōsa* 6:2 (February 1974), 15. See also Sōrifu kōhōshitsu, "Kōgai" [Pollution], *(Gekkan) Seron chōsa* 8:2 (February 1976), 28, for an October 1975 survey corroborating earlier findings.

38. Steiner, *Local Government*, pp. 207–230; Shōji Hikaru and Miyamoto Ken'ichi, *Osorubeki kōgai* [Fearful Pollution] (Tokyo: Iwanami Shoten, April 1964), p. 195.

39. Shōji and Miyamoto, *Osorubeki kōgai*, pp. 194–196; Tsuru Shigeto, *Gendai shihonshugi to kōgai* [Contemporary Capitalism and Pollution] (Tokyo: Iwanami Shoten, March 1968), pp. 271–286; Matsubara, *Kōgai to chiiki shakai*, pp. 179–191; Jūmin ni yoru

theless, early movements were patient at this stage and repeatedly asked their local *yūryokusha* ("powerful people") to deliver their petitions to the authorities. However, patience was not rewarded; the struggle of a petition-stage movement usually revolved around persuading local authorities simply to receive the petition, let alone to heed its contents. The rise of opposition to the idea of regional development dumbfounded politicians who built their careers by promoting industrial expansion. They usually resolved their conceptual dilemma by regarding the citizens' movements in their area as a vocal but bizarre minority that lacked any political potential and could thus be safely ignored. There is apparently no single case of a movement that obtained satisfaction by relying only on the method of petition.[40]

If the local residents were dissatisfied with the verbal agreements and reassurances (never legally binding contracts at this stage) elicited on their behalf by neighborhood leaders, then citizens' movements took shape. The early movements that persisted after disappointing failures with petitions had few helpful precedents to guide them in other directions, and were uninformed and inexperienced about other methods available to them. Most citizens' movements eventually uncovered serious transgressions of ethics, if not blatant violations of law, in the way their local politicians had concealed facts, extended favors to polluting industry, or promised municipal services to a company planning to build in the area. In such circumstances, the energy of a petition-stage movement could explode in the form of direct action. Groups resorting to sit-ins and demonstrations were usually too desperate to consider the impact on public opinion that forceful means would have, and used direct action as an emergency measure—to bargain for time, to close down a polluting factory, or to obstruct new industrial construction. Although the use of direct action could force local government or the polluting industry to negotiate, it would also damage the movement's bargaining position and produce a relatively unfavorable settlement. Thus direct action rarely yielded conclusive results for citizens' movements.

Some movements faded away after early failures with petitions and direct action, but others moved into what Matsubara Haruo calls the citizen stage, in which tactics based on a fuller awareness of citizens' legal and political rights bring the greatest chances of success.[41] Today, cit-

---

Keiji baipasu kōgai kenkyū guruupu [Residents' Pollution Research Group on the Kyoto-Shiga Bypass], *Kōgai: yosoku to taisaku* [Pollution: Forecasts and Countermeasures] (Tokyo: Asahi Shimbunsha, March 1971), p. 251.

40. Matsubara, *Kōgai to chiiki shakai*, pp. 183–242; Miyamoto, "Jūmin undō no riron to rekishi," p. 64; Ui Jun, *Kōgai no seijigaku: Minamata byō wo megutte* [The Politics of Pollution: On Minamata Disease] (Tokyo: Sanseidō, July 1968), p. 197; Ui Jun, *Kōgai genron* [Lectures on Pollution], 3 vols. (Tokyo: Aki Shobō, 1971), Vol. 3, pp. 217–219.

41. Matsubara, *Kōgai to chiiki shakai*, pp. 183–242; Tsuru, *Gendai shihonshugi to kōgai*, pp. 256–259.

izens' movements enter the citizen stage rapidly, benefiting from the painful and protracted phases of experimentation conducted by their predecessors. We should distinguish at this point between compensation-oriented and prevention-oriented movements, because their differences in goals dictate different strategies at the citizen stage.

Generally speaking, compensation movements could not build a broad political coalition in their communities from which to approach local authorities, because they could not attract the sympathy of non-victims. Often the victims were restricted to particular occupations—farming or fishing—and were therefore isolated within their communities and from each other. This posed a particularly tragic dilemma for victims of pollution diseases, who were ostracized by non-victims as freaks or as dangerous carriers of some dread contagion until medical research established otherwise. With both Minamata mercury poisoning and Toyama cadmium poisoning in the 1950s and 1960s, community residents who were not diagnosed as victims did not believe that they too might become victims.[42] The complete lack of community solidarity and the existence of tremendous community pressure to endure in silence are blamed for the long years of ineffectual protest made by the victims of these diseases. Compensation movements also faced strong opposition from non-victims who benefited from a special relationship with the offending industry—from local elites whose personal fortunes improved and from those employed at the factory. Compensation-oriented movements therefore obtained their best results from court action, which resulted in awards of compensation for living expenses, lost income, medical care, and an additional solatium for mental suffering. Court orders accompanying the final settlement also provided the most effective way to force the offending industry to modify its productive processes and install pollution-control equipment.

In contrast, citizens' movements interested in preventing pollution before it occurs may not have the sort of grievances that can be taken to court, and their efforts have to be devoted instead to building a broad political coalition from a cross section of the community. This is possible because no group—other than hopeful landowners and local elites—has yet established strong ties of dependence on the company planning to build in the area. Nonetheless, the task of turning an apathetic population into a unified citizens' movement is a formidable challenge to the resourcefulness of a prevention-oriented movement.

First, because damage has not yet materialized, a prevention move-

42. For an account of this local opposition, see Ui, *Kōgai no seijigaku*, pp. 2–192; and Ui, *Kōgai genron* 1:73–129. Seirinsha Films (c/o Aileen Smith, New York City) distributes two excellent documentaries made by Tsuchimoto Noriaki on Minamata: "Minamata Revolt," and "Minamata: The Victims and Their World," which deal with the theme of local political conflict.

ment has trouble convincing residents of the community that the threat of pollution is real. Local residents of the community are often eager for the material prosperity and revitalization that new industrial construction may bring, and they prefer to believe the promises of industry and local government that sophisticated equipment to prevent pollution exists and will be used.

Second, a prevention movement faces considerable opposition from those who argue that the movement is "egoistic," simply attempting to protect one locality from an evil that will then be transferred to some other district whose residents are less egoistic, more pliable. This argument appeals in part to the traditional belief that individuals do not have the right to protect their own interests, that they must cooperate with the authorities' plans. Charges of "egoism" gain added appeal for critics of a citizens' movement whose participants are actually rather well-off. Most movements attempt to refute this charge, but some prevention-oriented movements have assembled their own doctrine of enlightened self-interest—if what they do can be called egoism, then maybe egoism is not all bad. They argue that the failure of people in other localities to protect their own interests is no reason for a movement to abandon its efforts, that egoism in terms of one's values is really the basis of any action, that a certain amount of enlightened egoism is actually desirable and commendable, and that everyone should be egoistic enough to protect himself, so that social evils will be eliminated altogether.[43] This is a very striking notion with respect to Japanese philosophical tradition, possibly the first truly indigenous advocacy of utilitarianism!

The first successful prevention-oriented movement, one that deserves examination here because it also illustrates the emergence of the "citizen" stage in Matsubara's scheme, was in Mishima, Numazu, and Shimizu.[44] The three mayors involved initially favored the amalgamation

---

43. For a defense of what their opponents refer to as "egoism," see Matsunaga Yasuhiko, "Yokohama ni okeru jūmin soshiki to undō" [The Residents' Organization and Movement in Yokohama], in Miyamoto and Endō, *Toshi mondai to jūmin undō*, pp. 202–212; *Kōgai: yosoku to taisaku*, pp. 254–267; Miyazaki Shōgo, "Jūmin undō wa nani wo mezasu ka" [What do Residents' Movements Want?], *Kankyō hakai* 1:4 (September 1970), 3–18; Miyazaki Shōgo, "Hantai undō mo shōnenjō: 'jūmin ego' kōgeki wo hane-kaeshite" [The Opposition Movement Also Has a Just Position: Repulsing the Charges of "Residents' Ego"], *Asahi jānaru* 197 (6 September 1974), 90–94; and Nakamura Kiichi et al., *Jūmin undō 'watakushi' ron* [The Theory of "Self" in Residents' Movements] (Tokyo: Gakuyō Shobō, 1976).

44. References concerning the antipollution movement in Mishima-Numazu-Shimizu are Kokumin kyōiku kenkyūjo, *Kōgai to kyōiku* [Pollution and Education], vol. 6 in the series Kokumin kyōiku [Education of the Japanese] (Tokyo: Meiji Tosho, July 1970), pp. 185–187; Matsubara, *Kōgai to chiiki shakai*, pp. 185–211; Miyamoto Ken'ichi, ed., *Kōgai to jūmin undō* [Pollution and Residents' Movements] (Tokyo: Jichitai Kenkyūsha, November 1970), pp. 189–212; Miyamoto, "Jūmin undō no riron to rekishi," passim; Tsuru, *Gendai shihonshugi to kōgai*, pp. 272–280; Ui, *Kōgai genron* 2:135–165; Hoshino Shigeo,

of their cities into one legal unit, which would then become an industrial zone, and actively worked to attract industry to the area. However, in 1964 movements began in all three cities to oppose both the amalgamation plan and the associated proposal to attract petrochemical industries. Through their wide support (estimated at 80–90% of the voting population), the Mishima-Numazu-Shimizu movement managed in less than a year to persuade pro-development city officials to cancel their plans.

Mishima already had one large petrochemical company—Tōyō Rayon—so it was not difficult to persuade people that serious pollution was a real possibility in the event of further industrial development of this sort. The opposition movement also organized field trips to other petrochemical complexes. The innkeepers' association went to Yokkaichi, the merchants' and manufacturers' associations traveled to the Tokyo-Chiba industrial zone, landowners from one projected construction site went to Mizushima, and even the Mishima branch of the LDP went to Yokkaichi and Mizushima. All returned convinced of the reality of the pollution threat; they publicized what they had seen, and the merchants displayed opposition slogans and posters in their shop windows. As a result of this campaign, virtually all of those who owned land involved in the projected construction sites signed a resolution not to sell their land to the incoming companies.

Developments in Mishima had a great impact on the delayed sensibilities in Numazu, where science teachers from Numazu's technical high school took the lead in preparing slide and film lectures on pollution. For several weeks in 1964, the teachers went every night to various neighborhood associations and other small group meetings (perhaps 500 in all). Eventually in all three cities, neighborhood associations adopted opposition resolutions, the city assemblies voted for resolutions opposing the development plans, and finally the mayors themselves decided to heed the views of their constituents by withdrawing the plans from consideration. Because of public opinion in the three cities and the reversal in attitudes of city officials, the companies ceased their efforts to build in the area. Thus the Mishima-Numazu-Shimizu movement succeeded in reaching all of its goals.

The movement in nearby Fuji city is considered the complete pro-

Nishioka Akio, and Nakajima Isamu, "Numazu-Mishima-Shimizu (nishi itchō) sekiyū kombinaato hantai tōsō to Fuji-shi wo meguru jūmin tōsō" [The Struggle to Oppose the Petroleum Refinery in Mishima, Numazu, and Shimizu, and the Residents' Struggle in Fuji City], in Miyamoto and Endō, *Toshi mondai to jūmin undō*, pp. 72–283. In English, see Jack G. Lewis, "*Hokaku Rengō*: The Politics of Conservative-Progressive Cooperation in a Japanese City," (Ph.D. diss. in Political Science, Stanford University, 1975); and Jack G. Lewis, "Civic Protest in Mishima: Citizens' Movements and the Politics of the Environment in Contemporary Japan," in Flanagan, Steiner, and Krauss, *Political Opposition and Local Politics in Japan*, chap. 8.

totype movement, because it passed through all of the stages described above, because it was first a compensation movement and then a prevention movement, and because it also went to court.[45] Fuji is a highly industrial city of small manufacturing firms, 150 of which are paper and pulp companies. Fuji is famous for the problem of *hedoro* (waste from paper-pulp processing) that clogs the once beautiful Tagonoura Port in Suruga Bay. *Hedoro* ("slime" or "sludge") is a mass of fine particles and other organic substances, including deadly gases, that accumulate and solidify in shallow bodies of water.[46] *Hedoro* wastes, along with poisonous gases and vibrations, caused crop damage on the land and completely exterminated the fishing groups in Tagonoura. The townspeople began petitioning the local authorities for compensation as early as 1957, and local fishermen soon joined in. By 1967 they not only wanted compensation but also prevention at the source. The *hedoro* problem had advanced to extreme proportions, making Tagonoura Port unnavigable, and the anti-pollution movement now wanted complete elimination of *hedoro* wastes, a dredging of the bay, and a total halt to construction of a thermal power plant on the Fuji River. The movement regarded the "solutions" proposed by city and prefectural authorities (the ocean disposal of *hedoro* and the construction of still more industries in Fuji) as utterly intolerable, destined to exacerbate pollution rather than to reduce it. At this point local teachers and other activists in Fuji adopted what was then known as the Numazu style and held over two hundred study meetings during 1968, in addition to publishing two regular newsletters and making their own scientific surveys of the *hedoro* problem.

The transformation of the Fuji movement's goals from compensation to prevention, along with the adoption of new mobilization tactics learned from the Mishima-Numazu-Shimizu experience, converted the movement into a political coalition with broad community support. The movement entered the realm of local elections by nominating its leader, previously a JSP representative to the prefectural assembly, for mayor. He defeated the candidate sponsored by the paper-pulp companies in January 1970. The movement continued its electoral successes in the April 1971 local elections, when the LDP lost seventeen city assembly

45. Materials on the antipollution movement at Fuji were obtained from Hoshino, Nishioka, and Nakajima, "Numazu-Mishima-Shimizu . . . ," pp. 210–283; *Kōgai Nenkan 1972* [Pollution Yearbook 1972] (Tokyo: Kankyō Hozen Kyōkai, May 1972), pp. 600–609; Kōda, *Waga sonzai no teiten kara*, passim; *Kōgai to kyōiku*, pp. 141–167, 234–264; Matsubara, *Kōgai to chiiki shakai*, pp. 221–242; Ui, *Kōgai genron* 2:166–186; Nishiyama Masao, "Fuji kōgai jūmin soshō no naka kara" [From Inside the Residents' Lawsuit against Fuji Pollution], *Shimin* 3 (July 1971), 101–107; Toshihiko Kōda, "Conflicting Philosophies of Gain and Abundance in My Hometown," *Japan Quarterly* 26:2 (April–June 1979), 188–198.

46. Kankyō kagaku kenkyūjo, *Kōgai yōgo jiten* [Dictionary of Pollution Vocabulary] (Tokyo: Nihon Sōgō Shuppan Kikō, March 1971), p. 83.

seats (out of forty), and the combined opposition parties more than doubled their strength from four to nine seats. The vice-president of the movement was the highest-ranking winner in the at-large race for prefectural assembly, and the secretary of the Fuji movement won a seat in the Fuji city assembly (both ran as JSP candidates).

Not content to stop with its success in making local government more responsive, the movement went on to pin down legal responsibility for Fuji's veritable immersion in pollution, thus demonstrating the utility of legal action for a prevention-oriented movement. In November 1970 the movement filed a civil suit against the prefectural governor and the four major pulp companies. An out-of-court settlement in December 1976 awarded ¥1.1 billion (about $5.5 million) to the prefectural fishing cooperative, and a Tokyo high court ruling of September 1977 declared the dumping of *hedoro* illegal and ordered the pulp companies to find other means of disposing of their waste and to reimburse the prefecture for the expense incurred in dredging Tagonoura Port.[47]

These thumbnail sketches of the "prototype" citizens' movements in Mishima and Fuji offer some striking contrasts with the state of political participation in the 1960s and local government policy and practice summarized earlier. These movements overturned time-honored plans for city amalgamation and industrial development that had never been questioned before. In Fuji the movement even took steps toward restoration of the environment or undoing pollution damage already done. These movements abandoned traditional political channels and instead created a broad popular coalition to engage in head-on confrontation with politicians and business leaders. Finally, they mobilized city-wide electoral movements that replaced local executives with their own candidates, and in Fuji they even won a lawsuit against the offending firm and the prefectural government for pollution and dereliction of duty respectively. In the remainder of this work we shall try to learn why pollution could be such an important force for change and how movements could acquire such broad support, not only to achieve their antipollution objectives but to become a major political force in their community.

47. Kobayashi Tatsumi, "Tagonoura kō hedoro kōgai jūmin soshō" [The Residents' Lawsuit against Hedoro Pollution of Tagonoura Port], *Jurisuto* 492 (10 November 1971), 253–255; Harada Naohiko, "Tagonoura hedoro hanketsu e no gimon" [Doubts About the Tagonoura Hedoro Verdict], *Jurisuto* 571 (1 October 1974), 100–104; *Asahi Shimbun* (*AS*), 27 December 1976 (ssb 826/3), 6 September 1977 (ssb 167/1,4,9), and 20 September 1977 (ssb 674/7).

Participation through Environmental Litigation

WHEN JAPANESE think of pollution, most of them immediately recall the celebrated Big Four pollution disease lawsuits. There can be no doubt that the attention focused on these cases turned pollution into a serious political issue of concern to all Japanese and not just to particular segments of the population. Whereas the well-educated upper middle class formed the backbone of the environmental movement in the United States, and their concern with ecology was regarded by other Americans as a noble but peculiar hobby, large majorities of Japanese in 1970 and 1971, when the pollution trials were being publicized, thought that the environment was more important than the economy, that government was handling pollution very badly, that industry displayed no sense of social responsibility, and that victims of pollution disease had not yet been adequately compensated.[1] Thus these cases broke through

1. See the following articles reporting results of nationwide surveys, all published in *(Gekkan) Seron chōsa*: Yomiuri Shimbunsha, "Kōgai mondai" [Pollution Problems] 2:8 (August 1970), 52–62 (May 1970 poll); Sōrifu kōhōshitsu, "Kokumin no shakai teki kanshin" [The Social Concerns of the People] 3:4 (April 1971), 2–26 (July 1970 poll); Mainichi Shimbunsha, "Kōgai mondai" [Pollution Problems] 2:11 (November 1970), 52–60 (July 1970 poll); Sōrifu kōhōshitsu, "Shakai ishiki" [Social Consciousness] 3:11 (November 1971), 3–49 (March 1971 poll); and Sōrifu, "Kōgai mondai" [Pollution Problems] 4:6 (June 1972), 2–28; and Sōrifu kōhōshitsu, "Kankyō mondai" [Environmental Problems] 4:7 (July 1972), 2–33 (both on a November–December 1971 poll).

the customary lethargy and apathy in public opinion and made pollution an issue of national prominence.

These cases also altered attitudes toward the clarification of negligence and responsibility in disputes. In Japan, responsibility was traditionally diffuse, and a figure at the top of a hierarchy who had no actual knowledge of misdeeds could assume displaced responsibility through an informal act of apology and thereby save the organization from further censure or a formal accusation of negligence. Traditionally, this informal act of atonement was humiliating enough to operate as a deterrent, and it was uncivilized for a victim of wrongdoing to demand more. Japan's pollution victims naturally wanted to satisfy their traditional sense of justice by ensuring that the industrialists involved were personally shown the tragedy that they had wrought and forced to make a degrading personal apology to each victim. But some of the victims in each case felt that this was insufficient, and they wanted the courts to pinpoint legal responsibility at the source, reveal the firms' negligence to the eyes of the world, and establish legal standards of corporate responsibility as a more effective deterrent. Their legal victories not only accomplished this in each instance but transformed society's perception of pursuing justice in the courts from greedy and indecorous foolishness to a perfectly appropriate vindication of rights.

The Big Four cases enlarged the boundaries of what constitutes citizens' rights. For almost a century preceding these cases, the prevailing view in Japan was that pollution was simply one of the prices of progress and that silent sacrifice was part of a citizen's obligation to cooperate with national objectives. By awarding their verdicts to the victims, the courts resoundingly proclaimed that such suffering represented a transgression of justice, not a duty like paying taxes, and that it was therefore appropriate for citizens to demand protection of their health and environment as a right.

Furthermore, these cases made litigation a legitimate tool for the assertive citizen and thereby made the courts a channel of mass, not merely elite, participation. Justice was indeed to be distributed according to merit and not according to the resources of those involved. Thus these cases can show us how pollution became an issue of national concern, how formal legal responsibility became a worthy objective, how protection from pollution evolved into a right, and how litigation joined the citizens' repertoire as a path to participation. This will become clear as we explore the historical background to pollution disputes, the Big Four cases (each of which eventually became a citizens' movement in itself), the legal theory embodied in the verdicts, and the effect of the cases on subsequent environmental litigation.

Observers familiar with Japan's "economic miracle" and the tragic pollution diseases of the postwar era readily assume that pollution is a recent phenomenon there, although Lynn White has shown that environmental disruption often occurred in preindustrial society and even in ancient civilizations.[2] In fact, serious pollution problems first emerged in the last century during the rapid industrialization in the Meiji period (1868–1912). The following review of the prewar cases is offered to remedy prevalent misunderstandings about Japan's more recent experience with pollution, and also to serve as a base point by which to measure the evolution of protest methods and the victims' relative success in eliciting responses from industry and government. The prewar cases also illustrate the origin of beliefs that became very important later: that pollution and the victims' suffering were inevitable and necessary prices for economic progress, that prevention was impossible, that damage should be compensated, and that litigation was an unnecessary and extreme tactic. Thus postwar victims drew upon a long tradition in demanding compensation, but for many years they and the rest of Japanese society shared a debilitating *acceptance* even of extreme levels of pollution as unavoidable rather than as an intolerable infringement on their rights.

Prewar Disputes

Today's antipollution activists consider the protest movements that took place at Ashio, Besshi, and Hitachi as their own historical roots. To be sure, these prewar movements did not develop into anything resembling the highly politicized movements that exist today, and the Meiji state had within its grasp legal and police powers that effectively minimized open social conflict and dissent. But these well-known incidents still provided today's citizens' movements with formidable precedents, in that all three provoked large-scale popular protests and eventually led to some sort of constructive response on the part of government or the industries concerned.

· The Ashio Copper Mine Dispute

By far the most noteworthy case was that at Ashio copper mine in Tochigi prefecture.[3] Owned by the Furukawa *zaibatsu* ("financial con-

2. Lynn White, Jr., "The Historical Roots of our Ecologic Crisis," *Science* 155 (10 March 1967), 1203–1207.

3. Material about Ashio is from several sources: Iijima Nobuko, "Ashio Copper Poisoning Case," in Ui Jun, Sonoda, and Iijima Nobuko, "Environmental Pollution Control and Public Opinion" [English excerpts], paper prepared for the first International Symposium for Environmental Disruption, March 8–14, 1970; Miyamoto Ken'ichi, "Jūmin undō no riron to rekishi" [The Theory and History of Residents' Movements], in Miyamoto Ken'ichi and Endō Akira, *Toshi mondai to jūmin undō* [Urban Problems and Residents' Movements], vol. 8 in the series Gendai Nihon to toshi mondai [Urban Problems in Contemporary Japan] (Kyoto: Sekibunsha, July 1971), pp. 23–42; Fred G. Notehelfer,

glomerate"), the Ashio mine provided 40 percent of Japan's total copper production by 1891, one of Japan's major exports at the time. Although Ashio quickly became one of the most technologically advanced copper mines in the world, copper refining at that time was still a very dirty process even with the best techniques, and the proximity of population settlements to the mines exacerbated the consequences of the resulting pollution. Smoke and sulfurous gases hung in the air just beyond the mining town of Ashio, eventually making the area uninhabitable for any plant or animal, a condition that persists today. Waste water and runoff from the slag heaps at the mine entered the Watarase River and traveled downstream, where river water was used for irrigation. Mining activity also destroyed the watershed, causing repeated floods, which spread acidic water and dangerous heavy metals over a large area of farmland. Fish could not live in the river, and soil in the affected floodplain became too toxic to support crops of any kind. As a result, fishermen and farmers in the area downstream from the mine were utterly destitute, and began petitioning the authorities for relief as early as 1890.

The government's initial response was to discount the reports of pollution damage and to deny responsibility for compensation. Furukawa was already undertaking technological improvements to retrieve more copper from low-quality ore, leaving less for the slag heaps, and the government was satisfied that these sedimentation pools and dust collectors would reduce the flow of heavy metals into the river. Using Tochigi prefectural authorities as mediators, Furukawa also negotiated a series of agreements in 1892, in which he promised to control ore-dust and to pay a small sum as annual compensation for damage to villagers. The farmers promised in return to abstain from any protest until June 1896, when the tests of the new equipment would be completed. However, these payments usually went to landowners and village leaders, effectively buying their cooperation and dividing the protesters over the next course of action.[4] Furukawa later managed to have these compensation agreements extended indefinitely without raising the sums provided.

Several factors combined in late 1896 to revive the farmers' protest. The new equipment at the mine did not improve the situation downstream, and in addition to totally unproductive land the villagers now

---

"Japan's First Pollution Incident," pp. 351–384, and Alan Stone, "Japanese Muckrakers," pp. 385–408, both in *Journal of Japanese Studies* 1:2 (Spring 1975); T. Okabe, "Mine Pollution," in Ui Jun, *Polluted Japan: Reports by Members of the Jishu Kōza Citizens' Movement* (Tokyo: Jishu Kōza, 1972), pp. 48–52; Ui Jun, *Kōgai genron* [Lectures on Pollution] (Tokyo: Aki Shobō, March 1971), 1:189–275. Material about the contemporary state of affairs in Ashio was available through interviews with antipollution activists there and from the pamphlets and newspaper clippings they provided.

4. Shōji Hikaru and Miyamoto Ken'ichi, *Osorubeki Kōgai* [Fearful Pollution] (Tokyo: Iwanami Shoten, April 1964), pp. 188–192.

faced health problems. Once the Sino-Japanese war ended in victory for Japan in 1895, the villagers felt free to display a new militancy, so they prepared for a massive protest to begin as soon as their period of promised silence expired. Their sympathetic representative to the national Diet, Tanaka Shōzō, also terminated the patriotic silence he had maintained during wartime and resumed spirited criticism of Furukawa and the government. In September 1896 the worst flood in decades extended the contaminated area to 24,000 hectares in six prefectures. Damage to soil, crop yields, and the livelihoods of afflicted farmers and fishermen was more severe at this point than has ever been the case since, and villagers demanded that the government close down the mine, stop collecting taxes in areas with the worst soil pollution, and rebuild destroyed irrigation works.

Tanaka Shōzō persuaded influential government officials to tour the site of damage and elicited a government order in December 1896 for unspecified additional improvements at the mine to reduce toxic runoff and flooding. Dissatisfied with the vagueness of this order, the farmers gathered for a series of mass marches to Tokyo in March of 1897. Because of the tireless persuasion of Tanaka Shōzō, the Minister of Agriculture and Commerce embraced the cause, and by May 1897 the government issued explicit orders to Furukawa to construct elaborate facilities to reduce pollution (precipitation ponds, filtration pools, equipment to reduce the release of sulfurous gases, and the relocation of veritable mountains of accumulated tailings on top of new, nonporous foundations). If the mine could not comply within specified deadlines, it would be closed down. Not only did Furukawa obey the order at tremendous expense, he undertook additional research to discover still better methods of controlling dust, acidic gases and waste water, and heavy metal runoff.

However, despite Furukawa's rapid compliance with the government order, the land downstream remained contaminated and unproductive, and there was no quick way to restore the ruined watershed, so floods continued to plague the district. In the meantime, the farmers' protest movement grew more aggressive, and the mass marches continued. In February 1900 a march of several thousand farmers actually overpowered local police, but their leaders were finally arrested. (Just one month later, the Diet passed the Police Regulation Law to control such events in the future.) After a brief trial the lower court convicted those arrested, but when the farmers appealed, the higher court gave a thorough airing to the entire sequence of events leading up to the protest march and ordered a retrial, in which the case was thrown out of court on a technicality and all charges were dismissed.

The benevolence of the court did not alleviate pollution along the Watarase River, and the protest continued. The government created what it considered a final solution—both environmental and political—when a secret session of the Tochigi prefectural assembly authorized the purchase of the entire village of Yanaka, the heart of the protest movement, as part of a government flood-control project. Thus the most active protesters were compelled, by the power of eminent domain, to sell their land to the state and disperse. Tanaka Shōzō's death in 1913 silenced protest for the rest of the prewar era. Measures taken by Furukawa did eventually stop serious flooding and prevented additional pollution by heavy metals, and the Watarase River is once again being used for drinking water and for irrigation.[5]

What stands out from an account of these events is the Meiji government's eventual willingness to heed the farmers' requests despite powerful incentives to ignore them. Copper production from the Ashio mine was of national importance, Japan was involved in two major wars during the period, the government had substantial police powers at its disposal to quell dissent, and official policy favored rapid industrialization rather than the well-being of the peasantry. Nonetheless, the government made many concessions to a group of peasants who did not even have the right to vote. It threatened Furukawa with closing the mine, and he complied at tremendous expense. Although the dissolution of Yanaka village was almost certainly an attempt to eliminate the protest movement, it also constituted one among several effective measures that gradually increased the productivity of the contaminated land.

· Besshi and Hitachi

Two similar incidents of copper mine pollution occurred at Besshi in Aichi prefecture and at Hitachi in Ibaragi prefecture,[6] bearing out what we have learned from the story at Ashio. Extremely severe damage due to mine pollution provoked the local populace into protesting through conventional means at first, but as damage persisted and petitions failed to achieve results, local residents engaged in demonstrations, which forced the authorities to acknowledge the problem. The authorities then responded with surprising effectiveness. What is different about the Besshi and Hitachi cases is that the government did not have to issue threats, because both mining companies voluntarily constructed preventive facili-

5. Nonetheless, visible crop damage still occurs; 917 farmers tried to obtain compensation for damage suffered from 1952 to 1971, and in May 1974 they accepted a settlement amounting to 40 percent of their monetary demands. The mine closed down in 1973 because it totally exhausted the copper supply, but according to the 1974 arbitration settlement, the Furukawa company is still responsible for preventing the seepage of toxic wastes from the slag heaps. See *Japan Times* (*JT*), 12 May 1974.

6. Material on Besshi and Hitachi was obtained from Miyamoto, "Jūmin undō no riron to rekishi," pp. 23–42; and Ui, *Kōgai genron* 1:8–32.

ties quite advanced for the period, having learned from the Ashio example to anticipate the government's orders.

In 1894, four villages near Sumitomo's Besshi copper mine complained of crop damage due to sulfurous acid gas, and residents surrounded the refinery. Sumitomo industries moved the refinery operations to an offshore island, to reduce the pollution damage to these farmers, at a cost almost twice the annual gross earnings of the refinery. Unfortunately, sulfur dioxide gas and smoke damage on the mainland grew increasingly worse after 1904, when the island refinery began operations. The farmers, growing in numbers as the extent of the damage spread, petitioned Aichi prefecture as well as Sumitomo, and in 1907 the prefecture sent an inspection team. Serious damage persisted, and in 1910 the Ministry of Agriculture and Commerce arranged for arbitration between the farmers and Sumitomo. The company agreed to pay ¥77,000 in compensation (a substantial amount at the prewar rate of ¥2/$1), to limit yearly production to a specific amount, to limit operations even further during the season when rice seedlings were delicate, and to cease production altogether during the ten days when the seedlings were most sensitive.

Though the farmers were still dissatisfied, they had extracted remarkable concessions from a vital industry run by one of the major *zaibatsu* families with the full support of the government behind it. Sumitomo was willing after only a year of protest at Besshi to move refinery and smelting operations to another site at its own expense, and later voluntarily agreed to cease operations briefly in order to reduce damage. Sumitomo also gave the farmers 70 percent of what they asked, a much greater portion of the complainants' initial demands than is the case in the first arbitrated settlements of the postwar period.

The 1910 agreement at Besshi did not prevent further damage, however. Even though Sumitomo complied with a 1915 law requiring the dilution of sulfurous smoke, damage became very severe, affecting the health of every island resident and even damaging coastal villages on the mainland. In 1916 another series of negotiations took place. In addition to continuing its restrictions on production, the company would build taller chimneys to replace the short ones, inspect these smokestacks four times daily, and even switch to low-sulfur copper ore. The company also undertook research on more effective devices to filter the smoke, so that by 1934 the mine was already complying with standards that would not be legally required until years later in the Smoke and Soot Regulation Law of 1962. From 1910 to 1939, Sumitomo gave the farmers a total of ¥8,480,000, an enormous sum at the time, all invested in educational and agricultural facilities. Thus Sumitomo altered the production process, carried out many corrective measures, and paid out large amounts of profits as damages, even when it was not being legally compelled to do so, just because of pressure applied by local farmers.

The events at the Hitachi mine of Nippon Kōgyō, owned by Kuhara Fusanosuke, also verify our impression that prewar industry and government were surprisingly willing to accommodate the requests of farmers protesting against mine pollution. In 1907 sulfur dioxide mist damaged crops and forests, and Hitachi began negotiating with the farmers' representative. According to most accounts, Kuhara accepted responsibility readily and agreeably, never refuting the farmers' contention that the damage was due to the mining operation. After the Ashio case, it was widely assumed that if Japan was to have heavy industry at all, there was no choice but to employ primitive dilution devices (such as the use of many small chimneys rather than one large one) and to follow this up with appropriate payments for the damage that would inevitably result. Once the routine was established, farmers negotiated easily, and the cost of restitution payments was figured into the company budget. To cover mental suffering, Hitachi automatically increased by 10 percent the sum of calculable, visible damage. At the same time, the company provided free medical care to all those suffering from smoke-related problems, as atonement for the damage done.

In 1909 Hitachi conducted a survey of smoke damage and the first major meteorological survey ever made in Japan. Pollution continued to grow worse as the mine expanded, and in 1911 damage from scrap rock and concentrated gases was so serious that some expressed fear that the whole region would die, as had happened at Ashio. The government's study commission on mine poisoning (established because of the problems at Ashio) advised the construction of low, wide-mouthed chimneys with a dilution device. Hitachi promptly complied with this suggestion, but the dilution devices made no more difference here than at Besshi: the same quantities of noxious gases and fine particles fell over the same area. Hitachi's own offices were so thoroughly enveloped in thick, dark, acidic smoke that office work had to be stopped.

In 1914, Kuhara decided on the basis of his own meteorological findings to construct the world's tallest chimney (156 meters) on top of a three-hundred-meter mountain to disperse the smoke into wind currents that would carry it out to sea. This was a risky decision. Not only might a tall chimney fail to alleviate the smoke problems, but there were real doubts about whether Japanese technicians were ready for an engineering feat of this magnitude. But the experiment succeeded, eliminating the problem of concentrated damage in the vicinity of the mine. Thus, under Kuhara's guidance, the Hitachi mine produced Japan's first contribution to pollution-prevention technology, and its first major meteorological survey.

Why does it appear that prewar pollution protesters did so well and that business and government were so generous? Part of the explanation lies in the severity of the pollution itself. The problems that led to protest were more severe in terms of visible, short-term damage than anything that occurs today, because industrial processes were much dirtier at that time. The farmers who protested were not particularly prone to complain and might have endured the sort of pollution that is at issue today, but they were often faced with total destitution, giving them no alternative but to protest. The severity of visible, localized damage also made it impossible for industry to escape blame.

Another explanation lies in the nature of the protest movements, guided by unusually strong personalities and supported by a broad alliance of Meiji intellectuals and by Diet representatives (who did not depend on these large numbers of poor, unenfranchised farmers at elections and probably risked more loss than gain in their careers by supporting the protests). Environmentalists today argue that the presence of a leader like Tanaka Shōzō at Ashio was absolutely vital to any kind of protest in prewar Japan. It is also important to note that prewar protesters asked for relatively small compensation to be applied only in their own case, not uniform policies or comprehensive responses, so industry and government did not have to worry about setting expensive precedents.

There was also the question of political pragmatism: the farmers' protests resembled traditional peasant uprisings, and the riots of 1900 in the Ashio case were actually the largest disturbance in Japan since the Satsuma Rebellion of 1877. Given the farmers' willingness to turn to direct action in such great numbers, it is not surprising that the government took their demands seriously. The removal of Yanaka village indicates how much the government feared such protests. At Besshi and Hitachi, industry dealt successfully with the protests before they became political problems, perhaps because of the lessons learned at Ashio.

There may also be some truth in the view that the prewar Japanese government felt bound by traditional social norms that extended the mandate of leadership only to those who could handle it with compassion, benevolence, and responsibility. The behavior of the higher court in the Ashio case signified a willingness to open up the entire issue to investigation without actually blaming any of the participants and, in effect, constituted an apology and the indirect acceptance of the responsibility of government.[7]

We can also explain the relatively accommodating behavior of industry and government in the prewar period by reference to the relationship between government and business at that time. Industry turned out to be rather tractable in all three cases, but this has not been true at all in

---

7. This is the contention of both Notehelfer, pp. 376–383, and Stone, p. 398, as well as contemporary Japanese activists familiar with the Ashio case.

postwar disputes, where industries boldly defy government orders, reject government surveys, challenge the scientific evidence presented by the protesters, and insist that they cannot possibly afford to install the preventive equipment asked for. In the early prewar period, business was still a creature of government, made respectable only by the government's sponsorship of industrialization as the key to Japan's survival in a hostile international environment.[8] Older values placing manufacturing and commerce at the bottom of the social totem pole probably survived for several decades, and entrepreneurs may have felt within themselves a sense of inferiority when dealing with the government. In any case, the state's goal of preserving the national integrity of Japan was far more important to all involved than the picayune preferences of individual industrialists, as the behavior of Furukawa and Kuhara showed. Thus, industry bowed to government orders or acted early to prevent orders from being issued.

Postwar Litigation

The outcome of World War II reversed the government-business relationship just described. Defeat was a failure for government, and it was business that paved the way for Japan's recovery and reemergence on the world scene as a respectable economic power. Japanese no longer accepted state goals without question as they once did, but the public extended admiration and even gratitude to business. As an ironic consequence of this transformation, postwar antipollution protesters faced very difficult struggles. In part, this was because they protested less visible forms of pollution (which were nonetheless more widespread and far more insidious in their effect on the ecosystem). But it was also because they had to confront a stronger, more secure, more defiant, and perhaps less socially responsible industrial sector than prewar protesters had to deal with. The much greater intimacy of government-business relationships in the postwar period allowed only timid and confused intervention by government until very recently.

The prewar and postwar cases were similar in that they both erupted in the wake of a surge toward industrial growth. In both periods, victims learned that they had to display their plight to the world in graphic detail in order to be taken seriously. Mass communication notwithstanding, the extent of damage and suffering in both periods was greater than words could properly convey, and victims had to bring potential sympathizers and government officials to view the pollution site firsthand, so

8. See William W. Lockwood, *The State and Economic Enterprise in Japan* (Princeton: Princeton University Press, 1965), and Thomas C. Smith, *Political Change and Industrial Development in Japan: Government Enterprise, 1868–1880* (Stanford: Stanford University Press, 1955), on economic growth and entrepreneurship as a product of state policy.

that they would appreciate the victims' accounts and claims as true instead of dismissing them as absurd exaggerations.

But there was a vital difference in the way that settlements were reached. The prewar cases established a pattern of utilizing local elites and political bosses as mediators. In this way, industry managed to arrive at the least expensive compromises that were also acceptable to the victims. Postwar cases followed this pattern at first, but victims gradually learned that they had to bypass the local elite in order to improve the terms of the settlement. As a result, the landmark postwar disputes did not end with informal out-of-court compromises, as in the prewar examples, but proceeded to the courts. The Big Four pollution lawsuits also had far-reaching consequences, unlike their prewar predecessors: they were the single most important cause of the nationwide concern about environmental problems, they were a strong stimulus for the creation of Japan's impressive package of environmental legislation passed since 1970, and the verdicts themselves constitute one of the most "environmentally progressive" bodies of case law anywhere in the world. The following discussion of the Big Four cases includes both the history of the litigation as episodes of political participation and protest, and an analysis of their legal significance.

Therefore, the account of these lawsuits will begin with a brief summary of the Japanese legal system and its multiple heritage.[9] Tokugawa Japan (1600–1867) had one of the most complex legal systems outside of the Western world, a system of "status law" which might be characterized as "rule-of-man-by-law" rather than "rule-of-law."[10] Legal scholars consistently refer to it as a relatively "developed" system, with legal outcomes no harsher than elsewhere for that period, but predictable and just in terms of the Confucian ethics on which they were based. One survey of premodern legal systems found that only in Japan and England were decisions based on judicial precedent.[11] The procedures of dispute conciliation at the local level, the growing body of private or customary law, and positive law created by Tokugawa administrators might have merged to form an independent judiciary based on common law, as in England.[12]

9. On the Japanese legal system, see Arthur Taylor von Mehren, ed., *Law in Japan: The Legal Order in a Changing Society* (Cambridge: Harvard University Press, 1963); Yoshiyuki Noda, *Introduction to Japanese Law* (Tokyo: University of Tokyo Press, 1976); and Hideo Tanaka, *The Japanese Legal System: Introductory Cases and Materials* (Tokyo: University of Tokyo Press, 1976).

10. Dan Fenno Henderson, *Conciliation and Japanese Law: Tokugawa and Modern* (Seattle: University of Washington Press, 1965), 2 vols. See vol. 1, p. 174.

11. Kenzō Takayanagi, "A Century of Innovation: The Development of Japanese Law, 1868–1961," in von Mehren, *Law in Japan*, pp. 23–24.

12. Takayanagi, "A Century of Innovation," pp. 23–37; Henderson, *Conciliation and Japanese Law* 1:55–62.

However, after 1868, Meiji reformers cut short any natural evolution of the legal order by introducing codified continental law instead, borrowing heavily from France and Germany in order to impress Westerners with a "modern" legal system and thereby eliminate extraterritoriality from Japan's treaties with Western powers. These reformers preferred the French inquisitorial system—in which the judge took the most active courtroom role in questioning witnesses and preparing legal arguments—to the Anglo-American adversary system, in which the judge passively observes (and occasionally regulates) the competitive performances of lawyers for the plaintiff and the defendant. Lawyers were barred from pretrial questioning of witnesses (in the interest of preserving "impartiality") and thus from preparation of their cases. In effect, they had few courtroom functions and tended to leave the clarification of a dispute and determination of a solution up to the judge. Such circumstances did not inspire public confidence in litigation as a process for resolving disputes. After World War I new laws discouraged litigation in certain types of cases by requiring the use of conciliation and mediation instead. Thus, for a variety of both practical and cultural reasons, Japanese used litigation less often than other peoples.[13]

A second wave of change in the legal order took place with defeat in 1945 and the American occupation. Eager to make the judiciary a strong protector of civil liberties and an enforcer of the rule of law, American reformers grafted certain features of the Anglo-American tradition onto the Japanese system.[14] They revised the constitution and the legal codes, and introduced the adversary system in hopes of better protecting the rights of criminal defendants and increasing citizen access to the courts (but they did not revive the brief prewar experiment with juries). They created a four-tiered pyramid of summary courts, district courts, high courts, and a Supreme Court with a Grand Bench of fifteen justices. The Legal Training and Research Institute (LTRI) was created out of public funds to train all lawyers and judges in Japan, to insure that practicing lawyers would have the same high-quality preparation as judges.[15]

However, these reforms did not all work out as intended after sovereignty was returned to Japan in 1952. A legal profession unfamiliar

13. Takeyoshi Kawashima, "Dispute Resolution in Contemporary Japan," in von Mehren, *Law in Japan*, pp. 41–72. The fact that the Japanese do not resort to litigation as often as other peoples is also supported by a recent revisionist investigation. See John Owen Haley, "The Myth of the Reluctant Litigant," *Journal of Japanese Studies* 4:2 (Summer 1978), 359–390.

14. Alfred C. Oppler, *Legal Reform in Occupied Japan: A Participant Looks Back* (Princeton: Princeton University Press, 1976).

15. See Kohji Tanabe, "The Process of Litigation: An Experiment with the Adversary System," pp. 73–110; and Takaaki Hattori, "The Legal Profession in Japan: Its Historical Development and Present State," pp. 111–152; and Hakaru Abe, "Education of the Legal Profession in Japan," pp. 153–187; all in von Mehren, *Law in Japan*.

with the adversary system found it confusing and demanding. Citing cost as a concern, the government refused to expand the size of the LTRI, which produces only five hundred new lawyers and judges per year, severely constraining the capacities of the courts and the availability of lawyers to potential litigants. One unusually ironic twist is that the LTRI, intended to elevate the capabilities and prestige of the legal profession and thus enhance its independence, is a government body with an effective monopoly over that profession. On occasion, LTRI graduates selected for judgeships have been denied appointments, apparently because of their leftist leanings.[16] Because of the strain on the capacity of the courts, trial procedures remaining from the prewar period, and the preference of both lawyers and judges to allow ample time during trials for preparation demanded by the new adversary system, hearings may be scheduled one month apart rather than in concentrated spurts. As a result, one trial can take several years. Litigation is still not used even as frequently as it was in the prewar period, although there are signs that the legal profession and the Japanese public alike are becoming adept at the use of their new amalgamated legal order for new objectives. The number of lawsuits filed to evict tenants or to collect payment from defaulting debtors has fallen since the prewar period, whereas the number of suits filed to recover damages has increased.[17] The Big Four pollution damage suits took on special significance because they conclusively demonstrated to a skeptical public the independence of the judiciary and the effectiveness of litigation in promoting justice.

• *Itai-itai* disease (Toyama prefecture)

Itai-itai disease, now known to be a result of long-term cadmium poisoning, first appeared among farmers who lived on the Jinzū River in Toyama prefecture, perhaps as early as the 1920s.[18] The contaminated water of the Jinzū was used to irrigate rice paddies, particularly in the agricultural town of Fuchū, and victims ingested cadmium when they ate contaminated rice. Dr. Hagino Noboru, who first diagnosed the disease

---

16. "Seiji ni kusshita shihō gyōsei" [The Administration of Justice Bowed to Politics], *Sekai* 307 (June 1971), 200–203.

17. Haley, "The Myth of the Reluctant Litigant," pp. 366–370, presents statistical data confirming this, although Haley himself discounts it.

18. Material reported here concerning *itai-itai* disease came from several sources. See Kaji Kōji, *Kōgai gyōsei no sōtenken: kaiketsu no michi wa* [A General Examination of Pollution Administration: A Road to Solutions?] (Tokyo: Gōdō Shuppan, May 1971), pp. 105–127; Kankyō hozen kyōkai, *Kōgai Nenkan 1972* [Pollution Yearbook 1972] (Tokyo, May 1972), pp. 518–520, 562–578; Kokumin kyōiku kenkyūjo, *Kōgai to kyōiku* [Pollution and Education], vol. 6 in the series Kokumin kyōiku [Education of the Japanese] (Tokyo: Meiji Tosho, July 1970), pp. 30–42; Miyamoto Ken'ichi, *Kōgai to jūmin undō* [Pollution and Residents' Movements] (Tokyo: Jichitai Kenkyūsha, November 1970), pp. 288–307; Shimizu, "*Itai-itai* Disease," in Ui, *Polluted Japan*, pp. 17–21; Toyama Shim-

in 1946, claimed in 1972 that at least 120 had died of it since 1946 and that he had seen a total of 280 cases in Toyama prefecture, as well as a few others in Hyogo prefecture and on the island of Tsushima.

The disease is associated with massive neuralgic pain and with the gradual decalcification of the bone structure (particularly in the pelvis and legs), skeletal deformation, and extreme vulnerability to bone fractures. Pain due to acutely heightened sensitivity results from the slightest degree of body activity (even from respiration and digestion). Death eventually results from loss of appetite and physical weakness. All of the known victims have been women, except for six men who consumed the water of the Jinzū directly as drinking water. Women apparently have greater need for calcium than men, who can ordinarily tolerate greater levels of cadmium than women without experiencing the same risk of decalcification.

Based on the geographical distribution of the disease and chemical analysis of body tissues of the victims, Dr. Hagino hypothesized that it was caused by industrial wastes containing cadmium, zinc, and lead, which were released upstream by the Kamioka plant of Mitsui Mining and Smelting in Gifu prefecture. The Kamioka plant had expanded rapidly during the war years, releasing large quantities of heavy metal wastes, which surfaced in the postwar emergence of many cases of *itai-itai* disease. Although Toyama prefectural authorities established a Special Local Disease Countermeasures Committee in 1961 as a result of the controversy his theory aroused, Hagino and his associates were pointedly excluded from the committee, despite the fact that so far they alone had conducted systematic research on the disease.

While the Japanese scientific community sought other explanations for the disease—that it was a freakish result of climatic peculiarities in the area, that it was a hereditary problem, or that it was a result of nutritional deficiencies—Hagino received a grant of $30,000 from the United States National Institute of Health to pursue his own research at other sites of potential cadmium poisoning. Wherever the refining process was of considerable size, where the cadmium-bearing wastes were released as fluids rather than in dry form, and where this liquid waste entered the

bunsha, *Kōgai depaato: itai-itai byō, sono ato no Toyama ken* [A Department Store for Pollution: Toyama Prefecture After Itai-Itai Disease] (Kanazawa: Hokkoku Shuppansha, December 1970), pp. 7–35, 211–216; Ui, *Kōgai genron* 2:104–135; Ui Jun, *Kōgai rettō 70 nendai* [Polluted Islands: The 1970s] (Tokyo: Aki Shobō, June 1972), pp. 200–213; Additional information was obtained from the plaintiffs' newsletter, Itai-itai byō taisaku kyōgikai [Council for Countermeasures against Itai-itai Disease], *Itai-itai byō* [*Itai-itai* Disease]. Dr. Hagino's findings are also well documented in medical and scientific publications. Finally, on the new controversy over the cadmium theory, see Kondō Chūkō, "Itai-itai byō gen'in ronsō mushikaeshi no nerai" [The Objective of Steaming Up the Debate over the Cause of Itai-itai Disease Again], *Zen'ei* 383 (June 1975), 200–207, for the plaintiffs' lawyers' viewpoint.

underground water supply or the drinking water of a community, cases of *itai-itai* disease were found. In 1964 Dr. Hagino announced that he had diagnosed several cases in Tsushima.[19]

Dr. Hagino experienced tremendous social and political pressure to give up his research. His tax returns were audited unnecessarily, and he received poison-pen letters, threatening telephone calls, and bomb threats. There were accusations from many quarters that he was taking bribes to certify people who were not really victims, and that the cadmium theory was a grandstand play for money and personal fame. The prefectural governor publicly called Hagino insane (*kichigai*). Dr. Hagino encountered such pressure because he played such an extremely important role in the discovery of and research into *itai-itai* disease. For years, the victims suffered in silence, and it was Dr. Hagino who first noticed that they all shared similar symptoms and who devised experiments to locate the chemical origins of the disease. Because he had his own medical practice he could not be threatened with unemployment, as were many of the technicians and experts in other cases. Finally, Hagino persuaded the victims to go to court, where they would be guaranteed a forum for the orderly presentation of their evidence, and where Mitsui's responsibility for damages could be pursued.

With Dr. Hagino's encouragement, the victims began to organize and to petition the prefectural government and the Kamioka smeltery of Mitsui for financial compensation for their living expenses and medical bills. In September 1966 the prefectural countermeasures committee, in association with the Ministry of Health and Welfare (MHW) and the Ministry of Education, concluded its several years of study, and reported that *itai-itai* disease was a combination of cadmium poisoning, hormonal imbalance related to the lack of calcium, and nutritional deficiencies. As a result of this partial verification of the cadmium theory, the victims gained confidence, and in November 1966 they created the Council for Countermeasures against Itai-Itai Disease, thus formally becoming a citizens' movement. In January 1968, twenty lawyers decided to take the case into court. They found 28 victims who were willing to file a lawsuit as their last resort, and in March this first group of plaintiffs filed suit. Eventually the *itai-itai* case became the biggest of the Big Four lawsuits,

19. The government consistently discredited these diagnoses until a former director of Tōhō Zinc in Tsushima admitted in 1974 that he had ordered his employees to tamper with soil and water samples in order to deceive government inspectors looking for cadmium contamination. Nagasaki prefecture then asked Dr. Hagino to examine potential victims there once again. The Environment Agency's final determination was that there were twenty-two victims of kidney ailments caused by cadmium poisoning in Tsushima (though these cases were not identical to *itai-itai* disease in Toyama), and that these victims would be eligible for compensation under the pollution disease victims' relief system. See *JT*, 9 March, 13 March, 27 March, 23 May, and 26 May, all in 1974; and *JT*, 5 February 1976.

with 512 plaintiffs (including surviving victims and the immediate families of deceased victims).

At the same time that the victims began mobilizing and preparing to initiate litigation, the rest of society began to change its view of *itai-itai* disease. For humanitarian as well as practical political reasons, various leftist groups (labor unions, the JSP, the JCP, and others) within Toyama prefecture formed their own support group to publicize cadmium pollution. The committee on pollution in the upper house of the Diet took up the problem in May 1967. Both MHW and the Ministry of International Trade and Industry (MITI) began additional surveys in June 1967. In May 1968, shortly after the first group of plaintiffs filed suit, the MHW released its conclusions on the causes of the disease, supporting all of the major contentions of Dr. Hagino's cadmium theory and naming Mitsui Mining and Smelting as the most probable source of contamination. Thus *itai-itai* disease was the first to be formally recognized by the government as a pollution disease.

The mobilization of victims and their support groups and the national publicity given to *itai-itai* disease also affected prefectural and municipal politics. In July 1967 Toyama prefecture conducted medical examinations of 1,816 potential victims, and in the following year the prefectural assembly passed a pollution-prevention ordinance, which also provided two million yen per year in medical and living expenses to the certified victims. The municipal assembly of Fuchū (four progressive and twenty conservative assemblymen) passed a unanimous resolution in support of the victims in March 1969, one year after the first plaintiffs had filed suit. This remarkable resolution criticized the court for restricting public attendance at the sessions, called for government subsidies to cover the victims' court costs in view of Mitsui's tremendous financial resources, and donated one million yen of the municipal treasury to the victims for their court costs. The assembly also appealed to the other municipalities in Toyama prefecture, and in response thirty-two of the other thirty-five cities and towns in this traditionally conservative, uncomplaining region of Japan passed similar resolutions.

The prefectural governor, long known for his defenses of the Mitsui operation and Mitsui's various explanations of the disease, condemned these municipal resolutions, saying that it was illegal to donate money in this manner and that it was inappropriate for local governments to express an opinion on a matter still in court. The victims and their supporters replied that as long as local governments had to bear the costs of research and medical care they had a legitimate interest in seeing Mitsui declared responsible, and that it was surely the responsibility of local governments to be interested in the welfare of their citizens (which the victims were, and Mitsui, located across the boundary in Gifu prefecture, most definitely was not). The new prefectural governor elected in April

1971 adopted a more neutral position, friendly to both Mitsui and the victims.

During the same period, heavy concentrations of cadmium were found in Kurobe city (cadmium-bearing rice was eventually found throughout Japan), leading to a general demand for stricter provisions in the prefectural pollution-prevention ordinance passed in 1968. In July 1970, Toyama citizens resorted to the new method of direct-demand initiative: signatures from 2 percent of the eligible voters in the prefecture would require assembly action on a question within twenty days. The initiative petition needed only 14,000 signatures, but 21,400 valid signatures were quickly obtained, and the governor had to call a special session of the assembly. Although conservative assemblymen handily defeated the measure, this was an important moment for citizens' movements. Not only was this Japan's first antipollution initiative, it was also the first initiative campaign demanding consideration of legislation that citizens had drafted themselves.

Meanwhile, the lawsuit proceeded, at a reasonably fast clip for Japanese courts. Just a few months before the verdict was to be announced, Toyama prefectural authorities announced their intention to file suit against Mitsui to obtain financial compensation for the victims' medical expenses paid out of the prefectural treasury since 1968. The first such action ever taken in Japan, it was a tremendous boost to the morale of the plaintiffs. Their prefectural government was now as interested in pursing Mitsui's responsibility as they were, and did not want to use the taxpayers' money to pay Mitsui's bills.

The verdict was delivered on June 30, 1971. Although the *itai-itai* case was the third pollution suit filed, it was the first to arrive at a verdict, and thus played a very important role in setting precedents for future pollution litigation. The decision was virtually a complete victory for the plaintiffs, awarding the first group ¥57,000,000 of the ¥62,000,000 in damages that they had requested, a very important signal to Japanese industry. Neither prestige, status, influence, nor tremendous financial resources could guarantee a verdict favorable to industry in a pollution case.

Mitsui, shocked by the verdict, appealed. The plaintiffs, emboldened by their unexpected success the first time around, doubled their demands for damages and further increased these new demands by 20 percent in order to compensate their lawyers (who had worked virtually without payment thus far). Not only did the high court award the verdict to the plaintiffs again, it also gave them 100 percent of their newly enlarged demands for restitution. Mitsui's overconfident gamble cost the company almost three times what it would have had to pay if it had stopped at district court, in addition to another year of legal fees. The day after the verdict was announced, Mitsui also signed three additional agreements. Mitsui promised to pay commensurate restitution to all victims and their families who had not filed suit and to all subsequently certified victims, and to replace the contaminated topsoil of Fuchū with fresh soil; and the company signed a pollution-prevention agreement affecting its future operations. Firms involved in the other Big Four pollution cases did not make Mitsui's mistake, and instead accepted the decision of the district court.

• Organic mercury poisoning (Kumamoto and Niigata prefectures)

Unlike naturally-occurring inorganic mercury, methyl (organic) mercury compounds from industrial wastes can readily penetrate the chemical barriers that normally protect the human nervous system, gradually killing the brain cells and turning the affected areas into a black, spongy mass. Symptoms include the concentric constriction of the visual field, poor motor coordination, disturbances in sensation, loss of speech or hearing, and tremors and convulsions in the limbs, but there is considerable confusion over the diagnostic techniques in nonacute cases. Depending on the rate of ingestion of mercury, the disease can strike and kill in a matter of weeks, or it can attack very slowly over a period of years, often being confused with other ailments. No treatment has been discovered, and rehabilitation is successful only in moderate cases.[20]

20. Material concerning mercury poisoning, both in Minamata and Niigata, was obtained from the following sources: Bandō Katsuhiko, "Kōgai saiban no jittai" [The Realities of a Pollution Court], in Kainō Michitaka, Kankyō hakai [Destruction of the Environment], vol. 5 in the series Gendai ni ikiru [To Live in the Present] (Tokyo: Tōyō Keizai Shimbunsha, November 1971), pp. 141–162; Bandō Katsuhiko, "Niigata Minamata byō saiban ketsuban ni okeru genkoku gawa saishū chinjutsu" [Plaintiffs' Final Statement in the Concluding Hearings of the Niigata Minamata Disease Trial], Shimin 4 (September 1971), 196–206; Harada Masazumi, Minamata byō [Minamata Disease] (Tokyo: Iwanami Shoten, November 1972); Igarashi Fumio, Niigata Minamata byō [Niigata Minamata Disease] (Tokyo: Gōdō Shuppan, April 1971), pp. 110–191; Michiko Ishimure, "Pure Land Poisoned Sea," Japan Quarterly 18:3 (July–September 1971), 299–306; Kōgai nenkan 1972, pp. 532–593; Matsubara Haruo, Kōgai to chiiki shakai: seikatsu to jūmin undō no shakaigaku [Pollution and Regional Society: The Sociology of Livelihood and Residents' Movements] (Tokyo: Nihon Keizai Shimbunsha, October 1971), pp. 196–210; Miyamoto, Kōgai to jūmin undō, pp. 90–93, 238–287; "Niigata Minamata byō ryaku nempyō" [A Brief Chronology of Niigata Minamata Disease], Kōgai kenkyū 1:2 (October 1971), 42–43; K. Otani and Jun Ui, "Minamata Disease," Polluted Japan, pp. 14–16; Donald Thurston, "Aftermath in Minamata," Japan Interpreter 9:1 (Spring 1974), 25–42; Ui Jun, Gendai shakai to kōgai [Contemporary Society and Pollution] (Tokyo: Keisō Shobō, August 1972), pp. 67–130; and Ui, Kōgai genron 1:93–129, 162–189; Ui, Kōgai no seijigaku, pp. 1–192; Ui, Kōgai rettō 70 nendai, pp. 125–199; Ui Jun, "Minamata Disease," in Ui, Sonoda, and Iijima, "Environmental Pollution Control"; and Ui Jun, Watakushi no kōgai tōsō [My Struggle with Pollution] (Tokyo: Ushio Shuppansha, November 1971), pp. 106–121. On problems of diagnosis and future treatment, see Masazumi Harada, "Minamata Disease as a Social and Medical Problem," Japan Quarterly 25:1 (January–March 1978), 20–34.

The disease first appeared in Minamata in Kumamoto prefecture in 1953, in cats and dogs that ate large quantities of discarded fish taken from Minamata Bay. Soon afterward, the same difficulties in coordination began to appear in human adults. Congenital cases of the disease, caused when methyl mercury accumulates in the placenta of a pregnant woman (who might have no discernible symptoms) and is transmitted in a concentrated dose to the fetus, were discovered in 1958. The child's symptoms resemble cerebral palsy, but children with congenital Minamata disease are born with incomplete brains and cannot learn, unlike victims of cerebral palsy, who frequently have normal intelligence. The most seriously affected victims of congenital mercury poisoning are little more than vegetables, and have no control over any bodily functions.

During the period 1956 to 1960, a great deal of research on the disease was conducted, but the process of scientific examination was complicated by several factors: rivalry among government study teams from different ministries, the fact that the fish in Minamata Bay contained many kinds of contaminating substances, the fact that local industrial wastes included a wide variety of toxins in combination, an experimental emphasis on inorganic mercury in ignorance of the chemical changes that convert that substance to the much more lethal methylated, or organic, form of mercury, and outright suppression of scientific evidence.

Dr. Hosokawa of the Chisso Factory Hospital in Minamata began studying the disease and was joined in 1956 by scientists from Kumamoto University and by a study group in MHW. In 1957 these groups announced that the disease was caused by heavy metals which the victims ingested through the consumption of contaminated fish. Fishing families were the most seriously affected because they consumed the largest quantities of local fish. During this period of inquiry, the number of victims steadily increased and the general public grew wary of buying fish that came from Minamata Bay. The Kumamoto prefectural governor banned the sale of certain highly dangerous varieties of fish and shellfish from Minamata Bay, thus imposing great hardship on those fishermen who were also the most vulnerable to the disease. The fishermen petitioned the prefectural government for clarification of the cause of the illness, compensation for being unable to sell their fish, government aid to cover medical costs of the victims, financial and other aid for fishermen trying to adapt to other occupations, and an end to the pollution of fishing grounds.

In 1959 MHW announced that its investigations pointed to methyl mercury as the probable cause of the disease, and the Kumamoto University team named Chisso Corporation, a leading chemical firm, as the likely source of the mercury. Chisso's management hired other study teams with support from MITI, which argued that mercury was not the cause. Pressure from MITI resulted in the disbanding of the study team within MHW, and MITI then arranged for the Economic Planning Agency, over which it had more influence, to take over responsibility for the investigation. As a result, actual research was simply suspended.

Conclusive results were obtained, however, by Dr. Hosokawa while actually in Chisso's employ. Using secretly obtained Chisso waste water rather than samples from Minamata Bay, his experiments conclusively proved that Chisso wastes could produce Minamata disease in cats, with symptoms identical to those of human victims of the disease. Chisso's management discovered that Hosokawa was carrying out this research, prohibited him from continuing, and suppressed the evidence. Hosokawa quit his job to continue his research privately. He learned that inorganic mercury, a catalyst for the production of acetaldehyde from acetylene at Chisso, became organic, or methyl, mercury as a waste product, and that this was the critical ingredient that caused the disease. For reasons never made clear, Dr. Hosokawa remained silent until the second outbreak of mercury poisoning was discovered in Niigata prefecture in 1965.

The fishermen were in desperate straits by 1959. Local fishmongers formed an alliance and promised their customers that they would not buy any fish from Minamata fishermen. Even though the Hosokawa studies providing definitive evidence of links between Chisso wastes and the contamination of the fish were not yet public knowledge, the fishermen themselves had little difficulty in concluding that, as the only source of industrial contamination in the area, the mercury-dispensing culprit was most likely to be Chisso. Angry at the company's refusal to negotiate, four hundred fishermen locked the management into the factory, with the result that company executives and representatives of the fishermen finally negotiated terms of compensation in August 1959.

Although the fishermen demanded compensation of ¥100,000,000 to fishing families for damage to fishing grounds, the final agreement was that only ¥35,000,000 (less than $100,000) would be paid, as well as annual compensation thereafter of ¥2,000,000 ($5,555) to the cooperative. An arbitration committee including the prefectural governor was established to negotiate compensation for suffering and medical expenses for victims of Minamata disease. Chisso agreed in addition to reclaim a certain amount of land from the bay at its own expense and to give title of 10 percent of the reclaimed land to the fishing cooperative. Several analyses of this agreement pointed out that it was a net financial gain for Chisso, which acquired title to 90 percent of the reclaimed land without having to purchase the rights to the area from the local fishing cooperative.

During these negotiations, there were many demonstrations, sit-ins, and petitions to local government and to Chisso. New victims of Minamata disease were being discovered rapidly, beyond the borders of Minamata itself. Fishermen conducted an on-sea demonstration in their boats to demand that Chisso stop releasing wastes into the ocean, but Chisso brought criminal charges against them instead of negotiating. This so angered the fishermen that an even larger group assembled in the town of Minamata for a demonstration in November, to coincide with the arrival of a group of Diet representatives to study the problem.

The events of November 2, 1959, reveal a fascinating combination of passivity and rage among the fishermen. First, the housewife designated to speak to the Diet group made an extremely humble appeal:

We have regarded you Diet members as our parents. . . . It is indeed an honor that we, who would ordinarily be unable even to see you, can here present you with our petition. . . . We have been silent as our children died of Minamata disease . . . as our husbands became unable to catch fish, and as people kind enough to buy them from us even if we did catch any disappeared. We have not turned to stealing to live, but have resigned ourselves to our misfortunes. But now we have reached the point where we can no longer endure our lives. We can no longer trust anyone. . . . But now that all of you Diet members have so kindly come, we have the strength of thousands. We humbly beg that you have mercy upon us and help us somehow.[21]

Thus the fishermen asked for pity and compassion in return for years of silent suffering, as required by traditional Japanese norms that punish the open expression of anger against one's superiors.

This same group then proceeded to Chisso. Denied an interview, they stormed angrily into the factory to stop its operations by destroying the equipment if necessary. Riot police arrested the marchers, and the entire town of Minamata rushed to the defense of Chisso. Chisso employees approved a resolution to protect the factory against the fishermen's violent attacks. The regional labor association and twenty-three other groups passed similar pro-Chisso resolutions. Fifty influential citizens including the mayor (a Socialist), the president of the city assembly, and the head of the merchant's association, sent a petition to the prefectural governor saying that the economic survival of the city of Minamata depended on Chisso, and that the changes in methods of waste treatment which the fishermen demanded would mean death for the citizenry as a whole.

As a result, in December 1959, a final settlement for the fishermen and the victims was negotiated, but the demonstration and resulting community reaction had seriously damaged the bargaining position of the fishermen and the victims. Of the ¥35,000,000 which the company had already promised to pay, the fishing cooperative would have to return ¥10,000,000 to compensate Chisso for damage done during the

21. Ui, *Kōgai no seijigaku*, p. 101.

recent demonstrations. Chisso would pay ¥300,000 to the family of each deceased victim of Minamata disease, and an annual pension of ¥100,000 to each living victim. The victims had demanded ten times these amounts as *hoshōkin*, or compensation that connoted an admission of responsibility. Chisso insisted on offering the money as *mimaikin*, a solatium implying only charity, not acceptance of liability. Chisso also agreed to lend up to ¥65,000,000 to the fishing cooperative to help fishermen through periods of instability in their work.

The most controversial clause in the agreement required the fishermen and victims to forfeit the ¥100,000 pensions to survivors if Chisso was ever formally vindicated of responsibility, and to promise never to protest or demand greater compensation in the future even if Chisso were later found responsible. Such a clause frequently appeared in settlements for damages in Japan, but it is important to note that Chisso already knew of Dr. Hosokawa's conclusive findings implicating the firm.

The events of 1959 brought an official end to the problem of Minamata disease for the time being. Chisso's settlement with the fishermen and victims supposedly solved the problem of compensation. In addition, the 1959 report from MHW, which concluded that mercury was the probable contaminant and Chisso the probable source, forced MITI, its own studies to the contrary notwithstanding, to order Chisso to stop releasing its wastes directly into the sea and instead to install purification machinery within one week. Because of Chisso's new waste-treatment system, medical inspectors declared that congenital cases of Minamata disease could not occur in the future and would therefore not be certified (a subtle admission that Chisso had indeed caused the disease).

From 1960 to 1965, Minamata disease was considered a closed subject, official investigations were disbanded, and its cause was considered to be a moot but unimportant point. Then a few residents living along the Agano River in Niigata prefecture reported some unusual neurological symptoms. Autopsy evidence confirmed in June 1965 that a second outbreak of Minamata disease had begun. In contrast to the muddled reaction in Kumamoto, the reaction of the Niigata victims, the other local residents, and the prefectural government was swift and effective. The informed public was outraged that the lessons from Minamata's experience had been ignored and suppressed, thus permitting a second outbreak of the crippling disease. Niigata prefecture immediately began medical examinations to certify victims and prohibited the sale of fish taken from the Agano River. In August, twenty-two different local organizations (led chiefly by labor unions and the JCP) formed the Minsuitai (the Minamata Disease Countermeasures Council of Democratic Groups), and demanded a rapid investigation and solution to the problem. In December the victims themselves formed a group.

The MHW resumed its scientific investigation into the medical causes of the disease. In March 1966 the MHW concluded that Niigata Minamata disease was caused by methyl mercury originating in wastes from the Kase plant of Shōwa Denkō (which used the same process as Chisso) on the Agano River. In an attempt to protect Shōwa Denkō, MITI intervened in the publication of the report and insisted that MHW investigate in more detail before drawing final conclusions. The victims organized to demand ¥100,000,000 in compensation, but Shōwa Denkō refused to discuss large sums that might imply responsibility for the disease.

By this time the scientific debate had revived. In May 1966 moss growing beside the effluent conduits of Shōwa Denkō was found to contain organic mercury, refuting the company's claim that it did not discharge mercury at all and seriously challenging Shōwa Denkō's credibility. Counter-opinions which the firm submitted to the MHW study team contended that a prefectural warehouse for agricultural supplies had been damaged by the Niigata earthquake of June 1964, and that flooding and seepage into the underground water supply had carried mercury-bearing chemicals into the Shimano River. In order to explain how this mercury got into the Agano River, Shōwa Denkō said that the mercury had flowed into the ocean, and later during annual dry season when the freshwater level fell, high ocean tides had forced the mercury back up into the Agano River, where fish had consumed it.

In February 1967 the president of the firm announced over national television that no matter what the government findings turned out to be, his company would not accept them and would not comply with government orders. This announcement infuriated the victims and persuaded their lawyers to sue Shōwa Denkō even though everyone seriously doubted that such a powerful company could be defeated in court. The victims were worried about the time a lawsuit would take, about the cost of legal fees, and particularly about risking the loss of the prefectural aid they were getting to cover medical costs and unemployment relief. The lawyers visited all of the victims, one by one, until they found thirteen who were willing; on June 12, 1967, they filed Japan's first pollution lawsuit.

Scientific debate over the cause and transmission of the victims' ailment assumed critical importance during the course of the lawsuit. As late as January 1968, MITI continued to maintain that the origin of the organic mercury poisoning in Niigata was too complex to be specified. However, in September the Science and Technology Agency published the final report from the official investigative commission announcing that Shōwa Denkō was responsible for the poisoning and that the theory about agricultural chemicals could be dismissed as trivial. The crucial breakthrough was provided by Dr. Hosokawa, who finally ended his silence in response to the Niigata outbreak of the disease and revealed not only his definitive experiments but also Chisso's suppression of evidence in the Minamata case. Thus the government's official report also asserted that Chisso's wastes had caused Minamata disease in Kumamoto prefecture. Shortly after this announcement, all of the Niigata victims decided to join the lawsuit, on the prediction that they had a much better probability of winning now that the official government opinion, MITI notwithstanding, favored them.

Just two days before the final verdict was expected, Shōwa Denkō completely reversed the position it had adopted when there had been no threat of a lawsuit, and announced that it would accept the verdict and would not appeal the case. On September 29, 1971, three months after a district court had awarded its decision to the plaintiffs in the *itai-itai* disease case, the Niigata District Court similarly declared for the victims.

The course of events in the Niigata case and a visit by the Niigata victims to Minamata in January 1968 produced a dramatic change in the mood of both the victims and the other residents in Minamata. The speed with which Niigata citizens rose in defense of their victims was painful to Minamata residents who had ostracized the victims as potential carriers of a contagious disease and defended Chisso instead. Perhaps if they had supported the Minamata victims instead of Chisso, the second outbreak of the disease in Niigata might never have occurred. A JSP assemblywoman, Hiyoshi Fumiko, and a local poet, Ishimure Michiko, formed a citizens' council to defend the Minamata victims and pursue Chisso's responsibility.[22]

With considerable support this time from the local citizens and also from a faction of the Chisso labor union, Minamata victims renewed their own fight for recognition, relief, and legal vindication. However, the victims split into three groups (eventually into a total of *six* factions) over the proper way to do this.[23] The "entrustment" group feared defeat in the courts and instead agreed to an out-of-court settlement mediated by MHW. The settlement of May 1970 (before any of the pollution verdicts) provided a solatium of ¥3,000,000 to the families of deceased victims, and a lump sum payment of ¥1,900,000 plus an annual pension of ¥180,000 to the surviving victims. A second group of "new" victims, who were not yet certified and therefore had questionable standing to sue, opted for direct negotiations with Chisso. The third group insisted on the necessity of a court victory and of a legal declaration of Chisso's culpability, and on June 14, 1969, the "court" faction filed suit against Chisso.

On March 20, 1973, the court awarded the largest settlement thus

---

22. See Yutaka Sasayama, "Ishimure Michiko," pp. 69–70, and Jun Ui, "Aileen Smith," pp. 71–72, both in *Japan Quarterly* 25:1 (January–March 1978).
23. Thurston, "Aftermath in Minamata."

far in a pollution case, including sums of ¥18,000,000 to the seriously afflicted and to the families of deceased victims. Chisso was also ordered to pay commensurate amounts to all of the victims who had not filed suit, and to all victims who might be certified later.[24] This promise also brought the struggle of the direct-negotiations faction to an end. Led by Kawamoto Teruo, representatives of this group had camped out on the front steps of Chisso's main office in Tokyo, risking occasional beatings by company goons, from December 1971 to March 1973, demanding direct confrontation, a formal apology, compensation, a rehabilitation center, future medical care for the victims, and a more active search and certification of new victims. In July 1973 Chisso agreed to pay lump sums of ¥16, 17, or 18 million each to the Minamata victims who had not filed suit, plus lifetime monthly pensions of ¥20, 30, or 60 thousand (depending on the seriousness of the victim's illness), and to create a fund of ¥300 million for medical and economic aid to the victims. Chisso also promised to help pay for the educational expenses of congenital victims, and to offer written apology and an admission of responsibility.[25]

After the verdict, government surveys of potential mercury pollution that revealed contamination in all waters surrounding Japan; medical screening that found cases of mercury poisoning in unexpected locations; and MHW advice to households to limit weekly fish intake of certain species—all combined to stimulate nationwide panic and a drastic drop in fish prices. Fishermen facing bankruptcy blockaded harbors and dumped unsalable dead fish in the ports of industrial cities so that enterprises could neither receive nor send out shipments. Thus Chisso and similar firms had to negotiate additional compensation settlements with fishing cooperatives all over Japan.[26]

By March 1979 there were 1,765 certified victims in Kumamoto and Kagoshima prefectures, with 5,982 more applications pending and a potential total of 10,000 victims in all.[27] Chisso also agreed to an order from Kumamoto prefecture to pay 65 percent of the ¥20.3 billion expense of dredging contaminated sludge from the floor of Minamata Bay.[28]

24. *JT*, 21 March 1973.

25. *JT*, 10 July 1973.

26. See *Japan Times* from May 1973 through September 1973, but particularly 23 May, 26 June, 3–10 July, 18 July, 3 August, 8 August, 21 August, and 18 September. See also Norie Huddle and Michael Reich, with Nahum Stiskin, *Island of Dreams: Environmental Crisis in Japan* (Tokyo: Autumn Press, 1975), pp. 169–193.

27. See table 5 for recent victim statistics. See also *JT*, 5 May 1976.

28. *JT*, 29 February 1976, and *Asahi Shimbun* (*AS*), 1 September 1977 (ssb 3/1). In fact, dredging did not begin on schedule, because 1,817 residents of Minamata filed for an injunction in December 1977 to stop the dredging, which they now feared would stir up the mercury-containing sediments, cause mercury to reenter the food chain, and stimulate a new outbreak of poisoning. See *AS*, 26 December 1977 (ssb 823/1), and *Japan Times Weekly* (*JTW*), 7 January 1978.

By June 1976 Chisso had already paid out ¥22,790 million in compensation to certified victims and pollution-prevention programs, and was accelerating its perpetual search for new ways to obtain liquid funds to pay its rapidly increasing annual bill for compensation to victims, which ran to another ¥4 billion in 1977 alone.[29] Chisso, whose total indebtedness soared to three times its capital assets in 1977, canceled dividends to shareholders, sold several subsidiaries, and applied for emergency government loans. A protracted debate ensued over the appropriate government role in rescuing Chisso from bankruptcy and raised serious questions about who should bear the burden of relief to the victims, the real responsibility of polluting industries if the taxpayers bail them out, and government favoritism toward polluting firms. The Home Affairs Ministry opposed using public bonds to save a private firm, out of its concern for the health of local-government finances, but the Environment Agency endorsed the idea of saving Chisso so that the firm could continue to pay compensation to the victims. Finally, after receiving an informal guarantee of 100 percent financial backup at a June 1978 meeting of the ministers of the agencies involved, Kumamoto prefecture began issuing bonds to cover two long-term low-interest loans per year to Chisso through 1982. By December 1979 the prefecture had already supplied ¥7,861 million (about $35 million at 1980 exchange rates) in loans to Chisso.[30]

Because of the large settlement awards to Minamata victims, the Niigata victims renewed negotiations with Shōwa Denkō, which finally agreed to pay much larger sums (¥15 million to those most seriously afflicted) to the victims than those originally agreed on.[31] A similar settlement between Mitsui and *itai-itai* victims was concluded, increasing compensation and providing complete medical care and monthly allowances for nursing care. The amounts would increase in accordance with increases in the commodity price index, indicating that the pollution victims have grown quite adept at negotiations.[32] Thus the outcome of the Minamata case eventually extended to the others and demonstrated not only that industries would be held responsible for the pollution they produce, but that they might even be pushed close to bankruptcy to pay for their deeds. The Minamata case, once considered a failure by antipollution activists, now stands as a fearsome warning to industry.

29. On Chisso's indebtedness due to payments to victims, see *JT*, 26 January 1975, 28 June 1975, 9 June 1976. See also *AS*, 11 June 1977 (ssb 339/8).

30. On Chisso's attempts to obtain financial relief, see *JT*, 31 March 1973, 30 May 1974; and *AS*, 11 June 1977 (ssb 339/8), 17 November 1977 (ssb 535/10), 10 February 1978 (ssb 309/10), and 17 February 1978 (ssb 505/2). See also "Relief Measures for Corporate Castle Towns," *Japan Quarterly* 25:4 (October–December 1978), 389–392.

31. *JT*, 22 April 1973.

32. *JT*, 19 July 1973, 20 July 1973.

Recent legal developments have underscored this point. In December 1976, 362 applicants for certification as Minamata victims won a district court verdict, which ruled that Kumamoto prefecture had been negligent in processing applications too slowly and thus denying deserving victims the financial and medical relief they needed. In March 1979 the same court awarded damages to a group of uncertified victims and forced the prefecture and Environment Agency to overhaul the diagnostic techniques and screening procedures for certification.[33] Then in June 1977 the Tokyo High Court acquitted Minamata victim and activist Kawamoto Teruo of assault charges (Kawamoto had been charged with biting three people and hitting two others at Chisso's main office).[34] In May 1976, Kumamoto Public Prosecutors indicted the president of Chisso and the head of the Minamata plant on criminal charges of manslaughter. Although the charges were eventually reduced to professional negligence, in March 1979 the court handed down the first criminal conviction for pollution, and sentenced both Chisso executives to two years in prison.[35] The courts obviously faced the pollution issue head-on, rather than claiming, as they so often did in other controversial areas, that they had no jurisdiction, and demonstrated the ability to defend a controversial, though independent and forthright, position vis-à-vis the powerful pressure of industry.

• Yokkaichi asthma (Mie prefecture)

The Yokkaichi case was filed and concluded before the Minamata verdict, but it differed from the other three cases in two ways.[36] The other major pollution cases concerned water pollution caused by a single

33. *AS*, 15 December 1976 (ssb 493/1, 494/1), 29 December 1976 (ssb 868/1), 14 January 1977 (ssb 384/6), 28 March 1979 (ssb 1017/1, 1030/1).

34. Public Prosecutors, unaccustomed to defeat and offended at the ruling's criticism of their conduct, later appealed to the Supreme Court. *AS*, 14 June 1977 (ssb 457/1, 464/1, 465/1), 16 June 1977 (ssb 524/1).

35. On the legal issues in this case, see *AS*, 21 September 1977 (ssb 704/5), 22 September 1977 (ssb 735/1), 23 September 1977 (ssb 754/1), and 22 March 1979 (ssb 787/1, 788/1, 789/1).

36. Materials on Yokkaichi were Kaji, *Kōgai gyōsei no sōtenken*, pp. 19–104; *Kōgai nenkan 1972*, pp. 537–539, 593–600; S. Kitamura, "Yokkaichi Asthma," in Ui, *Polluted Japan*, pp. 30–33; Kondō Shūtaro, *Kōgai Yokkaichi no kiroku: aozora wo kaese* [A Record of Polluted Yokkaichi: Give Back our Blue Skies] (Nagoya: Fūbaisha, October 1967); Miyamoto, *Kōgai to jūmin undō*, pp. 214–237; Ono Eiji, *Genten: Yokkaichi kōgai 10 nen no kiroku* [From the Beginning: A Record of Ten Years of Yokkaichi Pollution] (Tokyo: Keisō Shobō, February 1971); and "The Graying of Japan: Petrochemicals, Pollution, Power Politics, and the People," *Rōnin* 1:12 (August 1973), particularly Sawai Yoshiro, "Summary of 1972 Yokkaichi," pp. 4–10. Information was also available from a newsletter published by the movement itself, Yokkaichi kōgai to tatakau shiminhei no kai [The Society of Citizen Soldiers Fighting against Yokkaichi Pollution], *Kōgai tomare*. A detailed description of the final verdict is in *Mainichi Shimbun* and *Asahi Shimbun* (evening editions), 24 July 1972.

source, whereas the Yokkaichi case concerned air pollution resulting from multiple sources. In 1955, local residents in the city of Yokkaichi were delighted to learn that an old naval fuel base was to be used as a site for the establishment of a large group (*kombinat*) of heavy industries.[37] By 1960 the phenomenon of "Yokkaichi asthma" was well known. The concern over pollutants released by these firms was first brought to the attention of the city authorities by fishermen, who demanded compensation for being unable to sell strange-smelling fish caught nearby (they won only one-thirtieth of what they asked).

In 1960 the city of Yokkaichi, along with Mie prefecture and Mie University, formed commissions to study the problem. The results—confirming the already obvious fact that the widespread asthma was a result of the sulfurous fumes produced by industries in the *kombinat* zone—were not published, but in the fall of 1961 the local labor union of civil service workers discovered some of these reports and published them. From 1962 through 1964, these studies continued to be made, though in a more open fashion, and the residents of the most seriously affected areas transmitted ten major petitions to the authorities through local neighborhood associations, which were dominated by old-fashioned political bosses with strong personal ties to the municipal offices. The only results were new air-pollution regulations, which set such weak standards of concentration (.18 ppm to .22 ppm for sulfurous acid gas, despite the fact that Yokkaichi asthma had been produced from concentrations of only .17 ppm) that the polluting industries did not have to take any action at all to meet the standards.

The first sign that Yokkaichi residents might change their tactics was the formation of a group built around the regional labor association, the JSP, and the JCP, which held the first citizens' assembly on pollution in July 1963. This meeting demanded that the city assembly take concrete measures to prevent air pollution, that the mayor negotiate with the prefecture and the national government to prevent the arrival of additional industries, and that the mayor take adequate control measures and force the polluting firms to install prevention equipment. In response, the mayor promised only to create a pollution patrol and an inspection committee. A similar citizens' assembly in July 1964 passed another resolution, demanding that the city finance evacuation and resettlement of residents away from the most dangerous areas of Yokkaichi. Local citizens learned at these meetings about their common problems and the alternatives available to them, but the group that organized the meetings soon dissolved, and little came of these resolutions.

37. *Kombinat* is a Russian word, pronounced *kombinaato* in Japanese, referring to a massive complex of manufacturing firms in related industries, all located in close proximity in order to minimize transportation costs.

At this point, the Yokkaichi case was considered a dismal failure by most activists and environmental writers, a typical example of what happens when victims rely on the traditional structure to solve their problems instead of turning to the new methods provided in the postwar political system. But then, in 1966 and 1967, two certified victims committed suicide, attracting nationwide attention. On September 1, 1967, only three months after the Niigata suit was filed, nine among the hundreds of certified Yokkaichi victims finally filed suit against six of the *kombinat* enterprises (Mitsubishi Yūka, Mitsubishi Kase Kōgyō, Mitsubishi-Monsanto Kasei, Chūbu Denryoku, Ishihara Sangyō, and Shōwa Yokkaichi Sekiyū). One observer suggests that the social pressure against filing suit was so severe that these nine persons only did so out of a sense of responsibility to the other victims, accepting the weight of social criticism directed against them much as martyrs might.[38]

During the course of the lawsuit the atmosphere surrounding public opinion, government action, and other pollution litigation grew increasingly supportive. In September 1971 the victims and their sympathizers formed the Society of Citizen Soldiers to Fight Yokkaichi Pollution, reflecting their new militancy. In June 1971, one of the defendant firms abandoned its plan to construct an additional plant in Yokkaichi. On July 24, 1972, after almost five years in court, the plaintiffs won their case. The court awarded them somewhat less than half of what they requested, but because they had asked for such large amounts per person, the final awards were in conformity with the general trend of steady increases established by other verdicts. Additional groups of plaintiffs filed suit, and non-plaintiffs negotiated independently for compensation.

The Legal Impact of the Big Four Verdicts

District court decisions are not binding on one another, and each pollution verdict had to stand alone as an independently reasoned interpretation based on the facts of the case. But they had a cumulative impact on legal theory, each verdict strengthening elements in the earlier ones and adding innovations of its own. The following analysis will be organized around the several themes where these landmark verdicts had their greatest impact.

• Causation

Generally, plaintiffs in any damage suit must demonstrate both causation and negligence—that the defendant's activity caused the

---

38. Frank K. Upham, "Litigation and Moral Consciousness in Japan: An Interpretive Analysis of Four Japanese Pollution Suits," *Law and Society Review* 10:4 (Summer 1976), 579–619.

damage suffered by the plaintiff, and that the defendant was at fault in not taking precautions to prevent this damage. Pollution suits pose a special problem in that they involve highly technical matters where solid scientific proof is not only difficult for victims with limited resources to obtain, but where definite proof would require experiments on human subjects. Even then, it would be next to impossible to duplicate the ecological conditions that prevailed at the time the suspected pollutant was transferred through the environment to the victim. In such circumstances the best available evidence is epidemiological—essentially statistical rather than clinical studies of a disease. The Toyama District Court broke precedent by accepting such evidence, and the Toyama High Court was even more explicit in specifically defining two levels of proof in a pollution case. The plaintiffs did not have to satisfy the definitions of causality in the natural sciences, and epidemiological evidence that was only indirect and probabilistic was satisfactory if the defense could not refute it with its own clinical or pathological evidence. Although Mitsui presented several alternative explanations of *itai-itai* disease—hormonal deficiencies, vitamin D deficiency, frequent pregnancy, menopause, and so on—none of these common conditions could explain the limited occurrence of the unique *itai-itai* symptoms, restricted to areas with cadmium-polluted water supplies. Nor did Mitsui demonstrate that the intensity, duration of exposure, or vehicle of transmission was the same in areas known to be contaminated with cadmium but where the disease did not occur.

Autopsy evidence in Niigata confirmed organic mercury as the causative agent of Minamata disease, so the arguments over causation revolved around whether Shōwa Denkō was the source of the mercury. The Niigata District Court again accepted epidemiological evidence, arguing that a point-by-point scientific verification would impede the relief of the victims' suffering. The same court also created the "doorstep" doctrine: if the plaintiffs offered a plausible explanation that traced the transmission of the responsible pollutants back to the doorstep of a particular firm, the onus would fall on the firm to prove that it did *not* discharge the substance in its wastes or that the plaintiffs' theory of transmission was flawed. The court argued that since the firm alone possessed the evidence concerning its manufacturing processes and waste products, if it was not the source of the pollutant the firm could easily produce evidence to disprove the plaintiffs' contentions. However, Shōwa Denkō ordered the destruction of charts describing the manufacturing process, and in 1966 it dismantled the Agano River plant and destroyed samples of waste water and other evidence. This suspicious conduct was probably meant to make direct scientific proof of causation impossible, but the court argued that Shōwa Denkō thereby deprived itself of the only evidence that might have cleared it of blame.

The Yokkaichi plaintiffs faced the most difficulty in establishing causation, because they suffered from respiratory ailments that were common all over the world and possible even in the absence of industrial pollution. Furthermore, there were many sources of air pollution and even of sulfur dioxide in Yokkaichi, so they could not trace a particular unusual substance from the point of discharge through the environment to themselves as victims. However, the court accepted epidemiological and other evidence showing that the six defendant firms were the major contributors to air pollution, that the victims' health problems were more frequent than could be explained by their previous medical histories and far more serious than could have occurred without the *kombinat*'s sulfurous emissions, and that weather conditions could explain the movement of *kombinat* emissions from the source to the areas where victims were concentrated. The defendants attempted to refute the plaintiffs' charges by arguing that their emissions had *not* contributed significantly to air pollution, that the victims were either feeble or hypersensitive, and that the real offenders were other "ravenous" consumers of oil, such as public bathhouses, ships docked in the harbor, hospitals, and schools. The court found these suggestions quite unconvincing.

It should be obvious that the meaning of these new legal, rather than scientific, standards of causality for pollution cases constituted a dramatic shift in the burden of proof from the plaintiffs to the defendants. Given the analogous position of defendants in civil and criminal cases, prevailing legal theory in Japan (and elsewhere) usually places the burden of proof on those who bring charges. But in a pollution disease case, the plaintiffs are sickly and lack both the resources and the scientific skill to discharge this burden according to prevailing standards of proof, particularly in comparison with the defendant industries. In all of the Big Four, the plaintiffs (victims) had only to demonstrate that their theory was plausible, to defend their theory against criticisms from the defense, and to show that the counter-theories put forth by the defense provided a less effective explanation of the available facts than their own did. This shift in the burden of proof and the evaluation of epidemiological evidence helped to equalize the resources of the two sides in a pollution case and to provide legal redress to victims who could not otherwise seek it.

· Negligence

Another vital innovation in the Big Four verdicts was their handling of the concept of negligence. Only in the *itai-itai* case, where the plaintiffs were able to rely on the no-fault liability clause in Article 109 of the 1939 Mining Law, was it unnecessary for the plaintiffs to demonstrate fault or negligence on the part of the defendants. But negligence was a major issue in the other cases, and the verdicts' newly widened interpretations of negligence virtually established the principle of strict or no-fault liability for all forms of industrial pollution, even though it does not exist in the Basic Law for Environmental Pollution Control.[39]

Article 709 of the Civil Code provides that "a person who violates intentionally or negligently the right of another is bound to make compensation for damage arising therefrom." The standard narrow interpretation of this article was that a defendant who could not be expected to have foreseen damage or who took "reasonable" measures to alleviate damage, even if these were insufficient to prevent it entirely, was not negligent. The Niigata court was the first to broaden this interpretation by establishing a "strict duty of care," ruling that chemical plants are apt to generate harmful waste products and are therefore obligated to manage their operations so as to ensure safety, to take "all possible" measures to prevent injury. Even if the firm uses the best available prevention equipment and the highest technical standards of the time, operations should stop immediately when there is any possibility of danger.

By these standards, the Niigata court found Shōwa Denkō negligent even though no evidence to show willful or malicious intent was presented. Mercury poisoning in Minamata was already a matter of common knowledge, and even though no particular scientific explanation of the disease was publicly confirmed before 1965, the scientific reports of 1959 named mercury in Chisso waste water as a probable cause. Shōwa Denkō used the same chemical processes as Chisso and therefore had a responsibility to exercise extreme care with its wastes. Thus the court found Shōwa Denkō negligent because it had not bothered to analyze its waste products, discarded its wastes untreated, and did not even notice that inorganic mercury changed into the more dangerous methylated form.

In the Kumamoto case, Chisso continued to release mercury wastes even after learning from Dr. Hosokawa's experiments that its wastes caused Minamata disease. The court regarded this episode as ample proof of malicious intent and negligence after 1959. The court also declared that Chisso's negligence extended back to the 1940s—even though Chisso violated no law or administrative standard, its waste disposal methods were superior to those used by similar firms, and there was no case of mercury poisoning yet to serve as a warning. In response to Chisso's defense that it could not have foreseen the creation of methyl mercury or the transmission of mercury through the food chain to hu-

39. On the insertion of an undefined and impracticable clause concerning no-fault liability (*mukashitsu sekinin*) into the Basic Law for Environmental Pollution Control (1967), and its subsequent removal in the 1970 revision of the law, see Margaret McKean, "Pollution and Policymaking," in T. J. Pempel, ed., *Policymaking in Contemporary Japan* (Ithaca, N.Y.: Cornell University Press, 1977), pp. 201–238.

mans, the court argued that it was common sense to regard Chisso's waste water as potentially dangerous, and that a 1921 article had already suggested the possibility of producing organic mercury as a by-product of the processes Chisso used. Much like the Niigata ruling, the Kumamoto court argued that nonnegligent conduct would involve continual analyses of waste water, extensive environmental surveys before the discharge of waste, and immediate suspension of operations whenever there was any doubt about the safety of plants or animals as well as people. Failure to foresee the possibility of damage was tantamount to experimenting on unwilling human subjects.

The Yokkaichi verdict ruled that firms are obligated to exhaust all possible measures to prevent pollution damage, transcending economic considerations, up to and including the use of the best technology in the world, in order not to be considered negligent. The most important modification of negligence doctrine in the Yokkaichi verdict was the court's decision that all six defendants were jointly and severally liable. That is, even if each single defendant released quantities of pollutants too small to damage human health, they were all located in close proximity and together produced massive pollution in a concentrated area. Even though there was no legal prohibition against industries clustering together, to the extent that their operations were related to each other and dependent on proximate location, they were all jointly liable for damages. If companies decided to locate together in *kombinats*, and if they were to engage in activities likely to release pollutants, then they had to discuss steps to avoid or alleviate joint pollution, to test their own emissions, and to install prevention equipment. Finally, the failure to use the world's best technology constituted negligence. This aspect of the Yokkaichi ruling compares favorably with the Federal Water Pollution Control Act of 1972 in the United States (which established 1977 and 1983 as the respective deadlines for installation of the "best practicable" and the "best available" technologies in polluting firms in America) because it had immediate, not future, application to other polluting firms. In short, the court ruled that it was the duty of firms in Japan to establish that their total combined emissions would not damage human health, *before* they built agglomerations of plants (*kombinats*). The six defendants did not make these advance preparations and were therefore negligent in their conduct. The Yokkaichi verdict had a far-reaching effect on cases involving other *kombinats* and put legal obstacles in the way of massive development schemes, even those already funded. Two of the huge projects planned before this verdict emerged, at Shibushi (Kagoshima prefecture) and Mutsu-Ogawara (Aomori prefecture) were subsequently reduced by more than two-thirds, in part because of the Yokkaichi verdict.

• Compensation

The Big Four cases also deftly handled the problems related to the compensation of pollution victims. An important feature of the Minamata ruling was its voiding of the 1959 solatium (*mimaikin*) contract between Chisso and the victims. Chisso argued that this was a legally binding compromise (*wakai*) under the civil code, but the court ruled that Chisso's suppression of Hosokawa's findings invalidated the agreement, which took advantage of the victims' lack of full information on causation of the disease and required them to surrender a legitimate right to claim damages in the future.

All of the courts awarded damages in amounts calculated to reflect the victims' suffering and individual circumstances, using varying schemes to take into account the victims' degree of disability, severity of symptoms, the extent to which their affliction interfered with their routine of daily life and work, and forfeited income. In addition, the Toyama High Court regarded Mitsui's appeal of the district court ruling as a barrier to relief that compounded the victims' suffering and therefore enlarged the compensation that Mitsui had to pay to the victims. Partly for this reason, appeals have been unusual in subsequent cases.

The courts recognized the rights of pollution victims, as disabled persons without employment or independent financial resources, to have government aid in the payment of their court fees. Americans are familiar with the defendant's right to counsel in a criminal case, requiring the courts to appoint a public defender when the accused cannot afford a lawyer. The Japanese system formed in 1952 extends this right to counsel to civil cases, and the *itai-itai* case established that pollution plaintiffs (victims) are eligible for aid under this system. Because the defendants lost all of the Big Four suits, the court ordered the polluting firms to compensate the victims for their legal fees (and refund the government for its expenditures on the victims' behalf). Fee-shifting depending on the outcome of a civil suit is familiar in both Japan and America, but three of the rulings (Kumamoto, Yokkaichi, and Toyama High Court) held that awards to cover the victims' legal fees, as a form of lost income, should be proportional to the severity of damages and the victims' increased suffering due to prolonged trials. Therefore these rulings set the sums for attorney expenses as a fixed percentage (10% or 20%) of the damage awards.

The plaintiffs' victories in the Big Four cases, along with these options to cover legal fees, influenced the community of trial lawyers and legal experts, and a group of young lawyers committed to handling pollution cases has emerged. They are willing to take these cases at very low fees or even on a contingency basis (otherwise unusual in Japan), knowing that they will eventually be compensated by the defendants if they win or by the government aid system for poor plaintiffs even if they lose the case. There is even a movement to establish an organization of public-interest lawyers whose task will be to take up such questions as environmental and consumer issues.[40]

Finally, the courts have gone beyond awarding compensation by issuing orders to polluting firms to do whatever is possible to restore the environment—in Toyama by bringing fresh topsoil to polluted paddies, and in Minamata by dredging the bay to remove mercury-contaminated sediments. Verdicts often include additional commitments of the polluting firm's resources to research, to the search for more victims, and to rehabilitation and treatment of victims. In most cases, victims and their supporters capitalize on the momentum created by the verdicts to extract a pollution-prevention contract from the polluting firms to apply to their future operations.

• Summary

The courts made it easier for victims to win pollution lawsuits by declaring epidemiological evidence acceptable and by shifting the burden of proof to industry. The courts went beyond the customary interpretation of negligence to create a standard of nearly strict (no-fault) liability, including sins of commission as well as of omission. Similarly, the courts stretched the polluter's duty of care to the farthest extent possible, to include failure to use the world's best existing technology and failure to stop operations when any damage is suspected. Finally, the courts went beyond standards and regulations in existing environmental policy to create a practical definition of pollution, which includes the total emissions from multiple sources even when pollutants released by each individual source taken alone are not sufficient to cause harm and do not violate the law.

All of the major cases were victories for the plaintiffs (the victims), and there is a clear trend for the damages awarded to increase in amount (see table 4). The largest lump sum paid to any individual plaintiff in the Big Four cases was ¥18,000,000 (awarded by the Kumamoto verdict in 1973). Since then, awards for suffering in pollution-related lawsuits have grown further, to over ¥50,000,000 in a Hiroshima district court ruling in February 1979. In accordance with this trend to regard with increasing respect and seriousness the suffering and costs of pollution, the payments awarded in the early verdicts have been supplemented as a result of renewed negotiations. Aware that non-plaintiff victims also could easily turn to the courts, industry has responded cooperatively to court orders

40. Julian Gresser, "A Japan Center for Human Environmental Problems: The Beginning of International Public Interest Cooperation," June 1973.

TABLE 4 | *Damages Awarded in Pollution Disease Litigation*

Case	Number of Plaintiffs	Total Award	Largest Award to a Single Plaintiff	Date Suit Filed	Date of Verdict
Cadmium poisoning Toyama DC	31	¥ 57	¥ 4	March 1968	June 1971
Mercury poisoning Niigata DC	77	¥ 270	¥10	June 1967	Sept. 1971
Air pollution Yokkaichi DC	12	¥ 88	¥15	Sept. 1967	July 1972
Cadmium poisoning Toyama HC	33	¥ 148.2	¥12	July 1971	August 1972
Mercury poisoning Kumamoto DC	138	¥ 930	¥18	June 1969	March 1973
PCB poisoning Fukuoka DC	46	¥ 683	¥25.7	Feb. 1969	Oct. 1977
SMON disease Tokyo DC—WAKAI	35	¥ 870	¥47	May 1971	Oct. 1977
SMON disease Kanazawa DC	16	¥ 431*	¥38.4*	May 1973	March 1978
PCB poisoning Fukuoka DC	729	¥6,000	¥17	Nov. 1970	March 1978
SMON disease Tokyo DC	133	¥3,251	¥49.7	May 1971	August 1978
SMON disease Hiroshima DC	43	¥1,070	¥53.7	April 1973	Feb. 1979

Note: All monetary values are in millions of yen. ¥1,000,000 has grown from $2,778 in 1971 to $5,556 in 1978 back down to $4,167 in 1979 when measured in dollars.

DC = District Court; HC = High Court; WAKAI = court-mediated settlement.

"Number of plaintiffs" refers only to the number of plaintiffs in the single civil suit in which the verdict was pronounced. There are additional PCB suits involving at least 331 plaintiffs, and in the case of SMON there are over 28 additional suits; 4,720 SMON victims have filed suit since May 1971, claiming over ¥190 billion in damages (nearly $1 billion at 1979 exchange rates).

* Includes interest (¥250 and ¥28 millions, respectively, without interest).

to negotiate commensurate settlements with non-plaintiff victims. It is now standard practice for compensation to consist of a lump sum for past suffering, a monthly pension for living expenses, and a monthly payment for medical care and the employment of a practical nurse in victims' homes.

Not only do pollution verdicts tend to benefit the victims, but appeals by industry to higher courts so far support the rule established in the *itai-itai* case, that the high court will be even more supportive of the victims than the district court. For example, the Tokyo District Court convicted Kawamoto Teruo (leader of the "direct negotiations faction" of Minamata victims) of criminal charges of assault and battery against Chisso executives, but in June 1977 the Tokyo High Court acquitted Kawamoto and instead reprimanded the police and the procuracy (in charge of prosecuting criminal charges on behalf of the state, similar to district attorneys and Justice Department prosecutors in the United States) for having abused their authority. Similarly, both plaintiffs and defendants in the Osaka Itami Airport noise-pollution case filed appeals because they were unhappy with the compromise decision of the district court in February 1974. The ruling by the high court in November 1975 was a total victory for the victims, granting all of their points and awarding them greater compensation for noise damage in the future than they had originally requested. The Transport Ministry appealed this case to the Supreme Court, making the Osaka airport-noise case the first environmental case to reach the highest level of the Japanese judiciary. The Supreme Court's First Petty Bench concluded final hearings in May 1978, and plaintiffs rejected the Court's suggestion of a mediated compromise instead of a verdict, which is not likely to be announced before the end of 1980. It appears that the Supreme Court is inclined to find for the plaintiffs on the basis of the facts and prevailing legal interpretations, but is reluctant to create a precedent which would put shackles on the government's entire transportation development program for the future.[41] In two recent cases (PCB poisoning and SMON disease), defendants have filed appeals following each of several district-court rulings in favor of the plaintiffs, but it remains to be seen whether these cases will also conform to the trend.[42]

The clearest evidence that the Big Four cases broadened the definitions of citizens' rights and established litigation as a respectable form of participation is the increasing willingness of pollution disease patients and victims of consumer fraud and dangerous products to go to court. Not only has the number of pollution-related lawsuits increased over time, but more cases now go to court than are settled out of court.[43] Among those who have filed damage suits are the following: newly discovered sufferers from chronic arsenic poisoning (due to arsenic trioxide released by mining operations), victims of hexavalent chromium poison-

41. *AS*, 23 May 1978 (ssb 732/1).

42. For recent developments in the PCB case, see *AS*, 5 October 1977 (ssb 161/1, 162/1, 170/1), 6 October 1977 (ssb 195/1), 10 March 1978 (ssb 337/7, 339/2, 350/1), 11 March 1978 (ssb 360/1, 375/1), 12 March 1978 (ssb 410/5), 19 March 1978 (ssb 645/4). For recent developments in the SMON case, see *AS*, 1 March 1978 (ssb 25/1), 8 March 1978 (ssb 258/5, 268/1), 14 March 1978 (ssb 472/1). On the recent SMON verdicts see *Yomiuri Shimbun*, 3 August 1978 (evening edition), p. 1, and 4 August 1978, p. 7; *AS*, 22 February 1979 (ssb 755/1), 6 March 1979 (ssb 210/7), 16 May 1979 (ssb 519/1, 526/1); and *JTW*, 2 June 1979.

43. The Justice Ministry indicates that there was a rapid increase in pollution litigation and formal arbitration from 1969 to 1972, with 409 lawsuits and 75 arbitration cases being processed as of December 1972. Unpublished statistics are available from the Saikō saibansho jimu sōkyoku minjikyoku [Supreme Court of Japan, General Secretariat, Civil Affairs Division].

ing, parents of babies poisoned by arsenic contained in a batch of Morinaga powdered milk, victims of SMON (a neurological ailment probably caused by the careless prescription of chinoform to control intestinal troubles), victims of AF-2 (a chemical agent used in the preparation of soybean curd), parents of thalidomide babies, victims of PCB (ingested orally in contaminated cooking oil), victims of noise pollution in congested areas or near airports or defense bases, victims of recognized pollution diseases who have not been certified by government screening, and many others. Similarly, those who suffered property damage rather than loss to their health have also filed large damage suits or entered into negotiations with polluters; these include fishermen affected by industrial construction, oil spills, oil-tank explosions, or red tides, and farmers with land contaminated by industrial chemicals. Although some of these cases end in court-mediated compromises or are appealed to the government's Environmental Dispute Coordination Commission, as a rule these mediated settlements are now commensurate with court awards, unlike the compromises of the prewar and early postwar eras. Pollution victims passed another legal milestone in March 1979 when a district court handed down the first conviction under Japan's unique law making pollution damage to human health a criminal offense.[44]

Similarly, because of the success of litigation to obtain compensation for pollution that has already occurred, antipollution movements trying to prevent the establishment of industries that would be likely to pollute the environment have also become increasingly interested in using litigation. Rather than suing a company for willful damage and harm to human health, these newer movements frequently sue governmental institutions for violations of administrative laws and procedures. Environmentalists presently have many cases in the courts to prevent construction of international airports, nuclear generators, conventional power plants, steel blast furnaces, petroleum refineries and storage depots, and similar industrial facilities. There are also suits to stop landfill operations, deforestation by paper-pulp and construction firms, and the construction of oil pipelines, highways, and railway track for Japan's noisy, high-speed, bullet trains.

Japanese Pollution Litigation in Comparative Perspective

The major Japanese cases were damage suits brought by victims demanding compensation because the most critical manifestation of environmental degradation in Japan was the emergence of disease in hu-

---

44. A Yokkaichi firm and four of its employees were found guilty of causing a chlorine gas leak in 1974 that affected over 10,000 nearby residents. *AS*, 7 March 1979 (ssb 251/1, 258/1).

mans. The greatest advances in pollution case law—the new interpretations of causation, negligence, and compensation discussed above—reflect this circumstance, and are likely to serve as a combined warning and model to countries that have not yet experienced or acknowledged pollution disease.

The advanced state of Japanese case law and policy where victims' rights are concerned is evident in the compensation system established in a 1973 law, passed after the first pollution verdicts, which extends automatic coverage to certified victims of recognized pollution diseases. Table 5 shows the numbers of certified victims of various pollution and related diseases. The government oversees the system, which is funded by a sulfur dioxide tax collected from industry and automobile tonnage taxes collected from car owners. Wherever a particular industrial source is found responsible through civil action for damage done to a certain class of victims, that source alone must provide total compensation each month (fixed at 80% of the average monthly wage of workers in each sex and age bracket). Otherwise, for each cubic meter of emissions, all polluting sources greater than a certain size in an area pay a fee into a general fund for the victims in that area. The fee varies by area according to ambient air-pollution levels. For example, because designated air-pollution zones (as are large portions of the major cities) have nine times the sulfur oxide levels prevailing elsewhere, polluting firms in those zones pay nine times the charge per cubic meter that firms elsewhere pay. As increases in the number of designated victims and their monthly compensation require increases in the total fund, the effluent charges also increase. From 1974 to 1976 the fees rose thirteen-fold, from ¥15.84/m^3 in air pollution zones and ¥1.76/m^3 everywhere else, to ¥209.97/m^3 and ¥23.33/m^3 respectively. By 1977 the fee in the designated area with the highest pollution had reached ¥536.63/m^3.

There are still many flaws in the system: controversy over the designation of diseases to be covered, the certification of victims, the delineation of pollution zones, the implicit encouragement to polluting firms to move into nondesignated areas in order to reduce their total pollution charges, and the assignment of charges based only on SOx emissions and not on other kinds of pollution as well. Nonetheless, it is the world's first automatic system for compensating pollution victims. It has low administrative overhead and pays for itself, it compensates victims "fairly" (compared with court awards in pollution cases), and by placing the financial burden on polluting industry it creates a direct incentive for firms to reduce their pollution in order to reduce their total effluent charge. Based on the OECD's Polluter Pays Principle, which in Japan is also called the Punish Polluters Principle (PPP), it is an efficient and effective example of the user-charge system, recommended by many economists and environmentalists around the world to force individual firms to pay

TABLE 5 / *Pollution Disease Victims*

Designated Pollution Diseases	Alive	Dead	Total	Applications Pending
Organic mercury poisoning				
Kumamoto and Kagoshima	1,478	287	1,765	5,982
Niigata	676	66	742	230
Cadmium poisoning[a]				
Toyama (*itai-itai* disease)	230	120	350	
Tsushima	22		22	
Chronic arsenic trioxide poisoning				
Miyazaki	99	10	109	
Shimane	17	3	20	
Air pollution diseases				
41 designated zones (January 1979)	71,190	625[b]	71,815	
Total designated victims receiving government aid in January 1979	73,189			
Total victims shown above	73,712			
Other Environmentally Related Diseases				
PCB (Kanemi cooking oil)[c]	1,578	51	1,629	
Morinaga arsenic powdered milk[d]	11,839	505	12,344	
Thalidomide[e]	253	?	?	
Hexavalent chromium[f]	191	41	232	
SMON[g]	approximately		11,000	

Source (unless otherwise noted below): Kankyōchō, *Kankyō hakusho 1979* [White Paper on the Environment 1979] (Tokyo: Ōkurashō Insatsu Kyoku, June 1979), pp. 285–303. Figures as of March 1979 except where noted otherwise.

[a] These are figures of victims receiving compensation through litigation and negotiation, larger than the numbers of victims of cadmium poisoning who receive relief from the government's compensation scheme (49 survivors and 81 deceased victims, totaling 130 with another 91 under observation as of March 1979). For the Toyama figures, see *JT*, 7 April 1976, and for the Tsushima figures, see *JT*, 5 February 1976.

[b] These 625 deaths as of March 1975 were reported in a mimeographed handout prepared by Isono Naohide for the Conference on Japanese Environmental Law and Policy in Comparative and International Perspective, held at the Japan Society, New York City, 2 May 1977.

[c] PCB, or polychlorinated biphenyl, contaminated a large batch of rice bran cooking oil produced by the Kanemi Company in Kitakyushu. The contaminated oil was sold throughout western Japan in 1968. The total of 1,629 victims shown here was the number of certified PCB poisoning victims as of October 1977 when the first 46 litigants won their damage suit in Fukuoka district court. This total rose to 1,665 in 1978, and there may be as many as ten to thirty thousand victims throughout Japan. For figures and estimates, see *JTW*, 15 October 1977, 15 July 1978, and 29 July 1978, as well as *AS*, 5 October 1977 (ssb 161/1, 162/1, 170/1) and 9 April 1978 (ssb 302/1).

[d] The Morinaga Dairy Corporation accidentally allowed powdered arsenic to enter a large batch of powdered formula for babies in 1955, and babies all over Japan were affected. The figures quoted refer to February 1976 totals provided in Isono Naohide, mimeographed handout, 2 May 1977 (see n. b above).

[e] The Japanese thalidomide disaster was settled out of court in December 1974, with awards to individual survivors ranging from ¥3 million to ¥40 million. For figures, see *JT*, 11 July 1975, and "Diary of a Plaintiffs' Attorneys' Team in the Thalidomide Litigation," *Law in Japan: An Annual* 8 (1975), 136–187.

[f] Hexavalent chromium poisoning victims are confirmed only among those who have handled the toxin during the course of their work. Figures quoted are unofficial ones collected by Kyodo News Service and reported in *JT*, 21 August 1975. Official Labor Ministry figures are a bit lower (191 total, including 24 dead) for the same date.

[g] SMON, or subacute-myelo-optico-neuropathy, is a disease resulting at least in part from the ingestion of large quantities of quinoform (or chinoform), a drug prescribed for stomach ailments. It produces a variety of chronic central nervous system disabilities up to and including paralysis and blindness. For figures, see *JT*, 11 June 1976; *JTW*, 11 March 1978; and *AS*, 6 March 1979 (ssb 210/7).

at least some of the costs created by their polluting activities which would otherwise be borne by society at large.[45] Japan is currently designing a similar relief system for victims of unanticipated side effects of medicines, to be funded by manufacturers and distributors of drugs.

The Japanese relief scheme should serve as a model to American policy makers for two reasons. Some American environmentalists object to the idea of an effluent charge that allows polluters to buy the right to pollute, but they overlook the possibility that the price can be set high enough to result in better pollution control than other systems produce. Furthermore, the effluent-charge system gives industry a stake in developing antipollution technology and an incentive to eliminate first that pollution which is most economically eliminated. By demonstrating the effectiveness of the effluent-charge system in covering some of the social costs of pollution and in encouraging the worst polluters to reduce their effluent most quickly, the Japanese system stands in direct contrast to the American preference for the bureaucracy-intensive regulatory approach. Although Japanese environmental legislation uses a regulatory approach in addition to the effluent-charge system, the American strategy relies totally on the setting of standards for emissions and ambient air quality which firms must meet regardless of technological and economic considerations. These standards are inevitably postponed rather than enforced when firms say they cannot meet the standards.[46] Second, the Japanese scheme for compensating victims may prove instructive as the problem of pollution disease grows in the United States, from such preliminary outbreaks of poisoning as kepone in Virginia, PCB in North Carolina, PBB in Michigan, tritium in Arizona, lead and uranium in the Rockies, sodium in the Snow Belt, and industrial chemicals at Love Canal in New York, to a deeper understanding of environment-linked cancers. The system is eminently workable where litigation is not—that is, when a certain level of damage is known to be caused by environmental pollution, but the polluting agent cannot be traced to particular sources.

Although there are highly developed bodies of tort law to deal with occupational diseases and pollution-related injuries to employees in the United States, victim-oriented developments in environmental law analo-

45. See Julian Gresser, "The 1973 Japanese Law for the Compensation of Pollution-related Health Damage: An Introductory Assessment," *Law in Japan: An Annual* 8 (1976), 91–135; and Organization for Economic Cooperation and Development (OECD), *Environmental Policies in Japan* (Paris, 1977), pp. 37–49. On possible changes in the relief system, see *AS*, 8 May 1979 (ssb 203/1).

46. It is impossible to go into detail here about the unintended inefficiencies in the American approach. For a thorough discussion of emission charges versus blanket regulation, see Allen V. Kneese and Charles L. Schultze, *Pollution, Prices, and Public Policy* (Washington, D.C.: Brookings Institution, 1975); and Robert Dorfman and Nancy S. Dorfman, eds., *Economics of the Environment: Selected Readings*, 2d ed. (New York: Norton, 1977).

gous to those in Japan have not occurred in the United States. Analysis of legal developments in the major American cases reveals an assortment of contrasts with the Japanese examples presented earlier. The American cases are different in purpose, in the nature of the charges brought, in the body of law relied upon, and in the identity and objectives of the plaintiffs and defendants.[47] The major American suits are designed to protect the environment itself from man, rather than to save human victims from the predations of their fellows. The charges involve failure to observe proper administrative procedure in designing or approving development projects, rather than liability for damage. Many of the American cases concern Section 102 of the National Environmental Policy Act (NEPA) of 1969 requiring environmental impact statements to be prepared before a federally funded project is approved; but Japan's Basic Law on Environmental Pollution Control has no such clause, and the major cases there were argued on the basis of laws that predated the bulk of Japan's environmental legislation. Finally, American defendants tend to be government agencies rather than industries, and plaintiffs tend to be environmental interest groups (Scenic Hudson Preservation Conference, Sierra Club, Wilderness Society, Natural Resources Defense Council, Environmental Defense Fund, and even Students Challenging Regulatory Agency Procedures, or SCRAP) rather than victims.

Because of these differences, the greatest developments in American environmental case law revolve around the issue of standing to sue.[48]

47. The closest analog to the Japanese cases is the Allied Chemical kepone (a pesticide) incident in Hopewell, Virginia, in which Allied Chemical and a subcontractor, Life Sciences, faced criminal indictments for conspiracy (Allied was acquitted) and violation of federal water pollution regulations (Allied pleaded no contest and was fined $13.2 million; in addition, two directors of Life Sciences were personally fined and convicted of violating federal water pollution and plant safety regulations). Allied also faced three major civil lawsuits. Workers at Life Sciences, which observed none of the standard practices for protecting employees from the kepone they handled, demanded $186.3 million; about 400 fishermen prevented from fishing in the James River settled out of court for $3 million in all; finally, 10,000 fishermen and marine industries filed a tremendous class-action suit for $8.5 billion. The State of Virginia also wanted $3.6 million for violations of state water-pollution regulations, and Allied may be required to dredge the James River. However, unlike the Japanese cases, the only human victims of kepone poisoning are employees at Life Sciences. There is no evidence yet of damage from indirect transmission through the environment, and such evidence is unlikely to appear in view of the discovery that the human body (and possibly other organisms) can metabolize kepone and eliminate it from the system. Thus far the kepone incident is really a problem of industrial safety rather than a pollution disease case. For a summary of the case, see Marvin H. Zim, "Allied Chemical's $20 Million Ordeal with Kepone," *Fortune* (11 September 1978).

48. The literature on American environmental law is enormous, but four useful works are Joseph L. Sax, *Defending the Environment: A Strategy For Citizen Action* (New York: Knopf, 1971); Frederick R. Anderson, assisted by Robert H. Daniels, *NEPA in the Courts: A Legal Analysis of the National Environmental Policy Act* (Baltimore: Resources

Whereas Japanese pollution plaintiffs had eminently clear standing by virtue of their suffering such severe physical and economic insult, American plaintiffs faced their greatest challenge in persuading the courts that they had standing. Reflecting the greater concern for wilderness and protection of nature in America relative to Japan, American courts gradually acknowledged standing to sue not merely on grounds that the plaintiff was threatened with economic or bodily harm, but also on grounds of possible harm to aesthetic, conservational, or recreational interests (*Scenic Hudson Preservation Conference* v. *Federal Power Commission*, 1965; *Sierra Club* v. *Morton*, 1972). In the case of *SCRAP* v. *United States* in 1973, the Supreme Court ruled that if federal action will harm the interests of a narrow group, then only members of that group have standing to sue; but if this harm will fall equally on the general public, then any citizen may sue. This development in pollution case law is incorporated into much recent environmental legislation in the form of citizen-standing clauses, giving any citizen the standing to sue if procedures stipulated by that law are violated.

Thus an association of environmentalists like the Sierra Club has standing to sue on behalf of a beleaguered environment if it argues that the association's interests in conservation or recreation are threatened by a particular project. In *Sierra Club* v. *Morton*, the Supreme Court ruled against the Sierra Club because it had failed to make these arguments, but the verdict provided the blueprint for future suits by outlining these new criteria to establish standing. In effect, through citizens who claim to represent the public interest in environmental protection, the natural environment itself has acquired standing to sue.[49]

American courts have also ruled that any citizen has standing to sue in case of a violation of NEPA's Section 102 and that the process of filing an impact statement is more than a bureaucratic ritual. Statements must be comprehensive and well documented, must take into account all environmental impact, and must compare the desired project with less damaging alternatives. Furthermore, federal agencies must consider criticism voiced in public hearings and must weigh environmental impact against potential benefits of a project before deciding to go ahead with it.

In none of these issues has there been much development in Japanese

for the Future, 1973); and Werner F. Grunbaum, *Judicial Policymaking: The Supreme Court and Environmental Quality* (Morristown, N.J.: General Learning Press, 1976); and Richard A. Liroff, *A National Policy for the Environment: NEPA and Its Aftermath* (Bloomington: Indiana University Press, 1976).

49. See Christopher D. Stone, *Should Trees Have Standing? Toward Legal Rights for Natural Objects* (Los Altos, Calif.: William Kaufmann, 1974), which originally appeared as an article in *Southern California Law Review* 45 (1972), and had great influence on the Supreme Court's Mineral King decision in *Sierra Club v. Morton* (1972).

environmental law. Environmentalists have thus far met strict definitions of standing even in filing preventive suits in Japan, either as taxpayers concerned about the misappropriation of public funds (the basis of the Tokyo High Court's 1977 ruling on behalf of citizens who sued Shizuoka prefecture for failing to insist that paper companies in Fuji city reimburse the prefecture for the cost of removing paper-pulp sludge out of Tagonoura Port), or as residents near a project that might cause future pollution (the only point granted in a Matsuyama District Court ruling of 1978 against plaintiffs who tried to challenge the constitutionality of nuclear energy).[50] The Matsuyama District Court foiled one recent attempt to establish a broader notion of standing when it rejected a suit filed by coastal residents to affirm citizens' right of access to publicly owned coastline (*irihamaken*). The court simply said that no such right is named in law and that the state has full decision-making power over the use of public lands, thus effectively denying standing in these circumstances.[51]

Impact statements for government projects are not required by national law except in the Inland Sea area (where oil spills and red tides persuaded the Diet to pass stringent emergency legislation). At the local level, most prefectures have informal guidelines or specialized environmental assessment teams that institutionalize the *idea* of impact assessment, but by 1979 only the city of Kawasaki and the prefecture of Hokkaidō had formal ordinances requiring impact studies.[52] Until the Diet passes the environmental assessment bill that has been under consideration since 1976 (so weak that environmentalists oppose it), impact studies and public hearings to discuss them are held only to comply with internal administrative regulations of various government agencies, another form of "administrative guidance" applied to environmental management as it also is to economic planning in Japan. As extra-legal arrangements, impact statements are not subject to legal evaluation at all, and they may be as empty and meaningless as the government dares to allow. Even the Yokkaichi verdict, which states that impact on the environment must be studied thoroughly before *kombinats* can be built, stands only as a warning. The decision does not automatically make the failure to conduct an impact study a violation of law in other instances. Until the law spells out the specific procedural requirements against

50. On recent developments in the *hedoro* pollution case in Fuji city, see *AS*, 6 September 1977 (ssb 167/1) and 20 September 1977 (ssb 674/1). On Japan's first nuclear power verdict in Matsuyama, see *AS* 25 April 1978 (ssb 863/1) and 1 May 1978 (ssb 3/8).

51. On *irihamaken*, see Keikichi Kihara, "Coastline Conservation—Establishment of Common Tideland Use Rights," *Japan Quarterly* 25:1 (January–March 1978), 35–42. On the recent Matsuyama verdict, see *JTW*, 10 June 1978.

52. Kankyōchō, *Kankyō hakusho 1979* [White Paper on the Environment 1979] (Tokyo: Ōkurashō Insatsukyoku, June 1979), pp. 415–417.

which impact studies could be evaluated and challenged in the courts, the only basis available for filing preventive lawsuits will be the charge that local governments violated other existing laws or abused their authority in the course of preparing for a development project. Most such suits charge either that there were violations of Japan's complex laws regarding the sale of land, classification of property for tax purposes, and the destruction of old roads or waterways, or that old-fashioned corruption paved the way for the development scheme in the first place. Naturally, the environmental legislation stimulated by the Big Four trials since the Pollution Diet of 1970 greatly expands the potential range of violations that can now be used as the basis for a lawsuit.

In the United States, damage suits in nonenvironmental disputes are so numerous, demands for compensation so huge, and some of them so absurd in content,[53] that the public's enthusiasm for this kind of litigation does not always appear to be the healthy assertion of civil rights desirable in a free society. Rather, it sometimes seems to be a new get-rich-quick game and a manifestation of the self-propelling cycle that results in a society where every action is circumscribed with legal risks. Cynics even suggest that the plethora of damage suits in America results from an oversupply of lawyers seeking to keep themselves busy (the United States has the largest number of lawyers per capita in the world). The situation in Japan is quite different. Though damage suits have increased fourfold in the postwar era, they are not frivolous. There is nothing absurd about pollution victims' claims of suffering, and the damages awarded, enormous only by Japanese standards, still perform the laudable function of serving as an incentive to industry to clean up pollution and observe higher standards of social responsibility.

The protracted struggles of these pollution disease victims, first with their illnesses, then with their local communities, and finally in the courts, have been recounted in detail to show how pollution could acquire such prominence as a political issue in Japan. No other nation has experienced a human tragedy of this magnitude which could demonstrate so clearly the failure of polluters to monitor themselves and therefore the need for government to intervene as regulator. Furthermore, by showing how in the absence of regulation industrial society inflicts its dangerous by-products upon innocent victims, these cases also served to

53. In recent years, Americans have sued the National Park Service (for insufficient warnings to park visitors) after being attacked by grizzly bears or being hit by lightning. A woman who was blown by powerful wind against a guard rail and broke her jaw sued the architect and manager of the Sears Tower in Chicago (for faulty building design). A woman who sued the city of San Francisco because her fall in a runaway cable car supposedly turned her into a nymphomaniac actually won $50,000 in damages. See Frank Trippett, "Time Essay: Of Hazards, Risks, and Culprits," *Time* 122:9 (28 August 1978), 76.

define pollution as a form of oppression of individuals requiring political and legal remedies.

These verdicts were crucial landmarks in the evolution of civil liberties doctrine in Japan. By transferring the burden of risk from the individual citizen and victim to the polluter (whether conceived narrowly as the industrial polluter or more generally as the society that consumes the services of industry), the Big Four verdicts collectively expanded the definition of civil rights to include freedom from pollution damage. The significance of this development stands out as a break with the past in comparison with the relatively lukewarm stance of the postwar courts on civil liberties,[54] requiring a reversal in prevailing legal doctrine with regard to the burden of proof, causality, and negligence. The casual attitude of the industrial defendants in these cases, who expected to win simply because the plaintiffs, however tragic their plight, could not possibly discharge the burden of proof as conventionally defined, showed how unexpected these changes in legal theory were. Moreover, the Big Four verdicts are extremely "progressive" in terms of defining a citizen's right to be free from pollution and the polluter's duty of care when measured against case law in the United States, whose legal system is one of the most libertarian and rights-conscious in the world.

These four pathbreaking cases also demonstrated that the judicial system could be used to protect ordinary citizens against abuses by powerful institutions, and thus to break down the well-known reluctance among Japanese to use the courts.[55] At the outset, lawyers had to recruit plaintiffs for the cases, but as a result other citizens' movements and pollution victims started using the courts with increasing frequency and for more complex purposes, not just to obtain compensation but also to prevent future pollution and to expose transgressions of the law by local governments. Thus these cases have greatly affected Japanese legal culture in addition to legitimizing litigation as a tool of citizen participation.

Finally, there is a fairly clear causal relationship in both directions between the Big Four cases and citizens' movements. The cases were filed from 1967 to 1969, and the verdicts were rendered from 1971 to 1973.

54. See John M. Maki, *Court and Constitution in Japan: Selected Supreme Court Decisions, 1948–1960* (Seattle: University of Washington Press, 1964); and Dan Fenno Henderson, ed., *The Constitution of Japan: Its First Twenty Years, 1947–1967* (Seattle: University of Washington Press, 1968).

55. Kawashima Takeyoshi, *Nihonjin no hōishiki* [The Legal Consciousness of the Japanese] (Tokyo: Iwanami Shoten, May 1967), contains the best-known development of the notion that the Japanese are reluctant to use the courts. Kawashima made the same point in English in "Dispute Resolution in Contemporary Japan." This notion has recently been challenged by Haley, "The Myth of the Reluctant Litigant," who argues that the Japanese may not use the courts as often as the most litigious peoples on earth, but that their reasons are practical rather than cultural.

Throughout this interval citizens' movements formed at an increasing rate. It would appear that media coverage given to testimony at the trials awakened the public to the dangers of pollution and thus contributed to the creation of citizens' movements. Though the tragedy in the cases themselves was certainly a factor in causing the courts to undergo such a dramatic shift in their legal reasoning, the courts must also have been responding to a rapidly changing political environment in breaking with conventional doctrine and in articulating the citizen's right to live without incurring the risk of pollution. Presumably the emergence of citizens' movements during the trials helped to change the political context in which verdicts were handed down, impelling the judges to find for the plaintiffs. Thus these Big Four cases converted the courts from a mechanism for orderly rule from above into a channel of participation from below.

Environmental Action
Japanese Style

SOME OF THE EARLIEST pollution disputes to generate citizens' movements led to pathbreaking litigation, acquired national publicity, and had direct impact on Japan's legal culture and the growth of other citizens' movements as well as indirect impact on environmental policy, as we have seen. But it would be a mistake to assume that the well-publicized cases were typical or that they permit us to generalize about citizens' movements as a whole. In fact, many citizens' movements cannot use the courts, because they do not have standing as plaintiffs, no justiciable issue is involved, or evidence sufficient for a legal resolution of the dispute does not exist. More often, the task of a citizens' movement is to become a credible political force which local governments and industries cannot afford to ignore. In order to fill gaps in our knowledge of the vast majority of lesser-known movements and arrive at a balanced understanding of the phenomenon, we need to examine a representative variety of different movements in different political settings. This chapter is devoted to case histories of each of the fourteen movements composing our survey, including developments since the interviews where newspaper coverage and personal correspondence permit, in order to provide concrete images of how citizens' movements come into being, how they function, and what sorts of obstacles they encounter. (See the Appendix for an explanation of how the sample was derived and how representativeness was insured.)

Rural Citizens' Movements

• Council for Countermeasures against *Itai-Itai* Disease

One group was included in this study to represent the famous court cases discussed in the previous chapter—the victims of *itai-itai* disease in Toyama prefecture. Although the course of the lawsuit was outlined there, it will be useful in this chapter to discuss the social and political setting, in particular the pressure experienced by victims as they prepared their court case.[1] Victims had always encountered informal prejudice and social ostracism simply because the surrounding community regarded them as hypochondriacs and freaks, also as the possible carriers of some dread contagion or hereditary defect.

But after victims began litigation, the hostility of other local residents crystallized. The theory that the cause of the disease was cadmium, absorbed into the body by way of locally grown rice, made consumers unwilling to buy products from this area. Local farmers, instead of feeling guilty about attempting to sell food that might be contaminated, vented their anger on the plaintiffs who were responsible for the publicity given to pollution of agricultural products in Toyama.[2] Families who did not fear that they would ever be affected by the disease, and even unaffected members of families with victims, argued that the plaintiffs were arrogant and pompous to go to court against a firm like Mitsui. Several informants said that because all but six of the victims were women, the group also experienced additional pressure to endure their pain in silence as a duty appropriate to their sex, but that their fortitude and perseverance constituted a victory for women's rights in Japan. Some townspeople "spied" on the plaintiff group and reported signs of internal weakness to Mitsui, in order to break the plaintiffs' determination to have Mitsui legally and publicly declared responsible. Mitsui hoped to settle quietly and cheaply instead.

However, as the trial vindicated the victims' suffering and strongly indicated Mitsui's culpability, the townspeople's hostility changed to sympathy toward the victims. There were also material reasons for this change in mood. The court's demand that Mitsui pay compensation even to victims who had not filed suit dissolved the mutual resentment that separated plaintiff from non-plaintiff victims. Moreover, the entire community of Fuchū entered negotiations with Mitsui to have the topsoil re-

---

1. Material concerning conflict between *itai-itai* victims and other community residents came from interviews with respondents and other informants. For additional sources, see items reported in chapter II, n. 18.

2. The same problem still exists. Toyama prefecture may have deliberately falsified data on cadmium concentrations in order to pass inspection and sell rice, even from areas where *itai-itai* disease does not occur but where cadmium levels are nonetheless very high. See *Japan Times*, 17 May 1974 and 18 May 1974.

stored, so formerly critical members of the community joined forces with the victims in order to share these benefits.

Another consequence of successful litigation against an illustrious firm like Mitsui was that residents reconsidered their relationship with political authority. The victims were angry at their prefectural governor when he criticized the MHW report concluding that cadmium was the cause of the disease. Victims regarded the governor's tenacity on behalf of Mitsui and the vitamin deficiency theory, even after a government report sanctioned the cadmium theory, as improper because it favored a private business outside of the prefecture over the governor's own constituents. Many suspected financial payoffs from Mitsui to several prefectural governments. Victims were also disillusioned with their Diet representatives, both LDP and JSP, who spoke a great deal about health benefits and compensation for the victims, but who did very little (and were probably unable to do much) in fact.

According to local informants, the clearest political manifestation of these changes in public attitudes was the election in April 1971 of reformist mayors in both Fuchū (where almost all of the *itai-itai* victims lived) and the city of Toyama, as well as an enlarged reformist delegation to the prefectural assembly. In the town of Fuchū there was a close relationship between *itai-itai* disease and the election of a reformist mayor, even, though the victims and their families could directly control only a minority of the votes. Fuchū, like many rural areas in Japan, had been a conservative stronghold, all the more so because its farmers had been relatively well-off. But in 1971 Dr. Hagino advised the victims and their families to mount a campaign for the JSP candidate for mayor in order to warn the LDP to start worrying about its constituents instead of its industrial friends. Although some of those who followed Dr. Hagino's advice may well have voted out of a sense of traditional obligation to a benefactor, most people in this town of 23,000 voters would have had no such sense of obligation toward Dr. Hagino—on the contrary, many had once hated him. Thus the furor surrounding the *itai-itai* case seems to have contributed to significant changes in the local political climate in Fuchū because of the pollution issue itself.

Similarly, although the city of Toyama contained few victims, its residents undoubtedly learned about industrial pollution and grew to believe that the local conservative party was more interested in its industrial connections than in the plight of pollution victims or in the danger of pollution to the population as a whole. Of course other factors explain a reformist victory in a city like Toyama, but it is significant that after the wide publicity given to *itai-itai* disease, many other movements arose in the prefecture to oppose pollution.

• The Citizens' Conference of Usuki

The spread of industry to rural areas is one of the most controversial issues in Japan today. Industrialists in urban areas facing increasing labor costs, higher property taxes, and opposition from antipollution movements see the opportunity to avoid all of these problems by moving to rural areas that would welcome them as a source of employment, local tax relief, and new prosperity. However, rural residents are also bitterly divided over the prospect of industrial development.

Our sample includes a group well known for preventing the construction of a polluting cement factory in their city.[3] In April 1969 Mayor Adachi of Usuki city in Ōita prefecture proposed that the city provide reclaimed land to permit Osaka Cement to construct a factory there. Along with many coastline cities in Japan, Usuki had previously used land reclamation projects to produce salable property as a device to rescue the city budget from serious deficits, and this proposal included plans for bay fill near the two hamlets of Odomari and Kazanashi, both fishing villages formally incorporated into the city of Usuki. The fishing cooperative, including its Kazanashi representatives, agreed to negotiate the sale of fishing rights to that part of the bay.

During the next few months, preparations did not go smoothly. It appeared that Mayor Adachi had promised various public facilities to Osaka Cement without surveying the costs or asking the prefectural government for funds beforehand. The quarrying company which hoped to supply Osaka Cement secretly bought up the land next to the site. During November and December 1969, opposition to the mayor's plan grew, centering around a few well-educated, outspoken residents of Kazanashi who had asthma victims in their families and feared pollution. As is common in Japanese fishing villages where the men were absent for many months of the year, the women were accustomed to making important decisions, expressing themselves openly and even aggressively, and being responsible for the running of their village. Angry with their menfolk for failure to oppose the mayor's plan, the women of Kazanashi began to organize an antipollution movement, an unusual feature of the organization that won wide publicity in the ensuing months.

Nonetheless, on March 21, 1970, the Usuki Bay fishing union reconfirmed the decision to sell fishing rights adjacent to the construction site.

3. The Osaka Cement case in Usuki was covered by Japan's national press. The leaders lectured at Ui Jun's Independent Forum, published in the *Kōgai genron* series for 1972. See also Gotō Kunitoshi, "Makoto no shūkaku wo mezashite" [Aiming at a True Harvest], *Shimin* 4 (September 1971), 82–85. The most comprehensive account is Matsushita Ryūichi, *Kazanashi no onnatachi: aru gyoson no tatakai* [The Women of Kazanashi: The Struggle of a Fishing Village] (Tokyo: Asahi Shimbunsha, August 1972). Additional information came from interviews and other informants.

A fishing cooperative consists of all the people who fish for a living in a particular area. Individual members apply to the cooperative for fishing rights to a particular area, for permission to use certain techniques, and for the rights to certain kinds of fish. The cooperative is a distribution center for collectively owned equipment, a labor union for bargaining with other industries or local governments, and a bank where members can deposit savings or take out low-interest loans, functions that are vital to the members of the cooperative. A fishing cooperative can decide to sell a certain portion of its fishing rights by a two-thirds vote (Article 50 of the Fishing Cooperatives Law and Article 8 of the Fisheries Law), and the proceeds received are divided equally among all the members, regardless of whose individual fishing rights have been sold. In effect, the fishing cooperative is capable of deciding to abolish the occupations of some of its members without their consent and without granting them any extra compensation for their loss. Controversy over the decision to sell was inevitable.

The hamlet of Odomari was in the affected site, but its fishermen were relatively poor and not optimistic about the future of their occupation in Usuki Bay. They caught low-quality fish, and they worked on the basis of a boss system, in which "the boss took 70 percent of the catch and his thirty employees took 1 percent apiece," according to one cynical informant. Thus residents there were eager to obtain whatever money they could by voting with the fishing cooperative to sell their fishing rights. Many of them expected to work in the quarry or later at Osaka Cement.

The neighboring hamlet of Kazanashi became the core of the controversy among the fishermen. A few households there did want to sell their fishing rights, because Mayor Adachi promised that the city would provide an improved road and a local harbor in return for their cooperation. It was later revealed that the national government had already provided a subsidy to pay for these projects, requested long before by Kazanashi as a whole. Mayor Adachi simply pretended that he had the power to deny harbor improvements on the basis of Kazanashi's political cooperation, and thus procured a few allies for himself there.

But the majority of fishing households in Kazanashi strenuously opposed the arrival of Osaka Cement and the decision of the fishing cooperative. The younger fishermen in Kazanashi fish with electric harpoon in the waters of northern Japan over a thousand miles from their homes. This fish is of the highest quality and brings a very good price in comparison with fish that struggle as they die on lines or in nets. The harpoon fishermen of Kazanashi frequently made incomes comparable to that of the mayor himself, a fact often cited to explain why the Kazanashi opposition was so invulnerable to bribes. These deep-sea fishermen obviously would not have lost rights to their grounds by the sale of fishing rights within Usuki Bay, but they wanted to preserve their clean community, and their dependence on good eyesight made them anxious to prevent air pollution in Kazanashi. Older fishermen in Kazanashi did fish locally and wanted to retain their fishing rights in the affected bay-fill site.

Thus, the hamlet of Kazanashi was deeply divided: of its 176 households, 33 were in favor of Osaka Cement (*sansei*), and 143 were strongly against it (*hantai*). *Murahachibu*—traditional ostracism—began to appear in February 1970. The *hantai* and *sansei* families became two separate hamlets, with separate arrangements for sanitation, garbage collection, public safety, and fire and police protection, and separate neighborhood associations, PTA, and women's groups. There was absolutely no interpersonal communication between the two sides.

Residents of the city of Usuki proper, stimulated by the antipollution movement in Kazanashi, began to take an interest in the controversy themselves. During early 1970, the regional labor association, the JSP, and the executives of five local food-processing industries became active in the opposition to Osaka Cement. Labor and the JSP had a understandable interest in protest and in opposing LDP programs, but the local industries also participated because they feared that the pervasive air pollution caused by a cement factory would contaminate their products, and in any case would damage their commercial image and ability to sell food products from Usuki. In April 1970, local assembly elections took place. The antipollution movement managed to publicize all of the candidates who promised to oppose the arrival of Osaka Cement and procured victory for all five of them. (Two later defected to the *sansei* side.)

At the same time, some Kazanashi leaders were already considering legal action. There were doubts about the validity of the fishing cooperative's decision to sell, because of a substantial likelihood that many fishermen who voted to sell were bribed. The figures usually quoted were ¥2,000, or several dollars, plus one bottle of sake for those who fished outside of the affected area, and several hundred thousand yen (several hundred dollars each) for the Odomari and Kazanashi fishermen who agreed to sell their own livelihood rights. Furthermore, lawyers thought that the law could be interpreted to require a unanimous decision on the sale of fishing rights of any individual members. Finally (and what was most important), the lawyers suggested that any decision of the fishing cooperative which deprived some members of their source of livelihood without their own consent would be unconstitutional. On these grounds, the disgruntled fishermen filed suit against the cooperative in June 1970.

The antipollution movement and the *hantai* fishermen faced severe pressure to abandon their suit. In addition to paying for their own legal expenses, the *hantai* plaintiffs actually subsidized the court costs of their opponents because they also paid dues to the fishing cooperative, which used its own funds in court. At the same time, plaintiffs were denied the financial services of the union—loans, health insurance, funds for equipment—as a punishment for challenging the union's decisions.

On September 9, 1970, the Citizens' Conference (Shimin kaigi)—the newly formed antipollution organization for Usuki proper—also filed charges against Mayor Adachi for incurring financial obligations for the city without first securing the funds. At the same time, the Citizens' Conference decided to recall him from office. During the course of the campaign to gather signatures for the recall, it was discovered that the city's financial obligations to Osaka Cement would make the factory a net liability for the city, not a net gain as Mayor Adachi had claimed. The Citizens' Conference calculated that the cost of providing sewerage, electrification, road widening, and other promised services was three times the size of the annual budget. Furthermore, the highly mechanized company would need only 150 employees, none of them local, rather than the 500 employees to be recruited from Usuki, as was originally planned. As a result of these revelations, the recall movement gathered the necessary 9,274 signatures within only five days, and over 14,000 signatures (out of 27,820 eligible voters) in the prescribed period.

Rather than be officially removed from office, Mayor Adachi resigned, so the recall vote became a regular replacement election. According to the final count of December 13, 1970, Mayor Adachi was reelected with 13,446 votes, though the Citizens' Conference nominee managed to win 11,647 votes. Ninety-two percent of the voters turned out, a much higher number than usual.[4] The close margin indicated that the anti-Adachi, antipollution movement had considerable support, in spite of the well-known Japanese reluctance to express hostility openly and the unfamiliarity of the recall method in Japan.

The majority of the Usuki population, who supported Adachi in his bid for reelection, probably did so largely from inertia and discomfort with the idea of recall. I was told of many specific examples of people who were personally opposed to Osaka Cement but who felt afraid to join the Citizens' Conference and even to vote by secret ballot to recall the mayor. It is highly significant that the antipollution movement in Usuki was strong enough to combat social pressure as well as it did, and to engage in open confrontation through electoral and legal channels.

Twice during the lawsuit, Osaka Cement tried to begin construction, and the antipollution activists had to resort to direct action in order to force the company to wait until after the court's decision. In February 1971, the women of Kazanashi occupied rafts in the bay for seventy-two

4. Voting turnout for Ōita prefecture in the local elections of April 1971 was 75 percent. See Mainichi Shimbunsha, *Mainichi nenkan 1973* [Mainichi Yearbook 1973]; and Sōrifu tōkei kyoku, *Japan Statistical Yearbook 1972*.

hours in an area where Osaka Cement tried to begin fill operations. This demonstration attracted the attention of the pollution policy committee of the Diet's lower house, and as a result Osaka Cement and the city of Usuki agreed to postpone operations until after the verdict. Then in June 1971, one month prior to the scheduled verdict, Osaka Cement again tried to bring fill dirt to the reclamation site by truck, so the women of Kazanashi again used direct action, crossing the street repeatedly (a perfectly legal device) and thus preventing the trucks from approaching the dumping site.

On July 20, 1971, the Ōita District Court handed down a verdict favorable in all respects to every argument the plaintiffs had made concerning the fishing cooperative's vote to sell rights to the bay shore. In the final summation, the judge declared fishing rights to be property protected by Article 29 of the Constitution, which no private party can "buy" without the owner's consent. Based on this interpretation, unanimous agreement to sell individual fishing rights to a private company would be necessary. Finally, the judge argued that in the case of deprivation of livelihood, protected by Article 25 of the Constitution, mere numerical comparisons were not sufficient to determine net financial loss or gain to the community, and in any case the possibility of grave environmental damage must also be considered. Ōita prefecture, the city of Usuki, and the fishing cooperative filed appeals, but the Fukuoka High Court upheld the district court verdict in October 1973.[5]

One month after the district court verdict, Mayor Adachi's term expired, and on August 22, 1971, there was a regular election for mayor. After near success in the recall attempt, and now with a favorable court decision, the Citizens' Conference fully expected to control the outcome of the election. Adachi did not run again, and the local merchants' association took the opportunity to promote one Niina Junji as an opponent of Osaka Cement and mayoral candidate, even though he had actually been Adachi's campaign manager previously. The Citizens' Conference considered nominating one of its own leaders (Gotō Kunitoshi) to run for mayor too, but in view of Niina's promise of no further industrial construction until the final legal appeals were over, conference leaders decided that it would be unwise to divide the antidevelopment votes between Niina and their own candidate. It was their intention not to take power themselves but to force whoever happened to be mayor to pay attention to the will of the citizens. (Though he resigned from the mayoral race, in 1975 Gotō won a seat in the Ōita prefectural assembly.)

Left with a choice between a conservative candidate in Niina and a JCP candidate, many members of the Citizens' Conference threw their votes to the JCP to indicate that they wanted the future mayor to take a

5. *JT*, 20 October 1973.

hard line against pollution. Some, unwilling to vote for a Communist, particularly after denying that their movement was Communist, voted for Niina. Many handed in blank ballots as a protest. Niina won comfortably, but the JCP candidate tallied up more votes than is customary for a Communist in Usuki, owing to the protest vote. Mayor Niina later revealed that he favored bringing Osaka Cement to Usuki, but after the unfavorable court rulings the company abandoned its efforts. The movement to prevent industrial pollution in Usuki became known as one of the most politicized and formidable in Japan. Informants revealed that Kazanashi in particular, long an LDP stronghold controlled by a party boss, later solidified behind the JSP, and members of the Usuki Citizens' Conference vigorously campaigned as individuals for the JSP candidate in the December 1972 general election; he not only won a Diet seat but outpolled all other candidates in the district as a whole by a comfortable margin.[6]

· The Liaison Movement to Prevent Petroleum Development in the Ōsumi Peninsula

Another group in the sample concerned about rural industrial development opposed the development of a petroleum refinery complex off the Ōsumi Peninsula, in Shibushi Bay, in Kagoshima prefecture.[7] The dispute began in 1970 when Shibushi Bay was designated as one of the areas slated for massive industrial development in accordance with the New

6. Probably the largest factor in the JSP victory in Ōita First District for 1972 was the JSP's decision to run a single candidate rather than split its votes between two candidates. By removing interest from the intra-JSP competition, this decision along with other factors actually decreased the total votes cast for the JSP, both in the district as a whole and in Usuki itself, from 1969 to 1972. Conversely, the total LDP vote increased from 1969 to 1972, both in the district and in Usuki. See Ōita ken senkyo kanri iinkai, *Senkyo no kiroku* [Election Records], (March 1970 and March 1973).

7. Information about Shibushi was available from interviews and pamphlets produced by several movements there. See also Fukada Shinsuke, "Shibushi-wan—subete wa kore kara hajimaru" [Shibushi Bay—Now It Will All Begin], *Shimin* 9 (July 1972), 152–167; Hayashi Takeshi, "Chiiki kaihatsu, kōgai to jūmin undō" [Regional Development, Pollution, and Residents' Movements], in Satō Atsushi, ed., *Chiiki kaihatsu, kōgai e no taiō* [The Response to Regional Development and Pollution], vol. 3 in the series Asu no chihō jichi wo saguru [Toward Local Self-Government for the Future] (Tokyo: Gakuyō Shobō, 1974), pp. 281–321; Kagoshima-ken kikaku-bu chiiki kaihatsu chōsa shitsu, *Shin Ōsumi kaihatsu keikaku (kasho)* [The New Ōsumi Development Plan (Provisional)] (December 1971); Shibushi-wan kōgai hantai renraku kyōgikai, *Shibushi-wan no jūmin undō* [The Residents' Movements of Shibushi Bay] (November 1972); Zen Nihon jichi dantai rōdō kumiai, *Shizen kankyō wo mamorō: Shibushi-wan sekiyu kombinaato hantai tōsō no kiroku* [Let's Protect the Natural Environment: A Record of the Petroleum Kombinat at Shibushi Bay] (August 1972); Zen Nihon jichi dantai rōdō kumiai Jichiken chūō suishin iinkai, *Shinzensō ni hantai shi hankōgai tōsō wo suishin suru kakuchi no tatakai no hōkoku* [A Record of the Fight in Each Region Promoting the Antipollution Struggle against Shinzensō] (September 1972).

Comprehensive National Development Plan (Shin zenkoku kaihatsu sōgō keikaku [Shinzensō]). In March 1971 the Kagoshima prefectural assembly and the Shibushi town assembly passed resolutions favoring the development, to the great consternation of the townspeople, who formed a group to oppose the plan the following month. The prefectural government enlisted the help of MITI (then headed by Tanaka Kakuei, soon to become Japan's prime minister and the sponsor of a controversial plan for massive industrial development in rural areas) to explain the plan at public question-and-answer sessions.

The prefecture's request in September 1971 that the Environment Agency remove the designation as a protected area or quasi-national park (*kokutei kōen*) from a forest bordering the development site stimulated the anti-*kombinat* movement into action. To save the coastal pine forest and to demonstrate that the local assembly resolution contravened the wishes of local residents, the Shibushi movement submitted a petition with 34,000 signatures to the Environment Agency, directly into the hands of Director-General Ōishi Buichi, in November 1971. This was a substantial number in comparison with the adult population of the area (the town of Shibushi itself, largest in the area, had less than 20,000 people, including children). In the town of Higashi-kushira, which encompassed the village of Kashiwabara where the refinery itself would be centered, 78.2 percent (4,832 persons) of the eligible voters signed the petition.

This drive for signatures became the foundation for a much larger liaison movement consisting of eleven citizens' movements in towns ringing the bay in Kagoshima prefecture and a parallel organization in Miyazaki prefecture consisting of seventy-two different civic groups. This large umbrella organization, which eventually brought thousands of local citizens into the streets to demonstrate, took shape in December 1971, twelve days after Kagoshima prefecture published the details of the development plan: an industrial zone of 2,850 hectares (including 2,470 hectares to be reclaimed from the bay) along a sixteen-kilometer strip of the coastline. This industrial zone would house an oil refinery with a daily capacity of a million barrels, a petrochemical plant with an annual output of 800,000 tons, as well as related structures and factories. It would be three times larger than any existing petroleum *kombinat* in Japan.

The controversy grew during 1972 as the liaison movement held study sessions, signature drives, parades, protest demonstrations, and meetings with Environment Agency and prefectural planning officials. They established contact with other well-known citizens' movements against industrial pollution and visited some of Japan's most polluted cities. The movement even collected enough money to send its leader to the United Nations Conference on the Environment in Stockholm. The liaison movement also lobbied heavily to have its petitions accepted as resolutions by local assemblies, in order to oppose the prefecture-wide associations of mayors and assembly speakers, which both passed resolutions in favor of the plan. The liaison movement won support from opposition political parties (Kōmeitō, JSP, and JCP), the General Council of Trade Unions (Sōhyō), regional labor federations (Chikurō), local government workers (Jichirō), the teachers' unions (Nikkyōsō), and an assortment of fishermen's cooperatives. In one case municipal workers held a sympathy strike for the liaison movement. The liaison movement's attempts to persuade local assemblies to support anti-*kombinat* petitions were more successful in neighboring Miyazaki prefecture than in Kagoshima, because officials and politicians in the former had no commitment to a plan prepared by another prefecture but several Miyazaki communities were definitely threatened with pollution if the *kombinat* were to be built. By June 1972, the only three municipal assemblies (Kushira city, Hinan town, and Minaminogō town) to adopt anti-*kombinat* resolutions were in Miyazaki prefecture, whereas four of the towns in the two-city seventeen-town cluster of communities ringing Shibushi Bay in Kagoshima prefecture had passed resolutions supporting the *kombinat*.

The feverish activities of June 1972 marked a turning point for the liaison movement. Most important was the pandemonium that broke out in the Kagoshima prefectural assembly during debate on citizens' petitions both for and against the *kombinat* plan, when several hundred opponents of the *kombinat* tried to present their petitions. The prefectural government responded by closing the assembly building and establishing a checkpoint at the door to allow entry only to prefectural employees and officials. Prefectural employees and ordinary citizens, both angry at this strictness and denial of access to their own elected representatives, joined forces to protest the procedure and to demand withdrawal of the *kombinat* plan. In a move reminiscent of national political confrontations in an earlier era, the prefectural government twice called the riot police to remove *kombinat* opponents from the premises. The assemblymen from the opposition parties left after the session was adjourned, and the riot police departed, but the remaining LDP and conservative independent assemblymen reopened the session and voted alone, by acclamation, to accept the pro-*kombinat* petitions. They ignored all of the anti-*kombinat* petitions.

As a result of this episode the LDP governor was sharply criticized for refusing to receive anti-*kombinat* petitions personally, for closing a public building to citizens, and for using deceit to arrange for the LDP assemblymen to consider only the pro-*kombinat* petitions without the presence of the political opposition. Only because of the anticipated legal costs did the JSP decide against filing an administrative lawsuit against the LDP. The major newspapers (*Asahi, Mainichi,* and *Minami Nippon*

Shimbun) all printed editorials criticizing the LDP for its conduct and for designing the plan in the first place without consulting the local populace.

The prefectural government's desperate measures to ignore criticism actually worked in favor of the anti-*kombinat* movement, which now found the task of extending the protest and mobilizing new activists much easier. The episode also politicized the anti-*kombinat* struggle by identifying the LDP as an enemy of the movement and by persuading the movement to accelerate its efforts through political channels, especially local assemblies. One immediate result was the first local assembly victory for the movement in Kagoshima prefecture. The municipal assembly of Higashi-kushira, where hostility to the *kombinat* was extremely intense, finally agreed to receive the petition signed seven months earlier by 78 percent of its constituents. While seven hundred vigilant opponents of the *kombinat* waited outside until 4 A.M. on June 29, 1972, the assembly resolved after twenty hours of debate to accept the first absolute opposition (*zettai hantai*) resolution, in a major victory for the anti-*kombinat* movement.

The disruptions of June 1972 also had an impact at the national level. The Kagoshima prefectural government now faced criticism from national LDP leaders and officials. Yamanaka Sadanori, a prestigious LDP Diet member from the *kombinat* district, announced that he opposed development based on petroleum and favored food-processing industries instead, to avoid pollution. The ten ministries concerned in the *kombinat* project (including MITI, the Economic Planning Agency, and the Environment Agency, among others) announced that the agreement of local residents was absolutely essential to such a plan even if this required revision and delay, and they canceled their arrangements to survey the *kombinat* site in preparation for construction. In July the new director-general of the Environment Agency in the Tanaka cabinet, Koyama Osanori (who happened to be an LDP Dietman from a district in Miyazaki prefecture), assured the JSP Diet members from Kagoshima and Miyazaki prefectures that he would not alter the designation as a protected area of the forest lining Shibushi Bay. He confirmed this again during a visit to Shibushi the following month, when he received the protest petitions ignored by the prefectural government, and said he would maintain the forest's designation as a quasi-national park as long as the anti-*kombinat* movement flourished.

In combination with several other events during the summer of 1972, this episode brought victory to the anti-*kombinat* movement in Shibushi Bay. The Transportation Ministry released a report concluding that the Ōsumi Peninsula development plan should be altered to give greater consideration to environmental protection and priority to the wishes of the local people. Shortly afterward, a group of consultants asked by Kagoshima prefecture to make a scientific study of the ecology of Shibushi Bay reported that the *kombinat* would lead to the death of all fish in the bay and in local rivers, oil pollution of the beaches, withering of the pine forest along the coast, and air pollution damage within a twenty-kilometer radius of the *kombinat*. Finally, the court handed down an unexpectedly strong verdict in the Yokkaichi case concerning air pollution from a petroleum *kombinat* much smaller than the one planned for Shibushi Bay.

On July 17, 1972, the Economic Planning Agency announced that it would shelve plans for development of the Osumi Peninsula. Although the governor of Kagoshima protested, he had no choice but to announce in August that in view of the plan's lack of citizen support, it would be revised; in December the prefectural assembly formally voted to suspend the plan.[8]

The arguments raised in this divisive conflict over development illustrate the controversy over rural development which besets Japan nationally. Shibushi activists feared that prevention technology would not be adequate to keep air and water pollution down to tolerable levels for such a large *kombinat*. Industrialists at Kashima (Ibaragi prefecture) won local support for their petroleum *kombinat*, also part of the Shin-zensō, by promising to use advanced pollution-prevention equipment to eliminate the problems that had plagued Japan's largest petroleum complex at Yokkaichi, but in fact the Kashima *kombinat* had produced severe air and water pollution even before it reached full operating capacity.[9]

The activists also saw flaws in the argument used by *kombinat* proponents that Shibushi could offer no alternatives to petroleum refining as a source of economic growth for the area, and they refused to accept the view that the *kombinat* would actually produce net economic gains for the area. The reclamation plans would ruin the abundant fishing grounds that provided a comfortable living for the majority of local fishermen, one of the area's most stable and lucrative occupations. Apart from their own personal stake in their livelihood, the fishermen with rights to these productive grounds inside the bay argued cogently that destroying the bay's most profitable industry in order to establish a profitable industry did not make sense. Destruction of the fishing within the bay would cause a chain reaction, in that schools of fish attracted to the mouth of the bay by the choice morsels within would no longer be available, and fishermen who expected to retain their fishing rights after the *kombinat*

8. *JT*, 18 January 1973.
9. Kondō Junko, "Chiiki kaihatsu to Kasumi-ga-ura no kōgai" [Regional Development and Pollution in Kasumi-ga-ura], in Kōgai mondai kenkyūkai, *Kashima kaihatsu to kankyō hakai* [The Development of Kashima and Environmental Destruction] (September 1972), pp. 67–76.

was built would nonetheless quickly become unable to catch fish. In any case, opponents of the *kombinat* argued that Shibushi Bay had plenty of other economic resources yet unexploited (orange groves, eel farms, cattle grazing, tourism, and the like), which would permit development with much less pollution and much less destruction of the natural environment.

Those opposed to the plan also argued that the *kombinat* would not employ local people, but would require highly trained technicians from the cities. Farmers who planned to sell their land and fishermen who considered selling their fishing rights would not be able to support themselves forever on the sums they received, and might still have to turn to poorly paid unskilled labor, or to leave home as seasonal migrant labor. Those who had actually visited the industrial zones of the north were likely to oppose the *kombinat*, preferring to continue to work away from home as *dekasegi* laborers in order to have pollution-free homes to return to, rather than work at home amidst pollution.

But the Ōsumi Peninsula was the poorest and most conservative portion of Japan's poorest and most conservative prefecture, and many local residents wanted desperately to believe that the Shibushi *kombinat* could provide them with material benefits and that the side effects of pollution could be ignored. Some were willing to trust the *kombinat*'s promise of pollution-free technology. Others believed that Shibushi was undeveloped because it was economically unattractive, and that the only way to obtain economic improvement was to accept the industries that other Japanese would not tolerate. One woman in favor of the *kombinat* told a news reporter that she was willing for local children to die from air pollution in order to bring petroleum to Shibushi.

The opponents of petroleum development in Shibushi had more success with arguments based on the threat of a cultural invasion by the impersonal, material values of industrial society. They argued that the LDP had abandoned its rural roots in favor of industrialists who wanted to sacrifice Japan's agricultural sector (in order to meet the demands of foreign powers that Japan import agricultural products in exchange for its manufactured exports). In this way, the LDP had betrayed the rural electorate on which it depended for votes and instead responded to the interests of heavy industry. The agricultural population thus paid more heavily for, and reaped fewer benefits from, industrial expansion than other Japanese. Similarly, population pressure and the high profits available from industrial or residential use of the land raised land values, so the Japanese government accordingly raised the tax rates to force farmers off the land. These arguments, echoed by various groups on the left and right in Japan as well as by agricultural and fishing cooperatives, seemed plausible to many Shibushi citizens, and they saw their opposition to one particular petroleum *kombinat* as part of a larger strategy to defend Japan's agricultural sector against the malicious scheming of industrialists who ran the LDP and the government.

Activists also appealed to regional pride by saying that industrial development threatened their distinct Kagoshima subculture with its special dialect and historical heritage. The most active group of anti-*kombinat* fishermen was known as the Apaches, some of whom also assumed Indian names. The Apaches said they would resist industrialization because it represented the culture of the West and of the white man, which other Japanese had unwisely adopted. Using this full battery of arguments, the coalition to oppose the Shibushi Bay *kombinat* became one of the most powerful citizens' movements in Japan.

The *kombinat* issue did not die with the first plan, and the liaison movement realized that its own vitality was crucial if anti-*kombinat* views were to have any impact on the revised plan, so in December 1972 the movement endorsed reformist candidates in the general election for the House of Representatives. Kagoshima Third District had three seats in the Diet, all of which were filled by LDP members. Two of these were extremely influential LDP leaders whose efforts were significant in having Shibushi selected as the *kombinat* site—Nikaidō Susumu and Yamanaka Sadanori, both of whom had been cabinet ministers. The leaders of the anti-*kombinat* movement had once been their proud and loyal supporters, capable of delivering thousands of votes. Much to the dismay of Nikaidō and Yamanaka, these local bosses encouraged the movement to endorse JSP and JCP candidates in the election. One former Nikaidō supporter who had been Nikaidō's classmate at middle school explained to compatriots in the movement that he had a long record of service to the community and loyalty to Nikaidō, that he did not approve of socialism, and that he supported the JSP, not in expectation of a Socialist takeover but for its potential effects on the behavior of the LDP. Currently, he continued, the LDP had so much power and was so overconfident, almost tyrannical, that it ignored the wishes of even its most faithful supporters. This imbalance between political parties was undesirable, and if the LDP lost one of its "secure" seats in Kagoshima it might pay more attention to local problems and stop the *kombinat*.

Actual election results revealed that the movement was not quite able to displace any of the three LDP incumbents, but that its campaign efforts caused a net movement of votes from the LDP to the opposition parties, and increased absolute turnout even in this area of declining total population. The election figures for Kagoshima Third District show that even though total turnout increased by over 8,000 votes, the LDP percentage of the vote fell from 86.2 percent in 1969 to 79 percent in 1972. These stray votes went not to independents or splinter candidates, but to the left: the JSP and JCP combined vote grew by 15,622 votes, or from

13.8 percent of the total vote in 1969 to 21 percent in 1972. This was a significant change in such a conservative district, particularly one where the LDP slate consisted entirely of incumbents, two of whom were major figures in the national party organization. Moreover, a breakdown of votes within Kagoshima Third District (see table 6) shows that these changes were particularly sharp in the towns of Shibushi and Higashi-kushira. Yamanaka clearly lost votes in Shibushi (the core of his voting base) to Nikaidō and, more important, to the JSP candidate in 1972. Similarly, Nikaidō lost almost one-third of his customary tally in Higashi-kushira (the core of his voting base), where the Socialist and Communist vote in 1972 was an astonishing 37.4 percent of the total vote (it was 7.4% in 1969).

TABLE 6 / *Changes in Voting Patterns from 1969 to 1972: Kagoshima 3*

December 1969 House of Representatives Election

		Higashi-Kushira	Shibushi	Kagoshima 3	
Winners					
Nikaidō Susumu	LDP	63.52%	19.30%	29.92%	(57,733)
Yamanaka Sadanori	LDP	11.39%	52.74%	31.03%	(59,880)
Hashiguchi Takashi	LDP	17.68%	6.83%	25.23%	(48,674)
Losers					
Arima Terutake	JSP	5.93%	17.74%	12.16%	(23,461)
Matohara Isao	JCP	1.47%	3.40%	1.66%	(3,201)
Total LDP vote		92.59%	78.87%	86.18%	(166,287)
Total JSP & JCP vote		7.40%	21.14%	13.82%	(26,662)
Total vote		99.99%	100.01%	100.00%	
Total valid votes		5,005	10,073	192,949	
Percent turnout		81.74%	71.48%	78.21%	

December 1972 House of Representatives Election

		Higashi-Kushira	Shibushi	Kagoshima 3	
Winners					
Nikaidō	LDP	42.71%	25.62%	30.35%	(61,085)
Yamanaka	LDP	4.16%	37.96%	24.80%	(49,911)
Hashiguchi	LDP	15.72%	7.29%	23.84%	(47,971)
Losers					
Kaminishi Kazurō	JSP	34.76%	25.68%	19.27%	(38,773)
Matohara	JCP	2.69%	3.45%	1.74%	(3,511)
Total LDP vote		62.59%	70.83%	78.99%	(158,967)
Total JSP & JCP vote		37.45%	29.13%	21.01%	(42,284)
Total vote		100.04%	99.96%	100.00%	
Total valid votes		5,273	11,034	201,251	
Percent turnout		86.83%	79.34%	82.71%	

Source: Kagoshima-ken senkyō kanri iinkai, *Senkyō no kiroku* (1969 and 1972).

Clearly the anti-*kombinat* movement's support of leftist candidates acquainted many voters with the strategy of a protest vote. Moreover, it is highly likely that there were many more protest votes than those cast for the JSP and JCP in 1972. The multimember district system in Japan pits candidates of the same party against one another, so in most rural districts LDP politicians try to collect the bulk of their votes from small, safe *jiban* (bases) rather than evenly across the whole district. As a result, voters think of themselves as supporters of particular candidates, not of parties.[10] Movement leaders explaining to other activists in 1972 how to register an unmistakable protest by voting for the left were certain that many movement members would fail to comprehend fully the rationale and would attempt to vote against the *kombinat* by abandoning their "regular" candidate merely to switch *within* the LDP, canceling each other out without realizing it. The figures demonstrate that many Shibushi voters, unable to bring themselves to break away from the LDP, tried instead to express disapproval of the *kombinat* just as their leaders anticipated, by abandoning Yamanaka (their regular candidate) in order to support Nikaidō. One survey suggests that whatever the anti-*kombinat* movement's effect on actual voting was, 38.4 percent of Shibushi voters no longer described themselves as LDP supporters and now claimed that they were disenchanted with all parties and preferred to affiliate with none (in contrast to those who had no affiliation simply because they were apathetic about politics). Thus many of the votes for the LDP in 1972 probably represented disenchanted protest votes too.[11]

Although the anti-*kombinat* movement failed to elect a reformist member to the national Diet in 1972, it has thus far prevented the construction of the *kombinat*.[12] In June 1976, Kagoshima prefecture unveiled a revised plan, reduced to less than one-third the size of the original (1,160 hectares of landfill to accommodate a refinery with a daily capacity of 300,000 barrels). Although the mayor of Shibushi, reelected in October 1977, supported the revised plan, the liaison movement still opposed local development based on a petroleum *kombinat*, since the

10. Nathaniel Thayer, *How the Conservatives Rule Japan* (Princeton: Princeton University Press, 1969), pp. 82–147; and Bradley M. Richardson, *The Political Culture of Japan* (Berkeley and Los Angeles: University of California Press, 1974), pp. 102–127.

11. Hashimoto Akikazu, *Shiji seitō nashi: kuzureyuku "seitō" shinwa* [Nonsupport of Political Parties: The Crumbling Myth of "political parties"], (Tokyo: Nihon Keizai Shimbunsha, 1975), pp. 58–60.

12. For recent details on the Shibushi *kombinat*, see *JT*, 15 June 1976; and *AS*, 6 June 1976 (ssb 173/6), 14 June 1976 (ssb 448/1), 16 June 1976 (ssb 494/4), 4 July 1976 (ssb 126/3), 24 October 1977 (ssb 790/10), and 20 February 1978 (ssb 622/5); and *Mainichi Daily News*, 1 March 1980. See also Fukushima Yōichi, "Shibushi wan wo mamoru—undō no kadai to hōkō" [Protecting Shibushi Bay—Problems and Directions in the Movement], *Jurisuto (zōkan) sōgō tokushū* 15 (Summer 1979), 160–163.

smaller project would also spoil the seaside pine forest and destroy fishing within the bay. Though not compelled to do so by law, Kagoshima prefecture conducted an environmental impact study, but both the Environment Agency and the governor of neighboring Miyazaki prefecture questioned the adequacy of the report, which did not even consider impact on Miyazaki even though it is certain to be affected. Miyazaki prefecture therefore undertook its own impact study, but in February 1980 it announced that, like the 1978 Kagoshima report, its own findings indicated that the *kombinat* would not cause pollution in excess of existing national standards. The liaison movement vigorously criticized both reports as incomplete and biased, and the Environment Agency has thus far maintained the designation of the quasi-national park along the bay shore.

Another important obstacle is the problem of fishing rights. Though a small cooperative within the fishing union agreed to sell its rights to a much smaller area of the bay for a different project to build a harbor and food-processing industry immediately adjacent to the town of Shibushi, most fishermen are still strongly opposed to anything larger, and developers have not yet managed to purchase fishing rights for the petroleum *kombinat*. In 1972, 90 percent of the fishing cooperative members in Shibushi Bay were unwilling to sell their fishing rights to the bay-fill zone to the *kombinat*'s private developers, who could not use eminent domain to force the fishermen to sell. Some pessimists worried that a majority of the fishing union might eventually be bribed to sell their rights, but the legal precedent established at Usuki (above) makes a less than unanimous decision of this sort unconstitutional. If the state does not find a way to use eminent domain, one determined fisherman could still prevent the land reclamation on which the entire *kombinat* project depends.

· The Society to Protect Nature and Culture in Ōiso

Another group formed to prevent further development, both residential *and* industrial, was located in Ōiso, a small but wealthy resort town in the rural portion of Kanagawa prefecture, which has served as a beach resort and a traveler's rest stop outside Tokyo for several centuries.[13] The founding members of this group began their career of preventing further development in their rural community in the early 1950s when the neighboring industrial city of Hiratsuka attempted to build a crematorium for its own use within Ōiso. Then in May 1967 they formed the Society to Protect Nature and Culture in Ōiso when the mayor and the prefectural governor proposed to convert Ōiso's famous white sandy

13. Information was obtained from interviews, leaflets, and the group's official records.

beaches into a harbor for the use of companies wishing to market the high-quality gravel and sand from Ōiso's shoreline. The group managed to stop the harbor plan after only one-sixth of the work had been completed. The Society next (in 1968) campaigned unsuccessfully against the construction of a national highway that separated the most sumptuous shoreline homes from the beach. Instead of planning the road to be built slightly inland and adjacent to the old Tōkaidō railway where it would not lower the scenic or financial value of the land so much, the national government built the road along the beach because the shoreline was already government-owned and required no expensive purchase of private property. The Society's most serious efforts were directed against the construction of a chemical plant in Ōiso, in concert with the group described below. The Society was instrumental in initiating lawsuits to enforce environmental quality standards and obtain financial compensation.

This group was the most thoroughly and hierarchically organized one in the sample, with a written constitution listing its principles and detailed procedures about election of officers and agenda at meetings. It was also the only group in our sample with an official list of members (then a hundred), each of whom regularly paid high dues (¥6,000 per year, about $20 at the time) to remain voting members. This society did not have any general interest in environmental issues or in the relationship between human society and the natural environment. The group specifically avoided policy statements concerning the directions of development elsewhere in Japan, and the leader confessed that he personally favored former Prime Minister Tanaka Kakuei's plan to industrialize rural areas, so long as Ōiso was not one of the areas designated to receive more industry. The group was deeply enmeshed in local politics and was willing to accept help from leftist parties and labor unions and to endorse reformist candidates in its local confrontations, but it was unwilling to support leftist activities in return on any large scale.

· The League Opposing the Establishment of the Johnson Factory

The Society to Protect Nature and Culture in Ōiso faced its most difficult challenge in the form of a proposed chemical plant, to which it responded by launching a much larger community-wide movement.[14] In August 1969, the Johnson Company (the well-known American makers of wax) made arrangements to buy a site, the most fertile and profitable farmland in Ōiso, to which its main plant in Osaka would move. In order to change the zoning designation of the site, the mayor simply convened an unannounced but technically "public" session of the local assembly

14. Information was obtained from interviews and handbills prepared by the activist group.

which no community members knew about. When residents later objected to the effect of a polluting industry on their farming and demanded a more consistent zoning policy, the assembly went on to rezone the entire surrounding farm area as appropriate for industrial development.

The mayor argued that Johnson would increase tax receipts and jobs for Ōiso and make possible the public facilities that opponents of the factory wanted. The antifactory movement retorted that Ōiso was a very wealthy town and had never been short of public funds, and that there was no unemployment problem. Furthermore, the particular site chosen for the factory was fertile enough to permit double-cropping of high-profit produce. The opposition was also worried about pollution from a chemical plant like Johnson, which would threaten local fishing and destroy the beautiful beach, which attracted a healthy tourist trade every summer.

The efforts of the Johnson company to buy the land, along with behind-the-scenes pressure exerted by the mayor and his supporters, created much ill feeling within the community. First, Johnson provided free gifts and a trip to Osaka to visit the main plant there (proudly rejected by members of the antifactory movement). Johnson even provided a few free trips to their plants in the United States, including tours of the homes of some Johnson employees. Many Ōiso residents were entranced by the tales of luxurious living among Johnson employees in the United States and unrealistically expected to be employed by Johnson and to enjoy similar standards of living. Some who sold land to Johnson actually imagined that Johnson would employ them simply as a gesture of goodwill in return. According to opponents of the Johnson plant, the mayor of Ōiso also visited all of the homes of people who owned land in the factory site and begged them to sell. Rumor has it that much money illicitly changed hands during these late-night visits. Other community leaders acted to suppress opposition, and as a result many movement members chose to leave neighborhood associations, the PTA, and local women's groups in order to avoid this pressure. Many of those who sold land were so ashamed that they kept the very fact of sale, and of course the price, a secret. Some held out, either to oppose the factory or to drive up the price, and some thus bargained so skillfully that Johnson bought replacement lands for them elsewhere and paid the three sets of taxes involved in the circumlocutious transfers of land.

With these methods, and also because rising land taxes made it very difficult for farmers to retain the land for agriculture, Johnson managed to buy all of the needed land and began construction in early 1971. Even though it did not prevent construction of the factory, the antipollution movement persisted. In the April 1971 local elections, the movement put up its own candidate for city council. The JCP, which had supported the movement, overconfidently nominated three instead of its usual two candidates, thus dividing the protest votes too thinly. As a result, only one of the JCP nominees won a council seat, and the movement's own nonpartisan candidate missed election by just a few votes. Wisely, the mayor did not run for reelection in April 1971 and stood for prefectural assembly instead. The antifactory movement campaigned on his opponent's behalf, persuading many Ōiso residents to vote for a nominee from another town rather than for their native son. The mayor lost his bid for a seat in the prefectural assembly, and his political career came to an end.

Although the Johnson company built its plant, brought its employees from Osaka, and began production in September 1972, the antifactory movement filed two civil suits against it, charging that illegal procedures were used to procure collectively owned land within the site. The first suit was based on laws providing that collectively owned lands used for agricultural roads, waterways, and irrigation ditches cannot be exchanged for other land, moved, or divided up, and that Johnson's destruction of irrigation channels not only was illegal in and of itself but ruined rice paddies in the area, which would otherwise have continued to be productive. Though the letter of the law was clearly on the plaintiffs' side, the factory's actions could not be undone, and this suit finally ended in a court-mediated settlement (*wakai*) in which the company paid damages to the aggrieved farmers. The second suit concerned the mayor's questionable manipulation of the town treasury during his efforts to bring Johnson to Ōiso. Although the antifactory movement believes that its material evidence of illegality is strong, by 1980 the court had not yet rendered a verdict.

Some members of the movement wanted to file a third set of charges against Johnson for violating water quality standards, because immediately after production began dead fish were found below the point of discharge, and visible water pollution was noted. Johnson discharged waste water through a concealed pipe running beneath a surface channel of clean water containing goldfish, and both emptied into a local stream. Although chemical analysis indicated that the effluents were much dirtier than existing standards permitted, this would not serve as grounds for a lawsuit unless it were to happen repeatedly. The company apologized and maintained that the bubbly, yellow, waste water was an accidental discharge. Legal responsibility for pollution damage downstream or in the bay beyond would be difficult to pinpoint in any case because Johnson discharged its effluents into a stream that also contained wastes from a new residential development on a nearby mountainside and from several pig and chicken farms located upstream. Therefore the antifactory movement abandoned the idea of a pollution lawsuit per se. As of 1980, Ōiso residents are disturbed by the odors emanating daily from the Johnson plant, which the factory is either unwilling or unable to control, but they are also relieved that serious pollution of the sort they most feared has not yet materialized.

Urban Citizens' Movements

The following nine movements were active in the Greater Tokyo area, so a prefatory note is necessary to explain the unique administrative structure of the capital region. The metropolis of Tokyo is actually a prefecture, whose elected chief executive is therefore a governor. The prefectural bureaucracy is known as the Tokyo Metropolitan Government (TMG), and the prefectural assembly is known as the Tokyo Metropolitan Assembly (TMA). The core of Tokyo prefecture is its twenty-three special wards (which in the prewar period constituted subdivisions of the then *city* of Tokyo), or *tokubetsu-ku*. Many of Japan's larger cities are subdivided into wards (*ku*), but only in Tokyo are these considered municipalities in their own right, fully equivalent to cities rather than mere subdivisions of them, with ward assemblies and ward mayors serving as the municipal level of government. One unusual feature of Tokyo's special wards is that ward mayors were indirectly elected by ward assemblies until the April 1975 local elections (in which they were directly elected by ward voters, as are the mayors of all other cities in Japan).[15] Outside of the twenty-three-ward area, Tokyo prefecture also includes many other municipalities with mayors and assemblies—cities, towns, and even villages in rural areas (*gun*) to the west.

15. Reforms conducted by the American occupation of Japan (1945–1952) required that all executives of local levels of government (prefectures and municipalities) be directly elected, in accordance with Article 93 of the 1947 Constitution. But in 1952 the Local Autonomy Law was revised so as to label the twenty-three municipal units (essentially the equivalent of cities) in the center of Tokyo prefecture as "special wards" (*tokubetsu-ku*) rather than the "local public entities" to which Article 93 referred. The mayors of the twenty-three special wards were thenceforth to be indirectly elected by the assembly and appointed with the consent of Tokyo's prefectural governor, rather than directly elected by the ward residents themselves. Several lawsuits challenged this revised system as unconstitutional. However, the Supreme Court ruled in February 1956 that indirect selection of ward mayors did not transgress any legal right of the voters, so there was no controversy to adjudicate. A later verdict of March 1963 went beyond this to affirm the constitutionality of the system. Since then the movement to amend the Local Autonomy Law in order to restore direct popular election of ward mayors has succeeded, and ward mayors were directly elected again for the first time in 1975. See Kurt Steiner, *Local Government in Japan* (Stanford: Stanford University Press, 1965), pp. 122–126; and Tōkyō tosei chōsakai, *Kuchō junkōsen: sono shisō to hōhō* [Direct Election of Ward Mayors: Theory and Practice] (1972). For details of an unusual lawsuit filed by citizens of Edogawa ward against their ward government over this issue, see AS, 19 May 1978 (ssb 626/1), 20 May 1978 (ssb 648/3).

· The Garbage War between Suginami and Kōtō Wards

In September 1971, Tokyo's Governor Minobe Ryōkichi declared war on garbage with the opening of the *gomi sensō* campaign—the citizens of Tokyo versus their own garbage.[16] At that time, 72 percent of the solid wastes of Tokyo were collected at sites throughout the city and transported by truck via Kōtō ward to landfill sites in Tokyo Bay. In addition to pollution of bay waters, the hazards of land reclamation by garbage included the extreme instability of reclaimed land, leading to ground subsidence and serious flooding. Rather than continuing this primitive procedure for the disposal of solid wastes, the Tokyo Metropolitan Government proposed to build enough high-temperature furnaces to burn all of Tokyo's garbage, evenly distributed throughout the twenty-three wards. Furnaces operating in 1972 (some of them ancient and filthy) were only capable of burning 27 percent of Tokyo's garbage, and the resulting ashes (10% of the volume of the original material) were still being transported to the same land reclamation projects in Tokyo Bay.

Moving all of Tokyo's garbage to a single disposal site was an extremely inefficient and unjust method of disposal. Kōtō ward, providing closest access to the bay-fill sites, processed nineteen times the amount of garbage it created in 1972. A tremendous percentage of the traffic on its main streets was garbage trucks, traveling at breakneck speeds, scattering loose refuse along the way, causing odor and sanitation problems. Greatest of all was the injustice to the neighborhood Edagawa-chō (not to be confused with Edogawa ward) situated next to the wharf where all of the trucks eventually gathered to wait for hours at a time to unload. The leader of Edagawa's neighborhood association decided that the people of Edagawa and Kōtō ward should not put up with this any longer, so he converted the association into a citizens' action group and convinced the community that protest was an acceptable activity. The neighborhood

16. For information about Tokyo's garbage problem, see Ōsumi Hiroto, *Gomi sensō* [The Garbage War] (Tokyo: Gakuyō Shobō, March 1972); San guruupu, *Kōgai zensen wo hikaeru: shufu no gomi hakusho* [To the Battlefront: The Housewives' White Paper on Garbage] (Tokyo: Jichi Nipposha, August 1972); Tokyo Metropolitan Government, "Garbage Disposal in Tokyo," *Tokyo Municipal News* 22:2 (March–April 1972), 1–16; Tokyo Metropolitan Government, *Tokyo Fights Pollution: An Urgent Appeal for Reform* (Tokyo, March 1971), pp. 219–244; Tōkyō-to kōgai kenkyūjo, *Kōgai to Tōkyō-to* [Pollution and Tokyo] (Tokyo, March 1970), pp. 113–166; Tōkyō-tominshitsu, *Tomin no Koe '71* [Voice of the People '71] (Tokyo, March 1971), pp. 36–39, 155–159. Additional information was available in pamphlets distributed to the public at ward offices. Information on the specific groups in the sample was obtained from interviews and from pamphlets and handbills provided by the various movements. One group published its own periodical newsletter, Suginami seisō kōjō kami-Takaidō chiku kensetsu hantai dōmei, *Tōsō nyūsu* [Struggle News].

association took on a dual character—it acquired a second name and held separately scheduled meetings on the garbage problem. The group began to protest in the summer of 1971, arguing that Tokyoites with more money, higher living standards, and more pleasant surroundings than they had should take care of their own garbage and not force the unpleasantness onto one tiny segment of Tokyo's population. Gradually their demands grew more specific—they wanted financial compensation for damage (to cover such things as the extra disinfectant they had to use in Edagawa and the medical expenses incurred to treat infections arising from poor sanitation), traffic lights to slow down the garbage trucks, and a community hall for Edagawa so that they could have a bit of cultural activity in their own locality.

Leaders of the Edagawa group were political conservatives who felt that Governor Minobe's leftist inclinations were an obstacle. Yet they admitted having better experience with him than with his conservative predecessors during their thirty-year period of cooperative silence. When they realized that those who remain silent cannot compete for a government's attention against those who articulate their opinions, and that the TMG would not change its policies simply out of sympathy, the group began to advocate direct action. After threatening massive sit-ins to obstruct the garbage trucks, the group eventually won the support of the Kōtō ward assembly, vis-à-vis the TMG. It was chiefly in response to these new demands from Edagawa and Kōtō that Governor Minobe declared the war on garbage in September 1971. Minobe also provided a written guarantee to Kōtō ward that by December 1972 garbage would stop going through the wharf at Edagawa and would travel by barge from a different embarcation point. He agreed to stop filling the fifteen sites in Tokyo Bay (which are euphemistically named the Island of Dreams) by November 1973, and to consider the opinions of residents in determining the use of the reclaimed land.[17]

The modern furnaces planned as part of the "garbage war" are intended to achieve complete combustion and to prevent the emission of polluting by-products from the combustion process. The heat energy released during combustion generates sufficient electricity to run the treatment plant and usually enough to provide hot water and heating for nearby buildings. The plants are being designed as handsome public buildings, in broad open spaces that function as parks with recreational facilities. Nonetheless, there is still very strong sentiment against living near one of these plants. People fear loss of property value, and they object to the high volume of traffic and the resulting hazards of noise, air pollution, and accidents created by the daily arrival and departure of

17. *AS*, 24 May 1977 (ssb 724/1), 25 May 1977 (ssb 758/1).

hundreds of garbage trucks. Some also fear that the burning of plastics will release toxic gases in spite of sophisticated antipollution technology in use at these plants.

Edagawa activists were of course enthusiastic about Minobe's plans to build a modern, clean incinerator in every ward, and they were placated by the TMG's assurance that Kōtō ward's incinerator would soon be built on the reclaimed land nearest Edagawa. However, Tokyo had considerable trouble persuading residents of more attractive areas of the city to agree to the construction of treatment plants near their homes. By far the best-known controversy was that in the Takaidō area of Suginami ward, a very comfortable upper-middle-class residential area. In November 1966 the TMG under Governor Azuma Ryutarō announced that it would buy land in Takaidō to build an incineration plant. Previous plans had involved plots of land that the TMG already owned, so Takaidō residents were upset to learn that a large, valuable expanse of land adjacent to their train station and elementary school had been selected instead. An opposition movement formed immediately.

Five months later Minobe Ryōkichi was elected governor and simultaneously the Construction Minister gave his permission to the TMG to use the power of eminent domain to acquire the site in question, thus saddling Minobe with a problem not of his own making. In July 1967 the twelve landowners who refused to have their land expropriated and 4,746 residents of the area filed suit against the construction minister for having acted unreasonably in granting permission for the use of eminent domain, on the grounds that the site was inappropriate, no prior consultation had occurred, and that the TMG already owned land that had long been announced as the projected site.

With the declaration of the "garbage war" in September 1971, aimed at the rapid construction of a treatment plant in every ward to distribute the burden of collection and treatment more equitably, Minobe's government renewed its efforts to build on the Takaidō site. On October 13, 1971, Minobe announced that he would use the power of eminent domain to seize the land. The TMG attempted forcible seizure, but the residents squatted on the site for several days. One Takaidō leader warned that the group was willing to risk bloodshed and loss of life—he referred to the turmoil at Tokyo's new international airport at Narita—if necessary. After a series of discussions, on February 26, 1972, Minobe promised in writing that he would not use eminent domain to appropriate the land. Thus the Takaidō residents seemed to have attained their most important aim—they would not ever be forced to accept compensation for land they did not want to sell to any government body, local or national. In April 1972 the TMG assured the Takaidō movement that it would consult with representatives from all districts in Suginami to find a mutually agreeable site elsewhere.

The written guarantees given to both groups created a temporary stalemate, but in December 1972 the "garbage war" became an explicit contest between Kōtō and Suginami wards when leaders of the Kōtō group used physical force to prevent garbage trucks from unloading in Kōtō ward. They agreed to allow the trucks to unload only on the condition that Suginami ward make a rapid decision on where to build its own sanitary treatment plant. Suginami failed to come up with a site by May 1973, so the entire assembly of Kōtō ward decided to set up the blockade once again. The ward mayor and all forty-eight assemblymen picketed access roads themselves.[18] At this point, Governor Minobe himself changed tactics, "allied" with the Kōtō group, and suspended garbage collection in Suginami ward altogether to initiate negotiations with Takaidō once again. In November 1973 he retracted his earlier written promise to Takaidō and once again invoked the power of eminent domain. In April 1974 litigation was suspended in order to negotiate an out-of-court settlement; in November 1974 an agreement on the conditions of land sale and the design of the plant was reached.[19]

Even though an incinerator would be built, the press considered this agreement a success for the Takaidō movement because the plans included many advanced features which Takaidō activists, increasingly well informed about the technology of waste disposal, demanded. Although the Takaidō activists could not keep the incinerator out of their area, they won the right to have great influence over questions of plant design, pollution control measures, and traffic flow (trucks would approach the plant via underground tunnels). The movement was particularly pleased with the elaborate provisions for popular participation and consultation, which gave neighborhood residents the power to inspect the plant and order stoppages if it violated the strict antipollution standards included in the agreement.[20] TMG was also pleased with the Suginami plan despite its high cost, and viewed these negotiations as

18. *JT*, 18 December 1972, 18–25 May 1973.

19. On the final settlement, see *Yomiuri Shimbun*, 16 November 1975, and *AS*, 25 November 1975 (evening edition, p. 1). See also *AS*, 2 November 1975 (evening edition, p. 1), 13 November 1975 (p. 9), 15 November 1975 (p. 20), 19 November 1975 (p. 22), 26 November 1975 (p. 20, p. 22). See also TMG publications describing the negotiations, the final plant design, and the agreement itself: Tōkyō-to seisō kōjō kensetsu suishin hombu [TMG Main Office to Promote the Construction of Sanitary Plants], *Suginami seisō kōjō no wakai jōkō* [Provisions of the Agreement for the Suginami Sanitary Plant] (November 1974).

20. In fact, these provisions for citizen participation further delayed actual construction. In July 1976, Takaidō residents objected to the TMG promise to other wards that if their plants burned Suginami garbage until the Takaidō plant was ready, then the Takaidō plant would later burn some of their garbage in exchange. Takaidō residents immediately noted that this arrangement would violate the November 1974 agreement. Not until December 1976 did the last of the residents who owned homes on *top* of the land that TMG

proof that a compromise acceptable to the most demanding citizens Tokyo has yet encountered was indeed possible. The compromise in Suginami did much to accelerate negotiations in Tokyo's other middle-class residential wards (Shinjuku, Nerima, Meguro, and Shibuya), which along with Suginami were the last to agree to construction of sanitary treatment plants.

The Takaidō movement's level of success can be attributed to its skillful use of every available political technique. In addition to relying on direct action and traditional methods of submitting petitions full of signatures to the local and national legislatures, the group also filed lawsuits and participated in local elections to place three of its own members in the ward assembly. It wisely argued that the principle at stake was not the question of a garbage incinerator per se, but rather the political right of citizens to be consulted by government. The group carefully avoided naming any other district in Suginami as a preferable site, and emphasized instead the importance of open negotiations with the people concerned as the proper means of selecting a site. Thus they won wide support from other community groups, who did not have to fear that Takaidō's victory might turn into their own loss.

The Takaidō and Edagawa groups were both represented in our sample. Both saw themselves in mutual conflict, and not only because their goals contradicted each other. The Edagawa group was outspokenly resentful of the higher status of people in Takaidō and other Yamanote districts of Tokyo, and to some extent their jealousy was well founded. The skills, knowledge, education, money, and useful experience were indeed concentrated in the comfortable Yamanote neighborhoods of Tokyo, which still seemed to have more real influence in local government. The Edagawa group felt that Minobe paid much more personal attention to the Takaidō protest than to their own, for he visited Takaidō several times and received its leaders at his downtown office, but he did not speak with Edagawa leaders. Although the incineration plant for Kōtō ward has even more frills than Suginami (the Kōtō plant houses a seaside park, a botanical garden, a gymnasium, an athletic field, a heated swimming pool, a community hall, and housing for ward employees), Edagawa activists did not participate in its design, nor did they have any elaborate agreement with the TMG giving them participatory rights after the plant begins operations.

---

purchased in November 1974 agree to leave. Not until December 1977 did residents agree on final details of the plant design (height, depth of excavation for the foundation, actual position of the plant on the designated site). Construction did not actually begin until November 1979. See AS, 1 July 1976 (ssb 20/1), 9 July 1976 (ssb 294/1), 24 July 1976 (ssb 780/1), 17 September 1976 (ssb 548/10), 11 December 1976 (ssb 368/1), 14 December 1976 (ssb 458/1), 25 June 1977 (ssb 833/4), 23 August 1977 (ssb 672/7), 27 December 1977 (ssb 843/4).

Even the immediate material rewards that the Edagawa group won were not precisely what they had in mind. The wharfside neighborhood of Edagawa asked for compensation and improvements for itself, on the grounds that Tokyo's garbage policy caused them more suffering and inconvenience than was felt by any other neighborhood in Kōtō ward. But the community hall, three gifts of land, a pollution-prevention agreement governing transport of garbage by truck and the financial compensation from TMG belong to Kōtō ward at large rather than to Edagawa-chō in particular, and Edagawa people feared that they might be "squeezed out" by the ward leadership. Thus they won only a modest improvement in their *own* circumstances.

Moreover, although the physical burden of handling Tokyo's garbage has been alleviated to some extent by the construction of the Kōtō incinerator as well as the others in progress, Kōtō ward continues to serve as Tokyo's dump yard, and the Edagawa neighborhood continues to bear a disproportionate share of that already large burden. The Kōtō incinerator, finished in 1978, is Japan's largest and burns more than 16 percent of Tokyo's garbage, far more than Kōtō's own share. It has a daily capacity of 1,800 metric tons, three times the size of the scaled-down 600-ton plant in Suginami's Takaidō, scheduled for completion in December 1982. Furthermore, the land reclamation sites near Edagawa remain the final destination for the garbage that will be dumped untreated and for the ash produced at all of Tokyo's advanced treatment plants. Because the TMG could not build incinerators in each ward rapidly enough, the need for additional reclamation sites became so pressing in 1977 that Tokyo gave Kōtō ward three valuable pieces of land in exchange for "permission" (necessary by the terms of the September 1971 agreement) to develop additional sites, also accessible from Kōtō wharves, beyond the breakwater. Still another recent proposal will exacerbate the burdens suffered by Kōtō ward, though it makes good ecological sense. The TMG plans to excavate the decomposed material from the filled sites in Tokyo Bay every ten years, sell it as fill to make low-lying land acceptable for construction development, and put more garbage into the resulting holes. Thus in one form or another, either as untreated material or as ash, all of Tokyo's solid wastes will be transported through the streets of Kōtō ward to landfill sites offshore, which the TMG will operate as gigantic dirt farms.[21]

During its eight-year resistance to the TMG, the Takaidō group learned many sophisticated lessons about democracy in action (electoral tactics, the art of lobbying, litigation, and more). But the Edagawa group made and won fewer demands, largely by accident rather than from any skillful use of political resources. Tokyo faced a serious crisis in its garbage treatment methods and had to adopt a more efficient, sanitary

21. *AS*, 24 May 1977 (ssb 724/1), 25 May 1977 (ssb 758/1), 29 June 1977 (ssb 984/1).

method of treatment that would extract utility out of the garbage, such as heat, and reduce the final quantity of material to be deposited in the rapidly filling land reclamation projects. What the Edagawa group advocated was what Tokyo had to do anyway. In fact, the material extras granted by TMG to Kōtō ward as a whole, in the form of public facilities to accompany the Kōtō incinerator, were actually modeled on detailed suggestions from Takaidō activists. Edagawa demands provided Minobe with an occasion to launch the "garbage war," but Takaidō demands provided him with guidelines as to how to proceed.

• The Movement to Decrease Garbage in Chūō Ward

The high-temperature modern furnaces that TMG planned did not address the long-term questions of solid-waste disposal—the consequences of putting even sanitarily treated ashes somewhere, the threat of soil and water pollution due to contaminants (such as heavy metals) within waste products wherever they are disposed of, and the inherent wastefulness of failing to utilize garbage for other purposes. This study included two other groups concerned not simply with getting away from garbage but with reducing the volume of waste that society produces, recycling rather than discarding, and promoting long-term solutions. One of these was another neighborhood association from Chūō ward, which the TMG considered a "cooperative" group rather than a "protest" group. Using funds from the ward office, this group organized recycling bazaars and the separate collection and recycling of reusable commodities. It distributed information to each household explaining what materials could be recycled and how to be frugal consumers. The group also approached local industries, schoolteachers, women's groups, and major department stores to obtain cooperation with their efforts. In a strict sense it was not a grass-roots movement, because the neighborhood association did not decide on its own how to tackle the garbage problem. Instead, the ward office asked the association to cooperate with an effort to reduce the total volume of garbage generated in Chūō ward, which was too small, congested, and valuable (Chūō ward contains Ginza and Nihonbashi) for a sanitary treatment plant to be built there.

• National Liaison Council of Regional Women's Groups (Chifuren)

The last of the garbage groups in our sample most closely resembled the recycling efforts familiar in the United States. This was a group of women involved in Chifuren (Zenkoku chiiki fujin dantai renraku kyōgikai, or the National Liaison Council of Regional Women's Groups), an alliance of local groups with 5,477,448 members in September 1972.[22]

22. Materials about Chifuren's activities to tackle long-term problems of garbage pollution are available in their annual conference bulletins. Still further information was

Although Chifuren often cooperates with the Housewives' Association (Shufuren), a smaller but well-known national women's group, and with Japan's League of Women Voters, it has no exact American counterpart. It serves as an umbrella organization through which Japanese women become involved in charitable activities corresponding to volunteer work among American women. Chifuren was largely responsible for the successful boycott against color television, the boycott of high-priced cosmetics, and many protests against the use of detergents, petroleum protein, and dangerous food additives.[23]

Chifuren as a whole cannot be considered a single citizens' movement, in that its national organization is really an interest group, much more institutionalized than a social movement, and many of the local groups it subsumes are not interested in political protest. However, if environmental problems emerge as local issues, member groups of Chifuren often turn their attention to environmental protest. All of the Chifuren members in our sample were individually active in bona fide citizens' movements in their own communities and were currently involved in local efforts to promote recycling.

Chifuren was the backbone of the "no-wrap" movement in 1972, an effort designed to reduce the amount of wrapping and packaging used in Japan. Shoppers refused to buy products that were wastefully and deceptively packaged, requested stores not to wrap packages, and carried their purchases in a traditional cloth scarf (*furoshiki*) brought from home instead of in throwaway bags provided by the stores. But the Chifuren members in our sample each went beyond this to organize recycling campaigns in their own communities. One respondent represented a group that obtained its operating budget by donating time and labor to the sorting and collecting of recyclable materials and then selling them to scrap dealers. Her group negotiated with department stores, packaging companies, and manufacturers to decrease the wrappings used and to stop providing free shopping bags, and persuaded local businesses to eliminate the cost of unsolicited wrapping paper from prices and to charge an extra fee for wrapping paper.

Recycling in order to prevent pollution that emanates from discarded waste products in a throughput economy is a new notion in Japan, but recycling to conserve scarce resources is one of the secrets of traditional Japanese frugality. As Japanese society grew wealthier and materials became cheaper relative to average personal income during the

---

available in the form of interviews, leaflets, and handbills. Chifuren headquarters has its own library (Zenkoku Fujin Kaikan, 1-17-7 Shibuya, Shibuya-ku, Tōkyō-to 150).

23. Hirohata Takeuchi, "Consumerism in Japan" (M.B.A. thesis, University of California at Berkeley, 1972); Maureen Kirkpatrick, "Consumerism and Japan's New Citizen Politics," *Asian Survey* 15:3 (March 1975), 235–249.

1960s, most scrap dealers were driven out of business. The waste reclamation business also declined because modern garbage included many nonrecyclable materials and many substances that the old-fashioned small-scale scrap dealer was not equipped to process. However, two forces have revived recycling in Japan. Activity by citizens' movements like those above has increased public awareness of recycling as a solution to both the resources pinch and the pollution problem.[24] Thus Tokyo citizens now comply readily if reluctantly with new requirements that they sort their own household garbage into categories for separate treatment. Similarly, the scarcity of raw materials makes recycling economical, and sheer necessity has revitalized the small scrap dealer and thrust Japan into the technological vanguard of recycling and resource recovery.[25] Scrap dealers now drive "paper exchange trucks" (*chirigami kōkansha*) around residential neighborhoods to collect old newspapers and magazines, in exchange for which they distribute toilet paper and facial tissue, and enterprising citizens can now find buyers for their used glass, cans, and newsprint.

To summarize, then, the "garbage problem" to most Japanese means the "incinerator construction problem," and involves keeping garbage out of one's neighborhood. But to some activists it also refers to the wasteful conversion of valuable resources into useless garbage which accumulates and threatens to contaminate soil, water, and air.

• The Society to Protect Life and Nature in Musashino

It is well known that Tokyo is one of the world's largest and most densely populated cities (see table 7). Although Tokyo does not have a highly concentrated core of population comparable to the City of Paris or the Borough of Manhattan, 78 percent of its entire population (8,900,000 people) lives in an area smaller than New York City, at a population density over 15,000 persons per square kilometer, far denser than any other urban area of comparable size in the world. Tokyo is almost twice as congested as New York City and Moscow, its closest rivals, and is several times denser than other major cities.

24. Though there is no Japanese equivalent of Goodwill Industries or the Salvation Army which depends on a regular supply of freely donated household throwaways which it recycles and sells, the exchange of used household items through flea markets and local newsletters is catching on. See *Japan Times Weekly (JTW)*, 10 February 1979.

25. By 1974 Japan's paper recycling rate was probably the highest in the world at 40 percent, compared with 33 percent for West Germany, 30 percent for France, and only 19 percent for the United States. Japan expected to raise this rate to 55 percent by 1980. See *JT*, 26 February 1974, 20 June 1974. Similarly, a pilot recycling project in Yokohama, "Stardust 80," which converts unsorted household waste into compost, paper pulp, and gas for heating, is the envy of foreign engineers, particularly because it promises a more economical operation than its equivalents abroad. See *JTW*, 7 April and 14 April 1979.

TABLE 7 / *Comparative Population Densities*

Nations in 1970	(per square kilometer)
Bangladesh (East Pakistan)	473
Taiwan	390
Republic of Korea	323
Netherlands	319
Belgium	317
Japan	280 (1,557 per level km^2)
Federal Republic of Germany	240
United Kingdom	228
France	93
Indonesia	81
United States	22
World Average	26

Urban Areas in 1970	Area (km²)	Population	Density
Borough of Manhattan	59	1,539,000	26,085
New York City	830	7,800,000	9,398
City of Paris	105	2,590,000	24,667
Greater Paris	12,000	9,251,000	771
Tokyo (23 wards)	577	8,900,000	15,425
Tokyo Prefecture	2,133	11,400,000	5,345
Moscow	875	7,100,000	8,114
London	1,562	7,500,000	4,802
Hong Kong	1,034	4,089,000	3,955
Singapore	581	2,050,000	3,528

Park Space (in square meters) per Person in Major World Cities in 1967

Tokyo (23 wards) in 1969	1.25
Tokyo Prefecture in 1969	1.26
Japanese cities as a whole in 1969	2.43
Japanese cities slated for "city planning" or new-town development in 1976	3.40
Zurich	6.4
Moscow	9.7
London	10.0
Amsterdam	12.6
Berlin	14.4
Vienna	15.6
Cologne	19.0
New York	19.0

Sources: Tōkyō kōgai kenkyūjo, *Sūji de miru kōgai: kōgai shiryō shū* (March 1971), 1–14; Tokyo Metropolitan Government, Bureau of General Affairs, Liaison and Protocol Section, *Tokyo Fights Pollution: An Urgent Appeal for Reform* (March 1971), p. 16; Tachi Minoru, "The Inter-Regional Movement of Population as Revealed by the 1970 Census," *Area Development in Japan* 4 (1971), 7–12; "Graphic View of Five Large Cities in the World," *Tokyo Municipal News* 22:7 (September–October 1972), 8; Peter Hall, *The World Cities* (McGraw Hill, 1966); United Nations, Statistical Office, *Demographic Yearbook 1970*; United Nations, Statistical Office, *Statistical Yearbook 1976*; *Statistical Abstract of the United States 1976*; Environment Agency, *Quality of The Environment in Japan 1977* (November 1977), pp. 204–205.

It is not so widely appreciated that Tokyo's housing and those facilities which enhance the quality of life are poor in comparison with Japan's per capita gross national product. Tokyo grew with great speed in a haphazard fashion that compounded all of the major pollution problems that a great city has to deal with. The city was nearly leveled in two major disasters—the great earthquake and fire of 1923 and the firebombing of 1945. The provision of rudimentary food and shelter for the destitute was of much higher priority than the relative luxury of first stopping to lay out straight, wide streets, to zone separate residential and industrial areas, or to rebuild according to strict standards of construction. Japanese cities have far less park space per person than those elsewhere. The average living space per person in 1965 in Tokyo was only 6.78 square meters (only 8.43 square meters for Japan as a whole), less than one small room per person.[26] Finally, the resulting serious problems that face all Japanese cities are all the more difficult to solve because of high population densities and land prices.

A unique pollution problem in Tokyo is construction pollution, or the spread of high-rise buildings, which threaten the "sunshine rights" (nisshōken) of the surrounding residents.[27] This is often described as a frivolous and uniquely Japanese obsession, but Americans are growing more familiar with the problem as the increase in applications of solar energy in private homes necessitates legal protection of the right to "solar access," as it is termed in the United States. Japanese are concerned about sunshine rights, not simply to permit applications of solar energy but as a fundamental element of the "civil minimum" as well as good health. Deprivation of sunshine is a serious problem in congested Japanese cities but not in cities that are more carefully planned and that provide more open space per person. In 1972 Tokyo had a bare minimum of zoning ordinances to determine the height of buildings permitted, the use (industrial, commercial, residential) of these areas, and the percentage of each lot that must be left open (from 0% in industrial areas to 30% in a

26. 1965 census figures came from Tokyo Metropolitan Government, *Sizing Up Tokyo* (May 1969), p. 43.

27. For general information on the sunshine problem, see Igarashi Toyokashi, "Nisshōken to seikatsu kankyō" [Sunshine Rights and the Living Environment], *Shimin* 9 (July 1972), 77–83; Saito Kōji and Sawa Keitarō, *Jūmin pawaa nyūmon: kayowaki shomin ga jiei suru tame ni* [Introduction to Residents' Power: So That the Helpless Common People May Defend Themselves] (Tokyo: Shufu to Seikatsusha, April 1972); "Reurbanization Plan for Tokyo," *Tokyo Municipal News* 22:7 (September-October 1972), 12–14; *Tomin no koe '71* (March 1971), pp. 128–129; *Tomin no koe '73* (March 1974), pp. 95–105; Tōkyō tosei chōsakai, *Kenchiku kōgai, sōon* [Construction Pollution and Noise] (November 1970); Tōkyō tosei chosakai, "Tōkyō no jūmin undō: genjō hōkoku" [Residents' Movements of Tokyo: A Report from the Scene], a series of three articles in *Tosei* 1 (January 1972), 33–44; 2 (February 1972), 17–27; and 4 (April 1972), 62–66. Additional information was available through interviews, pamphlets, and handbills distributed by these groups at their demonstrations and meetings.

first-class residential area). Unfortunately, first-class residential areas (where buildings may not exceed ten meters in height) were often immediately adjacent to commercial or industrial zones where height limitations did not apply. Furthermore, many of the zones were so small that they amounted to no zoning at all, and in effect residential and nonresidential properties were thoroughly intermingled. Virtually all of eastern and northern Tokyo was one vast industrial-use zone, despite the large residential population. Local residents there had absolutely no legal recourse to complain about noise or tall buildings that block sunlight, because all kinds of activity and buildings were acceptable in an industrial zone.

Finally, high land values and respect for individual property rights weakened the enforcement of zoning restrictions. Private householders were tempted to erect tall apartment buildings on their land or to build on a larger portion of their lots than was permitted by residential zoning. Until recently, the surrounding residents felt that the right of property owners to do anything they wished with their own land outweighed the importance of zoning restrictions. Thus local authorities received no pressure to enforce the zoning ordinances strictly, but experienced tremendous pressure to grant construction permits without examining the regulations too closely.

After 1970 hostility to high-rise construction grew strong in some areas, and movements opposed to particular structures succeeded. Our study includes one of these groups, a cluster of housewives opposed to high-rise construction in Musashino city (western Tokyo prefecture). As a result of the group's activity, in late 1971 the mayor of Musashino, a reformist supported by the JSP and JCP, announced new city guidelines requiring anyone erecting a building over ten meters tall to obtain the permission of surrounding residents, or the city would cut off the builder's water supply. One very active member of this group submitted to the Musashino city assembly her own draft of an improved zoning ordinance, one that eventually influenced national legislation.

The Musashino group cooperated with a Tokyo-wide liaison organization of sunshine-rights groups, which successfully pursued litigation in sunshine-rights cases. In damage suits the courts required owners of tall buildings to compensate nearby residents for extra heating and lighting bills, to erect clotheslines on top of their homes to permit laundry to dry, and to block off high windows that overlooked the plaintiffs' homes. In 1972 the Supreme Court declared that Article 25 of the Constitution (which guarantees "the minimum standards of wholesome and cultural living") included the right to sunshine, and that anyone who infringed upon another's right to sunshine would be liable for damages.[28]

28. *Daily Yomiuri*, 28 June 1972.

Recent developments include the extension of the legal concept of "sunshine rights" beyond situations involving two private parties and the "right" to have sunshine on one's residence. The Sapporo District Court was the first to award compensation to residents in a *public* apartment building (in July 1976). In September 1976 Tokyo residents in Itabashi ward won the first damage award from a public facility (a highway) that blocked their sunlight, a decision expected to raise the cost of all public facilities. Owners of a high-rise condominium were ordered to pay compensation to a kindergarten next door in the same month. The Tokyo District Court established in March 1977 that citizens were entitled to sunshine in their gardens as well as on their dwellings. In August 1977, residents of Nishikamata in Tokyo won the first sunshine-rights case in an area zoned for commercial use; the Supreme Court confirmed this ruling in April 1978 by rejecting the defendant's appeal.[29]

This body of case law goes beyond a homeowner's or a tenant's right to compensation for deprivation of sunlight and now includes court orders to modify architectural plans and even to dismantle the upper stories of the offending building. As a result of the concern over sunshine rights, modern buildings in Tokyo display a unique architectural style, with their upper corners lopped off to approximate a pyramidal shape on top and shorten the building's shadow.

Sunshine-rights groups have not confined their attention to the settlement of private grievances, but have lobbied effectively for stronger zoning laws and ordinances, as our own group did in Musashino. Tokyo tightened its zoning ordinances and the procedures for granting construction permits and extended the total area designated as residential zones. In June 1973 the liaison group of sunshine-rights organizations gathered 177,000 signatures to sponsor a citizens' draft of a more stringent zoning ordinance. The Construction Ministry adopted many of the provisions of the citizen proposal into its working drafts of legislation.[30] A revision of the Construction Standards Law which became effective in November 1976 required local governments to develop their own sunshine standards (for minimum hours of unimpeded sunlight cast to the north of a building on the winter solstice, December 21), and accompanying construction standards (ratios of a building's square footage and total volume to its lot size). After a great deal of debate over how much participation and veto power to grant to residents near a construction project, the TMA passed two ordinances in July 1978 to satisfy the

29. *AS*, 3 July 1976 (ssb 103/4), 3 September 1976 (ssb 91/1, 103/1), 1 March 1977 (ssb 23/6), 31 August 1977 (ssb 944/7), 25 April 1978 (ssb 858/1).

30. *JT*, 17 February 1973, 3 June 1973, 4 September 1973. See also Kashiwagi Satoru, "'Hiatari jōrei' no imi suru mono" [What the Sunshine Ordinance Means], *Jurisuto (zōkan)* (special issue on sunshine rights, January 1974), pp. 202–207.

direct-demand initiative of 1973 and to comply with the November 1976 Construction Standards Law. According to the TMG, disputes over sunshine rights have decreased since the laws went into effect in October 1978.[31]

The most far-reaching consequence of agitation over sunshine rights and urban planning in Japan, as well as over environmental protection in general, is the growing government interest in comprehensive planning, not for promotion of industry but for protection of the environment. The Construction Ministry began granting subsidies to firms to construct green belts around their plants in 1968. Two recent laws restrict industrial development and require green belts as pollution buffers around industrial complexes in the Kantō (Tokyo) and Kinki (Kyoto-Osaka) regions. The National Land Utilization Program adopted in May 1976 resembles the Swedish concept of physical planning, in that it classified every square meter of land in Japan into one of five land-use categories (urban, agricultural, forest, natural parks, or nature conservation areas). Finally, the Central City-planning Council recommended in July 1976 the creation of green-zone master plans for urban areas, with goals of increasing the space devoted to urban greenery to twenty square meters per capita and raising the proportion of green zones in urban areas to 30 percent by the year 2000.[32]

• Residents' Council for Countermeasures against Highway 35-36

In addition to the problem of sunshine rights, Tokyo has more common problems related to pollution that are results of haphazard growth and high population density. During the feudal period, many of Japan's castle towns were purposely built with narrow, crooked streets and many dead ends, to foil an attacking army's approach to the center of the city. Most of the roads still lack sidewalks, and many are too narrow for one medium-sized Japanese car to negotiate a corner comfortably. The need to modernize such a system of roads is painfully obvious. Per capita hours of commuting time have increased over the years as Japanese people crowd into the cities and establish suburban bed-towns. Even with double-tracking and the addition of many express trains to the lines, existing mass-transit facilities are being strained to the limit. Until additional lines are built, no more trains can be squeezed onto the tracks at

31. *AS*, 19 September 1976 (ssb 620/1), 27 January 1978 (ssb 834/1), 15 March 1978 (ssb 455/6), 21 April 1978 (ssb 720/1). Additional information obtained from the TMG, 18 March 1980.

32. Environment Agency, *The Quality of the Environment in Japan 1977* (Tokyo: Ministry of Finance Printing Bureau, November 1977), pp. 204–221. On Sweden, see Organization for Economic Cooperation and Development, *Environmental Policy in Sweden* (Paris, 1977), pp. 74–90.

rush hour. Rush hour trains already carry three times the officially decreed safe number of persons per railway car.[33] They are often packed to the extreme limits of physical capacity, so that people inside suffer cracked ribs, and windows burst owing to the pressure of people inside.

The TMG has great difficulty in buying the land it needs to build new subways, train lines, and automobile roads. The large population residing near any projected construction site is certain to protest the severe side effects of construction and of the new transportation line (air pollution, dust, noise, vibrations, traffic congestion, and increased traffic accidents). Any construction project reduces the amount of land available for parks and residences, arousing further protest. And because of the disorderly pattern of urban development in the past, any attempt to lay out a more systematic network of streets or to construct a straightforward transportation line inevitably cuts through the built-up areas, slicing into schools and neighborhoods, disrupting the daily lives of many people, and arousing the opposition of threatened community organizations, merchants' associations, PTA groups, and so on.

Our sample includes one group that opposed construction of a highway and a subway through Nerima ward (Highways 35 and 36) on the grounds that air pollution, noise, and the risk of traffic accidents near the highway would be severe, and because the TMG did not consult them before designing the road and beginning construction at both ends.[34]

Air pollution from automobiles became a subject of great concern when it was discovered in 1970 that residents of the most congested in-

33. Hidetoshi Katō, "A View of Densely Populated Societies," *The Wheel Extended* 1:4 (Spring 1972), 10–15. See also "The Reality of Traffic and Transportation in Tokyo," *Tokyo Municipal News* 20:10 (December 1970), 1.

34. Information came from interviews and Hirai Eiko, "Ningen yūsen no toshi seisaku wo" [Toward Urban Policies with Priority on People], *Tōkyō no shakai kyōiku* 19:1 (30 August 1972); Nishimori Tatsuo, "Hōshin 35-36 go dōro mondai to tomin sanka" [Citizen Participation and the Problem of Highway 35-36], *Shimin* 5 (November 1971), 37–45; Tōkyō tosei chōsakai, *Tōkyō no jūmin undō: sono mondai to tembō* [Residents' Movements in Tokyo: Their Problems and Prospects] (Tokyo, September 1971), pp. 4–15; Umahashi Michio, "Todō 36 go to jūmin no ronri" [Highway 36 and the Residents' Logic], *Shimin* 14 (May 1973), 152–159. Among TMG publications, see *Tomin no koe '71*, pp. 16–20; *Tomin no koe '73*, pp. 37–42; two detailed pamphlets: Hōshin 36 go dōro no jūmin tōhyō ni kansuru chōsakai [Investigatory Committee for a Popular Referendum on Highway 36], *Dōro mondai no kaiketsu no tame no teigen* [A Proposal for Solving the Highway 36 Problem] (Tokyo, March 1975); and Tōkyō-to tominshitsu [Tokyo Citizens' Office], *Hōshin 36 go dōro no jūmin tōhyō ni kansuru chōsakai no tōshin kankei shiryō* [Materials Relating to the Report of the Investigatory Committee for a Popular Referendum on Highway Number 36] (Tokyo, March 1975). See also Haruo Matsubara, "The Local Government and Citizen Movements," *Local Government Review* 5 (1977), 52–69. Findings from a survey of leaders and group members are available in Kanagae Haruhiko et al., "Jūmin undō no jisshōteki kenkyū: undō sankasha no bunseki wo chūshin to shite" [A Concrete Study of a Residents' Movement Based on Analysis of Movement Participants], *Tōkyō daigaku kyōiku gakubu kiyō* 15 (1975), 69–85.

tersection in Tokyo (Ushigome Yanagi-chō in Shinjuku ward) were suffering from severe lead poisoning because of lead in the exhaust gas. Furthermore, the serious photochemical smog incidents in Nerima and
Toshima wards, causing school children to be hospitalized, occurred in
the summer of 1970.[35] Residents in these areas where weather conditions
caused pollutants to concentrate thus had extra reason to fear additional
air pollution, and on September 19, 1970, the local residents living near
the projected roadway formed an opposition group, Residents' Council
for Countermeasures against Highway 35-36 (Hōshin 35-36 go dōro taisaku jūmin kyōgikai).

After gathering ten thousand signatures in two weeks, they presented a petition on October 9 to the Tokyo Metropolitan Assembly, requesting that construction on the road be stopped, and that the subway
be built by special methods that would be quieter and safer for the local
community. The group persisted and eventually elicited a favorable response, meeting six times with the TMG during August and September
1971. Rather than working through the metropolitan assembly or the
TMG offices with jurisdiction over road construction as they had at first,
the Residents' Council had the best success working directly through
Governor Minobe and his Citizens' Office (a newly created complaint-
coordinating service at the TMG). Both the group and the TMG point to
this close dialogue as the first real example of citizen participation in
Tokyo government. It is generally agreed that through the TMG's flexible
and tolerant response the local opponents of the road gradually modified their views from total opposition to any road at all to acceptance of a
road on condition that residents' views and preferences about the construction methods and design be taken into account. In November 1972,
Governor Minobe presented six alternative plans: one, for example, was
to build on top of the subway a road twenty meters in width, bordered
on each side by ten meters of trees, sidewalks, and bicycle paths. In response to additional suggestions from local citizens, the TMG set precedents for all of its future projects by conducting an elaborate environmental impact survey during August and September of 1973 and printing
a series of special newsletters to inform the residents about the six plans.
The TMG then proceeded to conduct an opinion poll of local residents
and to publicize the findings. The TMG planned to conduct a citizens'

35. A survey done in May 1970 revealed that fifty-eight out of sixty-six residents living within seventy meters of Ushigome Yanagichō intersection in Shinjuku ward had lead
concentrations in the blood and urine higher than the "safe" level stipulated by the law on
labor accident compensation. Subsequently, in a more general survey of lead pollution,
seven other intersections were found as badly polluted by lead as Yanagichō. See "Lead
Additives in Gasoline Accused," *Tokyo Municipal News* 20:7 (August 1970), 6; "Thick
Oxidants Frighten Tokyo Citizens," *Tokyo Municipal News* 20:9 (October-November
1970), 3; and TMG, *Tokyo Fights Pollution*, pp. 75–78.

referendum to choose among the six plans but abandoned this expensive procedure as its own financial troubles worsened. After a lapse in construction plans because of financial stringency, the TMG's subway corporation finished buying up the land in the planned roadway, and the subway is now under construction with the road to follow later.

Women from the group are now working on citizen commissions to advise the Tokyo government on more general problems of city redevelopment, urban planning, zoning, highways, and mass transit. This group concerned with air pollution and other hazards that would result from the construction of Highway 35-36 was well known in Tokyo and was considered even by the TMG to be one of the most sophisticated and skillful it had encountered.

• Tokyo Sewer Workers' Pollution Study Group

Another group in the sample concerned with urban pollution was an activist segment of the labor union of civil servants working at the TMG's Bureau of Waterworks (Tōkyō-to suidōkyoku rōdō kumiai, abbreviated as Tōsuirō).[36] The Tōsuirō group operated both as a citizens' movement by lobbying with the metropolitan assembly and as a labor union vis-à-vis the TMG as its employer. The group first emerged after the Bureau of Waterworks announced in June 1970 that it would begin dumping sludge from the process of sedimentation (primary treatment) into the ocean, rather than on land or into the main rivers of Tokyo as in the past. Concerned members of Tōsuirō protested the bureau's decision to compound ocean pollution problems, and Governor Minobe intervened on their behalf with an alternative suggestion. Furnaces were built to burn the sludge, reducing its volume by 90 percent, and the ashes from this process were once again dumped on land or in Tokyo's rivers.

The labor union was concerned about the health of temporary workers hired for the dangerous task of cleaning these furnaces, arguing that the bureau did not properly inform these temporary workers of the hazards involved and paid them an unsuitably low wage for such work. As a by-product of this dispute, some Tōsuirō members became worried about the risks of air pollution resulting from the incineration of the sludge, and about the risks of water and soil pollution resulting from the dumping of the ashes. The most dangerous ingredients of these final waste products were heavy metals (lead, mercury, chromium, cadmium,

36. Most of this information came from interviews in 1972 and 1980. See also Kawada Osamu, "Kokuhatsu—tachiagaru suidō rōdōsha" [Indictment—The Sewer Workers Rise Up], *Shimin* 4 (September 1971), 156–157. The group also published a periodical presenting its scientific findings: Tōkyō suidō rōdōsha kōgai mondai kenkyūkai [Tokyo Sewer Workers Pollution Problems Study Group], *Kōgai mondai chōsa kenkyū tsūshin* [Pollution Problems Survey and Research News]. The labor union's monthly newsletter also covers the activities of the group: Tōkyō suidō rōdō kumiai, *Tōsuirō Shimbun*.

and so on) from industrial waste water, which might seep into the underground water that supplied drinking water to the majority of Tokyoites still served by well water. The bureau's dumping sites were on inexpensive land near low-cost housing projects that were not served by sewers, so the underprivileged residents of such areas ran the greatest risks from the dumping of burned sludge.

This solution aroused the interest of some members of Tōsuirō for obvious reasons. As a socialist labor union they were interested in any social injustice. In addition, by 1972 they felt that the labor movement should improve its public image on the pollution issue, because unions in Japan were being lambasted for their silent loyalty to management in pollution cases. Japanese antipollution activists argued that workers within a polluting enterprise were in a particularly knowledgeable position about polluting substances and wastes released during production, and should reveal this information. As civil servants, members of Tōsuirō were protected against the loss of their jobs, so they were relatively free to publicize the potential polluting effects of Tokyo's sewage treatment process. Finally, they viewed their antipollution activities as a contribution to Minobe's reformist objective of being responsive to the needs of the people. Thus the antipollution activists in Tōsuirō agreed that they had a responsibility to publicize what they knew.

From 1970 through June 1972, these activists within Tōsuirō launched a movement to protest the dumping of burned sludge near Shikahama *danchi*, a low-income housing project in Adachi ward. According to their own scientific data, the burned sludge had a high concentration of heavy metals, which could rapidly seep into the surrounding soil over a twenty-four-hour period, especially during rain. The Shikahama group of housing project residents and Tōsuirō members argued that the Bureau of Waterworks should stop dumping ashes near residential areas that relied on well water as long as heavy metals were present in the sludge.

Although no method exists to remove heavy metals from water or sludge when they are present in combination with each other, there are simple inexpensive processes to remove individual metals (and salvage them for potential reuse) before they are combined with water containing other metals. The Tōsuirō activists argue that firms should be required to use these methods to process their own effluent before discharging it into public sewers. Not only would such a policy apportion the financial burden of waste treatment more fairly by eliminating a taxpayer subsidy to private industry, but it would be more economical in the long run than collective treatment without imposing a tremendous financial burden on industry. Public sewage facilities could then use sophisticated biological techniques (tertiary treatment) to reduce BOD (biochemical oxygen demand, a measure of organic water pollution) in the organic waste produced by households and thus convert sewage into sludge safe for use as fertilizer and water clean enough to drink. However, as long as the heavy metals and other inorganic contaminants are present, the final products of sewage treatment are dangerous sources of pollution wherever they go. Therefore, Tōsuirō activists insist that until the TMG requires individual industrial treatment of waste water, it is the responsibility of TMG and the Bureau of Waterworks to tell the public that they cannot remove heavy metals from the sludge, which thus enters the underground water table and the ocean, affecting both the water and the food supply for Japan.

Tōsuirō activists regarded the Shikahama movement as a failure when the self-government association of the housing project and the Bureau of Waterworks signed an agreement in June 1972 in which residents said that they were satisfied with the bureau's reassurances about their drinking water. The document provided that the bureau would accept full responsibility for any damage caused by the burned sludge and that the housing project could appoint members to a team that would regularly inspect the ashes, but the disturbing clause in the agreement was the residents' promise never again to start a protest movement. Nonetheless, the antipollution activists in Tōsuirō persevered despite the Shikahama failure, and subsequently organized into a study group that aimed at collecting data, informing the public, launching movements in other areas to improve the treatment of water, politicizing the public, and making local governments more responsive to the interests of their own residents.

Since then the group has evolved in several ways to become perhaps the most influential and institutionalized one in our sample. First, it broadened its concern from the problem of collective treatment to recycling, a pressing question for a city that faces a critical water shortage every summer. Since 1972 Tokyo has been forced to abandon the Tama River as a water source because the volume of treated sewage entering the river was three times the amount of the freshwater flow, utterly overwhelming the river's ability to purify itself. Though Tokyo has reduced the release of sewage into the Tama by 75 percent, it now draws water almost exclusively from the Tone River, which drops every summer. This recurring crisis lends credibility to the Tōsuirō study group and focuses the attention of citizens and policy makers alike on its claims.

As a result, the study group has had considerable impact on policy, largely through the merits of its arguments. In 1973 Governor Minobe outspokenly adopted the position of the Tōsuirō study group in criticizing his own Bureau of Waterworks for doing a poor job of sewage treatment. He also inaugurated restrictions on total quantities of pollutants in industrial effluent to prevent firms from simply diluting their wastes with fresh water to meet the earlier standards of concentration.[37] Similarly, by informing residents of Kōtō ward about the dangerous ingredients in sludge, the study group stimulated a citizen protest there and thus forced the TMG to stop dumping burned sludge into reclamation sites in Kōtō ward that were intended for solid waste. Instead, Tokyo adopted a safer process of compacting a mixture of sludge and sludge ash into cement-like cakes, which are now deposited in a special reclamation site near Haneda airport. Although it is impossible in the short term to achieve separate treatment of industrial and household waste in the developed sections of Tokyo where sewer lines have already been laid, the TMG applies stricter standards of in-house treatment to firms that build new factories in outlying areas. In western Tokyo where sewage is predominantly from households rather than factories, the TMG is experimenting with the conversion of sludge into compost.

An even more interesting development since 1972 is the new cooperation between the original members of the study group and Tōsuirō as a whole. In 1972 the antipollution activists in Tōsuirō complained that because they were leftist activists within a left-wing labor union, protesting the acts of a leftist prefectural government, their efforts were an unwelcome embarrassment to the labor union officers, the TMG (which prided itself on antipollution crusades), and the JSP and JCP members of the TMA. The officers of Tōsuirō tried to pressure the core of activists into silence, and the activists' appeals to assembly members and the assembly's pollution policy committee were treated with hush-hush delicacy. The fact that Tokyo had a reformist government also made it difficult to arouse the citizenry against it. Governor Minobe's enormous personal popularity caused people to give his administration the benefit of the doubt in the face of criticism, and even the antipollution activists in the study group themselves shared this admiration for Minobe.

However, the increasing severity of Tokyo's water problems eventually persuaded the Tōsuirō leadership and important elements in the TMG bureaucracy of the wisdom of the group's recommendations. This change began well before the transfer of leadership in April 1979 from Minobe, who retired after his third term as governor, to his conservative successor, Suzuki Shun'ichi, so it cannot be attributed to the unification of reformist forces against new conservative leadership. Thus Tōsuirō as a whole now promotes the goals of separate treatment and recycling, and even Jichirō (the national union of municipal employees) lends its aid to the group's various campaigns. The group's clearest success in winning formal recognition came when the TMG Bureau of Waterworks appointed four members of the union (including one member of our sam-

37. *JT*, 7 March, 18–19 May, and 19 July, all in 1973.

ple) to a committee of ten in January 1977 that was asked to report on various alternatives for treating pollutants in sewage. The final report, published in December 1979, came out strongly in favor of treating sewage as a renewable resource by recycling both water and sludge, along with other recommendations that have been made by the Tōsuirō group for years, and it is expected to influence development plans at the national level.[38]

In addition to this new pattern of intra-institutional cooperation, the Tōsuirō group is also reaching outward to other citizens' movements and interest groups that share its concerns. It is working with many local movements as well as the national Consumers' League (Shōhisha renmei) and Chifuren to ban the use and sale of synthetic detergents. Shiga prefecture has passed such an ordinance to protect Lake Biwa. Twenty-five prefectures and several large cities have adopted restrictions on the use of phosphate detergents as administrative policy pending legislation (fifteen other prefectures are considering similar moves), and most recently the Environment Agency asked national government offices to exercise voluntary restraint in the use of such detergents.[39] Finally, the Tōsuirō study group has joined an ad hoc coalition backed by most reformist forces in Tokyo to collect signatures for a direct-demand initiative to force the TMA to reconsider the Minobe draft of a powerful environmental assessment ordinance that his successor, Governor Suzuki, removed from consideration in October 1979.

In sum, the Tōsuirō study group broadened its activities in three ways: its objectives grew from short-term to long-term solutions to a problem, it succeeded in persuading a much larger and more powerful organization (Tōsuirō and occasionally Jichirō) to adopt its objectives, and it began cooperating in national coalitions of other citizens' movements. Its origins within a labor union gave it a unique potential for organizational development and acceptance by formal institutions that was not shared by any citizens' movement that had to build its own organization from scratch.

· The Society to Think about Nature in the Mountains (Yama no shizen wo kangaeru kai)

American environmentalists concerned about nature talk about protecting the wilderness from the onslaughts of man, but most Japanese groups that described themselves as concerned about the destruction of

---

38. Gesui odei shori chōsa iinkai, *Gesui odei no shori shobun nado ni tsuite* [Concerning the Treatment and Disposal of Sewage Sludge], (Tokyo: Tōkyō-to gesuidōkyoku shisetsu kanribu gyōmuka, December 1979), 3 vols., consisting of a summary (31 pp.), basic report (149 pp.), and supplementary documents (195 pp.).

39. *Mainichi Daily News*, 22 February, 27 February, 4 March, 11 March, and 26 March, all in 1980.

nature in 1972 turned out to be worried not about the wilderness or nature in the raw: they were concerned instead about parkland in the cities, space devoted to private gardens, and greenery along the streets. Some were "front" groups for merchants and businessmen who wanted to attract tourists to their area. To Americans, "environmental rights" can refer to the right of a defenseless and voiceless natural environment to exist without being violated by man, whereas to Japanese activists it more often refers to the right of society to maintain that natural environment for its own enjoyment.[40]

But there are some groups in Japan concerned with nature in the wild, and these have been increasing in number as the environmental movement as a whole has grown in strength and broadened its scope. The Wild Bird Society (Japan's counterpart to the Audubon Society or the Izaak Walton League) was concerned about wilderness areas occupied by wild birds. Other groups wanted to protect marshlands, establish protected zones within national parks, prevent the construction of superhighways through national parks, or oppose construction within the boundaries of national parks where land was still privately owned.

Our study included one group concerned about the destruction of nature wherever it was threatened by excessive human contact. It consisted of mountain climbers who decided that it was their responsibility, as people who appreciated wilderness and knew about the destruction, to protest the spoiling of wild areas.[41] They organized the group in late 1971 and acquired members all over the Tokyo and Yokohama areas by advertising in mountain-climbing magazines. Members were of all ages and occupations. They decided to devote their energies to a succession of movements to combat particular incidents of environmental destruction. During 1972 the group was involved in an attempt to halt construction of an enormous (150 kilometers, ¥70 billion) sightseeing highway, the Rempō Skyline Drive connecting Fuji-Hakone and Chichibu-Tama National Parks, along a mountaintop ridge in Yamanashi prefecture. The highway was proposed by the prefectural governor, who was elected in April 1971 in part because he promised to bring construction and sightseeing development to Yamanashi by building the road. Private developers intended to buy land near the road for tracts of cottages, restaurants, and other sightseeing facilities. Sixty percent of the planned road would traverse national parks, and 10 percent of it would actually pass through

40. Christopher D. Stone, *Should Trees Have Standing? Toward Legal Rights for Natural Objects* (Los Altos, Calif.: William Kaufmann, 1974).

41. Information was obtained from interviews, leaflets, and handbills prepared by the group. See also Ueda Yoshiaki, "Rempō sukairain hantai undō" [The Movement to Oppose Rempō Skyline Drive], *Shimin* 11 (November 1972), 116–117; and Satō Atsushi, "Shizen kankyō hozen to chihō jichitai" [The Preservation of the Natural Environment and Local Government], in Satō, ed., *Chiiki kaihatsu, kōgai e no taiō*, pp. 247–256.

special wilderness zones of the park where all man-made construction was supposedly forbidden.

The group filed petitions, met with prefectural officials, and held study meetings to inform the Yamanashi population about environmental damage. They consulted lawyers about the possibility of filing charges against the prefectural governor for violating the national parks laws, but decided against it because a similar lawsuit in Shikoku failed. Director-General Ōishi Buichi of the Environment Agency opposed the road, and through his jurisdiction over the national parks he was able to prevent its construction. His successor, Koyama Osanori, was less amenable to persuasion by environmentalist groups but did promise to reroute the road around the special wilderness zones in the national parks. As a result of public pressure the prefecture submitted a revision in June 1973 which removed most of the objectionable features of the plan. The new plan transformed it into a "nature road" to discourage heavy traffic, rerouted it around the special wilderness areas by lowering it four hundred meters in altitude, and attempted to follow the path of existing logging roads. Following this and similar successes by other groups of conservationists, new legislation expanded the authority of the Environment Agency to design a long-term plan for the conservation of nature and the preservation of rare species, and within the boundaries of the national parks to buy up privately owned land, monitor deforestation, curtail development of tourist or other economic activities, and even to restrict public access.[42]

· Independent Forum

Finally, the sample was filled out by the inclusion of one group that did not restrict its interests to one issue or locality, but worried about environmental degradation in whatever form, wherever it occurred: the Independent Forum (Jishu kōza). Independent Forum first took shape as a series of public lectures held monthly at Tokyo University beginning in October 1970, by Ui Jun, an assistant in Urban Engineering there.[43] It gradually evolved into an environmental watchdog for the entire nation, publishing the contents of lectures and other environmental news regularly in books and serial publications. In addition to the public lectures, Independent Forum sponsors workshops and seminars at Tokyo Univer-

42. *Quality of the Environment in Japan 1978*, pp. 225–237.
43. The activities of Ui Jun's Independent Forum are the most thoroughly documented of all. The group publishes its public lectures in a series of magazines named *Kōgai genron*, and then in book-length volumes of the same title. The first series of three volumes was published in 1971 by Aki Shobō, and the second series of four volumes was published by Keisō Shobō during 1972 and 1973. The Forum also publishes several periodicals including *Jishu kōza*, *Human* (in English), and the *Joint News Letter* (in English) with the Citizens' Research Institute on Energy and Environment.

sity, accredited but also open to the general public, whose members do laboratory and field research on pollution issues of their own choosing. Independent Forum is virtually the only channel through which university students participate in citizens' movements. Unlike any single environmental organization in the United States, Independent Forum has no official organization or membership list, and considers anyone who attends the lectures, the workshops, or the planning meetings a member. For our purposes, the interview sample is drawn from the 1972 participants in planning sessions and laboratory groups.

Although the Independent Forum does not officially engage as a group in activities to oppose specific outbreaks of pollution, it functions literally as a forum for spokesmen from citizens' movements all over Japan, and as an ad hoc nerve center for the environmental movement as a whole. Those who attend the lectures regularly usually develop personal interests in specific movements, devoting their time to organizing support groups in many cities and raising money. The Forum is now involved in the effort to challenge nuclear power. Ui Jun himself is probably the best-known leader of the antipollution movement in Japan, having appeared often in the mass media and attended numerous international conferences on environmental problems.

Rather than offering tentative conclusions about the nature of citizens' movements from this collection of case studies, we shall first go on to examine individual participants within these movements. We may then draw upon these case histories as useful background material as we try to interpret the findings that follow. Chapter IV deals with the mobilization of citizens' movements into effective pressure groups; chapter V examines what the activists think about politics; chapter VI analyzes how participation in citizens' movements changes both political attitudes and behavior of the activists.

iv

Mobilization
and Strategy

THIS INVESTIGATION of citizens' movements at the individual level begins with four topics. First, the recruitment process: who are the participants and what motivates them to join? Second, activists' views of environmental problems: how do they define the issues and what implications do their views have? Third, movement structure: what are the patterns of leadership and internal structure in citizens' movements and what do activists think about organizational matters? Fourth, what tactics do citizens' movements use and how do activists evaluate different resources available to them? By learning why activists join and how they are mobilized to act around the pollution issue, we can understand more about why citizens' movements have come into being. Similarly, by investigating mobilization, structure, and tactics, we can compare citizens' movements with similar phenomena—other social movements, protests, and communal political activity. (Wherever activists are quoted, they are identified by a case number. For a discussion of the statistical techniques used in the next three chapters, see the Appendix.)

Recruitment of Activists

To begin with, where do Japan's antipollution activists come from, and how were they drawn into citizens' movements? The demographic profiles in table 8 show that the activists differed from the general population in certain ways. Although activists were equally divided among men and women and were predominantly urban, as was the general population, antipollution activists were distinctly better educated, somewhat older, and (according to data not shown here) highly placed in the occupational strata relative to the larger population, as we might expect from their high levels of education. Seventy-nine percent of the sample could recall at least two other nonpolitical groups in which they were involved, indicating that the sample was considerably more sociable than the general population.[1]

Japanese observers often note the predominance of women in the antipollution movement, and this was markedly the case in three urban groups composed entirely of women.[2] It may be that the majority of the rank-and-file members of citizens' movements in Japan were in fact women, but because our sample also tapped leadership levels it included more men. Indeed, except for the all-women groups, the leadership of antipollution groups in our sample was entirely male. Observations from this study provided the following hypotheses (although I had neither the opportunity nor additional data to test these).[3] (1) In Japan, where social welfare and the well-being of the family are considered acceptable concerns for women, women outnumber men at the rank-and-file level of membership in voluntary associations devoted to social amelioration. (2) There are many such associations composed entirely of women whose civic consciousness and activism can be viewed as part of the highly professional role of the Japanese housewife,[4] consistent either with the dominant "Neotraditionalist" view or with the more flexible "New Woman" definition of self among Japanese women.[5] (3) Nonetheless, there are implicit limits placed on the activities of the women in groups that also contain men, and leadership activities in such groups tend to be performed by the male members. (4) Whenever traditional beliefs about female roles are stronger, the differentiation between male and female roles in voluntary organizations is greater, with women accepting decisions made by

1. See Sidney Verba, Norman H. Nie, and Jae-on Kim, *Participation and Political Equality: A Seven-Nation Comparison* (New York: Cambridge University Press, 1978), pp. 101–102; and Ikeuchi Hajime, ed., *Shimin ishiki no kenkyū* [A Study of Citizen Consciousness] (Tokyo: Tokyo Daigaku Shuppankai, 1974), pp. 439–454.

2. Others have observed the prevalence of housewives in the environmental movement. "Nihon repooto" [Japan Report], *AS*, 21 May 1973, p. 4; and Watanuki Jōji, *Nihon seiji no bunseki shikaku* [Analytical Viewpoints of Japanese Politics] (Tokyo: Chūō Kōronsha, 1976), pp. 76–81.

3. These hypotheses are supported by evidence collected by Ikeuchi in 1966. See *Shimin ishiki*, pp. 290, 441, 450.

4. Suzanne H. Vogel, "Professional Housewife: The Career of Urban Middle Class Japanese Women," *Japan Interpreter* 12:1 (Winter 1978), 17–43.

5. See Susan Pharr's useful typology in "The Japanese Woman: Evolving Views of Life and Role," in Lewis Austin, ed., *Japan: The Paradox of Progress* (New Haven: Yale University Press, 1976), pp. 301–328.

TABLE 8 / *Demographic Profiles*

	Activist	General Population
Age (arithmetic mean for adults over 20)	47	36
Sex		
Male	52%	49%
Female	48%	51%
Residence		
Rural (occupation in farming or fishing, or resides in town under 40,000)	38%	32%
Urban (resides in city over 40,000, generally Tokyo-Yokohama among activist sample)	63%	67%
Education		
Low (prewar primary & higher primary, postwar elementary and junior high)	16%	55%
Medium (prewar middle, girls' schools, postwar senior high school)	35%	36%
High (prewar higher, normal, technical schools, postwar vocational and liberal arts colleges)	49%	9%

Sources (for data on general population for 1970): *Nihon tōkei nenkan* [Japan Statistical Yearbook] 1972, 1975.

men, the women acting only in their own neighborhoods, and the men conducting communication outside of the group.

Men and women in our sample were considerably older than the general population. The antipollution movement in Japan (and probably elsewhere) consisted to a great extent of people worried about their immediate environment, their health, and their future well-being. Such people tended to have lived for a long time in their community;[6] not only were they attached to the locality but they had observed the ravages of rapid industrialization over time and could compare present environmental despoilation with a cleaner past. Most of the sample members had grown children, and had thus reached a stage in life where they had more time to devote to activities of this sort. They worried not only about their children's welfare but also about the well-being of later generations.

One unique feature of the Japanese environmental movement was the relative absence of young people. The American environmental movement receives a large portion of its strength and force from the efforts of young people, not only because Americans are relatively free at that point in the life cycle to devote their time and energy to political causes, but also because young Americans have the option of developing

6. This is also true in the United States. See Lester Milbrath, *Political Participation* (Chicago: Rand McNally, 1965), pp. 48–49, 110–141.

alternative lifestyles which can function as examples to the rest of the public that what they advocate is actually possible.[7] Similarly, in the interim between "examination hell" and absorption into the obligations of employment, marriage, and family, young people in Japan are also in the freest and most flexible period in their lives. We would therefore expect them to have a disproportionate presence in the environmental movement in Japan, but they are mysteriously absent. The explanation usually given by Japanese environmentalists is that those young people who are interested in any sort of social or political change tend to advocate total revolution, while the rest are absorbed in leisure or intellectual pursuits. Those few young people in our sample agreed that most of their peers found pollution an unattractive problem, requiring hard work without offering scope for revolutionary activity. Although interest groups in the United States often have a self-conscious concern with the recruitment of youth to assure the survival of the group in the next generation, Japanese citizens' movements are not sufficiently established to be concerned with their activity in the distant future. Only one of the respondents sampled revealed such a concern. The relative absence of young unmarried people and students in citizens' movements is not to be explained so much by the failure of citizens' movements to recruit them as by the lack of interest shown by young people themselves.

Because older people are usually *less* well educated in Japan, it is surprising that activists were so much *better* educated than the general population, but it is nonetheless a contrast to be expected. Education equips people with an interest in current affairs and with the scientific background to understand environmental issues. It is also true that education, especially in the postwar system, teaches people about their political rights and gives them some understanding of how to make their complaints heard.

This social profile describes the "average" activist in a citizens' movement as a well-educated, relatively well-off citizen with the wisdom of mature adulthood. Why, then, have people in such comfortable circumstances been transformed into angry activists? First of all, there is no "average" or "typical" activist; our image is really a composite, and it is possible to discern two very different sets of circumstances that produced the decision to become active. One cluster of people were relatively wealthy and highly respected community leaders who benefited from postwar economic growth and felt themselves to be in control of their lives and their surroundings. The pollution threat provided the first occasion in which they found themselves disagreeing with conservative policies.

7. Denton E. Morrison, Kenneth E. Hornback, and W. Keith Warner, "The Environmental Movement: Some Preliminary Observations and Predictions," in William R. Burch, Jr., Neil H. Cheek, Jr., and Lee Taylor, eds., *Social Behavior, Natural Resources, and the Environment* (New York: Harper & Row, 1972), pp. 274–275.

When they discovered that they could not influence local authorities whom they once considered friends, they underwent an emotional crisis that transformed them into outraged protesters. At the opposite end of the spectrum were a few people from the socially disadvantaged sector of society, subjected to a long series of hardships, accustomed to a marginal existence, not quite sharing in postwar prosperity. They had endured silently in the past on the assumption that they could do nothing effective or that vocal complaint might even be counterproductive. But pollution arrived as an awesome and final threat to their well-being, perhaps to life itself, an intolerable intrusion where silence threatened to be fatal. Fed up, they abandoned their traditional definitions of social propriety and started to protest.

Second, all of the activists in our sample, and presumably most of the larger universe of activists in citizens' movements, embarked on citizens' movement activity out of pressing needs: dire personal fears or perceived threats to health, property, or (less often) deeply cherished values. It was commonly heard that Japanese were unlikely to mobilize in force around the environmental issue until they all had twisted fingers and convulsive seizures, and that citizens' movements were more likely to be concerned about seeking compensation for damage already done than about preventing pollution before it occurs. This was a mistaken impression, however, created by the publicity given to the earliest court cases. Admittedly, the first people to discover the pollution problem were those who suffered from it and sought restitution through legal action, but more recent citizens' movements, inspired by these frightening examples, have arisen to protest pollution before it reaches such dangerous levels.[8] This change in emphasis was already visible at the time of this 1972 survey, which revealed that 66 percent of the activists were concerned with prevention of pollution before the fact, and only 31 percent of the sample became active after direct personal losses to health or property (19% of the sample fit both categories). Although survey respondents themselves shared the skeptical view and bemoaned the difficulties of building a prevention-oriented movement, that is precisely what two-thirds of them were doing.

Another misconception arising out of the fact that activists initially joined citizens' movements out of selfish concerns was that their interests remained selfish, and that citizens' movements were therefore prevented by the "egoism" of their members from cultivating a "civic conscience." However, many activists remained involved long after their initial "selfish" concerns were disposed of and they could no longer benefit materially from continued effort. At the time of this survey, a surprising 42 per-

8. "Nihon repooto," *AS*, 21 May 1973, p. 4.

cent of the sample had become principled "altruists," who continued their activism in order to benefit others like themselves.

In summary, then, the Japanese who joined citizens' movements were somewhat better equipped than the general population to comprehend a complex issue like pollution and to be aware of methods to combat it, through their relatively high education and ample experience in other community activities. Most were also somewhat better off than the general population and more able to afford the "luxury" of opposing further industrial development in order to prevent pollution. In that their social makeup was consistent with that of communal participation in Japan in the 1960s, citizens' movements blended more than they contrasted with their antecedents.[9] That is, both citizens' movements and earlier communal activities were egalitarian in that they included people from all socioeconomic levels, although in the most activist and voluntaristic forms of participation the well-educated had a slight edge. Similarly, young people were conspicuously absent, and the median age of forty-seven in our sample was consistent with the finding that Japanese reserved their most energetic participation in politics for their forties and fifties.[10] Finally, all were initially mobilized out of fear of an imminent threat to their lives and circumstances, but over time many self-interested activists acquired an abstract, even altruistic, concern with basic environmental issues and political principles.

Activist Views of Environmental Problems

Several patterns can be discerned in activists' views about environmental problems. Activists in Japanese citizens' movements seemed to be deeply concerned and quite knowledgeable, but in contrast with American environmentalists they defined pollution narrowly, focused their explanations and goals sharply on a limited number of targets, and perceived themselves rather than the environment as victims. An exploration of these views also serves as a surreptitious test to distinguish between casual or accidental involvement in citizens' movements and

9. Verba, Nie, and Kim, *Participation and Political Equality*, passim; and Ikeuchi, *Shimin ishiki*, pp. 401–466, on communal activity in Japan in the 1960s.

10. See Norman H. Nie, Sidney Verba, and Jae-on Kim, "Political Participation and the Life Cycle," *Comparative Politics* 6:3 (April 1974), 319–340. Young people in their twenties and thirties are more visible in citizens' movements in newly developed suburban apartment towns consisting entirely of young families. See Satake Hiroshi, "Shimin undō to chihō senkyo" [Citizens' Movements and Local Elections], in Nihon seiji gakkai, *Nempō seijigaku 1974: seiji sanka no riron to genjitsu* [Annual of the Japanese Political Science Association: The Theory and Practice of Political Participation] (Tokyo: Iwanami Shoten, March 1975), pp. 166–193.

self-conscious involvement based primarily on a deep concern with the issue itself.

· Causes of Pollution

When asked to select the underlying causes of pollution problems in Japan from a list of eight possibilities, respondents revealed much basic agreement. Sizable majorities of them blamed (1) excessive concern within government and bureaucracy about economic growth and industrial development (84%), (2) industry's attitude that pollution-prevention equipment was a waste of investment funds (75%), and (3) government laziness with respect to the establishment and enforcement of strict standards (63%). These most prevalent explanations accused large, powerful institutions of being either too lazy, too concerned about inappropriate goals, or outright stingy. It follows that if these institutions changed their motives, goals, or mode of operation, pollution would decrease.

Activists were much less likely to attribute pollution to underlying traits of society. Only 50 percent of the sample said that consumer ignorance about pollution was a cause; only 44 percent blamed population density (explained in the questionnaire to mean that production, consumption, and treatment of waste were too concentrated); and surprisingly, only 27 percent blamed the fact that Japan was an industrial society with a high level of consumption. Thus our sample of activists preferred explanations that carried accusations of neglect or malicious intent, rather than those that actually had broad explanatory powers.[11] They did not consider responsible those who were ostensibly weak and therefore blameless—the people as a whole—for insufficiently opposing pollution, or for insisting on buying the goods produced by polluting industries. Thus activists' intense concern with immediate problems made them more interested in finding culpable parties to accuse than in searching for real explanatory power, and unfortunately the most fundamental causes of pollution cannot be manipulated as easily or altered as rapidly as can specific institutions.[12]

· Responsibility for Pollution

When activists were explicitly asked to identify who was responsible for alleviating pollution (not who caused it), they again demonstrated a

11. For an authoritative analysis of ecological problems, see Paul H. Ehrlich and Anne H. Ehrlich, *Population, Resources, and Environment: Issues in Human Ecology*, 2d ed. (San Francisco: W. H. Freeman, 1972).

12. This tendency to blame particular institutions, rather than society as a whole, was also prevalent in the general population. See Yomiuri Shimbunsha, "Kōgai mondai" [Pollution Problems], *(Gekkan) Seron chōsa* 6:2 (February 1974), 20 (October 1973 national poll).

consensus: 73 percent considered industry responsible, and 69 percent considered the government responsible as well.[13] There was even greater agreement (92% of the sample) that the responsible party could not be trusted to attend to pollution problems on its own initiative, a view explained by one activist's account:

We appealed to everyone to explain to us why there was no need to worry about pollution, but you just can't talk to these people; you can never get a dialogue going. Whenever we asked for proof—why is the factory safe? what proof have you?—we got no answer. . . . We went to look at the existing factory, and the company said it could install preventive facilities to reassure us. So we asked what kind they had—and they never told us the details. (K2)

Given the high level of consensus on industrial responsibility for pollution, it is not surprising that activists were adamant about industry's financial responsibility for compensating victims and installing anti-pollution technology. All but three members of the sample said that industry should foot the entire bill, preferably out of "excess" profits without raising retail prices or relying on government aid. Several respondents argued that the taxpaying public should assume financial responsibility only in unusual circumstances: where the responsible industries could not be identified, or where polluting firms were too small to pay. Some said that firms which could not compensate society for the costs they imposed on the public should be allowed to go bankrupt.

Such views are probably due in part to the influence of Japan's more sophisticated environmental theorists, who usually argue that commodity prices should not have to rise to pay for pollution prevention, in contrast to their American counterparts, who are often willing to consider higher prices or taxes for certain products as a method of reducing pollution (for example, differential taxes on large cars, or higher prices for soft drinks purchased in cans or no-return bottles). American advocates place much more responsibility for pollution on the consumer—it is the consumer who wants, at low prices, the products that pollute—whereas Japanese environmental theorists do not conceive of consumer demand as a potent economic force. Leaning further to the left than the Americans, they regard Japan's affluence as a quality forced on society by profit-seeking industrialists dependent on the perpetual expansion of markets, and many believe that Japanese consumers would readily surrender this affluence if offered a choice and a respite from advertising.

13. Seventy-seven percent of a Tokyo-Osaka sample in May 1972 agreed that the government was "soft" on industry with respect to pollution policy. See Sankei Shimbunsha, "Kyō no seron" [Opinion Today], in *(Gekkan) Seron chōsa* 4:7 (July 1972), 81. In a national survey conducted in November 1971, 50 percent named industry's lack of a sense of responsibility as the primary cause of pollution, up from 33 percent of a national sample polled in 1966. See Sōrifu kōhōshitsu, "Kōgai mondai" [Pollution Problems], *(Gekkan) Seron chōsa* 4:6 (June 1972), 18.

Thus only 25 percent of the activists extended responsibility to the people at large, and even then only assigned to them the duty of insisting that industry and government carry out *their* respective responsibilities to solve pollution problems. Activists who were concerned chiefly with a specific incident of industrial pollution were even less likely to see any way that the ordinary public could contribute to solutions. Only a few added that it would, in the final analysis, be the people's responsibility to adapt their living standards and frivolous consumption habits to a more austere lifestyle.

· Definition of the Issues

The reasons for activists' intense feelings about industrial and government responsibility for pollution became clearer when we examine their opinions about specific environmental issues. The questionnaire asked them about nine topics: urban density and transportation, construction and deprivation of sunshine, air pollution, waste disposal, industrial water pollution, economic growth, rural development, destruction of wilderness, and overpopulation.

Most activists believed environmental disruption to be chiefly a result of haphazard industrial growth, and that slow or zero growth was necessary to alleviate the problem. Although the debate over the no-growth society was not the chief preoccupation of any of the groups sampled, feeling on the subject of further industrial development and rapid economic growth ran very high. Seventy-eight percent said that they would unquestionably prefer both growth and pollution to stop at present levels or decrease rather than continue; 47 percent quickly named pollution as the chief evil of economic growth, and many added that even the improved standards of living created by economic abundance had unwelcome social repercussions; 27 percent volunteered the opinion that there were *no* desirable aspects of economic growth, affluence notwithstanding. Only two mentioned shortages of energy and resources as a dangerous consequence of rapid economic growth, although presumably the oil crisis of October 1973 clarified the links between economic growth and environmental risks even more sharply for activists. The sample also took a dim view of industrial development as a device to revitalize poor rural areas. They were extremely critical of former Prime Minister Tanaka Kakuei's Kaizōron (a plan to break up cities and distribute both people and industry more evenly throughout Japan, and to pay for pollution prevention with continued rapid growth), with 78 percent arguing that this proposal (now shelved) would be disastrous. In contrast, the general population was very enthusiastic about the plan at this same time.[14] Fifty-five percent of the sample thought that only tradi-

14. Sōrifu kōhōshitsu, "Nihon rettō kaizōron" [On Reconstructing the Japanese Archipelago], *(Gekkan) Seron chōsa* 5:1 (January 1973), 2–23 (September 1972 national poll).

tional farming and fishing should be permitted in rural areas, although 31 percent took the more moderate view that nonpolluting industries, such as tourism and traditional cottage industries, would be acceptable ways of improving the rural standard of living.

Japanese environmentalists held strong opinions about economic aspects of environmental problems, but on two issues of great concern to American environmentalists they showed very little interest. Although 65 percent of the sample agreed that population problems were a major contributing factor to pollution, they meant not quantity but maldistribution (overcrowded cities and abandoned rural villages). Only thirteen respondents thought Japan's absolute population was too large in spite of the nation's remarkable achievements in lowering birth rates and reducing the annual increase in population. As evidence that pollution and population levels were not related, several pointed out that countries (underdeveloped and industrial) with larger populations than Japan had less pollution. In fact, when the Japanese government toyed with the idea of encouraging population *increase* after 1969, public criticism came only from women's groups who were angry that the LDP wanted to make abortion illegal in most circumstances; environmentalists remained silent.[15]

It is remarkable that in such a densely populated country environmentalists would ignore the contribution of population pressure to environmental stress. Outside observers of Japan's pollution problems invariably comment on the importance of population density per se and the imbalance between the Japanese islands' ability to support human activities and the absolute numbers of people who live on them.[16] Furthermore, most demographers and ecologists argue that both population size and density have multiplicative effects on the pollution produced at a given level of industrialization, and therefore on the number of people exposed to pollution damage.[17] Nonetheless, Japanese activists take little

15. See Charles F. Gallagher, "Prosperity, Pollution, Prestige—The Population Dilemma in Japan," *American Universities Field Staff Reports: East Asia Series* 18:3 (July 1971), 1–8; and in the same publication, F. Roy Lockheimer, "Japan's New Population Politics—Concern over 'Labor Shortage' Provokes a Controversy over Population Policy," 17:5 (March 1970), 1–13; and Lockheimer, "Population Review 1970: Japan," 18:1 (November 1970), 1–10.

16. See Paul Ehrlich and Anne Ehrlich, *The End of Affluence* (New York: Ballantine, 1974), pp. 117–138; Norie Huddle and Michael Reich, with Nahum Stiskin, *Island of Dreams: Environmental Crisis in Japan* (Tokyo: Autumn Press, 1975), pp. 313–320; and Donald Kelley, Kenneth Stunkel, and Richard Wescott, *The Economic Superpowers and the Environment: The United States, The Soviet Union, and Japan* (San Francisco: W. H. Freeman, 1976), pp. 45–48.

17. Paul Ehrlich, *The Population Bomb* (New York: Ballantine, 1971), may overstate the case but is well accepted. See also articles by Kingsley Davis, John P. Holdren, and Norman B. Ryder in Mancur Olson and Hans H. Landsberg, *The No-Growth Society* (New York: Norton, 1975), which originally appeared as *Daedalus* 102:4 (Fall 1973).

notice, and it was the consensus of our sample as a whole that population, whether conceived as a problem of size or as one of distribution,
was among Japan's lesser worries.

A second issue that did not attract much attention was the destruction of wilderness, although this concern has increased since 1972, and
the government passed amended legislation to strengthen protection of
wilderness and national parks, to require green belts around industrial
zones, and to restore greenery in urban areas.[18] Strictly speaking, only
the six members of a group specifically devoted to wilderness preservation worried that man's encroachment on the natural environment would
eventually affect his life-support system. In general, our sample of activists viewed the destruction of nature as a secondary side effect of industrial pollution, and problematic largely because it robbed humans of one
of their pleasures. In spite of a philosophical and religious tradition emphasizing harmony between human society and nature, it would appear
that most Japanese today, even environmentalists, have a view of nature
common in the West—that it is here for humans to tame, use, and enjoy.

In the United States, wilderness and the destruction of nature headed
the list of concerns because the American environmentalists emerged
from the nineteenth-century conservationist movement. But in Japan, industrial pollution was the first environmental issue to attract attention,
and the preoccupation with the damage to human life caused by industrial pollutants, already visible in the form of disease victims, seems to
have delayed the development of a sensitivity to broader ecological issues
until after the most pressing crises were dealt with. The contrast between
the classic writings of the environmental movement in the two countries
is a case in point.[19] Whereas Rachel Carson's *Silent Spring* (1962) was an
impressive treatise on ecology showing that human activities have begun
to damage the eco-system that supports those activities, Shōji Hikaru
and Miyamoto Ken'ichi's *Osorubeki kōgai* [Fearful Pollution] (1964) be-

18. The general population grew more concerned about the relationships between nature and human survival by October 1973, and the same transformation presumably took
place within the environmental movement after 1972 also. See Sōrifu kōhōshitsu, "Kōgai
mondai" [Pollution Problems], *(Gekkan) Seron chōsa* 6:2 (February 1974), 19. See also
Kihara Keikichi, Miyamoto Ken'ichi, and Sakai Ken, "Tenkanki no shizen hogo seisaku to
jūmin undō" [The Turnabout in Nature Preservation Policies and Residents' Movements],
Kōgai kenkyū 4:2 (Autumn 1974), 47–57; and Shibata Tokue and Matsuda Katsutaka,
Kōgai kara kankyō mondai e: shizen to ningen no kaifuku [From Pollution toward Environmental Problems: Nature and the Recovery of Man] (Tokyo: University of Tokyo Press,
1976). Similarly, there is now great concern over coastal conservation and the newly developed notion of the public's right of access to publicly owned coastline. See Kihara Keikichi,
"Coastline Conservation—Establishment of Common Tideland Use Rights," *Japan Quarterly* 25:1 (January-March 1978), 43–50.

19. Rachel Carson, *Silent Spring* (Boston: Houghton Mifflin, 1962); Shōji Hikaru
and Miyamoto Ken'ichi, *Osorubeki kōgai* [Fearful Pollution] (Tokyo: Iwanami Shoten,
April 1964).

gan with a chronicle of pollution "incidents" in each of Japan's prefectures, bolstered by quantitative evidence as to the number of outbreaks and the number of victims affected, and went on to discuss different kinds of *industrial* pollution and to provide a social, economic, and political analysis of pollution problems. In a sense, the tragic severity of pollution in Japan has forced Japanese activists to single out the most serious cases of human suffering and to forego (or delay) the luxury of considering ecological problems as a whole.

Tsurumi Kazuko, one of today's leading exponents of the work of folklorist Yanagida Kunio, argues that in the Japanese view, man and nature are so intimately intertwined (i.e., man is part of nature and thus a part of his own environment rather than a creature unto himself) that the conspicuous victim-consciousness in the Japanese environmental movement does not rule out a sensitive concern for the state of the larger environment.[20] However, to define an emphasis on victims as equivalent to an emphasis on the beleaguered natural environment is simply a semantic device, one that is not supported in any case by our earlier evidence. Activists in citizens' movements are deeply concerned about their own role as potential victims, and not nearly so worried about the natural environment as victim.

In fact, our sample shared a strong consensus that only the victims or potential victims in a particular dispute belonged in a citizens' movement. Such attitudes are likely to prevent the Japanese environmental movement as a whole from becoming much more than a collection of disparate episodes of conflict for some time to come. Although the early disputes seem to have cultivated a crop of full-time environmental lobbyists who are now trying to build national organizations in an attempt to influence government policy,[21] the prevailing image of the "movement" consists of famous disputes each limited to particular localities—thus the environmental movement in Japan consists of the major court cases, the antidevelopment movements in Mishima-Numazu, Fuji, Shibushi, Mutsu-Ogawara, Kamakura, Kashima, and so on. In contrast, when one thinks of the "movement" in the United States, one thinks of issues rather than places and begins naming organizations: Sierra Club, Audubon Society, Friends of the Earth, National Wildlife Federation, Conservation Foundation, Natural Resources Defense Council, Environmental Defense

20. Discussion at a conference on "Japanese Environmental Law: Lessons for America?" sponsored by the Japan Society, held in New York, May 2, 1977.

21. Ui Jun's Independent Forum has grown into a large organization with numerous national publications, whose subscription fees provide funds for nationwide activities against pollution. Similarly, national organizations to protect endangered species and preserve the natural environment have grown stronger, and organizations once devoted to protesting nuclear weapons and the U.S.–Japan Security Treaty (Gensuikin, Gensuikyō) have emerged as leaders of a national movement against nuclear power.

Fund, Environmental Action, Zero Population Growth, and the like. Whereas American environmental groups are relatively powerful national organizations, Japanese groups concentrate largely on local disputes, and are necessarily weak as lobby organizations.

· Knowledge and Commitment to Environmental Issues

Given activists' narrow definition of pollution problems and their strong sense of themselves as victims, it is possible that their banding together into citizens' movements might have little to do with any informed commitment to environmentalism. Some might join simply for the sake of narrowly defined personal advantage, without learning about the issue itself (for example, to stop construction of a particular road without acquiring interest in the larger problems of highway development and urban transportation). Others might participate solely because of ties to some other group that served as an organizational funnel to recruit citizens' movement activists. Assuming that one indicator of individual commitment might be information or concern about the issue that worried the citizens' movement as a whole, I constructed five indices from the nine questions about individual pollution issues, shown in table 9.

The first measure (Knowledge of Pollution Terms) revealed that the vast majority of activists were familiar with conventional pollution jargon of the day used in the questionnaire, which is no surprise. The next three measures (Information, Emotion, and Generality) were indices created by rating each respondent on each of the nine pollution issues according to levels of information, emotional investment in the issue, and general knowledge about the issue, respectively. A respondent could earn a low rating only by explicitly revealing ignorance or lack of concern or the inability to generalize beyond his own community. Similarly, a respondent could earn a high score only by demonstrating impressive knowledge, intense feeling (usually punctuated by extreme remarks, gritting of teeth, or pounding on the table), or specific knowledge of conflicts elsewhere over the same issue. Thus respondents were not graded on a curve that compared them with each other, but were measured against absolute standards.

The most important conclusion to be drawn from these measures is that Japanese activists were indeed worried about the issues their groups were involved in, and were well informed not only about those issues but about others as well. Respondents had very strong feelings about their own group's particular issues (sunshine rights, rural development, or whatever), but were considerably calmer about other problems, even those they knew a good deal about. Only 25 percent of the sample belonged to groups devoted to general rather than specific issues (for example, the recycling of solid wastes per se rather than the construction of a particular sanitary-treatment plant), so it is important to note that 41

TABLE 9 / *Dimensions of Interest in the Pollution Issue (in percentage)*

Indices	Low	Medium Low	Medium	Medium High	High	Total
Knowledge of Pollution Terms (n = 62)	3	5	2	7	84	101
Pollution Information Index (n = 64)	2	6	41	41	11	101
Pollution Emotion Index (n = 64)	17	20	22	30	11	100
Pollution Generality Index (n = 64)	19	—	41	—	41	101
Pollution Concern Index (n = 64)	2	19	33	38	9	101

Note: The Pollution Concern Index is composed of the Pollution Information, Pollution Emotion, and Pollution Generality Indices

percent of the sample earned high scores on the Generality index. Therefore, in spite of victim-consciousness, the inattention to global ecological problems, and the involvement in groups with relatively narrow objectives, these activists were capable of generalizing beyond their own antipollution struggles—for example, from their own efforts to prevent the construction of a local petroleum refinery to the general question of environmentally sound alternatives for rural development. Furthermore, they were not passive or accidental members of citizens' movements. Regardless of the circumstances in which they joined citizens' movements, they were clearly committed to citizens' movements on the basis of a common objective with the group, and appeared to learn, during their participation, more about other pollution issues as well.

In conclusion, we should note several themes that pervaded the activists' beliefs about pollution. First, activists engaged in a lot of hostile blaming behavior as they described the origins of pollution and recommended solutions. They believed that government and industry knew that their policies exacerbated pollution and persisted with those policies anyway, not out of lack of alternatives or because of technological bottlenecks, but rather out of malicious negligence, financial greed, and callous indifference to human suffering. They still expected the solutions to come from established authority. Not all activists integrated their disillusionment with industry and government into a revised set of expectations about the sources of new policies and initiatives. Only some of them explicitly stated that they had expectations of the people too, that it was the people's responsibility to demand, supervise, inspect, or contribute to the process of solving pollution problems.

Another noteworthy feature of respondents' beliefs about pollution is their demonstration of substantial social responsibility, in contrast to the egoism of which their critics accused them. Of course we have no idea what their behavior would be if they were actually confronted with a situation where responsible environmental action and individually self-ish action would be two different things, but activists did know the "right" answers. (For example, they would use public transportation in preference to personal automobiles, or they would not mind living near a sanitary treatment plant if the appropriate pollution controls were built into it, and so forth.) Despite their concern with immediate and narrowly defined problems in individual citizens' movements, activists understood that solutions to their "own" pollution problems were not simple, that every alternative involved some sort of adjustment and sacrifice, and that no answer would make all involved parties happy. Thus their intense feelings were tempered by some social and political realism.

The victim-orientation of Japanese activists had additional implications for how activists viewed the problem. Because they worried most about industrial pollution, they conceived of pollution as something evil that polluters (*kagaisha*) did to victims (*higaisha*). In the words of Ui Jun, neutrality in this issue was impossible because everyone was either a polluter or a victim.[22] Activists on both ends of the political spectrum regarded pollution as a variety of economic discrimination, something that the rich (anonymous invisible industrialists) did to those less fortunate than themselves, something that the very rich could escape from while everyone else remained behind as victims. In spite of the objective fact that activists as a group were slightly better off than average and as individuals came from a variety of socioeconomic circumstances, they identified themselves as members of an oppressed group.

Most activists in our sample were preoccupied with this piecemeal, dichotomous, divisive, discriminatory picture of pollution. They did not think much about the larger aspects of the issue: the relationships be-tween high consumption levels, population growth, economic growth, the occurrence of pollution, and the increasingly rapid depletion of natu-ral resources. They did not think about pollution as a threat to all human beings because of its threat to man's food sources and life-support sys-tem, nor about the effect of releasing high quantities of energy all over

22. Ui Jun, *Kōgai genron* [Lectures on Pollution], 3 vols. (Tokyo: Aki Shobō, 1971), 3:217. Ui Jun, *Kōgai no seijigaku: Minamata byō wo megutte* [The Politics of Pollution: On Minamata Disease] (Tokyo: Sanseidō, July 1968), pp. 209–210.

the surface of the globe (thermal pollution) on planetary weather or on the insulation of the earth from forces beyond our atmosphere. Nonetheless, Japanese antipollution activists showed considerable flexibility and foresight in terms of certain issues—urban density, for example, where they advocated long-term programs of drastic reconstruction—so perhaps these other limitations in their vision were simply a matter of exposure and priorities, not any basic rigidity of disposition. But it is nonetheless important to note that most activists at the time of the survey, even at leadership levels, did not seem to be aware of these global questions, which are considered fundamental by most environmentalists elsewhere.

In my view, American environmentalists have a broader understanding of the origins of environmental problems and a clearer vision of the extensive social changes involved in comprehensive solutions; but as a result, Americans flounder at the enormity of the task, creating stringent environmental legislation and stiff standards that were once world models, only to roll back, postpone, and create loopholes later.[23] In contrast, Japanese environmentalists define responsibility for pollution more narrowly, see pollution primarily as an economic rather than a sociocultural problem, and perceive its most important consequence as the creation of victims. Skeptics (including me) predicted in the early 1970s that this weak, fragmented, victim-oriented antipollution movement would never manage to stop the inexorable pollution-generating juggernaut that was Japan. But Japan *has* moved rapidly from being the most polluted nation on earth to being the nation most committed to environmental cleanup and the most advanced in pollution control technology.[24] By shaping the terms of the environmental debate even among policy makers, the narrow Japanese interpretation of pollution is indirectly responsible for the policy choices that made this remarkable transformation possible. In putting into operation the polluter-pays-principle, which puts the burden on industry through simple economic devices and devotes the proceeds to the relief of victims (see chapter II), Japan has adopted the most efficient way to create disincentives to pollute and thus to eliminate pollution at the source. This pragmatic emphasis on behavior modification may not be sufficient, but for the time being it is more effective than the

---

23. For a balanced appraisal of the environmental movement in the United States, see David L. Sills, "The Environmental Movement and Its Critics," *Human Ecology* 3:1 (January 1975), 1–41.

24. Those who want to study the world's most advanced pollution control technology now go to Japan for this reason. See *JTW*, 10 February 1979. On Japan's commitment and leadership in environmental cleanup, see Steven R. Reed, "Environmental Pollution Policies in Japan," paper presented to the annual meeting of the American Political Science Association in Washington, D.C., September 1979.

American value-oriented approach of asking people to adopt ecologically sound lifestyles without also giving them practical incentives to do so.

Structure of Citizens' Movements

There are parallels between activists' well-informed but nonetheless narrow victim-oriented interpretations of pollution and their strategy. As we shall see, activists have sober and carefully reasoned views about organizational matters but a relatively constricted emphasis on locally based groups and a cautious selectivity about tactics. One reason for our interest in the structure of citizens' movements is the frequent assertion that they teach their members about the actual procedures of democracy, not just through their activities vis-à-vis the political system, but particularly through stress on democratic processes and the abolition of status differences within the movement, in contrast to traditional emphasis on hierarchical structure and consensual decision-making. Endō Akira believes that a passive leader, or even no leader at all, encourages a relaxed, informal atmosphere in which the expression of opinions becomes easy and enjoyable.[25] Rather than regarding their activism as a time-consuming chore imposed on them by circumstance, members learn to participate on their own initiative because they enjoy the experience, not because they are enduring the trials of activism for a higher cause. Built into this view is the common but perhaps unwarranted assumption that traditional group structure and decision-making methods cannot be democratic.[26] In order to avoid imposing these assumptions onto our analysis, but in order to discover whether activists were sensitive to dimensions that could be labeled "democratic," I asked them for their own views on movement leadership, group structure, styles of decision-making, and the cohesion of the movement vis-à-vis outsiders.

• Leadership

The internal organization of a citizens' movement was of importance to many activists and a topic that the group discussed often. Some groups came to a decision about the mode of organization and the type

25. Endō Akira, "'Jūmin no toshi' e no jissen kadai" [Practical Issues in the Approach to "Cities for People"], in Miyamoto Ken'ichi and Endō Akira, eds., *Toshi mondai to jūmin undō* [Urban Problems and Residents' Movements], vol. 8 in the series Gendai Nihon no toshi mondai [Urban Problems in Contemporary Japan] (Kyoto: Sekibunsha, July 1971), pp. 462–463. Research on small-group behavior in the United States also shows that democratic structure produces happier group members. See Sidney Verba, *Small Groups and Political Behavior* (Princeton: Princeton University Press, 1961), pp. 226–229.

26. A review of forthcoming research on consensus versus conflict which challenges many of the stereotypes about traditional and current social values and practices in Japan is

of leadership they wanted and proceeded accordingly. Three of the groups (Independent Forum, the sunshine-rights group in Musashino, and the opponents of Highway 35-36, all based in the Tokyo area) refused to select a leader at all, out of the fear that members might slip back into traditional habits of deference toward leadership instead of asserting themselves, offering their own ideas to the group, and making sure that the leadership represented their wishes. These same groups were also fearful that whoever might be selected as a leader would gradually fall into a traditional leadership role emphasizing the tasks of building harmony and molding unity—and defer in turn to the local power structure rather than forcefully represent the group's interest vis-à-vis that power structure. The fear that such leaders could destroy the internal democracy and the external influence of a citizens' movement is frequently voiced in the environmentalist literature as well.[27] To Americans, who in small groups of three or more are inclined to hold elections for president, vice-president, and secretary, and who in larger groups seem at ease with *Robert's Rules of Order*, this concern for the fragility of internal democracy in a citizens' movement might seem exaggerated or unwarranted. But Japanese participants in citizens' movements felt that their political assertiveness is, paradoxically, new, delicate, and in need of protective nurturance.

Naturally, the dynamics that create division of labor and cause leaders to emerge also functioned in Japanese groups, and most citizens' movements did have leaders as a result. Eleven of the fourteen groups in this sample had a strong and narrowly focused leadership, which lent shape and direction, as well as social validity and respectability, to the movement. Therefore we asked respondents for their preferences about styles of leadership: should the ideal group leader "want members to agree on a course of action for the strength and unity of the group?" or "seek out different opinions in order to discover fresh ideas?" Only 18 percent of the thirty-four activists who responded preferred the first type of leadership, the sort required by traditional consensus politics, whereas 59 percent preferred the second type, a more democratic leader who would encourage the members to express themselves. Thus citizens' movement activists themselves have reservations about relying on traditional forms of leadership and are concerned about promoting internal democracy in citizens' movements. This conclusion is bolstered by the

---

available in Ellis S. Krauss, Thomas P. Rohlen, and Patricia G. Steinhoff, "Conflict in Postwar Japan," *Items* 32:2 (June 1978), published by the Social Science Research Council, 21–26.

27. Ui, *Kōgai no seijigaku*, p. 210; Ui, *Kōgai genron* 1:177–181; Ui Jun, *Kōgai rettō: 70 nendai* [Polluted Islands: The 1970s] (Tokyo: Aki Shobō, June 1972), 59; Tsuru Shigeto, *Gendai shihonshugi to kōgai* [Contemporary Capitalism and Pollution] (Tokyo: Iwanami Shoten, March 1968), pp. 270–286.

strong statistical relationships between activist preferences for "democratic" leaders and for other "democratic" practices within citizens' movements.

• Decision-making

Political scientists often argue that consensus politics as usually practiced is not democratic. The traditional concern for cohesion, harmony, and the appearance of unanimity results in aggressive attempts to persuade dissenters to go along with the majority, and in the reluctance of dissenters to speak their minds, resulting in majority tyranny over the rights of minorities within groups and in the suppression of truly free expression of opinion.

Decisions are made final only when unanimity is obtained even though it is forced and may actually be more in form than in spirit and substance. . . . Technically there may be dissenters, but as long as they do not register opposition it is quite enough to satisfy the passion for unanimity. Or if it is a small group, the majority will work on the dissenting minority until they are "converted" to the majority point of view either by moral suasion or even veiled threats.[28]

Nonetheless, it is theoretically possible for traditional consensus politics to operate democratically, if the final compromise is truly supported by a majority of members and no coercion has taken place to ensure loyalty to a group's decisions. Reflecting greater sensitivity to this possibility than much of the literature on the subject, citizens' movement activists had a finely tuned understanding of the paradoxes inherent in consensus politics, both of the potential authoritarian abuses just described and of the democratic possibilities of consensus politics in its ideal sense.

Advocacy of consensus politics and unanimous decisions was generally based on practical political considerations rather than on traditional moral values. Asked how they felt about majority rule and unanimity in decision-making, 70 percent of the sample said that majority rule should be sufficient, even though unanimity about particular points of action would be desirable to ensure a united effort. The 24 percent who said that a group should not take a course of action until unanimous agreement had been achieved usually added that the presence of a dissident minority might so impair the effectiveness of action that it would be critically important to hammer out a compromise permitting the dissidents to go along, to insure their contribution to subsequent efforts. They had no delusions about the ease of achieving unanimity, nor did they oppose

28. Chitoshi Yanaga, *Japanese People and Politics* (New York: Wiley, 1956), p. 86. See also Takeshi Ishida, "The Development of Interest Groups and the Pattern of Political Modernization in Japan," in Robert E. Ward, ed., *Political Development in Modern Japan* (Princeton: Princeton University Press, 1968), pp. 330–336.

the principle of majority rule. They did not advocate browbeating the dissidents into agreement, but instead suggested that the group refrain from acting at all until a satisfactory compromise was created.

This question often elicited two particular unsolicited comments: 16 percent of the sample added that whatever method of decision-making was used in a citizens' movement, it would have to respect dissent by accommodating minority views in the final compromise, and should not ride roughshod over minority opinion. Twenty-eight percent also added that truly unanimous decisions on major issues were actually impossible. These people disagreed with an excessive emphasis on harmony and unanimity, saying that some differences of opinion were bound to exist in a large group, and that insistence on unanimity would suppress minority views.

In general, most activists (whether they supported simple majority rule or unanimously acceptable compromises as a decision-making principle) had fairly sophisticated, realistic views about group processes, and were not particularly attached to the idea of consensus or conformity for its own sake.

· Organizational Principles

In order to round out the investigation of activists' beliefs about the principles for organizing a citizens' movement, I also asked about the relative importance of numerical strength versus group cohesion, about the place of political ideology, and about the controversial question of whether outsiders (in the form of students) should be allowed to participate. Activists were divided over whether numbers (38%) or unity (47%) was more important for the success of a movement. The basic idea that the number of people who favor a policy should have something to do with deciding whether to enact that policy might be considered a democratic one. In the past Japanese culture stressed the importance of spiritual fortitude in determining the outcome of a conflict—the group with the more cohesive spirit would win out. Thus the belief that unity outweighs numbers exhibits some allegiance to traditional values, whereas a stress on numbers would appear more congruent with the political realities of operating in a democracy.

The data support the idea that activists' beliefs about unity versus size as desirable traits in a citizens' movement represent underlying political values, in that activists who possessed nontraditional attitudes on other measures were most likely to emphasize numerical strength over unity. Emphasis on numbers was strongly associated with a preference for democratic leadership in citizens' movements (Tau-b = .391, $p <$ .001) and also with urban residence (Tau-b = .418, $p <$ .001), which is usually associated with nontraditional values in Japan. On the other hand, activists' own roles within citizens' movements and the circumstances peculiar to each movement may have been equally important determinants of belief on this issue. For example, group leaders tended to stress unity and cohesion, one of their main concerns as leaders, while rank-and-file members stressed the importance of group size, thus highlighting their own contributions as individual members to the group's chances for success.

Similarly, two features of circumstance made an emphasis on unity and cohesion vital as a matter of practical politics, not merely of traditional values, for activists in rural areas and those involved in lawsuits. First of all, because they were protesting policies of the local establishment and using unfamiliar methods, activists were rocking the boat, attracting attention, behaving in a conspicuous manner, embarrassing their community, and thus violating many traditional norms about social behavior and loyalty to the leadership of the local community. Activists in rural areas or involved in lawsuits invariably experienced tremendous social pressure designed to suppress their protests, and their best defense against this pressure was group cohesion and unity. As we have seen, the groups in Shibushi, Usuki, Toyama, and Ōiso all believed they were endangered by their opponents' efforts at infiltration and sabotage.

Furthermore, citizens' movements that survived this pressure actually won the respect and admiration of the surrounding community, which also held the traditional belief that devotion to principle and spiritual fortitude in spite of adversity were worthy of admiration. Therefore, not only because rural activists themselves believed that a unified group spirit was what counted, but also because the rest of a community would respect them only if they appeared unified and determined, rural activists and others operating in traditional settings found it vital to emphasize group cohesion, as opposed to numerical size, for purely pragmatic reasons.

Most activists agreed that one of the most serious threats to the cohesion and unity of a citizens' movement came from "ideology." Although their varied definitions of "ideology" posed analytical difficulties, these people all saw ideology in conventional terms as a highly systematized body of thought like Marxism. Almost half (47%) believed that ideology was a divisive and even dangerous force which could splinter the movement and alienate potential support. But 29 percent thought that ideology could be beneficial, by lending group cohesion and by laying the foundations for agreements on particular decisions. A few of them advocated reliance on an ideology like Marxism or Liberalism or New Leftism even at the risk of alienating potential support. But most were simply saying that a movement must agree on something in order to survive as a movement. What is significant here is that the majority of activists with definite opinions agreed with the professional environmental advocates in Japan, that the strength of a citizens' movement lay in its new role as a broad coalition of many kinds of people, built around a particular social problem, and that citizens' movements should reject the uses of ideology and patterns of organization presented by existing political parties and established interest groups on both the right and the faction-riddled left.[29]

It is necessary to point out that there was no statistically significant association between partisanship and beliefs about the suitable role of ideology. Although the term usually connotes leftist thought, in Japanese as in English, conservatives and reformists were equally opposed to the use of ideology. Conservatives wanted to make sure that they were not participating in a "red" group and that their friends and associates in the rest of the community could not possibly find one iota of evidence to ridicule them or to accuse them of being "duped" by the rest of the movement.

Reformists were equally disapproving of giving ideology any role within the movement. First of all, the majority of the reformist identifiers in citizens' movements were *not* themselves believers in Marxism or other left-wing ideologies (see chapter V). They supported the leftist parties, despite their ideological and philosophical disagreements with the left, because they were convinced that the JSP and JCP would listen to them but that the LDP would not. Second, even those activists who did espouse socialism or communism wanted to keep ideology out of the antipollution movement, and they needed support from as wide and diverse a public as possible. Even Tōsuirō, the group with the strongest ideological bent because of its roots in a labor union, had to stress ideological neutrality to prevent petty arguments among its own members and to maintain smooth public relations with Tokyo citizens and the TMG.

Just as many activists feared that ideology could destroy their movement, so also many feared student participation. Because these movements were acclaimed as residents' movements composed of people living in the affected area whose concern with the problem was immediate and intense and sincere, there was a good deal of debate over how these movements should react to offers of help from the outside. Over half (55%) of the activists agreed that offers of help from students should be rejected, that student participation was unacceptable, unwise, unnecessary, and downright dangerous. Several activists feared that students

29. Matsubara Haruo, *Kōgai to chiiki shakai: seikatsu to jūmin undō no shakaigaku* [Pollution and Regional Society: The Sociology of Livelihood and Residents' Movements] (Tokyo: Nihon Keizai Shimbunsha, October 1971), pp. 252–253.

would bring radical ideology with them, exploit the movement for their own purposes, and eventually destroy it.

I don't recognize the participation of students in citizens' movements. They are young and have no real life experience yet, so they have no earnest commitment to the goals but would turn it into a movement for the sake of a movement. (B1)

Citizens' movements have specific locations and specific problems, and other goals must not enter the question. . . . [Citizens' movements] shouldn't attract students in the first place. (K1)

Another 31 percent of the sample believed that only under certain conditions would student participation be acceptable—in particular, if students participated as local residents with the same concern about pollution that the rest of the community shared.

I am not dead set against students participating—people who have a [pollution] problem and happen to be students—but I would not welcome the student movement as a whole. Their violent means would offend all sorts of people whose sympathy we need . . . we would be a lot worse off. (B2)

Although 15 percent of the activists felt that hostility against student participation was unjustified, a prejudice manufactured by the mass media, animosity and distrust toward student participation were obviously the rule among a majority of citizens' movement activists. They were anxious to avoid outside support that might compromise their citizens' movement or deflect attention away from their original goals, in order to maintain emphasis on a single issue as the unifying force binding the citizens' movement together. Although critics in the early 1970s liked to think that citizens' movements were merely political illusions created by "outside agitators," the activists themselves placed great importance on local residence, and thus intimate involvement with the issue itself, as a credential for participation in citizens' movements.

To conclude, a majority of antipollution activists supported democratic methods for organizing and leading an antipollution movement, bearing out the assertion of hopeful observers that these movements were instructing their members in democratic principles through emphasis on a democratic structure within the movement itself. However, only a minority pursued this principle to the point of abolishing leaders, and most found strong leadership a vital asset. Because of their substantial pragmatic concern with maintaining cohesion of the movement as a defense against criticism, as well as a strong sense of possessive community loyalties, activists were generally wary about the use of ideology in citizens' movements and about the notion of participation by outsiders. Although most activists preferred loose internal structure and a free exchange of ideas within the movement, they also wanted to operate as a cohesive united front in the external political world.

Citizens' Movement Tactics

Finally, we shall examine the tactics used by citizens' movements and how activists evaluated the methods available to them. Although citizens' movements thought of themselves as protests and were certainly treated that way by a hostile establishment, as we saw in chapters II and III, they actually emphasized the use of legal methods and shunned controversial or violent ones. Nonetheless, within the realm of the acceptable, citizens' movements learned to use some unfamiliar methods and created some very imaginative ones.

• Pollution-Prevention Contracts

In addition to using the courts, citizens' movements also developed two novel devices, which require some explanation. The first is the pollution-prevention contract (*kōgai bōshi kyōtei*), usually between a potentially polluting firm and a local government (occasionally with citizens' movements as third parties), but sometimes negotiated directly between firms and citizens' movements. The Yokohama agreement of 1964 is generally considered the most important precedent for these agreements. The city of Yokohama drew up an agreement with several firms planning to build on reclaimed land, covering rapid construction of equipment to handle smoke, waste water, and noise, as well as compensation for damage that might arise in the future and a comprehensive policy for pollution prevention. The city required all business wishing to come to Yokohama to comply with the general form of this agreement; any enterprise wanting a weaker arrangement had to go elsewhere.[30]

Table 10 displays the rapid increase in the total number of pollution-prevention agreements. The majority provide for on-site inspection of the factory, and about one-third of them provide for suspension of operations and liability for damages if the firm causes pollution (defined either according to law or by the contract terms themselves, which are often more stringent than the law). The effect of growing citizen pressure is obvious from these figures, which show that local governments have grown increasingly able to demand unusually strong provisions in these contracts, such as penalties for breaching their terms. Finally, local governments have increasingly managed to extract from the firms a guarantee of absolute (no-fault) liability for damage done, regardless of whether effluent standards were violated in the process of causing the damage. An

30. Harata Naohiko, "Kōgai bōshi kyōtei to sono hōritsu jō no mondai ten" [Pollution Prevention Contracts and Related Problems from the Legal Point of View], *Jurisuto* 458 (10 August 1970), 274–279; Narumi Masayasu, "Kōgai taisaku 'Yokohama hōshiki' no naiyō to mondaiten" [Content and Problems with the "Yokohama Formula" for Pollution Countermeasures], *Kankyō hakai (bessatsu)* 2:7 (May 1971), 10; and Narumi Masayasu, "Kigyō to no kōgai bōshi kyōtei—Yokohama hōshiki" [Pollution Prevention Contracts with Industry—The Yokohama Formula], *Jurisuto* 458 (10 August 1970), 279–283.

TABLE 10 / *Pollution-Prevention Agreements*

	1971	1972
Direct agreements between firms and citizens' movements	223	395
Provisions of agreements between firms and local governments		
CM* participate as party to contract	18	40
	0.8%	1.2%
CM participate as observers	175	231
	8.2%	7.2%
Firm accepts absolute liability	1	10
	—	0.3%
Penalties for breach of terms	240	410
	11.3%	12.8%
Suspension of operations, liability for damages	804	1,104
	37.6%	34.5%
On-site inspection	1,509	2,271
	70.5%	70.9%
Total agreements between firms and local governments	2,141	3,202

Source: Kankyōchō, *Kankyō hakusho 1978* [White Paper on the Environment 1978] (Tokyo: Okurashō Insatsukyoku, June 1978), pp. 438–440; and *Kankyō hakusho 1979* (June 1979), pp. 413–417.

Note: Cell entry consists of the number of firms with the type of agreement described in the lefthand margin and the percentage of the total number of agreements between firms and local governments which constitutes this number.

CM = Citizens' movements.

extreme example of a strong pollution-prevention contract is the one negotiated between the fishing cooperative of Mutsu Bay (Aomori prefecture) and the national government. This contract provided financial compensation for fishing losses "suffered" while the fishermen were busy demonstrating to prevent the nuclear ship Mutsu from entering the bay, and guaranteed compensation in the future should the price of Mutsu fishery products fall, even if this were due to unfounded consumer panic and in the absence of any proof of radiation leakage or pollution damage to the products.[31]

• Single-Share Movement

The second of these innovative methods is the single-share movement,[32] in which members of a citizens' movement purchase single shares in a polluting enterprise in order to gain admission to annual shareholders' meetings (*sōkai*), where they have the legal right to question the board of directors and to introduce their own resolutions. Of course, cit-

31. *JT*, 12 August 1974, 16 October 1974.

32. Gotō Kōten, *Ichikabu undō no susume* [Promoting the Single-Share Movement] (Tokyo: Perikansha, July 1971); Ui, *Kōgai genron* 1:163–177; and Ui, *Kōgai genron* 2:51–54.

TABLE 10 / *continued*

1973	1974	1975	1976	1977	1978
796	1,113	1,394	1,821	2,127	2,453
45 0.9%	67 0.9%	76 0.9%	95 0.9%	318 2.5%	460 3.1%
276 5.4%	315 4.4%	337 3.8%	384 3.5%	408 3.1%	469 3.0%
37 0.7%	113 1.6%	510 5.7%	859 7.9%	1,135 8.7%	1,333 9.0%
945 18.5%	1,390 19.6%	1,985 22.0%	2,516 23.1%	3,244 25.0%	3,537 24.0%
1,777 34.8%	2,412 34.0%	2,808 31.5%	3,940 36.2%	5,113 39.4%	6,010 40.8%
2,603 51.1%	4,863 68.5%	6,062 67.9%	7,170 65.8%	8,508 65.6%	9,532 64.7%
5,097	7,096	8,923	10,899	12,978	14,730

izens' movement shareholders cannot ever hope to control a majority of the votes at shareholders' meetings, but they do have substantial influence through this method. Citizens' movements have purchased stock in Chisso to pursue company responsibility for Minamata disease, in the construction companies that planned to build the Japan National Railway freight line through Yokohama, in Shōwa Denkō (responsible for the second outbreak of Minamata disease in Niigata prefecture), and in Osaka Cement (the company that planned to build in Usuki).

Participation in shareholders' meetings provides several benefits to a citizens' movement. Company executives rarely deign to meet with antipollution activists; they can be represented in court by proxy and need not interrupt their daily routine to deal personally with their company's complicity in pollution incidents. But Japanese corporations are required by law to have two shareholders' meetings per year, open to any stockholder in the company, attended by the board of directors. Thus the single-share movement gives activists an opportunity to confront directors with their guilt and responsibility. It is a pleasurable irony to most owners of single shares within the antipollution movement that their one-time meager contribution of perhaps only ¥50 to the company store costs the company much more than that to administer every year.[33] Pam-

33. Advocates of the single-share movement in Japan are aware of Ralph Nader's Campaign GM in 1970, but beyond the long-range goal of democratizing the operations of large firms which they have in common, the two efforts are different. Campaign GM was

phlets describing the company's operations and budget must be periodically printed up and sent out, and announcements of decisions that are to be voted on must be sent out so that shareholders can mail in their votes. Most companies had to spend about ¥300 (U.S. $1) per shareholder per year in 1972, and ¥2,000 (U.S. $8) per shareholder in 1977.

To the extent that corporate executives are moved by traditional values, this confrontation with citizens' movement activists has an emotional effect on them, forcing them to face what they have wrought. But whether the executives are affected or not, the confrontation itself does wonders for activists' morale because the movement either wins concessions from the firm or galvanizes its energies against the intransigent enemy. That the presence of antipollution shareholders is disconcerting and upsetting to management is evident in the new corporate practice of hiring *sōkaiya* (a variety of gangster) to "keep order" at the meetings.[34] The single-share tactic wins favorable publicity for a citizens' movement, particularly if the firm indulges in the now common practice of hiring *sōkaiya* to silence the single-share owners or to prevent them from entering the meeting hall. Finally, the single-share method has legal value in that dissident shareholders may file charges against the firm for violating their rights. A verdict of March 1974 declared all resolutions made at a 1970 meeting of Chisso shareholders null and void because Chisso had forcibly prevented its shareholders from entering instead of protecting them.[35]

The above method can only be used in particular situations, and its future may be limited.[36] Informants in this study had little personal ex-

---

aimed at exerting real control over corporate decisions by attracting votes from existing shareholders to enact the proposals made by Nader's Project on Corporate Responsibility. The single-share advocates in Japan see their emphasis on "the masses"—having each individual purchase a single share—as an important difference. The Japanese movement is intended to take advantage of existing shareholders' rights as defined by the present Japanese commercial code, rather than to enlarge them. See Gotō, *Ichikabu Undō*, p. 15; and "Campaign GM: Corporation Critics Seek Support of Universities," *Science* 168 (24 April 1970), 452–455.

34. *Sōkaiya*—literally, those who take care of shareholders' meetings—also own shares in the firm and are involved in a highly specialized protection racket in which the *sōkaiya* force the firm to hire them, by threatening either to expose illicit corporate activities or to disrupt, rather than control, the meetings that they are also entitled to attend as stockholders. The *sōkaiya* may then blackmail the firm for having hired them in the first place. The Public Prosecutor's office took legal action on this problem, arresting a well-known *sōkaiya*, a member of Yamaguchi-gumi (Japan's largest "family" of "mafiosi"), and some of the company executives involved for extortion and bribery respectively. See *JT*, 5 February 1974, 5 March 1974. See also Ichiro Kawamoto and Ittoku Monma, "The *Sōkaiya*: Japan's Breed of Fixers," *Far Eastern Economic Review* 92:26 (25 June 1976), 55–58.

35. *JT*, 29 March 1974.

36. In 1977 the Justice Ministry proposed to eliminate the rights of single-share owners, ostensibly to discourage the hiring of *sōkaiya*, but also to eliminate the participa-

TABLE 11 / *Evaluation of Methods*

How can people express their expectations to the government: are there methods for people to make the government listen to their expectations and follow them? Which of the following methods are useful and which are not?

Method	Scale					Total	Mean Score
	−2	−1	0	+1	+2		
	Percentage						
Elections	0	15	16	0	69	100 (n = 61)	+1.2
Petitions	7	15	22	5	51	100 (n = 59)	+0.8
Lobbying	0	30	19	0	51	100 (n = 47)	+0.7
Letters	2	16	43	4	36	101 (n = 56)	+0.6
Sit-ins	5	18	27	15	35	100 (n = 60)	+0.5
Demonstrations	10	18	20	10	40	100 (n = 60)	+0.5

Scale:
−2 An immature, evil, or incorrect method.
−1 Useless.
0 Depends; not so good.
+1 Must do this anyway, whether useful or not.
+2 Useful; a good method.

perience with either the single-share movement or pollution-prevention agreements. However, respondents were asked for their opinions about several more frequently used methods, largely to learn how they regarded relatively traditional methods, relatively modern methods (or at least those that depend on the existence of a rather open society), and direct action techniques. Activists were asked about the utility of elections, petitions, lobbying, letter-writing, sit-ins, and demonstrations, and a scale of evaluation for each method was developed from the open-ended responses, to include their full range of comments. Distribution of respondents along the scales for each of these methods is shown in table 11 along with the mean scale score for each method.

• Elections

Citizens' movements have used the electoral process to elect executives and assemblymen who reflect their views on environmental questions. In addition, perhaps 10 percent of all movements have learned to

tory rights of minority shareholders in citizens' movements. The proposed change would allow only shareholders with ¥50,000 ($200 at the exchange rate of ¥250=$1) worth of shares to attend stockholders' meetings. *JTW*, 4 June 1977.

use some unconventional electoral tools not known in Japan before the American occupation: recall (for example, in Rokkasho, Uchinada, and Usuki), referendum (in Kagoshima and Tokyo prefectures), and initiative (in Kurobe city and Tokyo prefecture).[37] Citizens' movements have re-called mayors for illegal electioneering and for inviting nuclear power plants to their communities.[38] The Japanese electorate considers recall a suitable end for officials who commit major political or financial of-fenses, although many regard removal from office a drastic punishment for an official merely when they oppose his views. In the village of Rok-kasho in Aomori prefecture, the center of a raging controversy over *kombinat* development in Mutsu-Ōgawara, both the antipollution cit-izens' movement and the advocates of massive industrial development mounted recall campaigns against officials on both sides of the debate. In a fascinating pair of elections held two weeks apart in 1973, both offi-cials in question were honorably reinstated by narrow margins, indicat-ing that Rokkasho residents were indeed deeply divided over the issue at hand but considered recall too dire or too unfamiliar a method of attack on elected officials with controversial opinions.[39] Nonetheless, wherever recall is being used it serves as a clear reminder to politicians that an at-tentive and critical audience is evaluating their performance. Even when a citizens' movement fails to elect its endorsed candidates, it often achieves the same objectives by frightening the victors into adopting an antipollution stance (as happened in Mishima-Numazu-Shimizu), or by driving "propollution" candidates away from future electoral races (as happened in both Ōiso and Usuki in this study).

Thus it comes as no surprise that among our respondents, elections were by far the most popular method of influence, in that 69 percent of those replying considered elections useful. The 31 percent who had reser-vations about the utility of elections variously remarked that elections could not be successfully used by a minority movement, that it was still very difficult to persuade sympathizers outside the movement to alter their traditional voting habits and vote according to issues, that it was very difficult to compete with the funds that the established parties were able to distribute in order to control votes, and the like. These doubts did not reflect any alienation from the political system, but demonstrated these activists' awareness that election campaigns required a lot of effort

37. "Citizens' Movements," *Japan Quarterly* 20:4 (October–December 1973), 370. For details on Rokkasho, see note 39 below. On Uchinada, see *AS*, 21 May 1973, 4. On Usuki and Kurobe, see above in chapter III. On the Kagoshima referendum of December 1972, which defeated plans to build a petroleum kombinat in Shibushi, see *JT*, 18 January 1973, and chapter III above. On the Tokyo initiative that forced the metropolitan assembly to create legislation guaranteeing the right to sunshine, see *JT*, 3 June 1973.

38. "Citizens' Movements," p. 370.

and could be successfully used only in certain circumstances. Only one member of the sample (a New Left radical) argued that using elections as a tactic was no good, in and of itself, because no appropriate parties were available to choose from.

• Petitions

The second most popular method among activists was the use of petitions (*seigan*, *chinjō*). These terms do not refer to the petitions with signatures of eligible voters which are required to initiate recall elections or to put referenda and initiatives on the ballot. Rather, they are written appeals signed by many people, without legal power.[40] According to a survey of local governments by the Home Ministry, petitions are actually used by citizens' movements more often than any other single tactic.[41] In our sample, those who regarded petitions as an effective method tended to be those interested in highly specific pollution problems or in obtaining restitution for damage already done, presumably because these concerns were more amenable (than general problems or pollution prevention) to solution by petition. Prefectural assemblymen in Japan are bombarded with requests for specific favors, and they feel that attending to such tasks is one of their most important obligations.[42] Petitions requesting specific acts or compensation, which do not threaten to explode into important precedents, may well fit into local politicians' definitions of their responsibilities and thus succeed in having the desired effect.

Respondents generally agreed that petitioning was valuable not so much for any direct impact but for its indirect utility. As activists circulated petitions for signatures, they could publicize the movement, talk to their friends and neighbors persuasively, win support for the movement, and accurately assess community opinion on the issue. To the extent that they managed to gather many signatures, they could demonstrate that

39. *JT*, 10 January, 15 May, and 5 June in 1973.
40. *Seigan* and *chinjō* differ somewhat. An individual or a group may present a written petition to the local or prefectural assembly through a cooperative assemblyman. The assembly or one of its committees discusses the petition, and if it concurs with the request therein passes it on to appropriate officials to have the matter investigated and a report written. Such a petition meets the terms of Article 124 of the Local Autonomy Law and is a *seigan*. A petition presented without meeting these terms is a *chinjō*. The assembly has an obligation only to receive petitions, not to act. Even if the assembly sympathizes with the spirit of the petition, it need only request officials to investigate and report. Corrective action is not required. See Kurt Steiner, *Local Government in Japan* (Stanford: Stanford University Press, 1965), p. 365.
41. Environment Agency, *Quality of the Environment in Japan 1976*, pp. 80–84.
42. Young C. Kim, "Role Orientations and Behavior: The Case of Japanese Prefectural Assemblymen in Chiba and Kanagawa," *Western Political Quarterly* 22:6 (June 1969), 393.

the community felt widespread sympathy for their cause, and despite the legal emptiness of the petition, it could create indirect political pressure on local authorities who feared that community support could eventually be mobilized in more effective ways. Most activists who favored petitioning regarded it as a necessary initial phase for feeling out community support, creating cohesion within the movement by giving every member an important task to do, and publicizing the cause.

The remaining 44 percent of the sample were unimpressed with the use of petitions as a tactic, 15 percent pointing out that petitions carried no legal weight, and 7 percent arguing that the whole posture of petitioning was counterproductive, damaging to consciousness-raising efforts within the movement, and basically "feudal." They thus agreed with well-known environmental publicists and scholars who have concluded from detailed studies of individual citizens' movements that petitioning is based on traditional concepts in which people are not demanding what is their right and their due, but are begging for pity and sympathy from a posture of total humility, thus making no use of their real resources and placing no tangible pressure on the authorities.[43]

· Lobbying

The third method favored by activists was lobbying, which was usually explained as working through Diet representatives and assemblymen to influence legislation and policy. The whole idea of lobbying and negotiating with representatives over social issues is unusual to Japanese, even though they use the same sorts of procedures for private problems,[44] and some activists simply did not understand the idea well enough to evaluate it. They could comprehend the idea of making private appeals to individual legislators, but did not readily conceive of extending the same method to an issue with social or community-wide significance. Half of those who were able to respond thought that lobbying was a good idea, while the rest thought that it was unlikely to work, particularly if assemblymen refused to listen to them or meet with them or because the only legislators who would cooperate with them (JSP or JCP members) were outnumbered by conservative assemblymen.

43. Ui, *Kōgai no seijigaku*, pp. 196–210; Matsubara, *Kōgai to chiiki shakai*, pp. 179–180. It is not surprising that serious petitions have little success in view of politicians' conventional responses of disdain and amusement to groups of petitioners (*chinjōdan*) who travel to Tokyo ostensibly to make appeals but sometimes merely to make an exciting trip to the big city. Nathaniel Thayer, *How the Conservatives Rule Japan* (Princeton: Princeton University Press, 1969), pp. 221–224.

44. Young C. Kim, "Role Orientations and Behavior," p. 393; Ikeuchi, *Shimin ishiki*, pp. 274–288. Yanaga, *Japanese People and Politics*, pp. 107–108, describes how lobbying was a new addition to Japanese politics in the 1950s, and that "grass-roots lobbying" was virtually unheard of.

Those who said lobbying could be useful mentioned that legislators often operated in ignorance of the pollution issue itself and were unaware of the potential power of the antipollution movement. Face-to-face conversations could give the issue new importance and vitality in the minds of legislators, who in all innocence might have been unaware of the potential political importance (and utility to themselves) of pollution. An urban housewife said that "lobbying is effective, especially at the local level, because they see us and who we really are and what we really think. This makes them work hard for us" (F5). A respondent who had served as an assemblyman himself recommended persistence: "You can keep badgering the representative and his offices, with 'Whom are you supposed to represent? What am I to think if you continually ignore [me]?' You can use this to embarrass the representative [into working harder]" (J2). In this study, the skillful use of lobbying often led to regular citizen participation in planning commissions and the like at the local level, as local governments learned to recognize the wisdom of incorporating citizen views earlier rather than later in the policy process.

· Letters

Activists felt surprisingly ambivalent about writing letters to representatives, cabinet ministers, or the media, most frequently because they believed the letters would end up in some wastebasket without ever reaching their proper destinations. Particularly knowledgeable respondents described actual examples in which letters were counterproductive because hostile politicians won favorable publicity by appearing to make a fuss over some poignant written appeal, thus polishing their image without ever doing anything concrete. Many respondents, like the Japanese public at large,[45] viewed letter-writing as a tool only for making personal appeals to take care of private difficulties: "It's very good to write to someone powerful or appeal to him when it's for your own small advantage. But for any large complex problem it breaks down" (E5). Rather than writing letters to influence officials, activists concentrated on getting media coverage of their cause in order to influence public opinion.

No one thought about the tactical value of a massive letter-writing campaign to a large group of legislators. This tried and true method of interest groups in the United States has value because American congressmen, according to their own public testimony, pay a great deal of attention to their mail in calculating the opinions of their home districts. But in Japan most assemblymen and Dietmen follow their party's decision as to how to vote on a bill (and even independents in local assemblies usu-

45. Young C. Kim, "Role Orientations and Behavior," p. 393; Ikeuchi, *Shimin ishiki*, pp. 314–315.

ally behave as though they were LDP members),[46] so there would be no way for mail from constituents to make much difference in representatives' voting on bills.[47] In any case, the important decisions are made by the anonymous bureaucrats and LDP officers who prepare legislation for presentation to the legislature. Until recently, party bloc voting and solid LDP majorities in most assemblies made passage of LDP bills, as presented, almost automatic, and amendments by legislative bodies have been exceedingly rare.[48] Thus letter-writing campaigns addressed to elected representatives would have dubious utility in affecting the political process in any direct way.

• Direct Action

Finally, we come to the relatively unpopular methods of influence—direct action. Some activists opposed sit-ins and demonstrations because they regarded them as inappropriate, immoral, or evil methods associated with extremist groups. Others felt no sense of moral disapproval but feared that sit-ins and demonstrations could be counterproductive: "Those two methods just damage others, bring out the riot police, cost money, and injure the participants" (G4). If public opinion reacted in a hostile manner, direct action would bring no gains at all.

Despite these objections, half of the activists felt that sit-ins and demonstrations were occasionally necessary and even useful, to stall for time in tactical emergencies or to awaken public opinion to the existence of a problem that otherwise was receiving no publicity at all. Determined, well-supplied sitters-in could attract public sympathy (as in the case of Minamata victims who camped out on the doorstep of Chisso's Tokyo headquarters for over a year, or as in the thwarted attempt of anti-*kombinat* citizens in Kagoshima to present petitions to the prefectural assembly). Direct action could also prevent a company or the local authorities from carrying out illegal construction activities until a court injunction was obtained (as in the case of bay-fill operations at Usuki). As

46. Independents are frequently conservative politicians who did not receive the official LDP endorsement prior to the election, but they often join the LDP after victory. On party endorsement procedures, see Thayer, *How the Conservatives Rule Japan*, pp. 119–139. Politicians also run as independents to appeal to a wider public and also to indicate that they fulfill traditional norms of being above politics. On the predominance of conservative politicians making traditional appeals among candidates who are ostensibly independent, see Steiner, *Local Government in Japan*, pp. 393–408.

47. Yanaga, *Japanese People and Politics*, pp. 267–268. On party-line voting within prefectural assemblies, see Kim, "Role Orientation and Behavior," p. 397. See also Chong Lim Kim, "Consensus on Legislative Roles among Japanese Prefectural Assemblymen," in Allan Kornberg, ed., *Legislatures in Comparative Perspective* (New York: David McKay, 1973), pp. 398–420.

48. See Hans H. Baerwald, *Japan's Parliament: An Introduction* (New York: Cambridge University Press, 1974).

might be expected, political partisanship was the most potent predictor of attitudes toward sit-ins and demonstrations as techniques of interest-group influence, with conservatives strongly opposing the use of direct action and reformists willing to resort to it in certain circumstances.

Thus the most important influences on activists' evaluations of the various methods available to them were political attitudes and beliefs, exposure to the pro and con arguments surrounding these techniques, and actual experience using certain methods. Activists generally approved of methods that could be considered conventional, although many of these methods were actually newly established by the occupation and were only gradually being discovered by citizens' movements. Activists had strong reservations about tactics that might be labeled disruptive or violent, but the ultimate criterion used to evaluate a method was whether it worked.

Citizens' Movements as Social Protest

Individual motivations, issue orientation, sharply focused objectives, and structural traits of citizens' movements all indicate that citizens' movements easily fit the standard definition of a social movement. They are collectivities which seek to promote or resist change and which have indefinite and shifting membership, leadership determined more by informal response of members than by formal selection, and some continuity in objectives and strategy.[49] Early theories about social movements argued that they erupted during times of economic oppression or social chaos as expressions of rage by alienated or downtrodden victims of social pathology, whose irrational behavior threatened to replace a stable democratic order with mob rule. Social movements were therefore classified with panics, crowds, and riots. Then in the 1960s social movements that fitted the definitions but challenged the predictions of these theories emerged in most of the affluent democracies. Thus newer theories argue that social movements are a rational mode of action for people who are ignored or excluded by the prevailing system, properly seen as an outsiders' counterpart to the organized interest groups of the established elite. Participants in social movements are not totally without political resources, as it was previously believed, but form social movements in order to mobilize their organizational skills, creating a channel for influence and participation in the existing system.[50]

49. Ralph H. Turner and Lewis M. Killian, *Collective Behavior* (Englewood Cliffs, N.J.: Prentice-Hall, 1957), p. 308.
50. Early theories in the "collective behavior" school are represented by Hadley Cantril, *The Psychology of Social Movements* (New York: Chapman and Hall, 1941, reprinted by Wiley, 1963); Turner and Killian, *Collective Behavior*, especially Part Four; Neal J. Smelser, *Theory of Collective Behavior* (New York: Free Press, 1963). The newer school,

Our evidence indicates that citizens' movements verify the resource mobilization theory.[51] Activists in our sample did not join citizens' movements because they were disenfranchised, unemployed, isolated, alienated from society, or afflicted with anomie due to rapid social change, nor did they engage in undirected outbreaks of mass violence. They were not malcontents or rabblerousers, as the earliest theories of social movements would have predicted. On the contrary, although a small number worked in marginal sectors of the dual economy and saw pollution as insult added to injury, most activists had benefited materially from rapid growth and would have had little to complain about if environmental problems had somehow never developed. In fact, citizens' movement activists were slightly better off and more sociable on the average than the general population, and considerably better educated. Thus citizens' movements, along with social movements that emerged elsewhere in the late 1960s, were rational attempts by an aggrieved group to mobilize hidden resources which early social theorists failed to recognize.

However, the similarity between citizens' movements and other protests cannot be carried too far. Although citizens' movements conceive of themselves as protest movements and are regarded that way by their opponents, they avoid violence and illegal tactics and are not particularly disruptive as politics in the democracies go. Moreover, the literature on protest in Japan, the United States, and Europe concentrates on three things which citizens' movements turn out not to be: student rebellion (for which explanations revolve around alienation from middle-class materialism by idealistic youth);[52] racial or ethnic tension (where explanations concern rising expectations, cruelly disappointed in the encounter with persistent discrimination, low standards of living, and high unem-

---

which regards social movements as one among many rational tools for mobilizing existing resources in order to make claims on the system, is best represented by Anthony Oberschall, *Social Conflict and Social Movements* (Englewood Cliffs, N.J.: Prentice-Hall, 1973); William A. Gamson, *The Strategy of Social Protest* (Homewood, Ill.: Dorsey Press, 1975); and John D. McCarthy and Mayer N. Zald, "Resource Mobilization and Social Movements: A Partial Theory," *American Journal of Sociology* 82:6 (May 1977), 1212–1241.

51. Ellis S. Krauss and Bradford L. Simcock made this observation on the basis of data reported earlier from this study. See "Citizens' Movements: The Growth and Impact of Environmental Protest in Japan," in Scott C. Flanagan, Kurt Steiner, and Ellis S. Krauss, eds., *Political Opposition and Local Politics in Japan: Electoral Trends, Citizens' Movements, and Progressive Administrations* (Princeton: Princeton University Press, 1980), chap. 6.

52. See Kazuko Tsurumi, *Social Change and the Individual: Japan Before and After Defeat in World War II* (Princeton: Princeton University Press, 1970), pp. 307–389 on the student movement; Ellis S. Krauss, *Japanese Radicals Revisited: Student Protest in Postwar Japan* (Berkeley and Los Angeles: University of California Press, 1974); Kenneth Keniston, *The Uncommitted: Alienated Youth in American Society* (New York: Dell, 1960, 1962, 1965), and *Young Radicals: Notes on Committed Youth* (New York: Harcourt, Brace, and World, 1968), and *Youth and Dissent: The Rise of a New Opposition* (New York: Harcourt

ployment);[53] and class conflict (where neo-Marxist explanations relying on economic factors predominate).[54] In terms of predictions that this literature would have generated, citizens' movements contained the "wrong people." They were not composed primarily of students, Ainu, Burakumin, Koreans, blue-collar workers, or the poor. In fact, the socioeconomic egalitarianism in political participation found by Ikeuchi and by Verba, Nie, and Kim even before the growth of citizens' movements would indicate that the economically disadvantaged in Japan had no particular need to form citizens' movements.[55] Citizens' movements contained people of all classes and walks of life, and had considerably greater cross-sectional appeal than previous protests in Japan, which had been limited to certain segments of the population.

Unlike other protests, demographic and social traits had little to do with determining the need or inclination to protest pollution, a threat so severe in Japan that it mobilized all sorts of people, including many who would not ordinarily have been available for a protest movement. The perception of pollution as an instrument by which an evil conspiracy of polluters (*kagaisha*) exploited potential victims (*higaisha*) rationalized activists' anomalous position as opponents of established authority and vociferous critics of official policy. Hence their intense victim-consciousness, which corresponded neither to their relatively comfortable position in society, as measured by the usual indicators (which are insensitive to costs like pollution), nor to the reality that most activists were not suffering directly as victims but were in fact trying to prevent future pollution. Thus Japanese citizens' movements resembled both

---

Brace Jovanovich, 1971); and Ronald Inglehart, "The Silent Revolution in Europe: Intergenerational Change in Post-Industrial Societies," *American Political Science Review* 65:4 (December 1971), 991–1017, and *The Silent Revolution: Changing Values and Political Styles among Western Publics* (Princeton: Princeton University Press, 1977).

53. *Report of the National Advisory Commission on Civil Disorders* (New York: Bantam, 1968); Jerome H. Skolnick, *The Politics of Protest* (New York: Ballantine, 1969); Hugh Davis Graham and Ted Robert Gurr, *The History of Violence in America: Historical and Comparative Perspectives* (New York: Bantam, 1969); and Gurr, *Why Men Rebel* (Princeton: Princeton University Press, 1970). On ethnic minorities in Japan, see George DeVos and Hiroshi Wagatsuma, *Japan's Invisible Race: Caste in Culture and Personality* (Berkeley and Los Angeles: University of California Press, 1966), and Richard H. Mitchell, *The Korean Minority in Japan* (Berkeley and Los Angeles: University of California Press, 1967).

54. Marxism and emphasis on class conflict are particularly prevalent among Japanese scholars. This is somewhat less true in Europe since the rise of the neoconservative philosophes, but in both cases Old and New Left analyses are influential. For New Left writings on protest in Europe in the 1960s, see Gary L. Olson, ed., *The Other Europe: Radical Critiques of Britain, France, West Germany, and the Soviet Union* (Brunswick, Ohio: King's Court Communications, 1977).

55. Verba, Nie, and Kim, *Participation and Political Equality*, p. 75; Ikeuchi, *Shimin ishiki*, pp. 408–412, 441–454.

spontaneous protests by oppressed groups (especially in the minds of the participants) and more conventional interest groups skillfully using their resources to exert influence through perfectly legitimate channels.

Their cross-sectional appeal based on a single issue might appear to give citizens' movements the foundation for a powerful national organization, but such is not the case. Verba, Nie, and Kim discovered that the sense of community was extremely important in stimulating communal forms of participation, and citizens' movements reflected this fact.[56] Activists' motivations and beliefs about structure and tactics revealed that they were very protective of their movements, fearful of hostile outsiders who might damage the movement, and anxious even about sympathetic outsiders who might deflect the movement from its immediate purpose. Therefore, only local residents (*jūmin*) were eligible for membership, in the belief that only potential victims of local pollution had a legitimate and reliable interest in stopping it. This stress on the local community had two consequences of note. It certainly provided the cohesion and solidarity so important in achieving local success. But it also hampered the effectiveness of coalitions of citizens' movements, most of which must avoid engaging in any independent or comprehensive tasks that might undermine their primary goal, the individual victory of each of the component movements.[57] As a result, few citizens' movements are likely to evolve into national organizations or influence policy directly. The only clear exception in our survey is the Tōsuirō study group, which was able to take advantage of its origins within an established organization and of recurring crises that bore out its predictions to convert its persuasive message into the objectives of a larger institution. These fortuitous circumstances permitted the Tōsuirō group to become active in broad coalitions with the other few movements which built organizations at the national level.

56. Verba, Nie, and Kim, *Participation and Political Equality*, pp. 269–285.
57. "Jūmin undō no 'Kanagawa hōshiki': chūmoku sareru renraku soshiki" [The "Kanagawa formula" for Residents' Movements: A Liaison Organization to Be Noticed], *Kankyō hakai* 1:7 (December 1970), 21–23.

V

Political Attitudes
and Beliefs

AFTER THE examination of the mobilization, structure, and strategy of citizens' movements, the next phase is to probe further the minds of individual activists, to determine how the citizens' movement experience affected their attitudes and beliefs. This chapter analyzes activists' information, beliefs, and actual experience in politics, the new ideas to which they were exposed, and their unexpectedly hostile attitudes toward certain institutions. Once we appreciate the contours of their belief systems it will be possible to examine belief change and its effects on concrete behavior, in chapter VI.

Activists as Informed Citizens

Japanese observers assert that participation in citizens' movements causes activists to think more about politics and society, about a broader scope of social problems, and about the variety of political resources available to them—that activists become closer in character to the ideal participant citizen. To examine this claim, we shall look at activists' interest in politics and their levels of political information, the strength and clarity of their "democratic" beliefs, their general disposition toward the utility of political action, and their previous political experience.

· Information and Interest in Politics

It is not surprising that participation in citizens' movements was associated with high political interest. Thirty-seven percent of the sample said that they were somewhat interested in politics, and another 48 percent claimed to be very interested, with only 15 percent confessing that they were not really interested at all, in spite of their citizens' movement activity. Thus the citizens' movement sample was a good deal more interested in politics than the general population, among whom 30–45 percent usually disclaimed any interest in politics or elections.[1]

A simple measure of knowledge about local elections was built from responses to items asking about representatives in local, prefectural, and national legislatures and how respondents had voted in the most recent electoral contest for each of these legislative bodies. Activists were unexpectedly well informed: only 5 percent could say nothing at all about the elections, the nominees, or the victorious candidates; 63 percent knew about the candidates and the winner in all three of the elections mentioned; and another 13 percent displayed exceptional knowledge or had even run for office themselves. Some of the extremely well informed respondents were able to describe factional disputes during the selection of nominees and behind-the-scenes decisions, and one actually carried a small notebook at all times, containing voting statistics from his district for all recent elections at all levels. Only crude comparisons with similar measures in the general population are possible, but it would appear that in terms of political knowledge, these figures put citizens' movement activists well above their peers in the general population, among whom 15–50 percent usually fail even simpler tests of information.[2]

· Democratic Beliefs

Activists were also asked about their belief in a fundamental democratic idea, the notion of popular sovereignty. Sixty-four percent of the respondents agreed that "government should establish principles on the basis of popular initiative" (the most "democratic" option available to respondents), and 33 percent selected the statement that "government

1. Bradley Richardson, *The Political Culture of Japan* (Berkeley and Los Angeles: University of California Press, 1974), p. 48; and Ikeuchi Hajime, ed., *Shimin ishiki no kenkyū* [A Study of Citizen Consciousness] (Tokyo: Tokyo Daigaku Shuppankai, 1974), pp. 346–352. The same proportions of interest and disinterest prevailed in surveys done later in 1972, at the time this study was conducted. These surveys are available in Naikaku sōri daijin kambō kōhōshitsu hen, *Seron chōsa nenkan: Zenkoku seron chōsa no genkyō* [Public Opinion Yearbook: The Present Situation in Public Opinion across the Nation, 1973] (Tokyo: Ministry of Finance Printing Bureau, 1975), pp. 133, 140, 438.

2. Richardson, *The Political Culture of Japan*, pp. 149–151: Ikeuchi, *Shimin ishiki*, pp. 352–358.

and people should plan solutions from a position of equality" (not so clearly democratic, but a view that refrains from putting government in a position superior to the people). Only 3 percent (two persons) agreed with the explicitly antidemocratic idea that "people should rely on government guidance." It is difficult to interpret respondents' intentions in selecting from among these three fixed phrases after being asked a question of such broad scope. Support for democratic values as measured by this item presumably stemmed from experience and exposure to abstract democratic concepts since the beginning of the postwar period, and not merely from conscious opposition to traditional political values. Thus this measure probably tapped respondents' cognitive abilities and their social surroundings as much as it recorded philosophical beliefs.

Activists who agreed with the notion of popular sovereignty were also likely to favor elections and lobbying as successful methods for interest groups to use. Compared with the other tactics which they evaluated in the same question (sit-ins, demonstrations, petitioning, and letter-writing), the use of elections and lobbying as devices required perhaps the greatest level of political sophistication. Thus activists who approved of the idea of popular initiative were also the most enthusiastic about methods closely associated with the process of making popular initiatives work.

When we compare the activist sample's beliefs on the matter of the relationship between government and people with the views held by the Japanese population as a whole, it is obvious that citizens' movement activists as a group were considerably more supportive of democratic ideas. The Institute for Statistical Mathematics in Tokyo conducts a survey on "national character" every five years and reports that the proportion of survey respondents agreeing with the idea that people should discuss politics themselves rather than leave this task to politicians has been increasing steadily through the postwar period. However, the percentage willing to sacrifice the idea of democracy to benevolent paternalism by the state (43% of the sample in 1953) was still 30 percent in 1968 and 23 percent in 1973, much larger than the 3 percent of our sample who chose a similar option in 1972, that "the people should rely on government guidance," even though the people in our sample were older than the general population and many had received an explicitly antidemocratic education in the prewar period. It seems clear that citizens' movement activists were more democratically minded than the general population. Moreover, some would also attribute the drop from 1968 to 1973 in the portion of the general population preferring to rely on political leaders to the "democratizing" influence of citizens' movements on the general population.[3]

3. Jōji Watanuki, *Politics in Postwar Japanese Society* (Tokyo: University of Tokyo Press, 1977), pp. 32–42.

· Efficacy

Another dimension of citizenship of interest to us is the notion of individual or group action on behalf of the rights of citizens against encroachment either by some unjustly powerful minority or by the state itself—that is, precisely the task which citizens' movements set themselves. What impressions about civic action do they leave with their members?

The case histories included in our sample indicate that in general citizens' movements do rather well. Only 20 percent of our sample considered their citizens' movement a failure. Of course, the successful movements were never as successful as they had hoped to be. Litigants in court never won all the damages that they asked for, people who prevented factory construction could not be sure that the factory would never be built, and some people considered their movement successful only because they stalled proceedings sufficiently to predict that the worst would probably not happen. One Ōiso respondent evaluated his citizens' movement as a success, even though it had failed in its explicit objectives, because it had created a sense of community and caused many people to think about political issues and democratic values who otherwise would never have seen the relationship between politics and their own lives. Citizens' movement activists acquired the overall impression from their success that mobilizing in this new organizational form was a good idea. In spite of all the disappointment and frustration, activists usually felt buoyed up by the experience, convinced that voluntary association activity was a useful, and even a superior, addition to their political repertoire.

Activists thus acquired from citizens' movement participation the sense of involvement and efficacy that is usually regarded as a sign of "health" in a democratic political culture.[4] But Japanese society is known for an emphasis on group life and action within groups, so activists' new enthusiasm about voluntary associations constitutes no challenge to the traditional importance of the group. Did the experience of activism give participants any enthusiasm for *individual* action, any sense of individual efficacy? Interestingly, despite the fact that Japanese society as a whole supposedly provides individuals with few ways in which to act on their own,[5] our sample was relatively enthusiastic about the potential of individual action, and considerably more so than the general population

4. Both populist and elitist theorists (if they can be so crudely differentiated) agree on the personal traits that make up democratic citizenship and on the desirability of the democratic character in the abstract. However, they disagree on whether the democratic character is actually a vital necessity in a democracy and on the likelihood of cultivating it in more than a small minority of the population. See chapters VI and VII for further analysis and references.

5. On the traditional de-emphasis of the individual in Japan, see Takeshi Ishida, *Japanese Society* (New York: Random House, 1971); Chie Nakane, *Japanese Society* (Berkeley

had been before the emergence of citizens' movements.[6] Sixty-nine percent of the activists said individuals could be influential, and most of them provided actual examples. The 31 percent who said that individual action was futile did not even come up with as many negative reasons and examples as did those who favored individual action. In addition, activists who were hopeful about the potential impact of social activism in general (asked in another question) were also optimistic about the utility of individual action in particular.

Urban/rural residence had great bearing on efficacy (Tau-b = .383, p <.001). While 54 percent of the rural activists explicitly disparaged their influence as individuals and instead stressed the necessity of group action and the strength to be gained from the cohesion of a group (see chapter IV), urban activists expressed hope. It is tempting to conclude that the confidence shown by urban activists was simply a natural result of their favorable position in society—being closer to the cosmopolitan mainstream of Japanese life, recent intellectual currents, and the centers of power. Conversely, rural activists should have a lower sense of efficacy as individuals because of their social and intellectual isolation and the survival of collective traditions. However, this explanation, though plausible, does not square with the fact that urban/rural residence has *no* effect on political efficacy in the general population.[7] We must search for other explanations of these variations in activists' sense of efficacy. We find, for example, that involvement in litigation was also related to efficacy (Tau-b = .408, p <.001). Fifty-seven percent of those who resorted to litigation strongly believed that individual action was *futile*, no doubt because of their own experience in which methods short of group action like lawsuits did little good. Thus the sharp differences in efficacy between urban and rural activists were not automatic artifacts of residence, but indicated rather that the citizens' movement experience itself was somehow different for urban and rural activists, a point we shall examine carefully later in this chapter.

Regardless of variation in activists' sense of efficacy as individuals, the generally positive view of citizens' movement activity as a channel of influence contrasted with their rather pessimistic view of the prognosis for pollution problems. Fifty-three percent of the sample displayed great fear about the likelihood and potential magnitude of environmental holocaust. Only 17 percent expressed any optimism at all, and this was usually because their intense emphasis on present problems made them relatively less concerned about the future. Although most activists felt that

and Los Angeles: University of California Press, 1970); and Tadashi Fukutake, *Japanese Rural Society* (London: Oxford University Press, 1967).

6. Ikeuchi, *Shimin ishiki*, pp. 358–375.

7. Ibid., pp. 157–182, 375.

they were doing well with a piecemeal approach to the problem, their own citizens' movement successes did not give them simpleminded delusions about eradicating environmental problems in short order. Indirectly, then, activists' own evaluations validated the commonly made observation that what is important about citizens' movements is not their accomplishments in dealing with environmental problems, but their success in creating a new avenue by which ordinary citizens can influence politics.

· Political Experience

The general impression created by this data on activists' perceptions—their information, interest, and beliefs about participation—is that citizens' movement activists were more attuned to politics than the general population. However, this is precisely what we would expect from political activists, and it takes on significance only when combined with the fact that most citizens' movement participants were *not* seasoned political activists before joining citizens' movements. Two measures of previous political experience were devised from responses to several open-ended questions. Prior protest experience was defined as any participation in a group that opposed government policy on an issue, so that an antipollution activist who had already been through another citizens' movement or who had earlier opposed such things as defense or foreign policy, local industrial development, and so on, was for our purposes a veteran of protest. Conventional political experience consisted, on the other hand, of involvement in establishment politics (of either the right or the left) above and beyond the act of voting (in most cases, electoral campaign work in support of a political party), but excluding any act that should properly be considered protest.

This pair of measures permitted us to construct four categories which mapped out the prior political experience of incoming activists. Only 25 percent of the sample consisted of gladiators,[8] with both protest and conventional experience. On the other hand, 34 percent were veritable innocents, whose previous involvement in politics consisted of no more than voting. In between these two poles, 17 percent were veterans of protest without any experience in conventional electoral politics who thus adopted a new issue and a new organizational form by joining citizens' movements, and 23 percent were regular participants in establishment politics who changed their self-image from loyal supporter to protester for the first time by joining a citizens' movement.[9] In view of the 34

8. "Gladiator" is a term coined by Lester Milbrath in *Political Participation* (Chicago: Rand McNally, 1965), pp. 16–29.

9. This description also applies to those in this category who joined citizens' movements with leftist allegiances, in that earlier political efforts on behalf of opposition parties

percent of our sample for whom citizens' movements constituted a political baptism, and the total of 58 percent who had never participated in any kind of protest movement prior to joining citizens' movements, it is legitimate to conclude that citizens' movements do indeed mobilize large numbers of ordinarily quiescent citizens. Although citizens' movements are similar in important ways to the types of communal activity that preceded them in the 1960s, they bring a great deal of new blood into this most demanding form of political participation. Moreover, citizens' movements cannot be described simply as yet another manifestation of the old opposition in Japan.

Although a statistical comparison of the perceptions of participation discussed above and activists' political experience confirms the obvious—that interest, information, and democratic preferences *tend* to accompany greater experience—the "innocents" demonstrated high interest and competence also. Even if the gladiators possessed these qualities before joining citizens' movements, it is reasonable to conclude that among the less experienced activists citizens' movement participation was a crucial factor in producing high political interest and competence. Assessing the impact of citizens' movements in this respect, one activist said:

The problem is the idea of the *okami* [political overlords], bestowing government upon us the way the emperor did [in the historical past]. We leave politics up to others and never fight. That's a Japanese trait, but it's not citizenship [*shimin ishiki*], and that's why citizens' movements are important. We are developing the nerve to complain and demand what we want. (C3)

New Ideas Due to the Citizens' Movement Experience

It remains possible that citizens' movement activists were a self-selected group of people predisposed to acquiring and displaying the qualities of citizenship regardless of their involvement in citizens' movements. Fortunately, activists also provided their own testimony as to the sorts of changes that citizens' movements brought to their lives. Although we must rely on subjective, and possibly selective or distorted, reporting by respondents, an open-ended question of this sort has the compensating advantage of providing a filter, in that respondents reported the changes that were the most salient to them. They were encouraged to ramble freely in response to this item, and 80 percent answered in

---

would evoke feelings of allegiance, support, and affirmation on their part with respect to the parties they worked for, and their activities were entirely respectable and routine, in some cases the automatic consequences of their occupation or position in a labor union. In citizens' movements, the emphasis is on the policy one opposes and thus on political conflict itself.

TABLE 12 | *How Did Your Opinions Change as a Result of the Movement?*

	Learned Politics	Disappointed	Ideas Changed	Radicalized	Grew Hopeful	Average Number of Changes
Previous Political Experience			*Percentage*			
A. Political innocents (22)	45	41	23	14	9	2.09
B. Conventional experience only (15)	47	40	47	20	7	2.27
C. Protest experience only (11)	36	45	27	36	0	1.72
D. Gladiators (16)	44	19	19	31	19	1.81
Newcomers to protest (A + B)	46	41	32	16	8	2.16
Veterans of protest (C + D)	41	30	22	33	11	1.78
All activists (64)	44	36	28	23	9	2.00

Note: Cell entry is the percentage of individuals falling in the categories described in the lefthand margin who mentioned the changes in ideas listed at the top of each column. The Average Number of Changes in the right column is the number of changes in ideas mentioned for each category, divided by the number of individuals composing that category.

some detail. These replies were then coded into five general categories, which have been tabulated in table 12.[10]

The change most frequently mentioned (by 44% of the sample) was that citizens' movements had taught the activists a lot about politics. The politically inexperienced, particularly women, often said that they learned to appreciate the connection between politics and their own lives:

The movement turned into an education for me. I learned that I was a person myself, besides my husband, and began to look behind [politicians'] words for their real motives and behavior. I am much more concerned with politics now. (K6)

I have learned that we have to make demands ourselves and present them ourselves. Our lives are not unrelated to politics, as I used to think. (F2)

Others reported learning about the substance of politics:

I found out what real politics is like. . . . I studied a lot of law and procedure in order to draw up petitions and figure out what we could do. I really had to think a lot about practical politics. (E1)

10. Some of the following material is drawn from Margaret McKean, "Political Socialization Through Citizens' Movements," chap. 7 (pp. 26–28) in Scott C. Flanagan, Kurt Steiner, and Ellis S. Krauss, *Political Opposition and Local Politics in Japan: Electoral Trends, Citizens' Movements, and Progressive Administrations* (Princeton: Princeton University Press, 1980).

Detailed analysis indicated that those who reported learning the most were those who had the most to learn rather than those who were already knowledgeable about politics when they entered citizens' movements.[11]

Thirty-six percent of the sample mentioned being disillusioned about the LDP and about industrial indifference to environmental problems and general public welfare. The disappointed activists tended to be those who began with naive hopes for a simple and rapid solution but who instead endured bitter encounters with local government and surrounding communities, particularly in rural areas, where 63 percent of the activists were disillusioned. The association between rural residence and reports of disappointment produced a Tau-b = .451, p <.001. One rural activist described this transition:

I used to be "deaf" on the subject of politics, but I know how the city assembly works. This is true of all of us now; we all go to assembly sessions because we don't know what they would do if they thought they could fool us. We have to take an interest, go and ask questions, and watch them to see that they don't play any tricks on us. Now I always express my discontent, and I don't listen to what others tell me without making sure of my facts first. Unfortunately I have to doubt others before I act now. This is sad, but I can certainly protect myself better this way. (K2)

Only 9 percent of the sample said that they had grown "optimistic about our ability to make progress within the system" (F3) rather than outside of it, through the citizens' movement as a new mode of action. These few individuals, all urban reformists, had begun with such low expectations and cynicism toward the establishment that their unanticipated successes in citizens' movements could not help but lift their spirits.

Twenty-eight percent of the sample reported that their ideas had substantively changed in some way not already mentioned—a catchall description including remarks to the effect that respondents' ideas became more complex, more practical, more concerned with democratic values, or in other cases to the effect that respondents acquired new standards for voting or learned to think more independently. Some activists said that their old ideas were reinforced or strengthened, and their remarks were classified in this category also. Finally, some respondents (23%) said that the experience had "radicalized" them by changing their political posture a great deal. Several commented on the tradition of the *okami* (political overlords) from the past. Both of the following comments came from former conservative community leaders now active in citizens' movements:

11. More discussion of the relationships between reported change in ideas and other dimensions of citizens' movement activity is available in Margaret McKean, "The Potentials for Grass-Roots Democracy in Postwar Japan: the Anti-Pollution Movement as a Case Study in Political Activism" (Ph.D. diss. in Political Science, University of California at Berkeley, 1974), pp. 710–716.

I used to believe that we had to cooperate with the *okami* and *tonosama* [princes] and government offices, which are all the same thing, as superiors. . . . Such feudal ideas were strongly cultivated in us and in me too . . . but I changed to more democratic ideas, and opposed and protested. Now I don't like the idea of cooperating. It's gone. (E2)

Japan, from old times, has been [dominated by] centralized power—we listen and agree to the *okami*. We have the custom of *onegai* [begging] and *omakase* [relying on others], so government officials think that they can do anything they want. . . . So the people must unite and oppose this to get what *we* want. There is no other way. (J2)

Clearly, then, the experience of participating in citizens' movements modified the belief systems of activists as so many observers claimed, but citizens' movement participation was an even more important source of socialization for newcomers to protest than for veterans of protest. Newcomers were particularly more likely to mention that their ideas changed in content or that they grew disillusioned with the government, a threshold which previous protesters would obviously have passed earlier. Even among the newcomers there were important differences, in that those newcomers to protest who nonetheless possessed experience in conventional politics reported changes in ideas more than twice as often as the political innocents; the legacy of conventional experience was in part a burden to be unlearned, as well as an asset in ways to be discussed below.

Veterans of protest were of course susceptible to learning from citizens' movements also, and two patterns of belief change were clear within this group. Those veterans whose political experience was limited to protest were inclined to report having been powerfully disappointed and even radicalized by citizens' movements, shoved further leftward along the spectrum by yet another dose of political conflict. But the gladiators with more varied experience in conventional activity as well as protest were pleasantly surprised at the success of citizens' movements and newly hopeful about this mode of civic action, apparently more promising than the kinds of protest movements they had engaged in previously. In conclusion, most citizens' movement activists experienced belief change of some sort, but it was particularly the newcomers to protest who could not glide through citizens' movements impervious to what went on around them and who instead had to incorporate new information and adjust old ideas to fit accordingly.

Two Clusters: Sophisticated and Parochial Activists

Before we launch a more sharply focused investigation of the political attitudes of citizens' movement activists, it is necessary to introduce one of the findings to be used later in the analysis. The original intent of the activist survey was to examine how the citizens' movement experience affected the political consciousness of participants. I expected to find only minor differences among the activists, and in any case that such differences would fall in a normal distribution along a continuum, permitting us to locate a hypothetical "model" or "average" activist somewhere in the center of that distribution. However, extensive preliminary analysis (which need not be repeated here) indicated that certain dimensions having to do with social and motivational traits created sharp divisions among the sample and persisted throughout the data. It also appeared that these traits revealing sharp discontinuities in the attitude and belief profiles of activists might also share the same taproot, some underlying dimension which the interviews did not measure directly. I therefore attempted to test the possibility that the sample congregated into statistically discernible clusters or types.

Several methodological approaches were available, including factor analysis and its variants, but the data did not really meet their requirements.[12] Instead, I used the more conservative device of building an index. To select the independent variables that might produce two clusters of activists, a matrix of Tau-b coefficients of association among all such potential indicators was calculated. An index was then generated from those seven variables that turned out to be consistently interrelated (as well as another version of the index that excluded rural/urban residence so that it could be shown separately).[13] Three of these variables were background traits of the activists (rural/urban residence, education, and protest experience); three others referred to motives and goals with respect to pollution and citizens' movement activity (preventive orientation, self-interest vs. altruism, and group goals); the last referred to the use of one particular tactic (litigation). Thus these seven variables comprised measures of activists' social, political, and attitudinal traits as well

12. Factor analysis is used to explore the alignments among a group of variables, often to establish whether some underlying dimension or "factor" binds several variables together. Q-analysis is a reversal of factor analysis which treats individuals as variables and treats variables or traits as cases. Q-analysis can then be used to explore the clustering or alignments of individual cases (as opposed to variables) in a sample, to establish whether underlying groupings exist. However, Q-analysis requires a large number of variables (because they function as cases), but I had no reason to suspect that more than ten or fifteen characteristics of activists were involved. In addition, factor analysis requires interval level data, but I was willing to assume that our ordinal level data resembled interval level data only for minor manipulations. On factor analysis, see Benjamin Fruchter, *Introduction to Factor Analysis* (Princeton: D. Van Nostrand, 1954); and Harry H. Harman, *Modern Factor Analysis* (Chicago: University of Chicago Press, 1960). On Q-analysis, see Raymond B. Cattell, *Factor Analysis: An Introduction and Manual for the Psychologist and Social Scientist* (New York: Harper & Row, 1952). Professor Merrill Shanks of the Survey Research Center at the University of California at Berkeley also provided helpful advice.

13. Fuller discussion of data relating to this index can be found in McKean, "The Potentials for Grass-Roots Democracy," pp. 825–861.

Figure 1. Sophistication Index

A. Two Ideal Types of Antipollution Activists

Parochials	—	Sophisticates
rural residence	—	urban residence
low education	—	high education
newcomer to protest	—	veteran of protest
wanted compensation	—	preventive orientation
self-interested motives	—	altruistic individual motives
specific group goals	—	general group goals
had to use litigation	—	did not use litigation

B. Distribution Curve for the Six-Variable Sophistication Index (Rural-Urban Residence Excluded)

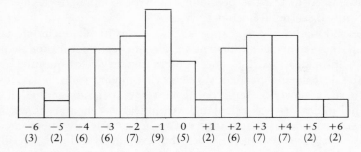

−6	−5	−4	−3	−2	−1	0	+1	+2	+3	+4	+5	+6
(3)	(2)	(6)	(6)	(7)	(9)	(5)	(2)	(6)	(7)	(7)	(2)	(2)

C. Distribution Curve for the Seven-Variable Sophistication Index (Rural/Urban Residence Included)

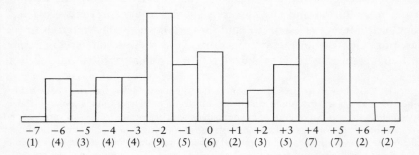

−7	−6	−5	−4	−3	−2	−1	0	+1	+2	+3	+4	+5	+6	+7
(1)	(4)	(3)	(4)	(4)	(9)	(5)	(6)	(2)	(3)	(5)	(7)	(7)	(2)	(2)

as an ingredient of actual experience. Figure 1 shows that both versions of the index did indeed separate the sample into two clusters.

One important qualification is that involvement in litigation was not associated with the "sophisticated" end of the spectrum as we would expect; the contrary was true. The sophisticated activists did not have to resort to litigation; the most severe and visible pollution affected those who were least prepared to deal with it and who eventually had no choice but to use this extreme device. Activists who became pollution plaintiffs did later acquire great familiarity with the legal system as a result of activism, in spite of their other characteristics labeled here as "unsophisticated." However, this variable should not be interpreted to represent knowledge of the legal system which an activist brought to his group.

Thus these background and attitudinal traits that were closely related to one another caused the sample to fall into a bimodal distribution, demonstrating the existence of two distinct clusters among the activists. The variables responsible for this clustering appear to have something to do with social and political savoir faire, awareness, an ability to relate abstract principles to one's daily life, and perhaps cognitive capacities. Although we call it the "sophistication index" below, no basic psychological measures were employed, and at most this index can only be regarded as a rough and primitive indicator. An activist's "sophistication" or "cognitive ability" refers not to inborn abilities but to what results from the combination of basic psychological equipment, personal development, and social environment.

What analytical utility do the "sophistication index" and the notion of clustering provide? First of all, in analysis too extensive to reproduce here, the index discriminates between these clusters of activists according to their belief sets, their political interest and knowledge, as well as their information about the issues that was the object of their activism. The sophisticates saw stronger connections between pollution and politics, judged various reference groups more harshly against higher standards of performance, indicated clearer support for democratic norms and procedures, favored the use of democratic methods and structures within citizens' movements, and had more information and general interest in politics, relative to the parochials.[14] Thus the sophistication index not only tapped such things as social environment and cognitive capacities, but also had to do with the substance of ideas and belief systems.

Constructing a typology from the six-variable sophistication index and rural urban residence indicates that there really were three types of activists: urban sophisticates (n=25), urban parochials (n=13), and rural

14. Almond and Verba used "parochial" to mean totally apolitical—having no orientation whatever toward political objects at any level; see Gabriel A. Almond and Sidney Verba, *The Civic Culture: Political Attitudes and Democracy in Five Nations* (Boston: Little, Brown, 1965), pp. 16–17. Verba recently extended the use of the term to refer to an understanding of government as provider of services and to a mode of participation labeled "particularized contacting" in "The Parochial and the Polity," in Verba and Lucian W. Pye, eds., *The Citizen and Politics: A Comparative Perspective* (Stamford, Conn.: Greylock, 1978), pp. 3–28. I use the term here in neither of these ways, but simply to refer to an orientation to citizens' movement activity that is narrower and simpler than that of the "sophisticates."

parochials (n=25). Only one individual fell into the "rural sophisticate" quadrant, which we may therefore discount as a rare event.[15] This information highlights several important points with respect to the analysis below. First, parochial activists were not confined to rural areas, as there were many activists in urban areas who also lacked the background traits and interest in broad issues which we might too quickly assume to be prerequisites for activism. In fact, a majority of our sample belongs in the "parochial" cluster rather than in the "sophisticated" one, signifying that such parochial characteristics were not the impediment to political activism that one might readily believe. Obviously, the social limitations leading to a "parochial" or an "isolate" score on the index did not preclude all forms of social or political activism, and even those who appeared isolated or provincial in some respects could nonetheless be concerned and involved members of their own local communities.[16] In view of the special effort made during selection of the sample to locate a group or two with general goals or preventive concerns, we have probably oversampled the sophisticates, and the citizens' movement population as a whole consists of an even larger proportion of "isolates" than our sample produced.

Second, just as a parochial orientation did not preclude activism, neither did it preclude the ability to learn. Isolates demonstrated the greatest amount of change and new learning due to the citizens' movement experience, precisely because the whole idea of protest was unfamiliar and disquieting to them at the outset, and they had to be prodded and shocked into activism by the sheer enormity of their problems. Even though the parochials were relatively less informed and somewhat limited in their ability to generalize or to comprehend the pollution issue in its entirety, they were perfectly capable of being emotionally upset about it and thus provoked to action. Table 13 shows that although the isolates were parochial in their vision, less informed and less involved in terms of an absolute comparison with their sophisticated compatriots in citizens' movements, they were much more likely to report that the experience altered their views, from disillusioning them to teaching them about politics. The only way in which the sophisticates changed more often than the isolates on this measure was in reporting that the citizens' movement experience had raised their hopes about the possibilities of so-

15. On the three clusters of urban sophisticates, urban parochials, and rural parochials, see Margaret McKean, "Citizens' Movements in Urban and Rural Japan," in James W. White and Frank Munger, eds., *Social Change and Community Politics in Urban Japan* (Chapel Hill, N.C.: University of North Carolina at Chapel Hill, Institute for Research in Social Science, 1976), pp. 78–81.

16. Rural Japanese in general tend to be intimately enmeshed in their communities and more involved in *local* politics in certain ways than city-dwellers. See Richardson, *Political Culture of Japan*, pp. 135–136.

TABLE 13 / *Background and Belief Change among Sophisticate-Isolate Clusters (Six-Variable Sophistication Index)*

	Sophisticates	Mixed	Isolates	Total
Residence				
Rural (24)	4%	44%	67%	38%
Urban (40)	96%	56%	33%	63%
Tau-b = −.544, p .001	—	—	—	—
Total	100%	100%	100%	100%
	(24)	(16)	(24)	(64)
How did your Opinions Change as a Result of the Movement? *				
Learned about politics	29%	44%	58%	44%
Disappointed, disillusioned	21%	63%	33%	36%
Substance of ideas changed	21%	19%	42%	28%
Radicalized	21%	25%	25%	23%
Grew hopeful about social change	21%	6%	0%	9%
Average Number of Changes	1.42	2.19	2.46	2.00
Sophistication Score [−6, +6]	+3.46	−.44	−3.46	−.11

* Cell entry signifies the percentage of activists in the columns identified at the top (sophisticated, mixed, or isolated) mentioning the type of change described in the left margin.

cial change, precisely because they had begun with grim attitudes on these prospects.

Because activists in both clusters were susceptible to change, they appear to have grown somewhat more similar to each other as a result of shared political experience. That is, at the outset the urban sophisticates were pessimistic about the likelihood of alleviating pollution, cautious in their expectations of citizens' movement success, and generally guarded about the impact that political activism would have on the larger society. After their participation in citizens' movements they remained relatively pessimistic but were nonetheless considerably encouraged and heartened by the unanticipated progress they had achieved. The same citizens' movement experience constituted a profound disappointment for the isolates, who began their activism with naive hopes about the responsiveness of the political system and fairly simple notions about pollution, and were naturally shaken as they grew to understand the nature of the obstacles they faced.

In summary, then, those who learned the most through the citizens' movement experience were those who had the most to learn. In this sense, citizens' movements served to enlarge the politically active public by mobilizing "isolates" who had not paid much attention to politics before, and turning them into seasoned political activists. The activist experience for isolates was a more critical one in causing them to think about political issues, and was a much more emotionally shattering one in terms of creating disillusionment with the political establishment.

Political Attitudes

This disillusionment with the political establishment shows clearly in a detailed examination of activists' evaluations of political parties, the national government, and other institutions, using three different rating schedules. We can interpret their responses both as realistic testimony concerning the environmental stance adopted by these institutions and as summaries of activists' own subjective perceptions of these institutions. In addition, evaluations made in terms of the environmental issue may tap attitudes born out of the exposure to citizens' movements, not merely inherited from previous experiences. These newly acquired attitudes will later be measured against partisan affiliations and actual voting habits to assess the influence of participation in citizens' movements on activists' larger roles as political beings.

The first series of questions asked activists to describe whether particular institutions selected from a list had assisted or hindered their citizens' movement. (Ns are low in some instances because these institutions were not always involved on the local scene, either for or against the movement.) A second series asked respondents to describe the policies of various figures and institutions, running from energetic efforts to fight pollution through malevolent efforts to suppress the environmental movement. The third series asked activists to analyze the obstacles faced by each of these institutions in its antipollution efforts—whether the institution tried to do its best, was hampered by a lack of resources, or actually felt no responsibility in the pollution issue. This third series was essentially a device to add depth to the other scales by gauging activists' willingness to sympathize with the political situation faced by each of these institutions.

The frequency distributions and arithmetic means on each of these rating scales are provided in tables 14, 15, and 16. It is obvious from these tables that activists agreed on which institutions constituted "enemies" of their groups and which were friendly allies. The business community, the conservative party, and the national government stood out conspicuously as enemies. The most consistent and conspicuous allies of the movement were the extreme opposition parties, the JSP and the JCP, but the Environment Agency was also favorably regarded despite its association with the government. It is also interesting to note that when labor unions, teachers, and students were involved in particular cases, activists considered them to have been quite helpful. However, when speaking in more general terms about labor unions (tables 15 and 16), activists were not so favorable.

• Views of the Political Parties

We have already noted the consensus among activists that the LDP's actions were a hindrance to the various antipollution movements

TABLE 14 / *Did the Following Groups Help or Hurt Your Movement?*

Group	−2	−1	0	+1	+2	Total	(N)	Mean Score
			Percentage					
Students	0	0	9	27	64	100	(22)	+1.55
Teachers	4	0	7	21	68	100	(28)	+1.50
Labor unions	0	9	3	19	69	100	(32)	+1.47
CGP	7	0	4	21	68	100	(28)	+1.43
JSP	14	0	0	10	76	100	(42)	+1.33
JCP	12	2	4	8	74	100	(50)	+1.30
Scholars	2	11	16	31	40	100	(45)	+ .96
DSP	23	8	8	15	46	100	(13)	+ .54
Fishermen	13	22	9	17	39	100	(23)	+ .48
Farmers	28	8	16	16	32	100	(25)	+ .16
Small business	25	25	13	3	34	100	(32)	− .03
Landowners	72	4	4	0	20	100	(25)	−1.08
Big business	82	6	0	0	12	100	(34)	−1.47
LDP	77	15	3	3	3	101	(39)	−1.62

Scale:
+2 They helped us.
+1 Most of them helped us.
 0 Half and half.
−1 Most of them hurt us.
−2 They hurt us.

sampled, and that the CGP, JSP, and JCP were very helpful and supportive of citizens' movements. In fact, the LDP made such a uniformly bad impression on most groups that there was very little variance within the sample. Activists said that at best the LDP talked about preventing pollution but avoided real action because of its dependence on industry, particularly the major polluters, for political funds. The DSP seemed to shy away from actual involvement in pollution disputes, and activists agreed that the DSP did little to distinguish itself from the LDP on this issue. Apparently the DSP's effort to serve as a moderate alternative to the LDP was lost on antipollution activists.

The CGP, on the other hand, seems to have made a favorable impression on antipollution activists, and this is all the more noteworthy in view of the fact that *none* of the respondents in the sample were CGP supporters either before or after activism. The CGP is known as a muckraking party, publicizing explosive social problems and reaping political advantages in the form of greater popularity in the meantime.[17] The CGP

17. The intense CGP interest in the pollution problem is noted in two party works on the subject: Kōmei Shimbun henshūkyoku, *Kōgai ni idomu Kōmeitō: tori modosō, midori to mizu to taiyō wo* [The Kōmeitō Challenges Pollution: Let's Bring Back the Birds, and Have Green and Water and Sunshine again] (Tokyo: Kōmeitō Kikanshikyoku, October 1970); and Kōmeitō kōgai taisaku hombu, *Kōgai zetsumetsu ni idomu: zenkoku kōgai chōsa repooto* [A Challenge to Extinction by Pollution: Report from Our National Pollution Survey] (Tokyo: Kōmeitō Kikanshikyoku, July 1971).

TABLE 15 / *How Would You Rate the Antipollution Activities of the Following Groups?*

Group	-3	-2	-1	0	$+1$	$+2$	$+3$	Total	(N)	Mean Score
				Percentage						
JCP	2	4	11	2	26	5	51	101	(57)	+1.67
JSP	2	3	19	3	34	9	31	99	(59)	+1.12
CGP	2	4	23	2	31	6	31	100	(48)	+1.00
Environment Agency	3	3	14	17	27	7	29	100	(59)	+ .97
Prefectural governor	13	5	14	4	21	7	36	100	(56)	+ .80
Labor unions	12	2	31	2	33	2	19	101	(52)	+ .25
Local mayor*	26	6	20	7	15	6	22	102	(55)	− .25
DSP	2	4	23	2	31	6	31	99	(55)	− .31
Bureaucracy	21	9	33	12	21	0	5	101	(58)	− .76
Tanaka†	29	11	36	5	7	0	11	99	(55)	−1.16
LDP	28	17	45	0	8	0	2	100	(60)	−1.50
Satō	36	9	51	0	5	0	0	101	(59)	−1.69
Big business	75	8	10	5	2	0	0	100	(60)	−2.43

Scale:
+3 Earnest about solving the problem, active, and trying as hard as possible to discover concrete techniques
+2 In between
+1 Sincere, but various obstacles interfere with their activity, such as the lack of technical understanding, or the fact that other people won't cooperate with them, or the lack of funds, or the fact that the problem is very serious
  0 In between (neutral point)
−1 Often simply talking about the problem, but disinclined to act, and often dependent on people who do not want to face the problem of pollution, so they avoid concrete activities
−2 In between
−3 Avoiding the problem is to their advantage; they think only about their own wealth and power

* Three respondents shown here as −3 actually insisted on being classified as −4 or −5, and these latter values have been preserved in calculations of means and in statistics measuring association with other variables.

†Two respondents shown here as −3 insisted on being rated as −5 and −7, respectively, and these latter values have been preserved in calculations of means and in statistics measuring association with other variables.

conducted its own scientific surveys of pollution to give credence to claims of local activists and offered specific assistance to some of the groups in our sample. The CGP share of the popular vote has never recovered its early record (15.4% of the national constituency in the 1968 House of Councillors election), and the CGP clearly saw an opportunity to attract support from the several million voters mobilized through the eruption of citizens' movements all over Japan. Among our sample, the CGP earned a good reputation on the pollution issue on the strength of its performance, but this favorable image did not create a single CGP partisan. Activists who offered criticism said that the CGP was good at discovering problems and obtaining publicity, but not at following through with help later on, and that the party's contributions to antipollution efforts were secondary to its interests in political advancement and therefore

TABLE 16 | *What Kind of Obstacles Make Antipollution Activity Difficult for the Following Groups?*

Group	−1	0	+1	Total	(N)	Mean Score
		Percentage				
JCP	17	40	42	99	(52)	+.25
JSP	20	50	30	100	(54)	+.09
Environment Agency	23	47	30	100	(47)	+.06
CGP	21	55	25	101	(44)	+.05
Prefectural governor	26	47	28	101	(51)	+.02
Local mayor	44	31	24	99	(45)	−.20
Labor unions	35	50	15	100	(48)	−.21
DSP	33	58	9	100	(43)	−.23
Tanaka	69	23	8	100	(48)	−.60
Bureaucracy	83	13	4	100	(53)	−.79
LDP	86	12	2	100	(57)	−.84
Satō	89	12	0	101	(52)	−.88
Big business	93	5	2	100	(60)	−.92

Scale:
+1 There are no obstacles; the institution helped us, worked hard for us.
 0 In a tone of sympathy: They are weak, disunited, lack money, have no practice, are only in the opposition and can't do much. They don't think very hard; they can't or don't understand the problem; they don't see the problem themselves yet; they are unrealistic; they see development and industry as desirable goals. They are powerless to act, dependent on others, and the situation is to blame more than they are; they are part of the capitalist system and can't help it; they are afraid to lose their jobs or their function.
−1 In a tone of anger or disgust: They aren't interested; they lack sincerity; they aren't responsible; they lack principle; they worry only about themselves; they are easily pressured to do other's bidding; they avoid the issue; they blindly obey their superiors; they only pretend to help us but abuse the movement for their own power; they take bribes from propollution forces; they are tied to industry; they get their money from people who don't care. They find it not profitable, even destructive to their power or profit to pay attention to pollution; they are unscrupulous and tyrannical.

suspect. The fact that the CGP share of the popular vote has leveled off in recent general elections (10.9% in 1969, 8.5% in 1972, 10.9% in 1976, and 9.8% in 1979) indicates that its reputation as a religious party still sets a ceiling on its ability to draw votes.

The JSP did not fare much better than the CGP in terms of activists' evaluations of its antipollution stance. Many again cited reservations about the JSP's political motives in assisting antipollution movements, and also added that the JSP was still to some extent a captive of organized labor, about which the citizens' movement activists were even less enthusiastic.

One outstanding feature of these evaluations is that only the JCP earned overwhelmingly positive scores from citizens' movement activists. In terms of aggregate measures, only the JCP managed to accumulate an unequivocally high positive score on the rating scale (table 15) and on the "obstacles" scale (table 16), which can also be considered a "sincerity" scale. The increase in JCP popular vote displayed in the 1972 general election (from 6.8% in 1969 to 10.5% in 1972) and subsequently maintained (10.3% in 1976, 10.4% in 1979), in spite of poor calculations resulting in a temporary loss of actual Diet seats in 1976, is probably a result of changes in partisanship and an increase in the floating vote stimulated by the phenomenon of citizens' movements. On the other hand, the decline in popular vote received by the JCP in the House of Councillors election of 1977 (8.4% in the national and 9.96% in the local constituencies) probably indicates the temporary political embarrassments suffered by the JCP that year (the Miyamoto scandal and difficult fisheries talks with the Soviet Union) and reveals that the floating vote stimulated by citizens' movements can float elsewhere.

• Views of the National Government

Activists were asked to rate the antipollution policy of and the obstacles faced by former Prime Minister Satō Eisaku, the then current prime minister Tanaka Kakuei, the bureaucracy as a whole, and the Environment Agency in particular. They agreed overwhelmingly (89%) that Satō's policies were entirely bad and that his motivations were in the worst category. Even a large majority (63%) of those who identified themselves as conservative after activism shared in this condemnation of Satō.

There was less agreement over the antipollution stance of Prime Minister Tanaka, who still benefited at the time of interviewing from the rosy glow that accompanied him during the first several months of his premiership. Eighteen percent of the sample had a positive view of Tanaka's position on the issue, stemming primarily from his drastic redevelopment proposal known as Kaizōron. Activists' views of both Tanaka and his plan were highly politicized, in that conservatives were enthusiastic about Kaizōron as a solution to environmental problems, whereas reformists cynically referred to the plan as "Kōgairon" (the plan to disperse pollution throughout Japan).

Activists shared less consensus on the role of the central bureaucracy with respect to pollution problems, in that responses spread broadly across the spectrum from good to bad, but as a whole the bureaucracy still fared rather badly, owing to its unavoidable responsibilities for policy design and implementation. The only readily identifiable subgroups among the sample who made favorable comments on the bureaucracy were diehard conservative partisans, who believed that the bureaucracy could be trusted to carry out environmentally sound policies if it were told to do so.

Alone among these symbols of the national government, the Environment Agency elicited positive reactions from activists, regardless of their political affiliations. The only noticeable cluster of skeptics was located among veterans of protest—those who were undoubtedly jaded by previous disappointments and viewed the creation of the Environment Agency as a clever government ploy to deceive and appease them, rather than as a sincere attempt to resolve environmental problems. Newcomers to protest were more inclined to be optimistic about any hopeful signs coming from government.

· Views of Economic Institutions

Japanese environmental activists conceived of pollution chiefly as industrial pollution and hence as a question involving powerful economic institutions, so they were asked about their perceptions of both labor unions and business enterprises. In general, labor was reluctant to endorse citizens' movements, insofar as labor shared the interests of industrial management in expanding production and improving efficiency (to increase wages rather than profits in this instance), and also in protecting firms from going bankrupt owing to high pollution-related expenses. Activists bemoaned the fact that organized labor as a whole had a passive, occasionally obstructionist role in the movement to combat pollution, but they were also sympathetic to labor's precarious position, many saying that it would be unfair to criticize the passive role of most workers. Some very emotional activists did say that labor unions were inexcusably selfish and unjustifiably afraid of taking risks on behalf of a higher cause, but the majority avoided sharp criticism.

The specific enterprise unions of offending companies invariably defended their firms, and urban citizens' movements almost never received any help from labor. However, regional labor federations in rural areas, consisting of workers whose jobs were not threatened and who were unconnected to the polluting industry itself, found it politically attractive to assist citizens' movements. Pollution problems in rural areas were usually more dramatic and provided organized labor with greater opportunities for combining its goals with those of the citizens' movements. The community-wide movements in rural areas often campaigned extensively in local elections, giving labor unions and their JSP or JCP candidates a useful issue. In rural areas where a smaller portion of nonfarm workers were organized into unions, the environmental issue also provided a potential foundation for the unionization of more workers. Thus the negative attitudes of urban citizens' movements toward organized labor were probably due both to objective fact (labor was actually more supportive of rural citizens' movements than of urban ones) and to subjective impressions (the rural groups were also probably more surprised and pleased at receiving help from labor, whereas the urban citizens' movements were somewhat disappointed at the shabby aid they received).

Turning to evaluations of the business community, we are not surprised to learn that activists had extremely negative views and blamed the evil motives of big business for this situation: only one respondent (naturally a conservative partisan) found it possible to view big business with even a morsel of sympathy, saying that business was sincerely trying to do its best. What is therefore surprising is that in specific cases businesses had in fact provided aid to citizens' movements when it was in their interest to do so. In Usuki, for example, the largest local firms were in food processing and vehemently opposed plans to bring heavy industry into town. The sympathy for business that we do find in the sample is based not just on spillovers from political conservatism, but also on an honest assessment of actual citizens' movement experience.

Two features that stand out from this review of political attitudes require further investigation. First, activists shared unusually hostile views toward a wide variety of objects ranging across the political spectrum. Second, activists displayed unexpected variability in their views of local authorities, differentiating between central and local government and displaying a motley assortment of attitudes toward their mayors and prefectural governors.

General Political Hostility

The remarkably negative reaction which activists had toward political institutions must be viewed in the context of the political cynicism displayed by the Japanese population as a whole. The Japanese public directs these feelings primarily at the occupants of present institutions—politicians, parties, and pressure groups—but not toward the fundamental features of democratic systems in the abstract, and the disaffected do not seem particularly prone to violent or disruptive behavior.[18] Rather than constituting alienation from the system, then, this expression of hostility and mistrust, which is commonplace in ordinary conversation and in response to surveys, may simply be a behavioral norm (*tatemae*, or outward appearance, as opposed to *honne*, or essence), and need not be salient or troubling to those who verbalize it. Obviously some portion of the hostility shown by our activist sample should be dismissed as "normal," though the incomparability of the measures used in different surveys makes it impossible to determine how large a residue of negative feeling we need to explain. Fortunately, the open-ended structure of the face-to-face interviews in this case encouraged activists to ramble so that

18. See Richardson, *Political Culture of Japan*, pp. 66–82; Scott C. Flanagan and Bradley M. Richardson, "Political Disaffection and Political Stability: A Comparison of Japanese and Western Findings," in Richard F. Tomasson, ed., *Comparative Social Research* 3 (Greenwich, Conn.: JAI Press, 1980); and James W. White, "Civic Attitudes, Political Participation, and System Stability in Japan," paper presented at the annual meeting of the American Political Science Association, Washington, D.C., September 1979.

they themselves generated the substantive content of their responses, assuring that they were not simply giving automatic responses to cues. The following analysis proceeds on the assumption that activists' hostility was both salient to them personally (*honne*, not just *tatemae*), and politically significant for our purposes (not just an artifact of being Japanese).

In order to examine all of these hostile attitudes in combination, I constructed composite scales of general dispositions toward the right and left wings—Attitude to the Right, Attitude to the Left, as well as two summary measures created by manipulating these first two. All were scored in the same way, from −3 (hostile attitudes) through 0 (neutrality) to +3 (favorable attitudes). These scales were based not only on selected items from the forty responses to the rating schedules explained earlier in this chapter, but also on every unsolicited remark made during interviews about referents which could easily be classified as either right- or left-wing. In this way, the composite scales took into account the salience of these attitudes for individual activists, and thus represented intensity as well as direction. "Right-wing" objects included the LDP, Prime Ministers Satō and Tanaka, and conservative mayors and prefectural governors where applicable. "Left-wing" objects consisted of the JSP, the JCP, labor unions, and reformist mayors and prefectural governors where applicable. References to the centrist parties were omitted, and remarks about economic institutions were excluded on the grounds that we would not be justified in considering them political judgments.

Table 17 shows arithmetic means for the total sample and important subgroups within it on all four scales. Citizens' movement activists were extremely hostile toward the political right, and rather favorable toward the political left, just as we would surmise from the discussion of individual attitudes toward specific referents so far. In fact, only fourteen members of the sample (22%) felt hostile toward the left in this absolute sense. Furthermore, activists were far more hostile to the right than they were favorable toward the left. It is important to appreciate the fact that activists were not overwhelmed by the left, and instead invested much more emotional energy in their disappointment with the conservative establishment than in any frantic grasping for solutions at the opposite pole of the political spectrum.

The two summary scales permit us to weigh these absolute attitudes toward right and left, respectively, against each other. Net Attitude toward the Left measured residual feeling—the difference between the scores earned on the Right and Left scales respectively—and was scored so that positive values represented a net preference for the left over the right. Attitude toward Political Objects was a similar summary measure, scored so that positive values represented favorable attitudes toward political objects of either left or right, and negative values represented hos-

TABLE 17 / *Political Hostility*

	Attitude to Right	Attitude to Left	Net Left	Political Objects
Total (64)	−1.94	+ .50	+1.22	− .72
Individual Motives				
Self-interested (37)	−1.65	+ .65	+1.15	− .50
Altruistic (27)	−2.33	+ .30	+1.31	−1.02
Group Goals				
Specific (48)	−1.67	+ .67	+1.17	− .50
General (16)	−2.75	0	+1.38	−1.38
Sophistication Index				
Isolates (24)	−1.33	+ .25	+ .79	− .54
Mixed (16)	−2.00	+1.31	+1.66	− .34
Sophisticates (24)	−2.50	+ .21	+1.35	−1.15
Previous Political Experience				
Innocent (22)	−1.95	+ .41	+1.18	− .77
Conventional experience only (15)	− .87	+ .33	+ .60	− .27
Protest experience only (11)	−2.64	+ .45	+1.55	−1.09
Gladiator (16)	−2.44	+ .81	+1.63	− .81
Residence				
Rural (24)	−1.92	+1.25	+1.59	− .33
Urban (40)	−1.95	+ .05	+1.00	− .95

tile attitudes toward political objects of either left or right. This final measure permits us to determine whether activists were essentially negative (or positive) in outlook regardless of the target of their remarks.

Activists displayed a sizable preference for the left over the right. Only seven respondents, or 11 percent, emerged with a net preference in favor of the right. However, activists' total view of the political objects included in these measures was essentially negative. Thus activists' net preference for the left was a bit grudging, not entirely enthusiastic; viewed another way, the activists' admiration for the left could not begin to compensate for their utter dismay with the right. One activist explained his anger:

The LDP's problem is money, their activity in real estate and construction, and the donations they get from industry. . . . The government, the prefecture, the mayor, and industry are all drinking and conspiring together so Japan can't [solve this problem]. . . . They say there's no pollution even though we can *see* it. . . . They're a bunch of liars. (G1)

These attitudes were conspicuously intense among certain subgroups of activists: those with altruistic (as opposed to self-interested) motives for participating in citizens' movements, those involved in groups with sweeping (rather than narrow) goals, and those with high scores on the "sophistication index" (which was of course composed in part of both of the preceding measures). Extreme hostility toward the right in combination with cautious reserve toward the left could result from both subjective and objective considerations. In terms of their own perceptions, the more sophisticated activists would also be more aware of political complexities in accomplishing any objective, more skeptical in their expectations of various institutions, and more sensitive to the gap between their final objectives and the status quo. The attitudes of the isolates were similar in direction but muted in degree because they lacked this skeptical awareness. Similarly, in terms of the actual goals sought and the obstacles interfering with them, the more ambitious activists would naturally face greater difficulty in persuading the powers that be to make major changes on a broad front, in comparison with the parochial activists requesting relatively minor concessions from the same institutions.

Thus far the hostility displayed by citizens' movement activists matches their circumstances, but these attitudes could result from the process of translating political attitudes held prior to citizens' movement membership into the pollution issue. To what extent then do these attitudes reflect characteristics which activists possessed before joining citizens' movements? Were activists simply a self-selected assortment of malcontents who already had chips on their shoulders? The political background of activists was related to their attitudes as assessed by the hostility scales, in that the well-rounded gladiators and those with previous protest experience were quite hostile toward the right, and as a result had an especially strong residual preference for the left. Thus we would suspect that hostility toward Japan's conservative establishment is cumulative, resulting from accretion over time, so that those who have protested before have already begun accumulating anger toward the right and simply have a head start over the politically innocent and those with conventional (and thus largely supportive rather than defiant) political experience.

Extrapolating from the well-known grass-roots conservatism of rural Japanese,[19] we would expect rural activists to be less hostile to the right, and more hostile to the left, than their urban counterparts. However, the facts contradict our expectations on both counts. Rural and urban activists were equally hostile toward the right, and, even more surprising, the rural activists were more favorable toward the left than the urban respondents. We shall explore this anomaly in greater depth in the next section, but it is clear that activists' attitudes toward political institutions did not come entirely from their past. Although a prior history of activism obviously left its mark, the character of the citizens' move-

---

19. Miyamoto Ken'ichi, "Grass-roots Conservatism," *Journal of Social and Political Ideas in Japan (Japan Interpreter)* 4:2 (August 1966), 100–106.

ment experience itself apparently overpowered the influence of socio-political environment prior to the emergence of citizens' movements.

The skepticism and hostility of the most experienced and worldly-wise activists performed a vital function for citizens' movements. Any group that feels defensive (as all citizens' movements do at first) must cultivate an in-group consciousness, a sense of separation between "us" and "them," just to verify its existence. This is particularly true of groups like citizens' movements which are embroiled in political conflict, obligating their members to be somewhat cautious in their relations with outsiders, both the forces that constitute the immediate enemy and those that extend aid for ulterior motives. Although activists' attitudes generally revealed some gratitude and pleasure toward those that offered help, maintaining a certain level of distrust and hostility against the enemy was probably more important than cultivating affection toward one's presumed allies. The important dimension of citizens' movement activity for activists to remember was what they were opposed to, and to continue that struggle in pursuit of their goals until they either won or lost. The hostility we discovered here was in part the reason that these people became active in a movement that was essentially a protest, but it was also a quality necessary for perseverence and continuity within the movement itself.

Views of the Local Political Setting

Neither rural activists' sense of futility as individuals nor their unexpectedly polarized attitudes of hostility toward the right and gratitude toward the left could have been predicted on the basis of what is generally known about rural/urban differences in Japan. Therefore rural/urban differences among *citizens' movements themselves* and special features of the local political setting must be examined as a source of explanation. There were obvious and recurring differences, both in details of the actual citizens' movement experience and in activist attitudes, between groups active in metropolitan and semirural areas (which we will simply label "urban" and "rural"). Tau-b values for most of the associations between urban/rural differences and other dimensions of activists' attitudes were usually greater than .40, and were statistically significant at p < .001. Furthermore, multivariate analysis revealed that urban/rural differences were often so sharp and so powerful that they overwhelmed other sources of variance.

We can begin to understand the differences between rural and urban activists by using fine tuning to examine their respective scores on some of the components of the hostility scales used above—their evaluations of the five major political parties on both the antipollution rating scale

TABLE 18 / *Activist Views of Political Parties and Local Executives*

	Urban	Rural	Total
Antipollution Ratings (scale of −3 to 0 to +3)			
Attitude to LDP (60)	−1.75	−1.13	−1.50
Attitude to DSP (55)	− .64	+ .18	− .31
Attitude to CGP (48)	+1.07	+ .89	+1.00
Attitude to JSP (59)	+ .77	+1.63	+1.12
Attitude to JCP (57)	+1.29	+2.22	+1.67
Attitude to prefectural governor (56)	+2.03	−1.40	+ .80
Attitude to local mayor (55)	+ .47	−1.26	− .25
Obstacles Ratings (scale of −1 to 0 to +1)			
Sympathy with LDP (57)	− .79	− .95	− .81
Sympathy with DSP (43)	− .32	− .07	− .23
Sympathy with CGP (44)	0	+ .13	+ .05
Sympathy with JSP (54)	− .06	+ .37	+ .09
Sympathy with JCP (52)	+ .03	+ .67	+ .25
Sympathy with prefectural governor (51)	+ .29	− .77	+ .02
Sympathy with local mayor (45)	− .07	− .46	− .20
Satisfaction with Local Representatives			
Satisfaction (scale of 0 to +3)	+1.03	+1.27	+1.12
Dissatisfaction (scale of −3 to 0)	−1.59	−1.41	−1.53
Net (Dis)Satisfaction (scale of −3 to 0 to +3)	− .57	− .14	− .41

Note: Cell entries are arithmetic means on the index listed at left for the group of activists (urban, rural, or all) described in the top of each column.

and its counterpart, the scale of sympathy with the obstacles faced by the five parties. Table 18 shows that rural activists displayed almost as much anger as the urban activists toward the LDP (their evaluation of the LDP's antipollution stance was not as critical as that of the urban activists, but they compensated for this by exhibiting almost unanimous disgust for the LDP in terms of the obstacles scale). More important, rural activists found the JSP and especially the JCP far more praiseworthy than did the urban activists. In general, the urban activists seemed to be somewhat freer with criticism, but much more sparing in passing out compliments to political parties. This finding also corresponds with what we know about the phenomenon of disenchantment with political parties in the general population, in that disengagement from partisan affiliations seems more prevalent in urban areas than in rural ones.[20]

20. Gary Allinson, "Japan's Independent Voters: Dilemma or Opportunity?" *Japan Interpreter* 11:1 (Spring 1976), 45–46; Hashimoto Akikazu, *Shiji seitō nashi: kazureyuku "seitō" shinwa* [Nonsupport of Political Parties: The Crumbling Myth of "Political Parties"] (Tokyo: Nihon Keizai Shimbunsha, 1975), pp. 21–24.

Activists' evaluations of their own mayors and governors in table 18 testify further to the differences between urban and rural citizens' movement experiences. The Tau-b association between residence on the one hand and antipollution ratings of prefectural governors on the other was an impressive .60, p < .001. Rural activists saved their harshest criticism for the antipollution stance of their local mayors and prefectural governors, who were almost invariably LDP members. Urban respondents, who were moderate in their praise of party organizations, became downright effusive when evaluating their prefectural governors. It should be pointed out that because most of the urban citizens' movements were drawn from the Greater Tokyo area, the object of this lavish praise was usually Tokyo's Governor Minobe Ryōkichi (a reformist independent sponsored by a JSP-JCP coalition), although some urban respondents were evaluating governors of prefectures surrounding Tokyo, not Minobe. The only negative evaluations of Minobe came from three conservatives in Tokyo who had no trouble rationalizing their criticism of a reformist governor with their citizens' movement activity in opposition to the prefectural government of Tokyo.

The urban/rural factor was not of such stark importance in affecting ratings of local mayors, because there was more variety in the kinds of mayors that activists were evaluating. Generally, rural activists were quite critical of the antipollution policies of their usually conservative local mayors. But these evaluations were muted by the fact that some of the rural movements managed to elect "antipollution" mayors to whom they now felt somewhat sympathetic. Urban activists' evaluations of mayors were even more varied. None of the urban movements had elected their own mayor (the larger the city, the more unwieldy a tool election campaigning becomes for a citizens' movement), but most mayors who received praise from urban activists were reformist mayors in cities in and near the Greater Tokyo area—in Yokohama and Kawasaki in Kanagawa prefecture, in suburban cities in Saitama and Chiba prefectures, as well as in Musashino and the cities of the Santama district of western Tokyo prefecture itself. In contrast, the urban mayors who received criticism from citizens' movement activists were conservatives from the twenty-three special municipal wards in Tokyo prefecture, where ward mayors were appointed rather than elected. To complicate the picture further, there was a reformist mayor in the Tokyo ward (Kōtō) where the most conservative citizens' movement in the entire sample was located. On the whole, though, while urban activists were not overly impressed with their local mayors, rural activists were utterly distressed with theirs.

Not only did the objective circumstances of rural and urban citizens' movement encounters with the political world differ, but the divergence between subjective citizens' movement expectations and actual experience dramatized this contrast. Rural activists, like Japan's rural population as a whole, tended to be conservative at the outset, when they believed that their group merely needed to bring its views to the attention of the conservative local government in order to have its grievances resolved. Instead, rural citizens' movements faced ostracism, official interference with their activities, and in many cases corrupt and illegal maneuvers to suppress the citizens' movements or to sidestep proper procedure so that the mayor's or governor's pet project could be presented to the public as a fait accompli as in Ōiso and Usuki. Thus rural activists usually were profoundly disappointed with local authorities.

It is extremely important to appreciate that this painful experience was equally disturbing to activists with either "democratic" or "traditional" values concerning the proper relationship between people and their leaders. To those who believed that leaders should be delegates or representatives chosen by the public to enact their wishes, the utter indifference—even hostility—which they saw in local government was intolerable, especially in view of the fact that most rural citizens' movements mobilized large pluralities, sometimes majorities, of the local community. And to the more traditional who believed that leaders should provide benevolent guidance to people in return for popular deference and humility, the behavior of local officials violated all standards of propriety, thus freeing them from any obligation to be deferent in return. One angry respondent described this sense of betrayal:

I voted for [the LDP candidate for the Diet] last time, and he won—darn it! We helped him but he wouldn't help us. I don't ever want to see his face again! He's afraid to make campaign appearances around here this time, you know. He's really heartless and cruel. (J4)

When rural activists then received help from leftist parties, from leftist assemblymen whom they had previously regarded as fanatics or cranks, and even from organized labor, they were delighted to receive this unexpected but welcome support from sources they once viewed with suspicion. Shortly after several JCP members who were helping their cause had been arrested in an antipollution demonstration, two farmers in Shibushi gave their impressions of the LDP and the JCP:

The LDP just comes in from the top, and we want to change that as much as possible. We don't want the LDP to order us around. . . . The JCP isn't so bad. . . . I really think people who go to jail aren't so bad. . . . I'd like a JCP candidate to run for mayor . . . we all think so these days. (J3)

[The LDP] only wants to help industries and people with big money. . . . I've come to think that the JCP is best of all, the most honest and sincere. (J4)

This new-found appreciation for the left probably occurred in direct proportion to the "trauma" of losing faith in conservative officials. The experience was particularly shattering to those activists who had once had intimate personal ties with the conservative establishment, either as neighborhood leaders, LDP bosses, or close friends of local officials:

I was angry because of the way the mayor [of Ōiso] seemed so bullheaded and stupid. . . . I personally went to the prefectural offices and talked with the governor. He made me so mad that I jerked him by the tie. (G1)

Our present mayor [in Ōiso] is the worst in Japan. . . . The previous mayor was so dumb he must also have been crazy, not to realize that he looked so dumb and that he did things so badly. (H1)

One respondent in Usuki was once a card-carrying member of the LDP and an LDP party boss of sorts. He took a petition containing eight hundred signatures to the LDP mayor he had helped to elect, but Mayor Adachi most unwisely told this man that he and his eight hundred friends "might as well go and die." The petitioner, shaken at this response to his first attempt to get something in return for his regular delivery of several hundred votes to the LDP in every election, withdrew from the party rolls, was censured by higher-ups in the LDP, and now takes great delight in supporting leftist candidates (K4).

The attitudes of urban activists evolved from a different set of experiences. Urban activists usually had to deal with a local establishment in which the reformists had already begun making impressive gains—either capturing the executive office or winning a substantial number (though rarely a majority) of assembly seats. Such a local government seemed to possess some sensitivity to environmental problems and often officially espoused strong antipollution policies. Thus urban activists usually expected sympathy, cooperation, and perhaps even a solution to their grievances, from local government. However, relative to these initial expectations they were usually disappointed:

It's funny for me, a socialist, to say this, but I don't really think that reformist local governments will be a quick solution to anything. . . . You find more democratic types among the reformists, but I don't think they're all so good. (K3)

Perhaps the most extreme example of conflict between a citizens' movement and a "pro" pollution reformist local government was in the city of Minamata, which had a leftist mayor for years. Because the Chisso employees' labor union was such a dominant political force within the regional labor associations and behind the leftist parties, the mayor of Minamata felt compelled to defend Chisso's interests, and from 1950 to 1957 and again after 1962, the same person served as president of the Minamata plant of Chisso and as mayor of Minamata.[21]

In congested urban areas, environmental problems are even more

21. Matsubara Haruo, *Kōgai to chiiki shakai: seikatsu to jūmin undō no shakaigaku* [Pollution and Regional Society: The Sociology of Livelihood and Residents' Movements] (Tokyo: Nihon Keizai Shimbunsha, October 1971), p. 200.

difficult to deal with than elsewhere.[22] In addition to the customary diffi-culties of assuming political responsibility for any allocation of scarce re-sources, as well as the overwhelming technological dilemmas presented by the pollution issue itself, governments must also tackle delicate re-distributive issues inherent in pollution problems. After all, environmen-tal policy is really the effort to arrive at a "just" distribution of filth, along with the associated risks and burdens. Thus the problems that con-cern urban citizens' movements present an extreme challenge to even the wisest and fairest of governments. Even a government which understands that it is now politically necessary to *attempt* to deal with these problems finds it difficult to please a citizens' movement, even one whose worries and goals it shares.

But the new reformist governments in Japan's major cities face addi-tional difficulties. Inexperienced at holding the reins of power, often de-prived of the resources and support which conservative regimes easily obtained from the national government, these new reformist govern-ments are anxious to accumulate a list of concrete achievements, to avoid embarrassment, and most of all to avoid glaring policy failures.[23] In ur-ban areas, then, reformist governments and their support organizations are in the embarrassing position of officially campaigning on behalf of citizens' movements and encouraging them in the pursuit of their objec-tives, while quietly discouraging specific movements that might discredit the reformist politicians in power.

Urban citizens' movement activists were often saddened by the equivocal or halfhearted responses they received from reformist local governments, but at the same time they sympathized with these govern-ments. Urban activists—including conservatives who were critical of re-formist local governments—all agreed that reformist local governments were much *more* cooperative than their conservative predecessors had been, and that they had achieved measurable progress in their negotia-tions with reformist local governments. Their disappointment with the left did nothing to moderate their residual anger toward conservatives, who often managed to obstruct citizens' movements even where they had experienced a relative decline in local power. For example, in the older sections of Japan's large cities, neighborhood associations below the ward level could be an important vehicle for conservative power even though they lacked formal legal authority. A Chifuren member who par-ticipated in a movement composed entirely of housewives complained:

22. Harvey Perloff, "A Framework for Dealing with the Urban Environment," in David F. Paulsen and Robert B. Denhardt, *Pollution and Public Policy: A Book of Readings* (New York: Dodd, Mead, 1973), pp. 74–90.

23. See Terry Edward MacDougall, "Political Opposition and Local Government in Japan: The Significance of Emerging Progressive Local Leadership" (Ph.D. diss. in Political Science, Yale University, 1975), pp. 279–489.

Our worst opponent was our local neighborhood association, which has power left from the feudal age and has always been in our way. . . . The sort of men [in the association] like to oppress women, so they don't appreciate our activities. They want to be great [*erai*] men, and that requires that we *not* do things. They actually do no work for the benefit of the neighborhood at all; they just eat and drink and then do what the ward government tells them to do. They don't take up people's needs and problems. . . . We've been working hard for ten years just to get the neighborhood association to leave us alone . . . but now we have succeeded where they didn't, and we can actually demand their cooperation for some things. (L1)

The scales measuring activists' satisfaction with their elected representatives,[24] shown in table 18, demonstrate that both urban and rural activists were unhappy with the quality of their local representatives,[25] although they could also single out a few whose performance was exemplary and whom they were happy to call their own. Returning to the interview transcripts to determine which activists were pleased or displeased with which representatives, we find that conservative activists directed most of their comments at conservative representatives, and reformist activists at reformist representatives. Conservative complaints invariably referred to LDP assemblymen whose behavior seemed indifferent or even irresponsible. On those few occasions when conservative activists did discuss reformist assemblymen, they did so with praise and admiration, as well as surprise.

It was the reformist activists who supplied most of the unfavorable commentary about reformist representatives, whom they accused of being too lethargic. When reformists did mention conservative assemblymen, they did so in a totally critical spirit, unless they happened to refer to one of that rare breed of antiestablishment conservatives who allied with citizens' movements. Naturally, activists who had entered the electoral arena to select one or more representatives on behalf of the environ-

---

24. Respondents were asked to describe their local representatives to the city assembly, prefectural assembly, and national Diet. From these responses were created scales of satisfaction, dissatisfaction, and net satisfaction, simply by counting the number of representatives whose conduct in office clearly pleased (or displeased) the respondents. Ambiguous or ambivalent references were excluded. The net satisfaction index was then calculated by subtracting Dissatisfaction from Satisfaction.

25. Although the local levels of government usually elect assemblymen at large, and not on the basis of districts, assemblymen tend to receive the vast majority of their votes from one particular area, and thus to "represent" the voters in that region. Called *jiban*, there is some evidence that these local power bases may be dissolving as the floating vote increases, even in local elections, although the slow and spotty occurrence of this decline is testimony in itself to the strength of the *jiban* pattern. On *jiban*, see Kurt Steiner, *Local Government in Japan* (Stanford: Stanford University Press, 1965), pp. 433–439; and Nathaniel B. Thayer, *How the Conservatives Rule Japan* (Princeton: Princeton University Press, 1969), pp. 82–110.

mental cause were understandably more satisfied with these, truly "their own," representatives than were activists who had not done so.

Summing up the general mood of disenchantment with present elected representatives and officials, one informant in Shibushi pointed out:

Our community is being ignored by everyone—mayors, governors, Diet representatives. . . . So *we* must protect our own community because no one else will do it for us. This is real self-government. I have only just begun to realize that *we* must fight to protect our *right* to govern ourselves. (J2)

Summary

Although we are unable to gauge how thoroughly citizens' movements "democratize" their members, activists were better informed and more interested in democratic values than the general population, in spite of the fact that only one-fourth of them had extensive experience in politics and as many as one-third were utter novices in politics.[26] Moreover, most learning and change in attitudes and beliefs occurred among the newcomers to protest; within this group, those who had engaged in conventional politics actually had a lot to unlearn. Similarly, "parochials" outnumbered "sophisticates," so parochialism was obviously no impediment to activism or intense feeling. The entire sample shared a highly emotional consensus on the identity of its allies (the left, especially the JCP) and its enemies (the LDP, national political institutions, and big business), and all agreed that reformist local governments, whatever their practical problems, were enlightened and energetic and that the conservative establishment was irretrievably compromised and unreliable on the pollution issue. This hostility toward political objects and activists' shared preference for the left over the right was due more to the character of the experience during citizens' movements than to personal background traits. Disillusionment was unusually sharp among activists in rural areas who had unexpectedly painful confrontations with conservative local governments unaccustomed to political challenges from their citizens. In such circumstances, the "trauma" of participation in citizens' movements had important influences on partisanship and electoral behavior, which we shall now investigate.

26. The apparent contradiction between our finding so many political amateurs among activists and Lewis's conclusion that Mishima activists had extensive background in civic and political associations and therefore that movements did not mobilize new recruits to politics is largely an artifact of sampling differences between the two surveys. Lewis excluded "mass action participants" from his sample, whereas I intentionally attempted to include "rank-and-file activists" here. See Jack G. Lewis, "Civic Protest in Mishima: Citizens' Movements and the Politics of the Environment in Contemporary Japan," in Flanagan, Steiner, and Krauss, *Political Opposition and Local Politics in Japan*, chap. 8.

VI

Movement Activists as Political Actors

PARTICIPATION IN citizens' movements was an emotionally jarring experience, which politicized activists concerning those elements of Japanese politics most intimately connected to their own citizens' movements. But did this experience function as the germ of any further change at a broader level, by affecting activists as political actors, not simply within their movements but in their roles as participants in the larger political system? In this chapter we shall investigate the impact of the citizens' movement experience on partisanship, general patterns of belief change, and voting behavior among activists.

Partisan Change

• Citizens' Movement Activists versus the General Population

Table 19 provides comparisons of party support (partisan identification in response to the question "Which party do you support?" and not actual voting habits at the polls) for both the activist sample and the general population in 1972, when interviewing took place, and in 1969 (selected as a base year because most of the activists in our sample were not yet involved in citizens' movements at that time).[1] As many other voting

1. In comparative terms, the Japanese party system is young, partisanship is weak, and voters' images of the parties lack substantive content. These facts create a methodologi-

196

and partisanship statistics also show, the entire Japanese population has been moving away from the LDP in recent years. Among the opposition parties, support for the JSP declined somewhat and support for the JCP rose dramatically. Within the general population, the most conspicuous change in party support was the unusual rise in nonsupport of any party at all.[2]

As we can see, approximately the same percentage of antipollution activists as in the general population were loyal to the LDP at the outset, and activists experienced the same move away from the LDP and also a slight increase in dissatisfaction with all the political parties taken as a whole. However, citizens' movement activists did not share the general population's tendency to remain aloof from parties; after all, they found it expedient to accept help from partisan sources willing to provide assistance. The clearest difference lay in the fact that citizens' movement activists were vastly more reformist than the general population, even at the outset of activism. Although we should attribute some of this disproportion to sampling error (for example, activists who were themselves reformists frequently mentioned that the general membership of their movement was either thoroughly mixed or predominantly conservative), citizens' movements probably *are* more reformist than the general population.

Within the reformist camp, it is noteworthy that there was such strong support among citizens' movement activists for the JCP in particular. Both the activists themselves and outside observers often expressed the fear of JCP influence within the environmental movement. Although these figures do not tell us anything about the actual patterns,

---

cal snag for any study of partisanship in Japan. We know that party identification—defined as a stable, enduring loyalty independent of occasional departures in particular elections—has tangible reality in the minds of voters in other political systems, but until researchers devise a way to learn what respondents are actually thinking when they report their "partisanship," we must accept the possibility that party identification is simply the same as one's most recent voting choice, for an unknown number of Japanese voters. Fortunately, this is not a serious problem in this study. Every member of our sample was able to name a partisan identity, whereas large percentages of the general public cannot or will not, suggesting that partisanship, whatever it is, has salience and real significance to citizens' movement activists. Although studies of party identification as an independent variable with all-encompassing explanatory powers is stymied if party identification *is* voting behavior, we are interested here in both partisanship and voting as dependent variables or consequences of activism in citizens' movements, whatever the intellectual difference or precise causal links between the two. See Scott C. Flanagan and Michael D. McDonald, "Party Identification as a Cross-National Concept: Comparing the Fit of the Party ID Model in Japan and the United States," paper presented at the annual meeting of the American Political Science Association, Washington, D.C., September 1979.

2. Several 1970s polls show that the most popular political party is no party at all, even outnumbering LDP partisans in the general public. See "Jiji seron" [Opinion on Current Affairs], *(Gekkan) Seron chōsa* 6:3 (March 1974), 80.

TABLE 19 / *Partisanship among Citizens' Movement Activists and within the General Population (in percentage)*

	General Population	Activist Sample	General Population	Activist Sample
	April 1969	Before CM	Sept. 1972	Fall 1972
Conservative identifiers	40.4	39.1	36.1	21.9
LDP	(33.4)	(34.4)	(29.5)	(17.2)
Independent	(7.0)	(4.7)	(6.6)	(4.7)
Reformist identifiers	29.2	57.8	29.0	70.3
DSP	(3.0)	(0)	(2.4)	(0)
CGP	(5.9)	(0)	(3.2)	(0)
JSP	(14.4)	(28.1)	(12.6)	(32.8)
JCP	(0.5)	(14.1)	(1.7)	(18.7)
Independent	(5.4)	(15.6)	(9.1)	(18.7)
Prefer to support no party at all	20.8	3.1	26.0	7.8
Other	9.6	0	8.8	0
Total	100.0	100.0	99.9	100.0

Source for general population: "Jiji Yoron," *(Gekkan) Seron chōsa* 1:1 (June 1969), 87; and "Jiji Yoron," *(Gekkan) Seron chōsa* 4:11 (November 1972), 72.

let alone directions, of political influence, they do indicate that the JCP has substantial opportunity to be influential. However, the movements themselves have strong incentives to resist JCP attempts to exploit its own supporters within citizens' movements, in order to maintain the allegiance of the other 80 percent of their members. Several respondents made this very point, that their group contained many JCP members and therefore tried to be careful to prevent excessive JCP influence: "We constantly had to fight the appearance that we were controlled by the JCP, because the JCP representatives in the city assembly were supplying us with information" (B1).

Table 19 demonstrates that there was an important shift in partisanship among activists during their participation in citizens' movements, and respondents themselves explained that this was entirely due to citizens' movement participation. Because the shift was all in one direction, away from the conservative party and toward the reformist parties, the 20 percent of the sample who changed their loyalties were labeled the "disillusioned switchers." "Conservative standpatters" (22% of the sample) were LDP supporters before participating in citizens' movements and remained so. "Reformist standpatters" (58% of the sample) supported the JSP, the JCP, or simply the reformist side before joining citizens' movements and continued to do so afterward. The few activists who said that they preferred to support no party at all (in table 19) were willing to indicate a preference if they had to select a party, so for simplicity they have been classified as partisans rather than as non-identifiers in the measure used below.

The reformist standpatters in our sample may be swollen in numbers because they include many recent recruits who were automatically classified as reformist standpatters if they shed their LDP loyalties *before* involvement in the particular citizens' movement in which they were sampled. Thus they were already reformist standpatters rather than switchers at the time of interviewing because one previous citizens' movement or protest experience had already converted them into reformist partisans. Although we have thus overrepresented reformists in our sample, this bias does not necessarily interfere with comparisons between reformists and conservatives, and we can also compensate for it somewhat by paying close attention to the underrepresented group of conservatives (both standpatters and switchers). One very important finding probably unaffected by oversampling of reformists is the fact that approximately half of those who joined citizens' movements as conservatives shed that loyalty as a result of the citizens' movement to become reformist identifiers instead. In fact, to the extent that we have oversampled reformist standpatters, we may thus be *underestimating* the role of citizens' movements in drawing disillusioned conservatives away from the LDP and turning them into reformists.

· Switching as a Consequence of New Learning in Citizens' Movements

In this chapter we shall investigate the respective roles of conservatives, switchers, and reformists within citizens' movements, and *why* this switching takes place. Do new attitudes and beliefs function as catalysts to cause changes in partisanship? If so, how? What difference does a change in subjective partisan affiliation really make to concrete political behavior?[3]

First of all, in order to learn why half of the conservative identifiers who joined citizens' movements broke the faith, we need to know what switchers think about pollution. Table 20 shows that on indicators

3. "Switching" as used here should not be confused with the inconsistencies in party identification and intended and actual voting choices found in the 1967 and 1976 election panel surveys in Japan. According to the activists' own testimony, the switching in this study, a comparatively large shift in a uniform direction, clearly represents a conscious and deliberate choice made over a period of one to two years in response to participation in citizens' movements. In contrast, the switching discovered in the national election surveys, whose pre- and postelection waves were only one month apart, probably represents random "noise" or "vibrations" among the most indecisive and politically indifferent segment of the electorate. Conversely, the standpatters in this study have preserved a stable indentification over a period of years with respect to a series of different elections, and not simply for the one-month duration of a single election campaign. See Flanagan and McDonald, "Party Identification as a Cross-National Concept."

TABLE 20 / *Attitudes and Beliefs Associated with Partisan Change*

	Conservative	Switcher	Reformist	Total
Views on Pollution				
Pollution Emotion Index				
Low (11)	36	23	8	17
Medium low (13)	29	38	11	20
Medium (14)	7	8	32	22
Medium high (19)	29	31	30	30
High (7)	0	0	19	11
Tau-b = .334, p < .001				
Pollution Generality Index				
Low (12)	64	15	3	19
Medium (26)	29	76	32	41
High (26)	7	8	65	41
Tau-b = .625, p < .001				
Pollution Concern Index				
Low (1)	0	0	3	2
Medium low (12)	43	31	5	19
Medium (21)	21	38	35	33
Medium high (24)	29	31	43	38
High (6)	7	0	14	9
Tau-b = .274, p < .001				
Motives and Goals				
Orientation to Pollution Problems				
Prevention only (30)	50	55	67	60
Mixed motivation (12)	8	31	26	24
Experience only (8)	42	8	7	16
Tau-b = −.203, p < .025				
Individual Motives				
Selfish (37)	79	62	32	58
Altruistic (27)	21	38	68	42
Tau-b = .228, p < .005				

of concern with pollution (the emotion, generality, and total concern indices introduced in chapter IV), switchers were considerably more alarmed than conservative standpatters, though not quite as much as the reformist standpatters. Theoretically, there are three different causal paths that would explain this relationship between the act of switching itself and attitudes toward pollution (or between switching and anything else, for that matter). Perhaps partisan switching raised consciousness with respect to pollution and thus induced changes in beliefs about it and related matters. Or perhaps activists who acquired certain views about pollution from citizens' movement participation eventually found conservative partisanship untenable and switched as a result. Or finally, we can postulate the existence of a third underlying dimension that could have caused changes in both partisanship and other traits. Although statistical methods of causal inference and path analysis have not been used

TABLE 20 / *continued*

	Conservative	*Switcher*	*Reformist*	*Total*
Political Beliefs and Attitudes				
How did your opinions change as a result of the movement? *				
Learned about politics	29	54	46	44
Grew disillusioned in government	21	77	27	36
Ideas substantively changed	36	17	30	28
Became radicalized	14	31	24	23
Grew hopeful about social change	0	8	14	9
Average number of changes	1.64	2.69	1.89	2.00
Political Hostility Scales $[-3, +3]$ †				
Attitude to right	$-.29$	-2.38	-2.41	-1.94
Attitude to left	$-.57$	$+.69$	$+.84$	$+.50$
Net preference for left	$-.14$	$+1.54$	$+1.62$	$+1.22$
Hostility to political objects	$-.43$	$-.85$	$-.79$	$-.72$
Reliance on Marxism				
None at all (19)	86	23	11	30
Some interest, no reliance (20)	14	54	30	31
Substantial reliance (14)	0	23	30	22
Doctrinaire (11)	0	0	30	17
Tau-b = .509, p < .001				
Totals	100	100	100	100
	(14)	(13)	(37)	(64)

Note: Vertical percentaging
  * Cell entry here is percentage of respondents falling in a particular category of partisan change who reported the changes in ideas described in the left margin.
  † Cell entry here is mean score on each hostility scale for each category of partisan change. The range for each scale is $[-3, +3]$, with negative scores representing hostility, positive scores representing favorable attitudes.

here (our data do not really satisfy the assumptions of such methods), a bit of careful thinking and examination of available evidence should lead to an explanation.

The first possibility—that switching precipitates other attitude changes—seems highly unlikely at least as a primary explanation, because it implies that partisan switching took place for no reason in particular, but that once it happened, switching punched a mental button that permitted the subject to advance to a new threshold of understanding with respect to the pollution issue. This seems too mechanistic, too much like passing "go" in Monopoly. Reversing the causal chain makes a good deal more sense. That is, those who developed a deep interest in pollution found the whole issue so important to them, so central a part of their belief system, that it displaced prior loyalties that were inconsistent with it, and a switch in partisanship was the automatic result.

As evidence, we should take note of activists' motives and goals in mobilizing around the pollution issue. Table 20 shows that switchers appeared to be in a transitional state, somewhere between the conservative standpatters they left behind and the reformists they later joined. They resembled the conservative standpatters with respect to the degree of self-interest underlying their activism; they were not nearly as altruistic as the reformist standpatters in their objectives. On the other hand, they closely resembled the reformists in being primarily concerned about prevention. Capable of fighting a threat which they had to imagine in the abstract, switchers did not need the direct stimulus of personal experience with pollution to push them into citizens' movements, whereas the conservative standpatters were more likely to require powerful incentives and even painful experiences with pollution to convince them to protest.

Switchers' surprising concern for preventing pollution, even in the absence of direct encounters with it, indicates a "higher" level of consciousness than is shown by the conservative standpatters. Furthermore, because this preventive orientation concerned activists' motives and goals at the time of joining citizens' movements, by definition it preceded partisan switching that resulted from participation in citizens' movements. The fact that measures of involvement and commitment to the pollution issue varied with partisanship also signifies the centrality of the issue to switchers' belief systems. In terms of our three competing explanatory models, these findings lend support to the notion that high concern in the subject of pollution preceded and contributed to partisan change, rather than the reverse. Still more persuasive evidence is available in the form of activists' own reports of how their beliefs changed because of citizens' movements:

Before, I was a supporter of the LDP, but finding that the LDP representatives wouldn't have anything to do with us but that the JSP and JCP gave us lots of help and made the group's success possible has made me change my mind, and now I support the reformist side. . . . Right now I feel very confused, very angry about the LDP, but unable to settle on the JSP or JCP as a preferred choice, although I think the people in the reformist parties tend to be a lot more honorable. (B2)

According to the third section of table 20, what activists claimed to have learned from the citizens' movement experience had a clear and unmistakable effect on their partisan affiliations. The switchers were more likely than any other subset of the sample to report having changed their thinking because of citizens' movements. Their average rate of 2.69 changes per person readily distinguished them from the standpatters on either end of the political spectrum. Moreover, these new ideas consisted in large part of new notions about politics and particularly of disappointment, disillusionment, and radical change. Obviously what the switchers learned during citizens' movement participation led clearly and directly to a reversal of party loyalties. As one urban housewife, a former political innocent, reported: "Before, I was for the LDP. . . . I am embarrassed about being for the JCP nowadays [laugh]. I never dreamed I would ever be voting for the Communists" (F2).

This reversal of loyalties is very clear when we examine the relationship between partisan change and political hostility as measured by the scales introduced in chapter V. A net preference for the left (on the Net Left Scale) was more closely associated with reformist partisan preference than any other single measure in the survey, with Tau-b = .461, p < .001. This relationship is also visible in table 20, where there is a consistent unidirectional change in the mean scores on each of the political attitude scales, as one moves along the rows of scores from conservatives to switchers to reformists. Among the standpatters, for whom partisan affiliation remained constant, partisanship served as a filter through which the citizens' movement experience could be interpreted. But among the switchers, the political attitudes and beliefs acquired during citizens' movements obviously played a part in engineering the partisan change and lowered the threshold at which a change in political loyalties became possible.

Conservative standpatters formed a distinct and conspicuous subgroup in their pattern of scores on the hostility scales. They were the only activists who were not enraged at the right, being able to summon up only a faintly negative attitude in the form of a mean score of −.29. Similarly, they were the only activists who had critical (as opposed to merely neutral or ambivalent) views of the left, and as a consequence a net preference for the right over the left. If we go beyond mean scores to explore further the individual scores of conservative standpatters, we find that in fact only seven of the fourteen had a net preference for the right over the left. These rare conservative diehards who remained more favorable toward the right than the left were all to be found among urban residents who faced a leftist local establishment and whose conservative political loyalties could be reconciled with a protest stance and thus survive the citizens' movement experience.

Thus half of the conservative standpatters were actually more favorable to the left than to their own end of the political spectrum, at least where the pollution issue was concerned. One such respondent (I5) clarified his views: with respect to pollution and other domestic issues, the LDP was unresponsive, inhumane, and callous, because of its unfortunate dependence on industry. But because foreign policy issues and the maintenance of Japan's American alliance were also important to him, he felt that he had to continue supporting the LDP at the national level, and thus he remained a conservative. The citizens' movement experience had not changed his partisan affiliation, but it had given him a positive image of the left. The fact that only half of the conservative standpatters could continue to view the conservative establishment favorably is an impressive statement of how very poor the LDP image is within citizens' movements as a whole.

Stated differently, the distinct and unusual attitude profile of the conservative standpatters signified that disillusioned switchers became almost indistinguishable in their political attitudes (at least on the pollution issue) from their reformist colleagues in citizens' movements, retaining no resemblance to their former conservative associates. Although the switchers appeared "transitional" in many respects, in this one sector they became full-fledged reformist identifiers, and the partisan identity that "counted" among these individuals was their new one.

Although switchers acquired a positive attitude toward the left in the absolute sense, they were by no means infatuated with the objects of their new political loyalties, nor did they become socialist ideologues. Two activists explained their support for reformist parties:

I resolved not to vote for the LDP, who are absolutely no good. . . . I have left the LDP and am now voting mostly for the JCP, although sometimes I vote for other reformist parties too. . . . But I do not at all want the Communists to win; I would hate to live in a country like Russia. But I think it would be good for the opposition to increase a good deal and make the LDP nervous so they'll try harder. The idea is to control the LDP by scrutinizing and frightening them. (B5, a switcher)

I have a policy never to vote for the majority party. . . . but I am definitely not a communist. But the LDP is negligent and tyrannical, and a majority that powerful can do anything and can afford to act selfishly without thinking of the people. So I want to decrease LDP strength. . . . But it may not help to increase reformist representation. I'm voting reformist only because it's bad for the LDP to have been in power alone so long. The reformists may not be any better when they're in power. (L1, a reformist standpatter who switched before her 1972 citizens' movement activities)

Citizens' movements drew their members leftward in terms of party affiliation but not in terms of ideological belief. The explanations of pollution as a product of capitalism and industrial society which circulated most widely among intellectuals and professional environmentalists in Japan contained many Marxist ingredients, although there was variety in these explanations, and not all owed the same debt to various schools of Marxism. Remarks made during the entire course of the interview were coded to indicate how much use respondents made of Marxist explanations, shown in table 20. Although there was a direct and obvious relationship between reliance on Marxism and reformist partisanship, the only doctrinaire Marxists were long-standing reformists, and comprised only 30 percent of them at that. Only 23 percent of the switchers relied on these explanations to any extent. The primary difference between conservative standpatters and switchers was that while the former knew

TABLE 21 / *Background Factors Associated with Partisan Change*

	Conservative	Switcher	Reformist	Total
Socioeconomic Traits				
Residence				
Urban (40)	71	46	65	63
Rural (24)	29	54	35	38
Labor Union Membership				
Not a member (48)	93	100	59	75
Unionist (16)	7	0	41	25
Tau-b = .373, p < .001				
Political Background				
Previous Political Experience				
Innocent (22)	43	46	27	34
Conventional experience only (15)	50	15	16	23
Protest experience only (11)	0	38	16	17
Gladiator (16)	7	0	41	25
Previous Protest Experience				
Newcomer (37)	93	62	43	58
Veteran (27)	7	38	57	42
Tau-b = .374, p < .001				
Level of Political Interest				
Local politics (21)	64	42	19	33
Prefectural politics (9)	7	42	8	14
National politics (23)	7	8	57	37
All levels (10)	21	8	16	16
Tau-b = .338, p < .001				
Open-mindedness				
Sophistication Index				
Sophisticates (24)	14	31	49	38
Mixed (16)	14	38	24	25
Isolates (24)	71	31	27	38
Tau-b = −.311, p < .001				
Totals	100%	100%	100%	100%
	(14)	(13)	(37)	(64)

Note: Vertical percentaging

very little about Marxist explanations of the pollution problem, the latter were conversant with these arguments.

· Underlying Causes of Switching and Belief Change

Learning acquired during the citizens' movement experience—new beliefs and attitudes, as well as hostile views of political institutions—had an obvious and direct impact on partisanship. But there remains the last of our explanatory models, the possibility that a third variable actually caused both the switching and the belief change explored above.

Such a causally prior factor might consist of activists' socioeconomic background, their political experience, or their psychological qualities. Table 21 displays the tabulations between partisan change and several indicators in each of these three categories.

Socioeconomic factors readily come to mind as possible explanations of switching and of belief change. Two prevalent concomitants of reformist political sympathies which emerge from most survey research on political opinion in Japan are labor union affiliations and urban residence. However, neither of these dimensions had the expected relationship with partisan change in our sample. Although many of the reformist standpatters had records of labor union membership, *none* of the switchers were in unions.

We might still expect to find that switchers were from urban areas, in view of the fact that the most dramatic recent increases in support for the leftist parties have been in large metropolitan areas. It is often speculated that the growing independent or nonconservative vote comes from recent migrants to urban areas, whose new surroundings expose them to stimuli directing them toward the opposition parties.[4] However, not only was there no such relationship, but the switchers in our sample were more likely to come from rural areas than the standpatters of either variety, almost certainly a result of the unpleasant encounters between citizens' movements and the local conservative establishment which were inevitable in rural Japan (see chapter V). It is ironic that the development projects originally designed to win rural support crucial to the LDP majority in the Diet threatened instead to erode the LDP's support base in some of its most secure strongholds.

Inquiring into other background factors that could create a predisposition among future switchers to turn to the reformist parties, we find some useful clues in indicators of previous political experience. Switchers were just as likely to be innocent of previous political experience of all kinds (other than voting, of course) as were the conservatives who stood pat, but among those who did have some sort of previous political experiences, there were significant differences. Experienced conservative standpatters had primarily conventional electoral experience only, whereas experienced switchers were more frequently involved in previous protests, not conventional politicking. Among conservative

4. Aggregate data by voting district definitely supports the notion that population movement increases support for the left. See Bradley Richardson, "Stability and Change in Japanese Voting Behavior, 1958–1972," *Journal of Asian Studies* 36:4 (August 1977), 683–685. It is usually assumed that in-migrants are the source of increased opposition voting in cities, but James W. White concludes from his data on migrants that the political consequences of urbanization are much more complicated. See *Political Implications of Cityward Migration: Japan as an Exploratory Test Case* (Beverly Hills: Sage Professional Papers 01-038, vol. 4, 1973), pp. 38–49.

standpatters, all but one were involved in protest for the very first time through citizens' movements, whereas 38 percent of the switchers (and a majority of the reformists) had engaged in protest at least once before. We may conclude, therefore, that conservative loyalties were difficult to maintain while protesting against conservative policies and institutions, and that the more often activists found themselves in this position, the more tenuous their conservative affiliations became. Clearly, then, prior exposure to protest (but not to politics-as-usual) predisposed certain conservatives to become switchers.

Another feature of activists' attention to political phenomena helps us determine why some conservatives switched while others stood pat. The standpatters had the most circumscribed political horizons, being almost exclusively interested in local politics. The switchers were somewhat less parochial, with 42 percent interested primarily in prefectural politics, and were thus more like reformists, who were largely interested in national politics.

A final possible source of "prior causation" was psychological makeup—the possibility that switchers differed from conservative standpatters in possessing an open-minded quality, the flexibility to absorb new information and, when necessary, new loyalties to match. Although I did not have access to activists' personalities and did not use psychological measures in the interviewing, the "sophistication index" introduced in chapter V seems to have something to do with activists' cognitive capacities. If so, then the rather strong association between "sophistication" on that index and partisan change in the direction of reformist loyalties shown in the last section of table 21 supplies evidence that switchers *were* more susceptible to change than the conservative standpatters. Whether the sophistication index was related to individual psychological dimensions or only to the social and motivational traits that actually composed the index, we should remember that the items in the index all referred to characteristics which activists either brought with them to activism or displayed very early in the citizens' movement experience. Thus the sophistication of the switchers relative to the conservative standpatters certainly means that predispositions of some sort did exist among those destined to switch later on.

In conclusion, then, it should be clear that switching was a result both of activists' personal susceptibilities and of the actual citizens' movement experience they encountered. It was a direct result of the new attitudes and beliefs on the pollution issue acquired through citizens' movement participation, and it was an indirect result of personal qualities ("sophistication") and the political background (exposure to prior protest, and moderately broad interest in political events beyond the local arena) which differentiated between switchers-to-be and conservative standpatters at the outset of citizens' movement participation.

Conservative Leadership

If we extrapolate on the basis of the preceding evidence and arguments, then the leftward leanings of citizens' movement activists are directly proportional to the intimacy of their involvement with citizens' movements, and more specifically to the brutality of their confrontation with Japan's conservative establishment. It would then be axiomatic to conclude that citizens' movements are indeed dominated, even controlled, by the left, the frantic disclaimers of citizens' movement supporters and the left alike notwithstanding. If citizens' movements are really leftist front groups, as their LDP critics and the targets of citizens' movements like to think, then we should expect to find that conservative identifiers within citizens' movements fall into the lower ranks of the movement, while the leadership positions are monopolized by leftists.

This makes a neat and tidy argument, but it is not true.[5] As table 22 instantly reveals, none of the disillusioned switchers in the sample occupied positions of leadership, whereas 50 percent of the conservative standpatters—an enormously disproportionate number—were leaders of their movements. Conversely, only 36 percent of the citizens' movement leaders in our sample were reformists, but *all* of the rest (64%) were conservative standpatters. How can we reconcile the existence of conservative domination with the customary citizens' movement stance of opposition vis-à-vis conservative local government (even in Tokyo, citizens' movements usually had more trouble with conservatives at the ward level than with reformist officials at the metropolitan level), and with activists' hostility toward conservative reference groups?

Our analysis must consider two problems. First, why are so many movements led by conservatives (or, conversely, why do conservatives gravitate toward the upper ranks of citizens' movements)? And second, how do these conservative leaders become deeply involved in citizens' movements while maintaining an attachment to the party they are protesting? To begin with, citizens' movements place great store by their claim to political neutrality, for the success of the movement and for the sake of their own political integrity. They must convince their opponents and the community around them that they are not what their critics like to think—tools of the leftist opposition—but represent something much larger and more serious. Moreover, citizens' movements must assure their own members that they will preserve neutrality within the group— that leftists in the movement will refrain from proselytizing—in order to

---

5. I have discussed the phenomenon of conservative citizens' movement leadership in "Political Socialization through Citizens' Movements," chap. 7 (pp. 35–39) in Scott Flanagan, Kurt Steiner, and Ellis S. Krauss, *Political Opposition and Local Politics in Japan: Electoral Trends, Citizens' Movements, and Progressive Administrations* (Princeton: Princeton University Press, 1979).

TABLE 22 / *Characteristics of Citizens' Movement Leadership*

	Rank & File	Officers	Leaders	Total
Partian Change		*Percentage*		
Conservative standpatters	36	14	50	100
Disillusioned switchers	54	46	0	100
Reformist standpatters	62	27	12	100
Tau-b = −.242, p < .0025				
Previous Political Experience				
Political innocents	77	23	0	100
Protest experience only	45	55	0	100
Conventional experience only	33	27	40	100
Political gladiators	50	19	31	100
Total	55	28	17	100
Political Hostility				
Attitude toward right	−2.20	−2.28	− .55	−1.94
Attitude toward left	+ .60	+ .61	0	+ .50
Net preference for left	+1.40	+1.44	+ .27	+1.22
Hostility to political objects	− .80	− .80	− .27	− .72

maintain the allegiance of members (including many reformist partisans) who do not want to be part of an obstructionist radical movement. Finally, citizens' movements, particularly those operating in hostile environments where confrontation and conflict are not quite acceptable, need as spokesperson and figurehead a socially respectable community leader, who is willing to entertain ideas on their merits, to challenge conventional ideas about Japanese economy and society, and to encourage creative and innovative tactics. Even when many citizens' movement members are frightened about open confrontation with established institutions or about unfamiliar methods, a leader who inspires confidence in the group because of other personal attributes can authenticate a movement's claim to decency and persuade both the surrounding environment and potential recruits to the movement that its objectives as well as its methods are reasonable. In traditionally conservative areas, the presence of a socially respectable leader who is personally capable of challenging his establishment cohorts on the basis of issues can be a critical catalyst in producing a strong citizens' movement.

Another reason for conservative leadership of citizens' movements is that veterans of protest and reformist partisans do not have a monopoly on political expertise. Protest was not nearly as important a qualification for citizens' movement leadership as conventional political experience was (see table 22). The vast bulk (77%) of political innocents, whether conservative or reformist, remained at rank-and-file levels. Those with a bit of protest experience did drift into the upper echelon, and protest experience affected beliefs about pollution and politics (see above). However, protest experience alone was not enough to create a citizens' movement leader, particularly if the movement needed to learn how to question and criticize government policy, to draft its own legislation, or to propose alternative development plans. Rather, the necessary and sufficient background criterion was familiarity with conventional politics.

Nor did reformists with experience in labor unions accrue any special advantages in seeking leadership of citizens' movements. Instead, those with social skills acquired through a multitude of nonpolitical social groups (PTA, women's groups, hobby clubs, professional or occupational associations, etc.) had much more organizational ability to offer citizens' movements. Such a background was closely associated with the tendency to gravitate into leadership positions in citizens' movements (Tau-b = .328, p<.001). Just as the leaders of protest movements elsewhere must be capable of appealing to four different clienteles or constituencies (movement members, the media, third parties from whom the movement receives aid, and those with the power to grant victory to the movement),[6] the maverick conservatives who lead many Japanese citizens' movements clearly fulfill this need with their respectability, skills, and useful knowledge of conservative local politics.

The question then becomes why there were conservatives willing to lead protest movements in an assault on their compatriots in the local establishment, and how citizens' movements found them. More perplexing, why did such persons often turn out to be motive forces in the creation of a citizens' movement? First, because of the enormity of environmental disruption in Japan, because pollution does not select its victims according to their partisan preferences, and because there are many reasons for even the most traditional conservative to object to pollution (the much-touted Japanese love of nature, affection for agrarian as opposed to industrial values, etc.), even some conservatives with strong loyalties to the LDP were capable of objecting to LDP policies at times. Naturally, loyal conservatives who became protest leaders were made of tougher stuff than those who were too docile to raise their voices in objection to party policy or to higher authorities. All of the conservative leaders of groups in this sample were strong personalities, with a conspicuous streak of independence vis-à-vis other community leaders.

They also tended to be extremely well educated, with a degree from a prewar university as a rule, a credential held only by a rarified group of older Japanese. Thus they were easily capable of cognitive manipulations permitting them to differentiate between conservative principles and con-

6. Michael Lipsky, "Protest as a Political Resource," *American Political Science Review* 62:4 (December 1968), 1144–1158.

servative politicians, or between the national LDP and the local branch, retaining affection for the former while reviling the latter. As table 22 shows, citizens' movement leaders shared the attitudes shown by their followers in feeling hostility toward the right and residual preference for the left. Dissecting the leaders' scores on the hostility scales in order to examine attitudinal components (not shown) indicates that the citizens' movement leaders reserved their greatest hostility for the LDP itself. Nonetheless, this hostility was very muted and restrained in comparison with the rest of the activists, reflecting the cognitive dilemma of citizens' movement leaders who maintained conservative affiliations and simultaneously disapproved of the conservative establishment with which they had to contend.

Alternate Paths of Change

The picture that emerges tells us a good deal about the changes in attitude that can be attributed to the activist experience, but it is necessary to fall back on social psychological theory to understand why change occurs. Theories of cognitive consistency posit that human beings desire consistency in their belief systems, and that they impose organization on their beliefs according to identifiable rules of psycho-logic.[7]

7. Growing out of an interest in applied psychology in the possibility of correcting false prejudices and stereotypes, the earliest models of cognitive consistency (Heider's balance theory, Osgood and Tannenbaum's congruity model, and others) assigned positive and negative signs to objects, discussed "valences" and "bonding" between objects, and even used matrix algebra or least squares solutions in order to seek mathematical laws that might predict attitude change. The early models applied only to simple combinations of attitudes and reference objects, necessarily omitting factors that were undoubtedly important in real, as opposed to hypothetical, minds. The simple models were easily tested, but they were also easily contradicted and therefore very weak as explanations of actual attitude change or as theoretical approximations of the processes that actually occur in the human mind. Leon Festinger then constructed a more comprehensive but more loosely defined theory of "cognitive dissonance." Generally recognized as a significant improvement, both plausible and powerful as an explanation, Festinger's theory is *so* flexible that it can be used to predict and explain almost any actual case of change or non-change. As a result, it is also criticized for being virtually unfalsifiable (or somewhat tautological).

Some critics also disagree with the basic assumption of consistency theory that humans seek consistency (or at least with the idea that this is a psychological compulsion rather than a consequence of social training), and suggest as an alternative the possibility of a curiosity or exploratory drive. But it is also reasonable to assume both—that people may well be curious and interested in change, and that they also want to make sense out of what they find. See Arthur R. Cohen, *Attitude Change and Social Influence* (New York: Basic Books, 1964), especially pp. 62–80; Jack W. Brehm and Arthur R. Cohen, *Explorations in Cognitive Dissonance* (New York: Wiley, 1962); Leon Festinger, *A Theory of Cognitive Dissonance* (Stanford: Stanford University Press, 1957), especially chapters on the role of social support, pp. 177–259; and Shel Feldman, *Cognitive Consistency: Motivational Antecedents and Behavioral Consequents* (New York: Academic Press, 1966), especially chapters by McGuire and Pepitone.

When confronted with dissonant or inconsistent information, people are forced to make some sort of change in the existing belief system: to revise existing beliefs so as to accommodate the new dissonant one, to make existing beliefs more complex through differentiation and compartmentalization so that they can be maintained for the most part but can now accommodate the dissonant belief, to distort or warp the dissonant element so that it can be absorbed without affecting existing beliefs, or finally to reject the dissonant element outright. Cognitive consistency theories would suggest that the citizens' movement activists who changed their ideas or partisanship were those who *had* to change them in order to understand and interpret the activist experience: Why had pollution arisen? Why had they been singled out as its victims? Why did other members of the community ostracize them for their concern instead of sharing it? Why did local leaders become difficult to approach or uninterested in lending aid to upstanding and responsible citizens such as themselves? And why did the methods of influence that they had counted on fail to work? For many activists, the citizens' movement experience constituted a collective intellectual adventure in search of new ideas and arguments which could explain their circumstances and suggest alternative tactics and satisfactory solutions to them. The particular arguments or explanations adopted by various activists would of course be influenced by several factors: the unique case history of their own citizens' movement, the ideas that percolated through their own circle of associates in the citizens' movement, and the intellectual sophistication or cognitive resources of different individuals—that is, the extent to which they could draw upon already existing beliefs to explain what they saw, and the cognitive acrobatics they could perform to maintain a comfortable level of cognitive consistency.

One ingredient in determining whether and how belief change took place in the minds of individual activists was their susceptibility to the packaged explanations made available by the respective political parties. The LDP's difficult position as the ruling party, which would inevitably be held responsible for existing problems, was to stress two inconsistent points: pollution was not a serious or widespread problem, and (for those who did not accept *that* argument) the government was trying to do as much as possible to solve it. The conservative party thus wanted to minimize the significance and breadth of pollution and to defuse it as a political issue by regarding each outbreak as an atypical accident, certainly not a symptom of any fatal flaws in the basic structure of society. Rather than accept blame for pollution, which the LDP argued was common to most industrial societies, the LDP held the view that only wealthy societies could afford to devote scarce resources to preventing pollution, and only under LDP leadership would Japan be able to continue rapid economic growth.[8] Although such a view obviously meshes with the self-interest of the LDP as the ruling party, the solutions to environmental problems it recommends have respectable advocates elsewhere also.[9]

For contrasting but equally pragmatic reasons, it was in the interest of the opposition parties to play up the pollution problem and to blame it on the LDP whenever possible. Thus the JSP and JCP interpretations of pollution resembled those of Japan's professional environmental spokesmen, viewing pollution problems as one composite phenomenon rather than as a collection of atypical, isolated industrial accidents, and pointing to the possibilities of environmental holocaust.[10] Furthermore, they argued that rapid growth would exacerbate the problem instead of providing the means to solve it, and a real solution would require thorough changes in the fundamental structures of society. Naturally, major changes could not be expected to come from the political party that benefited from the status quo, but only from those parties without a stake in the institutions and social patterns that allowed pollution to proliferate unabated. The opposition parties would then proceed to argue that they were also ideologically suited to the task of reshaping society because of their holistic approach to problems.

Naturally, preexisting partisan loyalties would create some inclination to adopt the encapsulated, distilled explanations offered by one's own party. But for citizens' movement activists, by definition already upset and angry about a local pollution issue, the opposition's arguments would appear more realistic and persuasive, though also unpleasant and frightening. The analyses of pollution which prevailed in our sample, dis-

8. For the LDP platform on pollution at the time of this survey, see Jiyūminshutō, *Kōgai to seiji—sumiyoi kankyō wo tsukuru tame ni* [Pollution and Politics—In Order to Build a More Pleasant Environment] (Tokyo, 1971). See also Kankyō hozen kyōkai, *Kōgai nenkan 1972* [Pollution Yearbook 1972] (Tokyo, May 1972), pp. 445–466. The official government view at the time is contained in *Kōgai hakusho 1971* [White Paper on Pollution 1971] (Tokyo: Ōkurashō Insatsukyoku, July 1971); and Kankyōchō, *Kankyō hakusho 1972* [White Paper on the Environment 1972] (Tokyo: Ōkurashō Insatsukyoku, June 1972).

9. Two serious works written in an attempt to counter the Club of Rome's Limits to Growth study, which warned that inaction now on environmental problems would eventually bring affluence as we know it to a sudden halt, are Wilfred Beckermann, *Two Cheers for the Affluent Society: A Spirited Defense of Economic Growth* (New York: St. Martin's Press, 1974); and Herman Kahn, William Brown, and Leon Martel, *The Next 200 Years: A Scenario for America and the World* (New York: Morrow, 1976).

10. For the JSP and JCP positions on pollution in the early 1970s, see Nihon shakaitō kōgai tsuihō undō hombu, *Jūmin no kōgai hakusho: inochi to kurashi wo okasu mono e no kokuhatsu* [The People's White Paper on Pollution: An Indictment of those who are infringing on our future and our lives] (Tokyo: Shakai Shimpo, October 1970); and *Kōgai nenkan 1972*, pp. 441–445, on the JSP. On the JCP platform, see "Jūmin undō wo kangaeru" [Thinking about Residents' Movements], *Bunka hyōron* 122 (October 1971); and *Kōgai nenkan 1972*, pp. 446–449.

Figure 2. Paths of Belief Change

	Reformist Sympathies		Conservative Sympathies	
	\	outset of citizens' movement		/
			leader & officer	rank & file
	reformist	disillusioned	conservative	conservative
	standpatters	switchers	standpatters	standpatters
Average Number of	(n = 37)	(n = 13)	(n = 9)	(n = 5)
Changes in Ideas	1.89	2.69	1.78	1.40
% reporting disappointment	27%	77%	18%	20%
Sophistication score [−6, +6]	+ .73	− .69	− .89	−3.60
Net Attitude to Left [−3, +3]	+1.62	+1.54	− .39	+ .30
Resulting Belief Set:	pessimism about pollution		optimism about pollution	
	optimism about civic action		pessimism about civic action	
	high individual efficacy		low individual efficacy	
		conclusion of citizens' movement		

cussed in chapter IV, drew largely upon the opposition parties' views. But we have also just seen that citizens' movements contained important pockets of resistance to the temptation to fall into step behind the opposition parties, in that some activists managed to become deeply involved in citizens' movements without becoming excessively enamored of the opposition parties. Therefore, in addition to partisan predispositions and the objective congruence between party platforms and activists' perceptions of their own circumstances, activists' ability to integrate new information into their belief systems—in short, their own cognitive capacities—also influenced their outlook.

There would appear to be two major paths of belief change, originating far apart but gradually moving closer together. Figure 2 displays these paths in simplified graphic form, along with empirical evidence. The length of each path is intended to be directly proportional to the extent of an activist's "cognitive crisis," and consequently to the extent of cognitive manipulations required to resolve inconsistency. First, there is the path taken by most of the reformist standpatters. As reformists at the outset they were accustomed to being "out," to having unanswered grievances, and to having little influence on social affairs. Upset about the pollution issue, they joined the antipollution movement, albeit with low expectations about their ability to have any impact or to succeed in achieving their objectives. Equipped through activism with a reasonable amount of information and awareness of pollution as a general problem, they developed ambitious goals beyond the mere protection of their own health and property. Through activism, these people were pleasantly surprised by the methods they used, by the utility of individual efforts, and by the modicum of success they achieved. Nonetheless, this encouragement and optimism about the possibility of using citizens' movements to have an impact on society did not give them exaggerated hopes for solving the pollution problem. Aware of the technological difficulties, of the sweeping changes in industrial management and investment priorities that would be needed to make major improvements in the situation, these activists remained relatively pessimistic about environmental cleanup. Receptive to the dire warnings issued by environmental experts, they did not consider the job done even when their own movements succeeded.

Another group of activists underwent almost the reverse experience. Largely conservative at the outset, these people needed compelling threats and incentives to push them toward social activism and protest against a conservative establishment. As conservatives who had never before been unhappy with the state of affairs or with the government policy, they assumed it would not be difficult to exert influence, and they had naively high expectations that their social and political connections would be useful and that their wishes would be respected because, after all, they were civilized adults and not helmeted troublemakers. These hopes were quickly shattered, and some were finally forced to go to court as a last resort. Nonetheless, they managed to do rather well in the end— not nearly as well as they had once hoped, and not nearly as easily as they had once expected, but they finally did achieve some of their immediate objectives. These were people who had defined their problems in very narrow terms at the outset, and they were largely preoccupied with their own self-interest. Once these narrow aims were satisfied, they considered their work to be successful.

However, this second group followed a path with two forks in it, which permitted those who traveled it to end up at three different destinations. Those who took the first fork and traveled the shortest distance, signifying the least cognitive change, were the conservative standpatters who were only marginally involved in citizens' movements and managed to insulate themselves from dissonant experiences. They went through little ideational change, either because they could tolerate high levels of cognitive inconsistency by failing to notice the inconsistency itself or because they absorbed only those new ideas which could fit into an unaltered original belief system. These people did not learn much about the overall pollution issue, and remained uninvolved and unexcited about pollution problems other than their own. As they were relatively isolated from the currents in the antipollution movement, their attitudes toward pollution changed only in that they became somewhat disillusioned with the conservative party and its leaders, as well as with other features of the political system, but without severing their loyalties.

A second group of conservatives went further along this path of "cognitive crisis and change," only just stopping short of the point at which their loyalties to the conservative party would have snapped. They became intimately involved in citizens' movements, often at the leadership level, learned more about pollution as a general problem, and gradually developed high standards of performance against which to measure their movement's activities and the response of local authorities. In comparison with these new higher standards, they were extremely unhappy with the conservative party and upset about the violations of law and the unethical conduct that they gradually discovered in local government. These conservatives compartmentalized, differentiated, and refined their old beliefs so that they could accommodate new information and simultaneously protect portions of their conservative loyalties, thus removing the contradictions between their roles as pillars of the conservative community and as citizens' movement protesters, all without too much cognitive strain. Hence we have the phenomenon of deeply involved conservative citizens' movement leaders who maintained loyalties to the LDP in the abstract while working energetically for the defeat of individual members of the local LDP establishment and their replacement by citizens' movement candidates.

Finally, a third group of conservatives who joined citizens' movements traveled the greatest distance and actually crossed the boundary of their conservative loyalties, turning into reformist partisans. They developed a higher sense of individual efficacy and optimism about civic action than the other activists who joined citizens' movements as conservative partisans. These switchers resembled the conservative citizens' movement leaders in attitude change quite a bit, the major difference being that they did not have such a fully developed web of personal and institutional loyalties to the LDP, individual LDP politicians, and other groups that supported the LDP. Instead of resolving cognitive strain by complicating and differentiating their belief systems, they threw out the single ingredient that created inconsistency—their conservative affiliation—and replaced it with reformist partisanship.

Electoral Behavior

· Voting

We have established that participation in citizens' movements did change partisan loyalties as well as a variety of attitudes and beliefs about both pollution and politics, but the acid test remains—did these hostile political attitudes and partisan changes matter in elections?

To make this observation, I constructed one measure of voting consistency and another to record campaign activism, both based on responses to inquiries as to how activists had voted in recent elections at several levels of government—in the December 1969 House of Representatives election and in the April 1971 local elections; and respondents were also asked, if possible, how they intended to vote in the December

1972 House of Representatives election. From these replies I built a measure of consistency or loyalty in voting over the course of several elections, distinguishing between the loyal conservative voters, the loyal reformist voters, and those who had a mixed voting pattern.

Both of these were cumbersome measures because respondents from different movements had to be lumped together. Different movements functioned at different times, which overlapped with scheduled elections in different ways, and some communities also had special elections at irregular times. As a result, when respondents reported their campaign activity and votes in the three most recent elections in their community, they were referring to different combinations of elections, citizens' movement participation, and partisan change. There were cases where activists reported change in party identification but had not yet had a chance to vote on the basis of the change, or where an activist did not always have candidates of his own party to choose from, or where the activist felt bound to support a citizens' movement candidate even when that individual nominee was not affiliated with the respondent's party of choice. This worked in both directions, with reformist citizens' movement members supporting conservative antipollution candidates, and less surprising, with conservative activists supporting reformist citizens' movement candidates.

Citizen's movement activists reported a total turnout of 89 percent, much higher than Japan's recent national averages. More important, many respondents could not resist the opportunity to add their thoughts on voting even though they were asked simply if they voted always, often, or seldom. Only one respondent referred to voting as *gimu* ("obligation"), whereas several others openly criticized this traditional approach to voting as a matter of obligation. One said, "I always vote, no matter what. It's the only right I have to express myself on politics, so I don't dare *not* use it" (F5). Many women in the sample had reached adulthood in the prewar period without the right to vote, and several of them remarked that they remembered finally receiving the franchise after the war and had never missed an opportunity to use it since. At some point during the interview quite a few respondents indicated that they regarded the vote as a right and as a political tool to be used to promote one's preferences on issues of importance. Explained an activist in Shibushi:

Old people here are very reluctant to vote JSP: they can't make this change of heart, and even consider it betrayal. They consider elections separate from the citizens' movement. To fight this attitude, our citizens' movement keeps trying to tell people that they should not consider elections separate. We argue that the conservatives are no good, and will not do us any good until there is balance between conservatives and reformists.

Table 23 shows the very close congruity (Tau-b = .605, p< .001) between respondents' stated partisan preferences and their actual voting habits, in spite of all the complications mentioned above which would have blurred this relationship.[11] Seventy percent of the conservative standpatters voted only for conservative candidates in the three most recent elections preceding the interview, and 74 percent of the reformist standpatters also voted as loyal reformists. The switchers reported the greatest quantity of mixed voting, reflecting both "split ballots" (for antipollution reformists at the local level and for conservatives at the national level), and a combination of elections occurring both before and after the change in partisanship. Eighty-one percent of the switchers had already demonstrated their commitment to the reformist parties in at least one election. Thus we come to the unavoidable conclusion that not only did citizens' movements alter many participants' ideas, political attitudes, and partisan preferences, but they also led to visible changes in voter alignment and actual votes cast.

Citizens' movements are probably doing much more to disturb voting patterns in rural areas than elsewhere, as is shown in the unusual level of mixed voting among rural citizens' movement activists. Moreover, only 9 percent of the rural activists were loyal conservative voters even though 17 percent of them defined themselves as conservative standpatters in terms of formal party identification. Thus even among activists who still call themselves conservative, citizens' movements contributed to a leftward drift in ballot box behavior. This is presumably a reflection of the bitter and brutal experiences which citizens' movement activists in semirural areas in Japan go through, and it should be taken seriously as a sign of rapid erosion of conservative support in these areas. Such a development is significant; citizens' movements outside of the Pacific industrial belt are Japan's best-known, in large part because they often mobilize large pluralities or majorities of their communities. The LDP depends on its support from such districts, where malapportionment turns rural votes into substantial Diet strength for the party, so that small losses are really large ones in the party's view.[12]

· Campaign Activity

If we extend our inquiry beyond voting to explore more active forms of participation, we learn that 62 percent of citizens' movement activists

11. As described in note 1 above, multicollinearity may be responsible for part of this relationship, but for 48 percent of the sample we can be certain that party identification and voting choice are conceptually separate, because partisanship and voting history do not coincide. For the rest, of course, we cannot know whether party identification and voting choice are separate factors which influence each other or are simply identical in the first place.

12. On malapportionment, see Ronald J. Hrebenar, "The Politics of Electoral Reform in Japan," *Asian Survey* 17:10 (October 1977), pp. 978–996.

TABLE 23 / *Voting Behavior of Citizens' Movement Activists (in percentage)*

Voting Loyalties	Loyal Conservative	Mixed Voter	Loyal Reformist	Total
Partisan Change				
Conservative standpatters (10)	70	30	0	100
Disillusioned switchers (11)	18	45	36	99
Reformist standpatters (35)	3	23	74	100
Tau-b = .605, p < .001				
Residence				
Rural (23)	9	52	39	100
Urban (33)	24	12	64	100
Total (56)	18	29	54	101

Extent of Campaign Involvement	None	Passive	Active	Ran for Office	Total
Residence					
Rural (24)	25	25	33	17	100
Urban (40)	45	20	30	5	100
Previous Political Experience					
Innocent (22)	68	14	18	0	100
Protest experience only (11)	73	9	18	0	100
Conventional experience only (15)	0	47	33	20	100
Gladiator (16)	0	19	56	19	100
Tau-b = .431, p < .001					
Partisan Change					
Conservative standpatters (14)	29	43	14	14	100
Disillusioned switchers (13)	62	0	31	8	101
Reformist standpatters (37)	32	22	38	8	100
Voting Loyalties					
Loyal conservative (10)	50	20	20	10	100
Mixed voting pattern (16)	25	25	31	19	100
Loyal reformist (30)	33	17	43	7	100
Total (64)	38	22	31	9	100

Note: Extent of Campaign Involvement:
None = no electoral activity other than voting.
Passive = listening to speeches, being a *kōenkai* member, talking to people, vague mention of "working for my candidate."
Active = passing out leaflets, organizing a *kōenkai*, working in elections for the antipollution movement.
Ran for Office = respondent ran for office as a citizens' movement candidate.

were active in election campaigns, including 31 percent who were heavily involved and 9 percent who actually ran for office themselves. This is much higher than we would find in the general population.[13] A good deal of this reported election campaign activity was directly related to the involvement of a citizens' movement in local elections.

13. Although the categories of campaign activity in this study are not smoothly comparable with those used in the Verba-Nie-Kim-Ikeuchi study, citizens' movement activists appear to be much more involved in intense campaigning. In contrast to the 40 percent of the citizens' movement sample who were heavily involved in a campaign or had run for

This is particularly clear in the case of rural movements: 75 percent of the rural activists in our sample engaged in some sort of campaigning, and 17 percent actually ran for a local office of some sort (table 23). In part this was simply a consequence of circumstance: urban electoral districts contained large populations, and even the smallest formal units of local government in the Tokyo area (wards, or *ku*) had several hundred thousand persons each, which discouraged election campaigning on the basis of one issue. Rural groups, on the other hand, were more favorably situated to use elections and thus looked upon them as a way to advance their cause. But two other reasons for the use of the electoral process by rural citizens' movements were the role of local elected officials—unresponsive and impolitic at best, corrupt and illegal at worst—in environmental disputes in rural areas, and the ingenuity of rural citizens' movements in injecting issues of substance into local politics.

The citizens' movements involved in electoral campaigns exploited both their old and their new reserves of talent. The second section of table 23 shows a strong association between conventional political experience (party work, campaign activity, and the like, for either left or right) and campaign involvement. We already know that citizens' movements drew upon people with expertise of this sort for their leadership; similarly, the pool of activists with *conventional* (not protest) political experience knew best how to turn a familiar event—with almost ritualistic character in the conservative strongholds of Japan—to the service of the citizens' movements. Yet, citizens' movements turned 30 percent of the activists who lacked this experience (innocents and those with protest experience only) into electoral campaigners on behalf of the citizens' movements, making a substantial contribution to the political education and training of fresh recruits.

Finally, although a majority of the sample was reformist in both partisanship and voting, reformists did not control citizens' movement campaign activities. In fact, there was no simple or systematic relationship between partisan affiliation or voting habits and campaign activity, other than the polarization among disillusioned switchers. Even the switchers produced their fair share of active campaigners and candidates for local office, but all the rest remained totally withdrawn from campaigning.

---

office themselves, only 4 percent of the Verba-Nie-Kim-Ikeuchi national sample were members of a political club or organization. In contrast to the 62 percent of the activists who had some experience in campaign work either before or because of citizens' movement participation, only 25 percent of the general population had been similarly involved. See Sidney Verba, Norman H. Nie, and Jae-on Kim, *Participation and Political Equality: A Seven-Nation Comparison* (Cambridge: At the University Press, 1978), pp. 58–59, 124–131; and Ikeuchi Hajime, ed., *Shimin ishiki no kenkyū* [A Study of Citizen Consciousness] (Tokyo: Tokyo Daigaku Shuppankai, 1974), pp. 401–418.

This was probably due to the traumatic nature of switching, often a very sensitive personal secret, not something which all switchers were prepared to shout from a megaphone car in an election campaign.

But the real importance of this non-relationship is that it validates citizens' movement claims to political neutrality. There is no tendency for citizens' movement activists of a particular partisan identity to dominate citizens' movement electoral activity. Campaigns really were wide open, all citizens' movement members really were welcome to participate, and even though a given movement might accept external help from, say, leftist groups, citizens' movements did maintain an internal sense of impartiality.

Summary

It should be clear that citizens' movements had a very strong influence on the political behavior of their members. One of the most apparent effects was the phenomenon of leftward shifts in activists' partisan affiliations, affecting one-fifth of our sample and, more important, half of the conservatives who entered citizens' movements as conservative identifiers. The socioeconomic traits ordinarily associated with reformist partisanship (urban origins and labor union experience) had no explanatory power, demonstrating that switchers were not a self-selected group of people on the verge of drifting to the left regardless of citizens' movements.

The factors that were important in producing switchers were personal traits of another sort, and the components of the citizens' movement experience itself. Switchers were more likely than conservative standpatters to have protest experience, to be concerned about pollution problems and prevention even in the abstract, and to resemble reformist standpatters in their level of "sophistication." Thus we may conclude that, relative to the standpatters, switchers were more open-minded about absorbing new information, more adept at abstract thinking (in that they were capable of developing an intellectual concern for environmental problems, on which they could then act), and as a result more likely to have cohesive or consistent belief systems.

In addition to these psychological characteristics of activists, the content of the citizens' movement experience itself affected switching, in that political attitudes concerning pollution were acquired during membership, preceded partisan switching, and obviously contributed to it. The chief catalyst of change (whether we are discussing partisan switching or the broader attitudinal change seen in the overwhelming majority of the sample) appeared to be the size of the gap between expectations and realities as newly appraised through citizens' movements. Those activists with the highest expectations and the most bitter encounters were therefore more vulnerable to switching and to other forms of attitude change.

The content of the new attitudes and beliefs that stimulated partisan change provided evidence that the fundamental lesson taught by citizens' movements was skepticism and caution in making political judgments. It is important to understand that severing ties with the conservative establishment was more important to switchers than the new affiliations which they absorbed through citizens' movements, and that their new-found reformist identity was a political stance adopted on the basis of pragmatism and convenience, not from new ideological beliefs. The significant role of conservative standpatters as leaders of movements and as conspicuous campaigners and candidates in the electoral activity of the movements also lends strength to claims of political neutrality and independence from ideology. What is significant about the act of switching was the unlearning and displacement of old loyalties, not by equally sentimental or unreasoned loyalties to new reference groups, but rather by a posture of individual independence, a new stress on the evaluation of political parties and objects on the basis of issues and rational calculation.

Finally, these attitude and belief changes had a visible and tangible effect on concrete behavior. Citizens' movement activists voted in accordance with new partisan preferences rather than old ones, and large numbers of them became personally involved in election campaigns on behalf of their movements. Only a tiny proportion of citizens in most democracies are ordinarily roused to political activism beyond the act of voting (5–7% in the United States).[14] It is remarkable that citizens' movements made campaign activists out of 30 percent of the political innocents—those totally lacking in prior political experience of either conventional or protest varieties—regardless of their parochial or "unsophisticated" orientations (as measured by the sophistication index).

In conclusion, citizens' movements transformed the orientations of their members from the passive acceptance of inherited or circumstantial political affiliations to an active (*shutaiteki*) exercise of cautious and independent judgment, leading to partisan change in half of the conservatives. Citizens' movements went on to give their members concrete experience, not merely in protest but also in confirming their new political identifications at the polls, and for many the experience also included vigorous involvement in election campaigns.

14. Lester W. Milbrath, *Political Participation* (Chicago: Rand McNally, 1965), p. 21.

Citizens' Movements
in Japanese Politics

WHAT CAUSES citizens' movements to emerge? Conversely, what effect do they have on their own members, on the surrounding community, and on Japanese politics as a whole? To resolve these questions, this chapter will draw together the evidence concerning environmental litigation, pollution disputes, and the attitudes and behavior of citizens' movement activists, integrate this evidence with more recent developments documented in the press or collected by others, and compare citizens' movements with social movements elsewhere.

Causes of Citizens' Movements

An explanation of the emergence of citizens' movements must be placed in the context of what we know about the concomitants and causes of participation in general, along with what we know about the state of participation in Japan in the 1960s. We need to ask what trends and events promoted the expansion of communal participation through informal groups (which became citizens' movements) both at the broader social level and at the level of the individuals who were recruited. I would argue that citizens' movements were neither predictable nor inevitable as an "epiphenomenon" or a "symptom" of secular trends in Japanese society, and that they arose instead from the simultaneous combination of three factors.

• Latent Capacity

The first factor is the latent capacity for democratic participation, which consists of (1) a population with sufficient education, material comfort, and similar resources to be capable of participating; (2) a political culture in which participation is acceptable behavior; and (3) institutions that guarantee the basic freedoms of speech, press, and assembly essential to effective participation. Philosophers and political theorists have long argued that democracy requires some mysterious minimum of such things, and as new social or political groups demand consideration in decisions, a participant political culture and free institutions gradually develop. Since 1945 Japan seems to have had a population with the "right" traits, the American occupation imposed the "right" institutions, and political culture began "catching up." Regardless of the anomalous sequence in which the Japanese polity acquired these three features, they each increased in strength during the postwar era. The public became more prosperous and educated, the political culture grew as accepting of the ethos of participation by the 1960s as in most democracies, and free institutions were securely established, no longer likely to be overturned by a "reverse course" in retaliation against occupation reforms. One might therefore expect that these trends over time would cause participation to increase. However, empirical research has greatly complicated our understanding of the necessary and sufficient conditions for participation.[1] The factors already mentioned create only the possibility and not the certainty of increased participation. Others (cultural heritage, socioeconomic stratification, organizational patterns, and many more) can be at least as important in determining the probability that opportunities for increased participation will be sought or achieved. Moreover, there is no universally reliable combination or threshold value for these factors, below which demands for participation cannot appear or above which such demands will definitely appear. People do not alter their behavior in obedience to coefficients in regression equations, and in the 1960s there was still a passive quality to Japanese political participation. Thus even if this latent capacity was a necessary precondition, it was not sufficient to stimulate more energetic participation. A population whose government

1. See Gabriel A. Almond and Sidney Verba, *The Civic Culture: Political Attitudes and Democracy in Five Nations* (Boston: Little, Brown, 1965); Seymour Martin Lipset, *Political Man: The Social Bases of Politics* (Garden City, N.Y.: Doubleday, 1960), pp. 27–63; Norman H. Nie, G. Bingham Powell, Jr., and Kenneth Prewitt, "Social Sructure and Political Participation: Developmental Relationships," *American Political Science Review* 63:2 and 3 (June and September 1969), 361–378, 808–832; Robert A. Dahl, *Polyarchy: Participation and Opposition* (New Haven: Yale University Press, 1971); Robert A. Dahl and Edward R. Tufte, *Size and Democracy* (Stanford:Stanford University Press, 1973); Sidney Verba, Norman H. Nie, and Jae-on Kim, *Participation and Political Equality: A Seven-Nation Comparison* (New York: Cambridge University Press, 1978).

appeared to be performing well in terms of expectations had few grievances to complain about, and most Japanese were satisfied with their rising standard of living and expected little more from politicians.

• An Issue

The missing ingredient was a pressing issue to make increased participation worth the bother. For circumstantial reasons explained in the first two chapters, the environmental crisis supplied this issue, rather than taxation, redistribution of wealth, incorporation of an excluded social group, a crisis in values, or some other problem more familiar as the stimulus to expanded participation and protest elsewhere. As the interview results indicated, activists were mobilized primarily out of their intense concern with this issue rather than inadvertently through affiliations with other groups, and their activism served instrumental rather than expressive needs. The combination of latent capacity and a pressing issue were now sufficient to guarantee three things: that participation would increase in the late 1960s in Japan, that pollution would be the focal point, and that activity would be aimed at making demands rather than expressing support. However, latent capacity and a pressing issue taken alone ensured only this much, and not that this increased participation would differ in nature from prevailing patterns.

• Closure of Existing Channels

What forced citizens to form new groups within which to participate was the fact that, one by one, the prevailing channels of participation disqualified themselves. The accounts of citizens' movements in the first three chapters indicated that particularized contacting and petitioning did not work. For the most part, attempts to use the formal institutions or networks which monopolized communal activity in Japan and created what Verba, Nie, and Kim termed "lockout" also failed. Political parties had no mass base. Agricultural cooperatives, neighborhood associations, candidate support organizations, and similar groups that ordinarily served as intermediaries between citizens and political institutions were unresponsive or even hostile to the pollution issue. Only in the rare situation where pollution threatened all members of a preexisting group equally—as in the garbage war in which neighborhood associations of Takaidō and Edagawa became the core of citizens' movements there—did these organizations perform the function of political intermediary.

Independent evidence suggests that existing institutions that might once have served community needs, either as channels of grass-roots influence or as forums for the resolution of disputes, no longer suffice. A study that compared opinions of neighborhood association leaders with those of their constituents for a sample of ninety-four Kyoto neighborhoods and eighty-nine Osaka neighborhoods showed that existing neighborhood associations functioned adequately as channels of political influence in the older neighborhoods, largely because the residents had few grievances. However, in the newer neighborhoods of *danchi* settlements, local residents had a high sense of dissatisfaction and numerous political grievances. They were very interested in participation and mobilized readily into ad hoc groups (essentially citizens' movements) to solve their problems, but they felt apathetic and distrustful toward the formal neighborhood associations. At best, these citizens regarded neighborhood associations as one among several organizational tools available for exerting pressure on city government.[2] Thus the Japanese public seems to be groping for new forms that would replace existing ones that have proven rigid or intractable as avenues of influence on new issues and would serve as new mechanisms for the resolution of conflict that is now out in the open.

Existing channels could not accommodate antipollution demands as they had handled other sorts of requests, largely because of the nature of the pollution issue itself. It was a more divisive issue than others, usually splitting members of the same group or constituency over vital interests: production, employment, and polluting activity versus health and safety. Moreover, the antidevelopment solutions that were proposed threatened the modus operandi of local politicians and industrialists for support mobilization and regional development. Pollution introduced a new dimension of conflict into policy choices which these existing channels could neither suppress nor resolve. As our survey findings indicated, the individuals concerned about pollution experienced tremendous disappointment and even trauma in their search for assistance. Drawing whenever possible on the social skills and political experience of their associates, citizens simply had to build their own organizations. They then had to abandon the methods customarily used by other groups in favor of pursuing redress either through the courts or through unfamiliar (though legal) techniques of exerting political pressure. Thus citizens' movements carried on the Japanese custom of participation through institutions and groups, but as newly formed informal groups, usually independent of preexisting organizations and having to use novel tactics, they contrasted with patterns prevailing in the 1960s from which they arose.

The unique circumstances that produced antipollution citizens' movements are clearer if we contrast the environmental issue with another, ostensibly similar, social welfare problem, which was handled

2. Muramatsu Michio, Ikeuchi Hajime, et al., *Chiiki jichikai no kinō ni kansuru kenkyū: Kyōto-shi no chōnaikai* [Research on the Functions of Local Self-Government Associations: Neighborhood Associations of Kyoto City] (Kyoto: Shisutemu Kagaku Kenkyūjo, March 1976), pp. 82–83.

quite differently: aid to the elderly. Considerable public discussion of this issue during the 1970s led not to controversy or citizens' movements but to the emergence of a national consensus on the importance of the problem and to the rapid and quiet growth of government programs to provide medical and other benefits to the elderly. With three-quarters of all old people living with their children, the plight of the elderly was of tangible concern to all Japanese, who knew that they too would eventually grow old. The economic adjustments involved in expanding such services were relatively small, and general government revenues supplied the benefits even to most locally initiated programs, preventing the division of each community or group into recipients versus chief bearers of economic burden. Finally, there were already plenty of existing groups with a built-in interest in social services to the aged to articulate public concern: municipal workers' unions (Jichirō), unions of workers in homes for the aged, doctors' associations, professional groups among social workers, and especially old people's clubs (rōjinkai), an important support network for the LDP. Politicians could integrate the idea of increased social services into their self-image as patrons and providers of pork-barrel rewards and government subsidies to their constituents. Similarly, policy planners in the relevant ministries readily accepted the importance of such programs as a professional responsibility and as a way to bring Japan's welfare policies into step with its new status as an affluent democracy. Thus Campbell found that the government took the initiative on these policies with little prodding from the public, and that the most important sources of policy were the natural competitive forces of partisan politics and bureaucratic entrepreneurship.[3] In this case, then, the nature of the issue allowed existing institutions to act quickly and imaginatively even while public demand remained at a low level.

But the very different issues and institutional behavior in the case of pollution forced citizens' movements onto the scene. At the outset most Japanese did not expect to become pollution victims. Defenders of the economy feared not just increased expenditure but a total industrial shutdown. Rather than having a natural interest in antipollution investment, established pressure groups and bureaucratic agencies had reason to oppose such a response. Finally, demands for attention to environmental problems contradicted most politicians' expectations instead of fitting smoothly into their customary routines. Unlike welfare for the aged, the problem was left to fester until controversy exploded.

Thus the citizens' movement phenomenon was generated by the simultaneous existence of a dormant capacity for increased participation, an issue (pollution) that generated conflict and defied conventional po-

3. John Creighton Campbell, "The Old People Boom and Japanese Policy Making," *Journal of Japanese Studies* 5:2 (Summer 1979), 321–357.

litical treatment, and the closure of existing organizational paths to participation. Citizens' movements were not surface phenomena easily predicted on the basis of underlying sociopolitical change or rates of urbanization and economic growth; they were an independent and unexpected development resulting from a unique combination of events, and a force for change in their own right.

The Effects of Citizens' Movements at Close Range

In order to design an orderly route through what remains the complex question of how citizens' movements in their turn affected Japanese politics, we shall proceed from the small to the large. First we shall discuss the effect of citizens' movements on their own membership and their immediate political surroundings. Then we shall look at their impact on local politics—the local elite, policy outputs, and the political process. Finally, we shall consider the long-term significance of citizens' movements for Japanese politics and compare them with similar social protest movements in the other democracies.

· Changes Within the Membership

Mobilization. Whether citizens' movements mobilize new recruits to the political public or simply enrich the experience of seasoned activists has been a subject of some argument, but our survey data provide the first opportunity to evaluate the question systematically. Citizens' movements performed three functions in the realm of political mobilization.

First, they constituted an introduction to vigorous political activity beyond voting, including aggressive participation in election campaigns sponsored by citizens' movements, for one-third (34%) of their members. These innocents consisted of two types: quiescent conservatives who had simply followed community norms without a second thought until joining a citizens' movement, and closet reformists who had concealed their affiliation with the opposition by withholding concrete support other than their vote from any political cause before citizen's movements. Moreover, citizens' movements seem to have mobilized people who would not otherwise have been "natural" or "self-selected" candidates for political activism. Although recruitment of urban sophisticates is not particularly surprising in view of their social characteristics, the participation of so many parochials, both rural and urban, could not have been anticipated on the basis of their demographic traits. Thus citizen's movements not only enlarged the political public but also brought new kinds of people into it.

Second, citizen's movements offered the first opportunity to engage in a new *form* of political activity to another 41 percent of their members. They provided an education in protest (in the sense that they definitely opposed certain established policies and tried to alter them) and taught those with conventional political experience how to use the system to obtain a redress of grievances, not merely to submit particularistic requests and not simply to engage in the politics of support and conformity. Citizens' movements also provided an education in conventional politics (in that they relied on legal methods) to those with prior protest experience, showing these people how to go beyond the mere expression of dissent to obtain solutions to their problems. Citizens' movements were by definition a formative experience for any of their members who had not done both protest and conventional politicking before.

Only 25 percent of the activists were gladiators (possessing prior experience both in protest and in conventional politics beyond the act of voting), but even for this subset, citizens' movements provided a valuable education by combining these two approaches to politics. In his survey of upper-echelon activists and leaders in Mishima, Jack Lewis found that even for this highly sophisticated and experienced group, citizens' movements provided a novel introduction to the techniques of political compromise, by teaching them to cooperate with others "previously perceived as political enemies," and thus transforming attitudes with respect to the "scope of permissible political cooperation."[4] In addition to their obvious contribution to the mobilization of the 75 percent of the membership with limited experience in politics, citizens' movements performed an important function in the political education of the gladiators as well, by providing them with a new understanding of political compromise and cooperation.

This suggests the third way in which mobilization is significant. Citizens' movements brought these disparate types of people together and forced them to cooperate with one another on behalf of their mutual interest in an issue. Raw recruits to communal activity joined company with seasoned politicos of both right and left—establishment conservatives and experienced leftists who had done union or party work before but never in collaboration with people of other persuasions. Even though citizens' movements are similar to the "network" pattern of mobilization so conspicuous in Japan, in that each citizens' movement in itself was really a network, their cross-sectional appeal to people of different backgrounds and political experience is new and significant. In part this results from the very nature of pollution, whose impact is indiscriminate and does not overlap with existing organizational boundaries.

4. Jack G. Lewis, "Civic Protest in Mishima: Citizens' Movements and the Politics of the Environment in Contemporary Japan," chap. 8 in Scott Flanagan, Kurt Steiner, and Ellis S. Krauss, eds., *Political Opposition and Local Politics in Japan: Electoral Trends, Citizens' Movements, and Progressive Administrations* (Princeton: Princeton University Press, 1979), pp. 28–48.

One activist described the random but sweeping effect of environmental problems: the men work hard for the industrial structure that causes pollution so that they can support nonworking wives and the growing consumer appetites of their families, thus freeing the women to devote their newfound leisure to protesting against the pollution generated by their husbands.[5] Such an issue can obviously create new patterns of cleavage and alignment, and the resulting political forms—citizens' movements—break down the rigid social and organizational boundaries that separate political actors into nonoverlapping segments and insulate them from one another. It is tempting to resort to the word "pluralist" in describing the social consequences of this phenomenon, a truly remarkable extreme in any discussion of Japanese politics.[6]

The fact that citizens' movements enlarged the political public and created a new community of political activists and opinion leaders should significantly alter our picture of Japanese politics. Until recently, scholarship on Japanese politics reflected an underlying view that Japanese society consisted of a political elite on the top, containing most of the objects worthy of our attention (the left and right establishments of parties, major interest groups, and formal governmental institutions), and a calm, cooperative, highly organized but apolitical public beneath it—with small knots of extremists of the left and right ranting irrelevantly off to the side somewhere. The major link between the two layers consisted of vertical threads (paternalistic *oyabun-kobun* ties) within organizations, as observed by Nakane Chie.[7]

Now we are beginning to see greater complexities within the elite and more interesting shadings and variations in the public beneath it, along with gentle disturbances in the neat vertical order of status (as opposed to class) consciousness in society. The recent scholarly discovery of such themes as conflict and competition in Japanese society is an appropriate, though belated, reaction to enormous changes in worldly realities. Citizens' movements are a manifestation of—and more important, a contribution toward—these developments. They are part of an intermediate layer taking shape between the top and bottom of the pyramid, recruiting most of its members from the vague void below, but with a significant number of converts from the elite above as well. Furthermore, this intermediate layer cuts through the vertical threads connecting top

5. Tokyo activist at a sunshine-rights meeting in Tokyo, 10 June 1972.

6. Muramatsu Michio, "Gyōsei katei to seiji sanka" [The Administrative Process and Political Participation], in Nihon seiji gakkai, *Nempō seijigaku 1974: seiji sanka no riron to genjitsu* [Annual of the Japanese Political Science Association: The Theory and Practice of Political Participation] (Tokyo: Iwanami Shoten, March 1975), pp. 48–68.

7. Chie Nakane, *Japanese Society* (Berkeley and Los Angeles: University of California Press, 1970).

and bottom and is held together instead by horizontal bonds based on the commitment to an issue.

Political scientists and sociologists have long debated the role of private associations in a democracy. On the debit side of the ledger, interest groups need not be democratically inclined themselves, they may enforce conformity rather than encourage self-expression, and depending on their sources of support they may overrepresent those who are already powerful in society rather than distribute power more widely. On the other hand, voluntary associations or communal activities are also vital to democracy by providing citizens the opportunity to express their views in much more specific ways than elections allow. Voluntary associations can counteract the centralization and concentration of power, socialize individuals in democratic practices, teach them about the nature of the political process in their society, and contribute to the orderly resolution of conflict and to social change.

Our findings clearly indicate that citizens' movements functioned as the sort of voluntary association which enhances rather than limits democracy. Verba, Nie, and Kim showed that if we include *all* groups in Japanese society in the 1960s, associational activity actually equalized participation in terms of resources rather than overrepresenting the powerful (see chapter I). However, most of these groups were apolitical, and participation was actually quite passive. Few would deny that among active political groups the well-organized interests of business and labor were overrepresented in the inner circles of Japanese politics before the rise of citizens' movements. On the other hand, citizens' movements articulated views that certainly were not being voiced by the more established political pressure groups in Japanese society; similarly, they mobilized the otherwise unorganized and formerly underrepresented interests of the political innocents.

Socialization. Our analysis of the effect of participation in citizens' movements on attitudes and beliefs among individuals serves as a study of political socialization, a field which until recently has emphasized childhood learning among middle-class whites in America. Practitioners in the still young field of socialization research have pointed out several deficiencies in it, particularly the inattention to adults.[8] First, until we

8. Theodore Newcomb's study of students at Bennington College in the 1930s is still cited as the most significant work on adult political socialization in America, and Krauss's work on radical students is virtually the only panel study of adult socialization in Japan. Theodore M. Newcomb, *Personality and Social Change: Attitude Formation in a Student Community* (New York: Dryden Press, 1943); and its follow-up study, Theodore M. Newcomb et al., *Persistence and Change: Bennington College and Its Students after 25 Years* (New York: Wiley, 1967). Ellis S. Krauss, *Japanese Radicals Revisited: Student Protest in Postwar Japan* (Berkeley and Los Angeles: University of California Press, 1974).

explore political attitudes through the life cycle by conducting expensive longitudinal studies on a sample of children (and possibly their parents) to maturity, we cannot assume that childhood learning is actually relevant to adult political behavior. Second, socialization is often regarded as a vehicle of system maintenance, betraying a conservative bias in favor of the status quo, and is rarely examined as a vehicle for system change or system creation. Third, socialization research is largely confined to studies in firmly established systems with relatively old political parties. We need to compare the "normal" or "obvious" socialization processes in such systems with socialization among adults as well as children in new or rapidly changing systems, in which family and peer group might have much less importance than direct personal experience with politics. Such a comparison would tell us much more than we now know about how the problem of socializing subsequent generations imposes limits on the pace of political change, or conversely, on the ability of a political system to survive in the face of discontinuous socialization. Japan experienced a massive collective crisis in the form of World War II and drastic reform afterward, which created an enormous gap between the generations who lived through the war and younger ones with only second-hand knowledge of it at most, and therefore is a very fruitful site for careful research.[9] As an analysis of political learning in response to a crisis faced in adult life in the context of a young political system, the present study of citizens' movement activists focuses on these neglected questions.

The fact that citizens' movements affect the attitudes, beliefs, and even the subsequent political behavior of their members demonstrates that they serve an important function in Japanese politics as agents of adult socialization. They do not simply recruit members for a brief flurry of activity from which people depart unchanged, but actually transform the political attitudes of those they mobilize. Through citizens' movements, activists learn how to build effective political organizations. They

---

For assessments of the field of political socialization in general and adult socialization in particular, see David O. Sears, "Political Socialization," in Fred I. Greenstein and Nelson W. Polsby, eds., *Handbook of Political Science*, vol. 2: Micropolitical Theory, (Reading, Mass.: Addison-Wesley, 1975), pp. 93–153; Roberta S. Sigel and Marilyn Brookes Hoskin, "Perspectives on Adult Political Socialization—Areas of Research," in Stanley Allen Renshon, ed., *Handbook of Political Socialization: Theory and Research* (New York: Free Press, 1977), pp. 259–293; and Richard E. Dawson, Kenneth Prewitt, and Karen S. Dawson, *Political Socialization*, 2d ed. (Boston: Little, Brown, 1977), especially chap. 5 on the adult years.

9. In addition to Krauss's work (see n. 8), see Joseph A. Massey, *Youth and Politics in Japan* (Lexington, Mass.: Lexington Books, 1976); Tadao Okamura, "The Child's Changing Image of the Prime Minister: A Preface to the Study of Political Socialization in Contemporary Japan," *Developing Economies* 6:4 (December 1968), 566–586; and Akira Kubota and Robert E. Ward, "Family Influence and Political Socialization in Japan," *Comparative Political Studies* 3:3 (July 1970), 140–175.

learn about newfangled methods of exerting influence, from litigation to recall elections and from single-share campaigns to pollution-prevention agreements. They acquire a more complex understanding of the political process, replacing benign idealistic images with more sophisticated perceptions of bargaining, political posturing, and the pressures that really matter to politicians and thus impinge on decisions. From the painful aspects of the experience activists develop a sharp hostility to most political and economic institutions, although their sense of efficacy either as individuals or as citizens' movement members prevents this hostility from spilling over into political alienation. They define new issue-based criteria for evaluating the performance of politicians and local governments. Thus activists learn about politics and their rights as citizens and acquire a healthy sense of independence vis-à-vis authority.

Moreover, evidence of political learning and attitude change is greatest among those with the least political experience and among parochials, who constitute too large a portion of most citizens' movements for their presence to be ignored as accidental. Citizens' movements include many people who do not fit the idealized description of the perfect citizen. Even parochial Japanese with traditional values and a sense of deference and humility toward authority can learn from their own experience that certain unfamiliar themes in democratic rhetoric actually mean something and can even do them some good.

An important consequence of this socialization process is that in 20 percent of the sample—or, more important, among 50 percent of the activists who began as conservative partisans—activism stimulated a change in partisanship (invariably from conservative to reformist) on top of these attitude and belief changes. In a larger number, citizens' movements created new voting patterns, particularly an increase in issue-oriented voting rather than voting based on personality and networks of *kankei*.[10] In view of the enormous attention given in the past to the motivations of Japanese voters, and the prevalent findings that voting was generally based on personal attributes of a candidate ("aura" and interpersonal connections, not to be confused with stance on issues), this change in voting orientations wrought by citizens' movements would be significant in its own right even if it extended only to the activists themselves.

We should not misconstrue this development to mean simply that citizens' movements are driving their members to the left. There are of course many ways in which a citizens' movement can benefit from help

10. On *kankei*, see Scott C. Flanagan, "Voting Behavior in Japan: The Persistence of Traditional Patterns," *Comparative Political Studies* 1:3 (October 1968), 391–412; and Flanagan, "The Japanese Party System in Transition," *Comparative Politics* 3:2 (January 1971), 231–254.

offered by the left—for example, confidential information or evidence about illegal preparations for inviting industry into the area often come from reformist assemblymen or members of the municipal employees' labor union. However, activists learn from hard experience that parties and unions may try to exploit the pollution issue to attract publicity, acquire a good public image, or win votes and increase union membership, without ever providing much concrete aid to the movement or working for real solutions to environmental problems. Recent developments in Fuji provide a good example. Although the anti-*hedoro* movement aggressively supported Socialist candidates for public office in the early 1970s (see chapter I), its leaders are disappointed with the reformists it put into office. Because the movement's loyalty is not to the left but to objective results, it now looks favorably on those local conservative politicians whose pragmatic instinct for survival taught them to be responsive to the movement.[11]

Therefore, even when movements gratefully accept assistance of this sort, most are careful to disavow any official ties to political parties or to ideology-based organizations, to assert that they want to accommodate all members of the community who share their antipollution views, and to refute the inevitable charge that they are "red." Only 22.4 percent of the citizens' movements questioned by *Asahi Shimbun* maintained ties with a single political party. To preserve their leverage in local politics, the rest either had links to several or all parties (36%) or refused to have anything to do with any party whatsoever (34.6%).[12] Similarly, to proclaim its neutrality the citizens' movement in Numazu (described in chapter I) had dual leadership, with one movement officer a conservative, the other a leftist.[13] These concerns for preserving ideological neutrality and placing issues above doctrine signify that the informal coalitions we occasionally find between citizens' movements and the leftist parties, along with the leftward drift in activists' personal affiliations, flow from a temporary marriage of convenience between two political forces that find themselves united in certain objectives.

Therefore, what we should stress in evaluating socialization and the changes in partisanship resulting from citizens' movement participation is that activism makes voting a political act based on individual judgment, rather than a social act defined by accidents of circumstance. The exposure to citizens' movements provided many activists with their first

11. Toshihiko Koda, "Conflicting Philosophies of Gain and Abundance in My Hometown," *Japan Quarterly* 26:2 (April–June 1979), 188–198.

12. Nakamura Kiichi, "Jūmin undō no soshiki to kōzō" [The Organization and Structure of Residents' Movements], *Chiiki kaihatsu* 154 (July 1977), 24.

13. Jūmin ni yoru Keiji baipasu kōgai kenkyū guruupu, *Kōgai: yosoku to taisaku* [Pollution: Forecasts and Countermeasures] (Tokyo: Asahi Shimbunsha, March 1971), p. 252.

real opportunity to think about issue-oriented voting. Rather than considering voting to be a duty, a time to express feelings of obligation toward a candidate, many learned to think of politicians as being somewhat obligated to their constituents, and to think of voting as the right of self-expression and as a way to influence political leaders and policies. Even among those activists who did not change partisanship, many heard for the first time, articulated by their own community members and not by a civics textbook, about the possibility of approaching elections with a political strategy in mind.

The greatest importance of these changes is the extent to which participation in citizens' movements brings activists an appreciation of themselves as independent political actors, with the sense of self (*koga*) that Japanese social scientists often describe as an essential ingredient of the ideal democratic "community." Muramatsu suggests that this sense of self must be based on personal experience and daily life, not merely on an intellectual understanding of the term.[14] Similarly, Richardson, noting a discrepancy between formal learning of democratic norms and the psychological internalization of these norms, concluded that in the 1960s most Japanese still lacked the concrete experience so crucial for internalizing participatory values.[15] I would argue that citizens' movements cultivate the confidence and independence which can be regarded as this essential sense of "self" and thus provide the heretofore missing experience with active forms of participation.

Moreover, citizens' movements were an important agent of *resocialization* to politics. In view of the age of our sample (an arithmetic mean of forty-seven) and the fact that 69 percent completed their education in the prewar period, citizens' movements may well have provided, especially for the politically inexperienced, a more intense immersion course in democratic politics than anything they had yet been exposed to. Adults are apparently capable of drastic change, even in a direction opposed to the "natural" forces of aging: our sample became demanding rather than resigned, less conservative and more inclined to experiment with new ideas and new political tactics. However, the literature on political commitment and belief change indicates that reinforcement and repetition of experience are important in creating new attitudes and beliefs, along with initial exposure. We have no direct way of evaluating the longevity of any transformation that citizens' movements may bring

14. Muramatsu Michio, "Jūmin no seiji ishiki to seiji sanka" [Residents' Political Consciousness and Political Participation], in Matsubara Haruo, ed., *Jūmin sanka to jichi no kakushin* [Residents' Participation and the Reform of Self-Government], vol. 2 in the series Asu no chihō jichi wo saguru [Toward Local Self-Government for the Future] (Tokyo: Gakuyō Shobō, February 1974), pp. 87–91.

15. Bradley M. Richardson, *The Political Culture of Japan* (Berkeley and Los Angeles, University of California Press, 1974), pp. 230–231.

about in the political behavior of their members without interviewing the same respondents again after the passage of time. Short of such an undertaking, we must be cautious about drawing conclusions.

Nonetheless, these findings do suggest that the fate of new political systems need not rest entirely on support from new generations and that they can, under certain conditions, win over older generations originally socialized in the values and beliefs appropriate to an earlier system. Perhaps societies have greater resilience in the face of rapid change than we realized. One might even faintly hope that new democratic systems have some chance for stable future development, a comforting thought in an age when the democracies appear to be declining in numbers and vitality with each passing decade.

· Impact on the Community at Large

Citizens' movements have some important effects on nonparticipants in their communities. Although the experience of attitude and belief change has to be more intense for the activists who are directly concerned, it is reasonable to extrapolate that citizens' movements have some influence on inactive but sympathetic observers by giving legitimacy both to the stance and to the strength of participatory and democratic values. Generally, citizens' movements are able to collect many times more signatures on petitions than their active strength would indicate, and when they manage to use elections as a tool of influence they often win many more votes than the number of their active members (as in Shibushi, Usuki, Ōiso, Takaidō, and Nerima in our survey). Although only 10 percent of the citizens in Mishima could be labeled activists in the anti-*kombinat* movement there, 82 percent of the city's population demonstrated sympathy with the movement.[16] Survey data of several types indicate that citizens' movements have helped to legitimize social activism in general and citizens' movements as a particular form, in spite of the "allergy" once displayed toward them by the general public. Supporters of citizens' movements (51.5%) outnumbered those who disapproved (10.6%) by five to one in a nationwide poll of March 1973. Similarly, 36.2 percent said that in order to correct the errors of a mayor or an assemblyman they would join either a recall campaign or a citizens' movement.[17] Citizens' movements are even more widely accepted among city dwellers: 23 percent of the respondents in a 1973 Tokyo survey said that there had been a movement active in their area during the previous

16. Lewis, "Civic Protest in Mishima," pp. 28–29.
17. Satō Atsushi, *Tenkanki no chihō jichi: atarashii shimin to gyōsei no hōkō* [Local Self-Government in a Time of Transformation: New Directions in Citizens and Administration] (Tokyo: Gakuyō Shobō, 1976), p. 113. See also Ritsuo Akimoto, "Japanese Political Awareness," *Local Government Review* 5 (1977), 5–16.

year, and 44 percent of these respondents had participated, indicating that in just one short year as many as 10 percent of all Tokyoites had been activists in citizens' movements. The same survey revealed that 68 percent of the Tokyoites who had not had a local movement to join would nonetheless be inclined to participate if a citizens' movement took form in their area.[18] Similarly, in surveys of two suburbs of Tokyo (Ushiku and Ageo), 75.7 percent thought citizens' movements were a suitable form of action, and 88.9 percent said they would cooperate in some way with such a movement.[19] Thus citizens' movements have definitely established themselves as a respectable form of activity even among nonparticipants.

Furthermore, just as a pebble cast into a pool of water sends ripples outward in all directions, so citizens' movements also affect their opponents in a community, who are forced by the movement's definition of the situation and by the movement's actions to adopt similar methods. Perhaps the clearest example of this phenomenon is available to us in the case of Rokkasho village in Aomori prefecture. In Rokkasho, sharply divided over the Mutsu-Ōgawara *kombinat* development project, both the citizens' movement against development and the portion of the community favoring development attempted to influence local politicians and launched recall movements against elected officials.[20] Thus the prodevelopment forces, which viewed the antidevelopment citizens' movement as a divisive body engaged in inappropriate behavior that would destroy the community, had to adopt similar methods to combat the movement, and quite possibly had to undergo certain similar transformations in attitudes and beliefs toward political tactics and conflict per se. Similarly, the ripple effect is probably responsible for the fact that people seeking all sorts of objectives had adopted the citizens' movement form, creating a multiplicity of citizens' movements and goals.[21]

Citizens' Movements and Local Politics

The simple fact that citizens' movements are a recent development imposes difficulties on any analysis of their consequences, but Jack Lewis's exhaustive study of one of the earliest movements shows how a

18. The Tokyo survey was reported in *Asahi Shimbun* (*AS*), 15 June 1973.
19. Kaoru Hamaji, "Consciousness and Attitudes in Residents' Participation," *Local Government Review* 5 (1977), 70–82; Akimoto Ritsuo, "Jūmin undō to jūmin sanka" [Residents' Movements and Residents' Participation], in Jichi Daigakkō kenkyūbu, eds., *Jūmin sanka to gyōsei* [Residents' Participation and Administration] (Tokyo: Daiichi Hōki Shuppan, 1976), pp. 164–166.
20. *Japan Times* (*JT*), 10 January, 15 May, and 15 June, in 1973.
21. Akimoto, "Jūmin undō to jūmin sanka," pp. 166–169.

citizens' movement can restructure local politics.[22] The citizens' movement that arose in 1964 in Mishima became a full-fledged political organization backing an unusual coalition of reformist and conservative forces, and it has dominated the political scene since then, united around a collective concern for balanced development, citizen welfare, local autonomy, and protection of the community and its environs against further damage. This coalition originally took form in the 1961 mayoral election in Mishima, *prior* to the emergence of a citizens' movement, when local progressives (the JSP, JCP, Sōhyō-affiliated unions, and other reformist independents) found themselves without a candidate for mayor. They finally managed to recruit Hasegawa Taizō, a man of conservative background willing to run on a progressive ticket. He won by a slim majority in a surprising upset in 1961, by emphasizing the issues of local autonomy (especially opposition to amalgamation with other cities) and citizen welfare, precursors of citizens' movement concerns. The citizens' movement that later erupted around the question of constructing a large petrochemical complex in the Mishima area in 1964 supported Hasegawa's coalition because he opposed the *kombinat*, and increased his majorities in subsequent mayoral elections. The citizens' movement survived after defeating the *kombinat* by becoming Hasegawa's support organization.

During the 1960s, Mishima was an astonishing exception to most of the rules of Japanese local politics. However, the subsequent eruption of citizens' movements all over Japan with similar concerns, many of them explicitly relying on the Mishima example as a model, has transformed Mishima from a deviant case into an important prototype in the survival of the citizens' movement as a political organization concerned with structure and process in local politics.

Nonetheless, before pursuing the complex relationship between citizens' movements since Mishima and the larger arena of local politics, we must address the problems posed by the available evidence. There is no systematic way to obtain irrefutable evidence about the impact of citizens' movements other than to examine individual cases.[23] There are

22. In addition to Lewis's article, "Civic Protest in Mishima," see "*Hokaku rengō*: The Politics of Conservative-Progressive Cooperation in a Japanese City" (Ph.D. diss. in Political Science, Stanford University, 1975); "Coalition Formation in a Local Multi-party System: Implications for Political Change in Japan," paper presented at the Association for Asian Studies, Chicago, March 1973; "Interparty Cleavage and Consensus in a Japanese City: A Report on Political Activitists' Election Campaign Behavior," paper presented at the Southeastern Region Japan Studies Seminar, Georgetown University, Washington, D.C., February 1974: and "Local Politics and the 'Displacement of Conflicts': A Note on Party System Change in a Japanese City," paper presented at the Southeast Regional Conference of the Association for Asian Studies, University of Georgia, Athens, Georgia, January 1975.

23. Satake Hiroshi, "Shimin undō to chihō senkyo" [Citizens' Movements and Local Elections] in *Nempō seijigaku 1974*, p. 166.

thousands of citizens' movements, mostly undocumented, but the fourteen movements in this study constitute a representative set of case studies. Using these along with case materials collected by others and press coverage of recent movements, we shall try to build a cumulative picture of citizens' movement influence on local politics.

Much of our evidence has to be indirect. Political upheavals and the fate of citizens' movement objectives in specific communities where citizens' movements have worked vigorously for or against certain electoral and policy outcomes tell us whether citizens' movements become an effective political force capable of influencing political actors and processes. Going beyond communities where citizens' movements erupted, we may note rough similarities between the policies citizens' movements demand and the programs recently created by local governments all over Japan. Finally, in order to assess their general significance we can examine political trends since the heyday of citizens' movements, although we certainly cannot assume that everything postdating the peak of citizens' movements in a community or in Japan as a whole is therefore a result of citizens' movements.

• Impact on the Local Political Elite

Citizens' movements naturally have an impact on the local political elite from whom they intend to elicit a response, though this effect varies enormously according to their choice of tactics, the political complexion of the local establishment, previous local experience with political conflict, the nature of the issue in question and its potential economic impact on the community, and many other factors. Even if we restrict our attention to the most common case of an ideologically neutral movement, willing to collaborate with local leftists on citizens' movement terms, facing a conservative local establishment at either the municipal or the prefectural level, there exists a vast range in the responses of local conservative elites. There are several cases in our own sample where some conservative neighborhood-association leaders were instrumental in the very formation of a citizens' movement because of their own early concern about an issue. In rare cases local conservatives holding formal elective office initiated citizens' movements. In Kashima, slated for *kombinat* development according to the New Comprehensive National Land Development Plan (Shinzensō) of 1969 and now the site of Japan's largest industrial complex, the mayor himself founded an antipollution citizens' movement, which extracted pollution-prevention agreements from the industrial firms in the zone.[24] Generally, though, where conservative local

24. Hayase Takeshi, "Chiiki kaihatsu—kōgai to jūmin undō" [Regional Development—Pollution and Residents' Movements], in Satō Atsushi, ed., *Chiiki kaihatsu, kōgai e no taiō* [The Response to Regional Development and Pollution], vol. 3 in the series Asu no chihō jichi wo saguru, pp. 308–309.

leaders work for citizens' movement goals, they are late recruits to the cause, having been transformed by the movement's own strength and presence, as well as by their own sense of political pragmatism. They are thus defectors from a much larger conservative elite which throws its weight against the citizens' movement. It is even more common for the local elite to be not only uninterested but intransigent, and the citizens' movement takes form because only a strong independent organization can create sufficient pressure to influence that local elite. Local officials who lay themselves open to charges of corruption and bribery, who react with callousness or indifference to particularly tragic cases, who elude requests to explain or justify official antipollution policy, and who make no attempt to heed the dissidents' opinions frequently provoke still more open confrontation.

Satake finds that citizens' movements are a major factor today in determining the outcome of local elections, often having a casting vote, and further finds that movements which resort to the use of elections (because their strength coincides conveniently with electoral district boundaries) are generally successful.[25] In Mishima, the anti-*kombinat* citizens' movement contributed to a permanent change in the structure of local politics, not only by helping to unseat mainstream LDP politicians, but also by strengthening the new governing coalition of progressive forces and maverick conservatives.[26] Movements in Usuki, Takaidō, Fuchū (Toyama prefecture), and Fuji managed to elect their own candidates and thus displace some portion of the previous elite. A May 1978 election in Hōhoku (Yamaguchi prefecture), in which 91 percent of the eligible voters turned out to elect a mayor opposed to the construction of a nearby nuclear power plant by a three-to-one margin, demonstrates how well citizens' movements have learned their electoral lessons.[27] Citizens' movements achieve their influence in elections by various means, differing in whether they concentrate on local executive offices or local assemblies, whether they promote candidates who come from within the citizens' movement itself or campaign for promovement candidates advanced by a local reformist coalition, or whether they remain aloof and independent from local leftist forces or work together with them. Even a citizens' movement that explicitly avoids electoral activity as a group can affect the outcome of local elections if many members of the movement decide to become individually active in favor of candidates who represent the views advanced by the movement as a whole, or if local politicians simply perceive the movement to be strong enough to control the outcome of an election. An effective movement may also cause selected

25. Satake, "Shimin undō to chihō senkyo," p. 166.

26. Lewis, "Civic Protest in Mishima," pp. 40–43.

27. AS, 6 February 1978 (ssb 214/8), 24 April 1978 (ssb 817/4), 15 May 1978 (ssb 444/7).

local officials to withdraw from politics to avoid the possible humiliation of losing an election, as in Ōiso.

Surveys of local officials' attitudes also demonstrate the impact of citizens' movements.[28] Elected officials approve of citizens' movements to almost the same extent as the general public does. Among civil servants, those in conservative areas and those occupying the highest ranks still regard citizens' movements as egoistic, obstructionist nuisances, but they are also resigned to them as a permanent feature of the political scene to which they must adapt. Most officials regard citizen participation in local government as essential, not only on principle but because in an age of financial stringency and increasing citizen demand they can prevent conflict and serve the community better if they maintain direct contact with local residents and listen carefully to their needs and grievances. Civil servants in large urban areas, particularly where reformist forces are strong, believe that they should encourage citizen participation and respond positively to citizens' movement pressure. Almost none of the officials in these several surveys thought that it was desirable or feasible to ignore citizens' movements.

· Impact on Policy Outputs from Local Governments

An indicator of the long-term effects of citizens' movements on the local level is the concrete result which they elicit from local government, either by forcing local government into more responsive behavior or by reconstituting that government itself, as was just described. Direct evidence is available from our cases—in which all but the movement in Ōiso achieved a substantial portion of their objectives—and also from recent studies of local government. Matsubara and Nitagai found that virtually all of the 185 municipal governments they surveyed in 1972–1973 responded to local citizens' movements with positive steps, though only in proportion to the pressure generated by the citizens' movement.[29] Local governments distinctly preferred ad hoc efforts to any act that might set precedents. The most prevalent response was to im-

28. See Hiromi Hidaka, "Citizens' Felt Needs and Those Needs as Perceived by Local Officials," and Chugoku Shimbunsha, "The Civil Servants and the Residents' Data Obtained from Two Attitudinal Surveys," both in *Local Government Review* 5 (1977), 36–51 and 83–99; Yasuo Watanabe, "Views of the Chief Executive Officer on 'Citizen Participation,'" *Local Government Review* 6 (1978), 58–76; Satō Atsushi, *Tenkanki no chihō jichi*, pp. 112–118; Satō Atushi, "Jūmin undō to jichitai gyōsei" [Residents' Movements and Local Government Administration], *Chiiki kaihatsu* 154 (July 1977), 43–55; Matsubara Haruo and Nitagai Kamon, *Jūmin undō no ronri: undō no tenkai katei, kadai to tembō* [The Logic of Residents' Movements; Developmental Process, Issues and Prospects] (Tokyo: Gakuyō Shobō, 1976), pp. 25–200, 247–330.

29. Matsubara and Nitagai, *Jūmin undō no ronri*, pp. 297–330; Haruo Matsubara, "The Local Government and Citizen Movements," *Local Government Review* 5 (1977), 52–69; and Satō Atsushi, *Tenkanki no chihō jichi*, pp. 108–122.

prove public relations activities (public discussion and explanation meetings, direct contact with the movement, the issuing of more information about the problem). Local governments could easily dispose of disputes over traffic safety, welfare facilities, and schools by such means and by manipulating the local budget, and they seemed willing to solve many other problems by taking action against local polluting firms or amending development plans.

But local governments had much more trouble and had to make more concessions in order to hammer out compromises with citizens' movements that challenged their own projects. In view of the increasing sophistication and expertise shown by citizens' movements, particularly on these more difficult issues, local governments indicated that they did not expect to succeed in the future with simple persuasion and would have to engage in mutual dialogue, hold more official public hearings, put local citizens on advisory committees, and survey the opinions of local residents. Perhaps the clearest evidence of a causal relationship between citizens' movement demands and local policy comes from a 1974 survey of eighty-five section chiefs in the Kyoto city administration, who agreed that over a ten-year period citizens' movements had become the most important source of policy initiative in Kyoto other than the mayor himself.[30]

What distinguishes citizens' movements from conventional pressure groups is that they want much more than a single act or concession, such as a playground, a traffic light, a lump-sum payment to an aggrieved group, a specific pork-barrel project on their behalf. Unlike the demands made by their predecessors, citizens' movements usually want new, long-term policies designed not merely to appease their group but to prevent similar problems from arising in the future. In addition to specific policies or institutional changes in the localities where they have arisen, citizens' movements have had indirect influence nationally by creating an atmosphere in which almost all Japanese prefectures and most of the municipalities in urban areas felt compelled to adopt similar changes in policy and procedure.[31]

The first local government bodies to respond to citizens' movement

30. Muramatsu, "Gyōsei katei to seiji sanka," p. 43. Additional findings from this survey of Kyoto city section chiefs are available in Michio Muramatsu, "Organizational Behavior of Local Public Officials," *Local Government Review* 4 (1976), 37–58. Ronald Aqua reports that officials he interviewed in eighty-eight Japanese cities also shared the view that citizens' movements were a powerful influence on local policy (personal communication, June 1976).

31. See especially Awaji Takehisa and Funada Masayuki, "Kōgai taisaku no tenkai to mondaiten" [The Development of Pollution Countermeasures and Their Problems], pp. 210–220, and Satō Atsushi, "Shizen kankyō hozen to chihō jichitai" [Preservation of the Natural Environment and Local Self-Government Bodies], pp. 269–280, both in Satō, *Chiiki kaihatsu, kōgai e no taiō.*

pressure by creating their own ordinances were of course in the most urbanized and polluted areas, such as Tokyo, Kyoto, and Osaka. Pollution problems provided reformist local governments in such cities with an important issue on which they could take policy initiatives.[32] The immediate result of these early efforts was to set off a full-fledged constitutional debate over the right of local bodies to create ordinances not already subsumed in existing national laws, which was resolved in 1970 when the Diet revised the Basic Law for Environmental Pollution Control to give local government bodies clearer authority over environmental problems. The Basic Law now explicitly allows prefectural and municipal ordinances to take into account special local characteristics (such as extreme environmental pollution), implicitly giving them the right to create legislation that is both innovative and more powerful than national laws. The Basic Law delegates authority for designing region-wide pollution-prevention plans in seriously polluted areas to the appropriate prefectural governors, and authorizes the prefectures and municipalities to initiate their own pollution control councils. Most important, the revised law guarantees greater national subsidies to local governments to assist with the cost of these enlarged environmental control programs.[33]

These revisions in the Basic Law stimulated the passage of additional environmental legislation and the creation of greater capacity to handle environmental complaints and countermeasures at the local level, now that local government bodies which lack the adventurous spirit of the reformist metropolitan governments have the state's guarantee that their policies will not be viewed as unconstitutional. A growing body of municipal and prefectural ordinances deal with environmental protection, often including higher ambient quality and effluent control standards as well as stiffer fines and jail terms for violators than do the laws passed by the national Diet (see table 24). By October 1975, forty-six prefectures had passed ordinances to deal with the protection of nature, and seven metropolitan prefectures with reformist governments had also passed comprehensive environmental protection ordinances. The Environment Agency claimed that the arrests for pollution offenses in-

32. Terry Edward MacDougall, "Political Opposition and Local Government in Japan: The Significance of Emerging Progressive Local Leadership" (Ph.D. diss. in Political Science, Yale University, 1975), pp. 387–411. MacDougall suggests that citizens' movements and environmental issues were important in stimulating and guiding the rise of local reformist forces. See "Japanese Urban Local Politics: Toward a Viable Leftist Political Opposition," in Lewis Austin, ed., *Japan: The Paradox of Progress* (New Haven: Yale University Press, 1976), pp. 31–56; "The Progressive Alternative in Japanese Local Political Leadership," paper presented to the Association of Asian Studies, March 1973, Chicago; and "Local Opposition and Big City Elections in Japan, 1947–1975," chap. 3 in Flanagan, Steiner, and Krauss, *Political Opposition and Local Politics in Japan*.

33. Environment Agency, *Environmental Laws and Regulations in Japan* (Tokyo: Ministry of Finance Printing Bureau, 1976), pp. 1–8.

TABLE 24 / *Local Government Countermeasures for Pollution Control*

	1971	1972	1973	1974	1975	1976	1977	1978
Pollution Complaints								
To local government	76,106	87,764	86,777	79,015	76,531	70,033	69,729	69,730
To police	nd	18,353	nd	36,373	33,714	31,181	33,350	36,148
Pollution Offenses								
Incidents	482	791	1,727	2,856	3,572	4,697	4,827	5,383
Persons arrested	nd	nd	3,922	4,531	5,506	6,236	6,453	6,288
Persons indicted	nd	nd	2,787	3,239	3,790	4,540	4,636	4,231
% of indictments	nd	nd	71.1%	71.5%	68.8%	72.8%	71.8%	67.3%
Pollution Disputes								
Newly submitted to environmental dispute coordinating councils	28	34	58	58	62	82	74	73
Prefectural Personnel in Pollution Control								
Specialists	—	3,609	4,292	4,810	5,239	5,117	5,444	5,303
Total personnel	2,634	4,568	5,284	5,852	6,614	6,267	6,620	6,299
Municipal Pollution Control Ordinances								
Pollution control	79	217	288	346	426	460	470	516
Environmental protection	7	39	71	75	144	178	180	214
Other related ordinances	48	48	49	63	65	164	267	304

Sources: Kankyōchō, *Kankyō hakusho, 1973–1980* [White Paper on the Environment, 1973–1980] (Tokyo: Ōkurasho Insatsukyoku, 1973–1980). Kōgai tōchōsei iinkai jimukyoku, *Kōgai kujō kensū chōsa kekka hōkokusho 1975* [Report on the Results of a Survey of the Number of Pollution Complaints] (January 1977), p. 2.

creased rapidly because the police paid more attention to environmental offenses and because citizens reported violations and assisted in the apprehension of offenders to a greater extent as well.[34]

Local governments also enlarged the staff assigned to pollution control and to the processing of complaints related to environmental quality. By October 1975, all forty-seven prefectures had sections specializing in pollution prevention, all but four had a department to promote environmental administration, and all but three had pollution control centers or research institutes. At the municipal level by the same date, 274 municipalities had a department or section to deal with environmental prob-

34. Police are not involved in the detection of pollution offenses in the United States, but in Japan most environmental laws include penal provisions for fines and imprisonment, and the National Police Agency and its prefectural branches are empowered to arrest offenders. Most arrests are of individuals caught disposing of individual or industrial wastes in violation of waste management and water pollution laws.

lems, and another 512 had assigned a subsection to the environmental issue; 49 municipal governments with high reformist strength even had their own pollution control centers or environmental research institutes.[35] The Central Environmental Dispute Coordinating Commission was created in November 1970 to relieve pressure on the courts and to provide binding solutions to complainants whose grievances were not suitable for litigation. By December 1975 it had received a total of 238 cases.[36] The number of pollution complaints received by local governments peaked in 1973, and this is usually explained by actual improvement in the environment and by the energy crisis, which had the double-barreled effect of temporarily displacing worries about the environment and reducing pollution as Japan sought greater energy efficiency. Another consequence of citizens' movement activity at the local level was the rapid increase in the number of pollution-prevention contracts (kyōtei) between local government bodies and industrial firms, and legal opinion is gradually shifting in favor of regarding them as binding contracts similar to any other business contract.[37]

In sum, then, citizens' movements have forced the local level of government in Japan to deal with an agenda set by their citizenry, to make decisions independently of guidance from the national government, and to create long-term policies designed to alleviate environmental problems.

· Impact on the Local Political Process

Citizens' movements almost always go beyond an interest in the substance of policies related specifically to the environment or consumer problems they are angry about, to cultivate a concern with the question of *how* local governments arrive at their decisions. Regardless of the extent to which they succeeded in achieving specific objectives, almost all of the movements in this study learned during the course of their dispute with local government that an important source of their difficulties lay in the absence of a free flow of information between local government and the public. In certain cases, the resulting decisions were demonstrably incompetent or even financially untenable because they were not subject to adequate external review or public criticism. Frequently it was the furor

---

35. Environment Agency, *Quality of the Environment in Japan 1976* (Tokyo: Ministry of Finance Printing Bureau, 1976), pp. 224–225.

36. Ibid., p. 218.

37. Awaji and Funada, "Kōgai taisaku no tenkai to mondaiten," pp. 199–208. See also Harada Naohiko, "Kōgai bōshi kyōtei to sono hōritsujo no mondaiten" [Pollution Prevention Contracts and Related Problems from the Legal Point of View], pp. 274–278, and Narumi Masayasu, "Kigyō to no kōgai bōshi kyōtei: Yokohama hōshiki" [Pollution Prevention Contracts with Industry: The Yokohama Formula], pp. 279–283, both in *Jūrisuto* 458 (10 August 1970).

over such a decision, arrived at without any consultation with the people to be affected, which stimulated the rise of a citizens' movement in the first place. Such a citizens' movement usually decided that the local elite, inbred and accustomed to going about its business unchallenged, might surrender on one issue or in one policy area, but would continue to abuse its authority unless firm procedural guarantees for citizen input were also created.

For these reasons, citizens' movements often develop deep concern with opening up the inner workings of local government to public scrutiny, increasing citizen access to the authorities, and creating guarantees to prevent any new procedures for citizen input from degenerating into perfunctory rituals. Citizens' movements with these concerns frequently force changes in the planning procedures of local governments whereby reports, proposals, the results of environmental impact studies, and the like are circulated to the local citizenry in advance of any action that might be taken. Citizens' movements insist that public hearings and conferences be well publicized so as to create for the citizenry an arena for the exchange of ideas and the expression of criticism. Sometimes movements manage to arrange for regular citizen representation on commissions involved with city planning and environmental management. Several movements in this study, in Tokyo, Usuki, and to a lesser extent in Ōiso and Shibushi, did this. There has been a steady increase in the use of direct-demand provisions (recall, initiative, referendum) to establish or revise local ordinances, particularly in pollution prevention, citizen control over local purse strings, and levels of local services, including some very innovative and significant legislation. Recall is being used to threaten or remove officials not because of scandal but increasingly in connection with controversies over basic policy and the constitutional responsibilities of those in public service.[38] Citizens' groups all over Japan have pressed local governments to pass ordinances modeled on the American Freedom of Information Act, an invaluable tool used by groups in the United States, to guarantee citizen access to public documents. Since May 1979, fifteen prefectures and four cities have begun deliberating measures

38. See also Satō Atsushi, "Chiiki kaihatsu no kōgai to gekika" [Regional Development and the Intensification of Pollution], in Satō, *Chiiki kaihatsu, kōgai e no taiō*, pp. 35–37; Satō Atsushi and Watanabe Yasuo, *Jūmin sanka no jissen: jūmin shitai no gyōsei wa dō kokoromirareteiru ka* [The Practice of Residents' Participation: How Is Administration by Residents Themselves Being Conducted?] (Tokyo: Gakuyō Shobō, 1975), passim; Abe Hitoshi, "Gyōsei no sekinin to jūmin sanka" [Administrative Responsibility and Residents' Participation], Jichi Daigakkō kenkyūbu, eds., *Jūmin sanka to gyōsei* [Residents' Participation and Administration], pp. 39–55; Satō Atsushi, *Tenkanki no chihō jichi*, pp. 227–249; Shindō Muneyuki, "Chokusetsu yōkyū seido to jūmin sanka" [The Direct-Demand System and Residents' Participation], Jichi Daigakkō kenkyūbu, *Jūmin sanka to gyōsei*, pp. 76–91.

to make more official information available to the Japanese public, and it is expected that local governments will initiate such legislation before the central government responds to similar pressure being exerted at the national level.[39]

It is particularly interesting that Japanese citizens' movements demand more opportunities to participate than their system provides them, in view of very different findings from a comparative study of local participation in fifteen Western democracies including the United States. In all of the Western nations under study, actual citizen participation lagged considerably behind the efforts of municipal administrators to elicit participation.[40] Together these observations suggest the ironic possibility that democratic values and institutions may atrophy in the nations that gave birth to them but may under special circumstances find greater nurturance and healthier support in a society like Japan which lacks a democratic tradition.[41]

In their effort to increase citizen access to local politics, citizens' movements differ as to whether they emphasize the legislative route—electoral involvement designed to improve community representation in the local assembly—or the administrative route—consisting both of election campaigns on behalf of a local executive who will reflect citizens' movement goals and of direct dealings with the local bureaucracy.[42] Movements favoring the former argue that what is important is to put into the local assembly trustworthy representatives who can give a citizens' movement a permanent voice. These representatives also function as a body of knowledgeable intermediaries to present citizens' movement views forcefully to the city government and to provide the movement with feedback from the system. Although these appear to be reasonable arguments, the legislative route to influence is not often the preferred choice of a citizens' movement strong enough to elect a mayor. More often, the legislative route is selected by citizens' movements that are strong enough to elect several representatives to a local assembly, but not strong enough to determine the outcome of a mayoral election.

39. *Asahi Evening News*, 3 March 1980.

40. *Studies in Comparative Local Government* 5:2 (Winter 1971, special issue on citizen participation), 52–57, 80–96.

41. Revisionists in the new field of people's history (*minshūshi*) in Japan would argue that citizens' movements constitute the revival of a democratic tradition that has been obscured by conventional scholarship. See Daikichi Irokawa, "The Survival Struggle of the Japanese Community," *Japan Interpreter* 9:4 (Spring 1975), 465–494; Carol Gluck, "The People in History: Recent Trends in Japanese Historiography," *Journal of Asian Studies* 38:1 (November 1978), 25–50. I have addressed this controversy as applied to citizens' movements in "Citizens' Movements in Japan: Rural Revivalism or Modern Democracy?" paper presented at the Association for Asian Studies, Chicago, April 1978.

42. Satake, "Shimin undō to chihō senkyo," pp. 167–183.

For both historical and practical reasons, citizens' movements with a choice usually select the administrative route.[43] First of all, in the vast majority of Japanese cities where both mayor and assembly are conservative, real decisions are made within the inner circle of the prevailing party before they reach the legislature, so the local assembly is not a significant decision-making body. Thus a citizens' movement has little reason to infiltrate the local assembly and instead wants to influence the local LDP party structure, the mayor, and the local bureaucracy where the stuff of politics really takes place.

There are also pragmatic motives for involvement in elections for local executives rather than assemblymen, the same as those which explain why the reformist parties have also emphasized mayoral and gubernatorial over assembly elections in their own growth at the local level.[44] Direct election of a mayor does not involve the complicated strategic decisions required for an assembly election. In prefectural and municipal assembly elections (with certain exceptions in the metropolitan prefectures) candidates run at large, rather than for seats in particular districts, and thus each candidate competes against every other candidate. Any group attempting to expand its influence by electing assemblymen must therefore calculate its total voting strength in the district, endorse the appropriate number of candidates (to avoid distributing votes too thinly or wasting funds on candidates who must inevitably lose), and, most important, control the distribution of its votes carefully (so that no nominee receives votes greatly in excess of the number needed to win, thus depriving other party nominees of votes). Even a citizens' movement with considerable voting strength would require substantial political skill—knowledge of the electoral habits of the district and the endorsement and vote-control methods used by other parties—to turn that strength into election victories in an assembly election. But in a mayoral election a citizens' movement need only endorse one candidate, who runs against a limited field of competitors, and campaign single-mindedly on behalf of that candidate.[45]

The incentives to continue working through the mayor and local bureaucracy are obviously compounded once a movement succeeds in electing a sympathetic candidate as mayor. A reformist mayor, whether placed in office by a citizens' movement or by an effective reformist coalition preceding the rise of citizens' movements, usually faces an assembly which still has a conservative majority. When assembly deliberation is

43. Ibid., p. 177; and Muramatsu, "Gyōsei katei to seiji sanka," pp. 53–56.
44. MacDougall, "Political Opposition and Big City Elections."
45. For an example of the problems involved in a movement campaign for assembly elections, see Satake on Shinza city, "Shimin undō to chihō senkyo," pp. 178–183.

necessary, the citizens' movement throws its support to the mayor to enhance his probability of winning in any confrontation with a hostile assembly. On other issues, the movement bypasses the assembly and the local conservative elite of *yūryokusha*, and instead works directly through the mayor and specially created citizens' consultation offices (*shimin shitsu*) in the local bureaucracy.

Muramatsu found this pattern in Kobe, Yokohama, Kyoto, and Tokyo, which all had reformist executives, and believes that the emergence of citizens' movements and the resulting increase in popular participation at the local level are likely to strengthen this trend for collaboration between citizen and official to the exclusion of local assemblies. Sakata investigated this question and learned that citizens' movements generally view their local assemblymen as ignorant, slow-moving amateurs, concerned primarily about favorable publicity for themselves. They get better and faster results by working through the local bureaucracy's staff of full-time professional specialists interested in solving problems.[46]

Whichever route they use, citizens' movements have opened up the local political process, not only in their own communities but elsewhere, where local officials try to head off confrontation by soliciting broad participation in controversial decisions. A clear illustration is the case of the nuclear-powered ship "Mutsu," for which the national government sought a permanent port and repair site in the city of Sasebo.[47] This ship was originally to have been based in the city of Mutsu in Aomori prefecture, but the furor that resulted after radiation leakage was discovered on the ship's maiden voyage in September 1974 gave rise to a very powerful citizens' movement against Japan's atomic energy bureaucracy. In an agreement with the movement in Mutsu, the government promised that it would seek a new home port for the ship by April 1977, that neither removal of the fuel rods nor repairs to the reactor would be carried out in Mutsu, and that local fishermen would be handsomely compensated for past and future damage to their fish sales.

In 1976 the Japanese government began negotiating for a new port with the city of Sasebo and the prefecture of Nagasaki, but by the dead-

46. Muramatsu, "Gyōsei katei to seiji sanka," pp. 48–68; Tokio Sakata, "Citizens' Movements and the Role of Local Assemblies," *Local Government Review* 6 (1978), 48–57.

47. On the "Mutsu" episode, see *AS*, 22 October 1973; *JT*, 22 October 1973, and August, September, and October in 1974, passim; "The Mutsu," *Japan Quarterly* 22:1 (January–March 1975), 3–6; Dane Lee Miller, "Drifting Ship, Drifting Government," *Japan Interpreter* 12:2 (Spring 1978), 201–222. On the final disposition of the "Mutsu," see *Japan Times Weekly* (*JTW*), 13 May, 10 June, and 29 July in 1978, and 27 October 1979.

line of April 1977 had received permission only from the mayor and municipal assembly of Sasebo, to allow only the repairs. Due to political pressure from fishing cooperatives, the city of Nagasaki, and organizations of atomic bomb survivors, Nagasaki's prefectural assembly refused permission until a severe slump in the shipbuilding industry threatened to bankrupt Sasebo Heavy Industries, the largest employer in the city of Sasebo. The central government finally succeeded in its efforts to bring the "Mutsu" to Sasebo for repairs by working out an agreement in July 1978 involving five concerned parties: the Nuclear Ship Development Agency, the Science and Technology Agency, the city of Sasebo, the prefecture of Nagasaki, and the prefectural federation of fishing cooperatives. The final agreement also provided the fishermen compensation for potential radiation damage and promised the prefecture extension of high-speed rail service to the city of Nagasaki. The prefectural governor promised to be cooperative about allowing tests of the fuel rods in the reactor vessel but insisted on retaining the rights of prior consultation and informed consent to such tests by keeping the key that must be used to lift the fuel rods for examination. The "Mutsu" was towed into Sasebo harbor in late 1978, but as of November 1979 the government had not even secured a wharf where repair work could take place, nor had any other city agreed to become the ship's home port.

It is significant that all of the local officials involved in these two years of negotiations—the assemblies and executives of Nagasaki prefecture, the city of Sasebo, as well as the city of Nagasaki, which was involved because it suffered an atomic bombing in 1945—proceeded with extreme care. They were sensitive to the potential controversy in the issue, anxious to conduct themselves with propriety and to consult adequately with all interested parties. The contrast with the behavior of local officials interested in promoting similar projects in the past (in Kashima, Shibushi, Usuki, Ōiso, and so on) should be obvious. Instead of working out the necessary decisions behind closed doors, obtaining assembly approval in a quiet and little-publicized session, and then announcing a fait accompli to the bewildered public, these executives and assemblies conducted their negotiations openly and cautiously. They constantly reminded negotiators representing the central government that any decision reached would have to be acceptable to their citizens, and they negotiated additional agreements with interested groups, such as local fishermen and dock workers, before rather than after the arrival of the "Mutsu." Although local leaders could not placate all of the opposition to repairing the "Mutsu" in Sasebo, their new sensitivity verifies the mixture of hopes, predictions, and assertions already voiced by Japanese scholars about increasing citizen participation.

Thus citizens' movements have played a significant role in democratizing local politics and changing the primary orientation of many local politicians and bureaucracies from their administrative functions (*gyōsei*) to those of representation and self-government (*jichi*).[48]

• Changing Images of Local Autonomy

Because citizens' movements know that they have influence at the local level where they can exert continuous pressure, they demand that jurisdiction over certain issues such as environmental problems be delegated to local bodies or that local authority over these matters be enlarged. The urban reformist governments were not the only ones that reacted enthusiastically to this call for independence. Hiroshima prefecture announced in 1978 that it would be the first to delegate 53 of a prefecture's 125 licensing powers to the municipal level and would review the possibility of similarly delegating the remaining 72 powers, in response to citizen demand.[49] Similarly, many prefectural or municipal ordinances concerned with environmental regulation, designed in response to citizens' movements, have served as models for national laws years later.[50] Shiga prefecture attracted national attention in 1979 when it announced the drafting of an ordinance to ban the use, sale, or gift of synthetic detergents and to restrict the discharge of nitrogen and phosphorous wastes into Lake Biwa, the water supply for 13 million people in the Osaka-Kyoto region. This ordinance is modeled on citizen movement demands and is the first to ban a substance before the national government does so.[51] Similarly, sympathetic local governments all over Japan are sponsoring novel experiments in energy conservation with alternative decentralized energy sources, quite unrelated to the central government's research on high-technology forms of energy.[52]

The success of citizens' movements in stimulating local autonomy requires us to rethink certain generalizations about Japanese local government. One view, which we acquired largely through studies of the occupation and the "reverse course," is that many of the democratizing reforms of the occupation, however well intended, were nonetheless fundamentally flawed in trying to decentralize power and create local autonomy, an organism that could not possibly be expected to survive in

---

48. Matsushita Keiichi, *Shimin sanka* [Citizen Participation] (Tokyo: Tōyō Keizai Shimbunsha, 1971); Matsubara Haruo, *Kōgai to chiiki shakai: seikatsu to jūmin undō no shakaigaku* [Pollution and Regional Society: The Sociology of Livelihood and Residents' Movements] (Tokyo: Nihon Keizai Shimbunsha, October 1971), especially pp. 176–183; and Matsubara Haruo, ed., *Jūmin sanka to jichi no kakushin*, especially articles by Matsubara, Yamamoto, Okuda, and case studies by Satō Fumio, Okamura, Yamauchi, Tanaka, and Watanabe.

49. *Mainichi Shimbun*, 13 October 1978, p. 3.

50. Satō Atsushi, *Tenkanki no chihō jichi*, pp. 227–249.

51. *JTW*, 25 August 1979.

52. *JTW*, 29 September 1979.

Japan. But citizens' movements' contribution to the transformation from *gyōsei* to *jichi* and the emerging local/national rivalries in Japanese politics suggest that the notion of local autonomy per se should not be regarded as absolutely alien to Japan. Apparently there is scope for an indigenous evolution of the ideas of decentralization and the desirability of local autonomy, even in a nation with high cultural cohesion and physical density and with such a strong recent tradition of political centralization.

Although Japanese citizens' movements inspired concern for local autonomy, environmentalists in other countries clamor for greater administrative centralization and uniformity and increased national and international regulation.[53] Perhaps this results from the fact that Japanese environmentalists were concerned not only about the consequences of industrial activity in its later stages as it encounters natural limits (pollution and environmental destruction), but simultaneously about other issues associated with earlier stages of economic development, chiefly the transition from agriculture to industry. In effect Japan endured a rough and rapid passage into the industrial age twice. The first period of economic takeoff began in the nineteenth century and continued until the 1930s. Then after World War II Japan had to repeat the transition from agricultural society all over again, artificially compressing both early and late phases of industrialism into the political experience of a single generation. Today's environmentalists in Japan resemble trust-busting populists and muckrakers of an earlier day in their concern for democratic reform, decentralization, and hostility to the concentration of power in a political and economic elite, in essence objecting to the social conditions left behind in the wake of excessively rapid expansion, which characterizes the earlier phases of industrial growth. In the United States today there is also concern for local control and an emerging hostility to bigness, but it derives from such issues as race relations, public education, and the tradition of states' rights, and is unrelated to environmental problems.

Another familiar precept about Japanese politics is the commonplace notion that local governments are hopelessly dependent upon the national government for financial support. This dependency creates an institutional necessity for local governments to serve at the beck and

53. Michael J. Brenner, *The Political Economy of America's Environmental Dilemma* (Lexington, Mass.: Lexington Books, 1973), pp. 121–132; Lettie McSpadden Wenner, *One Environment Under Law: A Public Policy Dilemma* (Pacific Palisades, Calif.: Goodyear Publishing, 1976), pp. 51–148; Walter A. Rosenbaum, *The Politics of Environmental Concern* (New York: Praeger, 1973 and 1977), chap. 10; J. Clarence Davies, III, and Barbara S. Davies, *The Politics of Pollution*, 2d ed. (Indianapolis: Bobbs-Merrill, 1975), pp. 220–224; and Cynthia Enloe, *The Politics of Pollution in Comparative Perspective* (New York: David McKay, 1975), pp. 145–149, 317–331.

call of the national bureaucracy, which awards stipends and subsidies, and prevents local bodies from being responsive toward the citizenry to whom they are ostensibly accountable. A favorite LDP campaign technique was to turn the financial vulnerability of local government to partisan advantage by arguing that the LDP's pipeline to the center would keep the local community supplied with development projects and subsidies. However, in their impact on local environmental policy and decision-making, citizens' movements loom as a force which can compete with these institutional imperatives and thus spoil the effectiveness of the LDP's appeals. Displeased with what the LDP did with its pipeline money, many voters were willing to risk losing this lucrative channel to the central treasury and instead to support reformist independents and citizens' movement candidates who promised democratic processes and accountability in local government. LDP hopefuls must now campaign on these same terms, promising to stand on the "residents' side" (*jūmin saido*) in any confrontation with the national government. Conservative resilience in the 1979 local elections suggests that the LDP learned its lesson well.

With citizens' movements insisting that local government protect the interests of local residents as they themselves define these interests, cities must choose between fulfilling old or new definitions of good performance. It would have been inconceivable before the era of citizens' movements for a local government to challenge the central government in court, but in 1973 the city of Settsu did just that. Settsu built four nursery schools for which the central government supplied only 2.7 percent of the cost, in spite of a provision in the Child Welfare Act stipulating that the central government would provide 50 percent of such funds. Although the city lost its suit to recover the missing funds in 1977, this example shows how local governments are redefining the concept of service to constituents.[54]

Thus an aggressive citizenry can compete with the constraints imposed by financial dependency to change fundamentally the role of local governments vis-à-vis the state, from deference and cooperation toward innovation and rivalry. This change demonstrates that local government need not inevitably serve the central government rather than its own constituents, and casts doubt upon one of our most convenient generaliza-

54. The Tokyo District Court ruled in favor of the central government on the grounds that giving every local government the automatic right to claim a subsidy (as opposed to giving the central government the right to review bids and to award a given total quantity of subsidies) would result in extremely inefficient and indiscriminate allocation of resources and unpredictable burdens on each year's budget. See Michio Muramatsu and Ronald Aqua, "Japan Confronts Its Cities: Central-Local Relationships in a Changing Political Context," in Douglas E. Ashford, ed., *National Resources and Urban Policy* (London: Methuen, 1980), pp. 163–181.

tions about the pyramidal nature of Japanese politics. In fact, the stimulation of local/national rivalry is one of the chief objectives of citizens' movements, which realize that direct impact on the national government is beyond the reach of any individual movement. Instead, citizens' movements try to win their own local governments over as allies in their conflict with higher authority.

The emergence of regionalism and local/national conflict are long-term trends in Japan, but we should acknowledge the importance of citizens' movements in contributing to these changes.[55] We have ample evidence, both where citizens' movements arose and in communities wise enough to learn from others, that citizens' movements have helped to change the style of some local politicians from traditional paternalism, usually benevolent in intent but limited in imagination, to more responsive attention to constituent demands. In effect, this is a shift in representational style from patron to caretaker in the terms Richardson devised to describe Japanese politicians, similar though not fully analogous to a shift from trustee to delegate in Wahlke's scheme of legislative roles.[56] Citizens' movements not only won more stringent environmental controls and more balanced approaches to regional development in the communities where they emerged, but they apparently sparked the creation of similar policies in most prefectures and many municipalities. The same ripple effects have occurred with respect to local political processes, so that procedures for planning and policy evaluation now allow for more citizen input and consultation. Finally, by competing with the national government for the attention of local government, citizens' movements provide a foundation for strengthening local autonomy and stimulate increased rivalry between center and periphery.

Citizens' Movements in Comparative Perspective

The preceding investigation into the causes and consequences of citizens' movements for members, their immediate surroundings, and local politics serves as an adequate basis for comparison between Japanese citizens' movements and environmental protests and social movements in other settings. This comparison can, in turn, add historical and spatial

55. Gary Allinson, "Japan's Independent Voters: Dilemma or Opportunity?" *Japan Interpreter* 11:1 (Spring 1976), 36–55; Taketsugu Tsurutani, *Political Change in Japan: Response to Postindustrial Challenge* (New York: David McKay, 1977), pp. 208–209; Michio Muramatsu, "The Impact of Economic Growth Policies on Local Politics in Japan," *Asian Survey* 15:9 (September 1975), 799–816; and Flanagan, Steiner, and Krauss, *Political Opposition and Local Politics in Japan.*

56. Bradley M. Richardson, "Japanese Local Politics: Support Mobilization and Leadership Styles," *Asian Survey* 7:12 (December 1967), 860–875; John C. Wahlke, Heinz Eulau, William Buchanan, and LeRoy C. Ferguson, *The Legislative System: Explorations in Legislative Behavior* (New York: Wiley, 1962), 272–280.

depth to our perception and thus contribute to our remaining objective of exploring the significance of citizens' movements for Japanese politics beyond the local level.

Japan and Germany are often compared because of obvious historical parallels—for example, the development of nationalism and an interest in empire in the late nineteenth century, a timid and unsuccessful experiment with democracy using similar constitutional foundations, followed by the rise of extremism and military expansionism in the 1930s, a devastating defeat in World War II, and a miraculous economic recovery afterward. Japan and West Germany also have many environmental problems in common because of the rapidity of postwar economic growth emphasizing heavy industry, the mixed spatial pattern of agriculture with industrial activity, high population density, and the visibility of pollution in daily life, in both nations. Thus it is not entirely surprising that there are also similarities between the environmental movements in the two countries. The German movement is composed of small groups organized at the local level, and there exists only one major national organization (the Burgerinitiativ, or "Citizens' Initiative"), whose purpose is to coordinate the massive demonstrations against nuclear power which have preoccupied the German movement recently. Naturally, these parallels are not perfect, and there are also important differences: the intense opposition in Germany to nuclear power rather than other environmental threats, the reliance on marches and demonstrations as tactics, and the conspicuous presence of young people all contrast with Japan. But in these two contemporary affluent democracies, which both saw attempts to establish parliamentary democracy earlier in this century overpowered by authoritarian and military traditions, a primary concern of both movements is citizen participation, not merely as a means but as an end in itself.[57]

If we then compare the environmental movement in Japan with that in the United States, the importance of political context and the potential variation in composition, goals, structure, and tactics of a movement become clear. First of all, the American movement is considerably larger, estimated to consist of 20,000 groups with a primary interest in environmental questions, along with 20,000 additional groups concerned about the environment as one among several concerns. There is an enormous

57. I am indebted to Linda Floyd for help with sources on the German environmental movement. See William Hines, "Anti-Nuclear Ferment in Europe," *The Progressive* 41:9 (September 1977), 19–21; "Nuclear Man at Bay," *Economist* 262 (19 March 1977), 12–13; "Rethink Urged on Nuclear Energy Programme," *German Tribune* 777 (6 March 1977), 4. See also *New York Times*, in 1975, 9 April (14) and 28 August (10). In 1977, see 20 February (7), 30 March (8), 2 August (6), 7 August (IV-18), and 10 August (IV-16). In *The Times* (London), for 1975, see 21 February (6), 25 February (6), 2 March (1), 10 August (13). In 1977, see 20 February (1), 23 February (6), 15 March (1), 22 March (9), 23 March (17), 14 April (14), 31 May (4), and 22 August (15).

core of 5.5 million dues-paying members just in the nineteen best-known national organizations. The National Wildlife Federation, with 3.5 million members, is the largest conservation organization in the world. One estimate, which makes no attempt to avoid double-counting of energetic individuals who belong to several national groups, is that there are approximately 20 million members (or about 9% of the entire population) in all 40,000 groups with some interest in the environment.[58] In contrast, the Japanese movement probably consists of only 3,000 or so individual citizens' movements, all organized at the local and not the national level. These groups may involve as many as 6 million members (about 5% of the entire population), a comparable total in view of the fact that this figure avoids double-counting by omitting coalitions. However, the hard core of regular members is probably only 135,000, according to our estimates in chapter I, and the largest Japanese organizations are regional coalitions of at most 300,000 members.[59] Obviously the American movement has considerably more political and financial power, reflecting not only the richer tradition of political participation but also the greater wealth of the society and the unusual willingness of Americans to donate to political and charitable causes.

The American movement is a peculiar amalgam of young people interested in a counterculture of alternative lifestyles, along with scions of the upper middle class. The Japanese movement, neither a youth crusade nor an establishment fad, represents a more balanced cross-section of society. The American movement's general interest in ecology contributed to such strong legislation to protect the natural environment that two endangered species, the three-inch snail darter and the Furbish lousewort, stalled the construction of hydroelectric dams in the United States. It is difficult to conceive of a similar event occurring in Japan, where environmental problems are defined more narrowly in terms of human health and well-being, reflected in the "victim consciousness" both of activists' demands and of Japanese policy.

The American movement tends to define the solutions to environmental problems in terms of increased regulation of economic activity but without any fundamental change in the structure of the economy. Japanese environmentalists are considerably more inclined not only to be suspicious of capitalism as an economic philosophy, but also to question the growth strategies Japan used in the past. Japanese environmentalists harbor basic doubts about the integrity and trustworthiness of political institutions, whereas their American counterparts have successfully infiltrated the environmental policy-making structure.

58. Odom Fanning, *Man and His Environment: Citizen Action* (New York: Harper & Row, 1975), pp. 116, 213, 214.

59. Nakamura Kiichi, "Jūmin undō no soshiki to kōzō," p. 23; "Citizens' Movements," *Japan Quarterly* 20:4 (October–December 1973), 368.

Perhaps the greatest contrasts occur in movement structure and tactics. It is probably inappropriate to conceive of the American environmental movement as a social movement any longer—it has fulfilled the predictions of Michels' iron law of oligarchy and evolved into a set of institutionalized interest groups.[60] The conspicuous environmental groups in the United States are highly structured, well-organized interest groups, which lobby regularly in Washington and participate actively (though of course not as effectively as they would like) in the design and modification of legislation. The American movement prefers the tactics of well-established interest groups: lobbying, organized letter-writing campaigns, fund-raising by mail, electoral campaigns against Congress's "Dirty Dozen," and so on. In contrast, the Japanese movement avoids institutionalization and concentrates on tactics suitable for influencing politics only at the local level.

Because of a strong political tradition that looks favorably upon voluntary action and citizen access to government in America, the environmental movement quickly worked its way into the political establishment, turned into a set of long-lived interest groups which lobby at the national level, and saw its goals accepted as national policy. Through the Citizens' Advisory Council on Environmental Quality, the Environmental Protection Agency actively solicits citizen input, partly to create a constituency that can strengthen its bureaucratic bargaining position and its ability to police the polluting activities of private industry and other government agencies.[61] The American movement's greatest impact has been on policy, not political culture. The Japanese environmental movement has clearly had an important indirect role in eliciting legislation and national policy to deal with environmental problems, but citizens' movements could not take for granted the notions of citizen participation, local autonomy, or access to the government, and have had to convert these into principal goals in their own right, rather than as means to more distant ends.

It is more appropriate to compare Japanese citizens' movements with American social movements that have proven to have greater historical significance thus far than the ecology movement. There are intriguing parallels between Japanese citizens' movements and American populism at the turn of the century. Both contained overtones of agrarian sentimentalism opposed quite simply to the conversion of agricultural life to industrialism. Both complained about the imbalance between the wealth associated with industrial activity and various symptoms of social "lag," such as the filthy or dangerous processes and working condi-

60. Robert Michels, *Political Parties: A Sociological Study of the Oligarchical Tendencies of Modern Democracy* (New York: Dover, 1915, 1959).
61. Fanning, *Citizen Action*, pp. 38–70.

tions which industry defended in a time of expansion as a necessity for profit and growth. Both objected to oligopoly and monopoly among industrialists and the resulting corruption and antidemocratic tendencies inherent in such a concentration of economic and political power. Thus both developed a concern with decentralization and grass-roots democracy as a form of insurance against the abuse of power by the concentrated economic institutions and political machines they feared. Similarly, like the antiwar movement of the 1960s, Japanese citizens' movements challenged some of the fundamental values and beliefs of the political establishment and exposed the gap between the system's democratic ideals and its actual mode of operation.

But we might best appreciate the excitement citizens' movements have generated in Japan by comparing them with the civil rights movement.[62] Both could be regarded as social movements demanding political power for a group that had not claimed it before—for blacks systematically disenfranchised and discriminated against in the United States, and for average citizens intimidated by the oppressive weight of an elitist, hierarchical social and political tradition in Japan. Both lend strength to the resource mobilization rather than the alienation theory of social movements. The American civil rights movement began in the established organizations of the black middle class, not among the ghetto unemployed with much more serious grievances.[63] Similarly, Japanese ac-

62. This discussion of the civil rights movement and local government in the United States draws upon Milton Kotler, *Neighborhood Government: The Local Foundations of Political Life* (Indianapolis: Bobbs-Merrill, 1969); Thomas D. Lynch, symposium editor, "Symposium: Neighborhoods and Citizen Involvement," *Public Administration Review* 32:2 (May–June 1972), 189–223; Erasmus H. Kloman, "Citizen Participation in the Philadelphia Model Cities Program: Retrospect and Prospect," pp. 402–408, and Howard H. Hallman, "Federally Financed Citizen Participation," pp. 421–427, and Robert A. Aleshire, "Power to the People: An Assessment of the Community Action and Model Cities Experience," pp. 428–443, and Richard W. Boone, "Reflections on Citizen Participation and the Economic Opportunity Act," pp. 444–456, all in *Public Administration Review* 32 (special issue, September 1972); Daniel Bell and Virginia Held, "The Community Revolution," *Public Interest* 16 (Summer 1969), 142–177; Edgar S. Cahn, ed., *Citizen Participation: Effecting Community Change* (New York: Praeger, 1971); Henry J. Schmandt, "Municipal Decentralization: An Overview," *Public Administration Review* 32 (special issue, October 1972), 571–588; Irving Kristol, "Decentralization for What?" *Public Interest* 11 (Spring 1968), 17–25; Joseph F. Zimmerman, "The Politics of Neighborhood Government," *Studies in Comparative Local Government* 5:1 (Summer 1971), 28–39; Douglas Yates, "Neighborhood Government," *Policy Sciences* 3:2 (July 1972), 209–210; and Douglas Yates, "Political Innovation and Institution Building: The Experience of Decentralization Experiments," in Willis D. Hawley and Michael Lipsky, eds., *Theoretical Perspectives on Urban Politics* (Englewood Cliffs, N.J.: Prentice-Hall, 1976), pp. 146–175.

63. Richard P. Gale, "From Sit-in to Hike-in: A Comparison of the Civil Rights and Environmental Movements," in William R. Burch, Jr., Neil H. Cheek, Jr., and Lee Taylor, eds., *Social Behavior, Natural Resources, and the Environment* (New York: Harper & Row, 1972), pp. 280–305.

tivists, though somewhat better off than the average, nonetheless come from all social strata, and as we have seen, citizens' movements draw considerably on the social and organizational skills contributed by their members.

Both movements must be credited with arousing great interest in increasing channels of citizen participation—through the Model Cities and Community Action programs of the Kennedy-Johnson era in the United States, and through the creation of citizens' complaint windows, "citizens' offices," citizens' oversight boards, and more public hearings to discuss local government projects in the 1970s in Japan. Both movements produced advocates of decentralization of authority, from the city to the neighborhood level in the United States, and from the national to the prefectural (analogous to state) and municipal levels in Japan. In fact, Americans have considered creating a layer of government at the lowest level corresponding to community associations which the Japanese have had for centuries. It was proposed in the city of Los Angeles that neighborhoods be governed by a directly elected neighborhood board whose full-time staff officer, a "neighborman," would serve as liaison between neighborhood and city levels of government.[64] This is very reminiscent of neighborhood associations (*chōnaikai*) and village headmen in Japan, though with a slightly more democratic flavor.

There were also confrontations between national and local layers of government in both countries, although the patterns of alliance were quite different. In the United States, the federal government took up the cause of the civil rights movement in confrontations with sluggish state and local governments, responding with legislation and funding devoted solely to encouraging political participation by ethnic minorities. In Japan, where there was no federal tradition of states' rights or decentralized power, the national government resisted citizens' demands for devolution of power to local units, and inadvertently forged an informal alliance against itself, between many citizens' movements and their respective prefectural and municipal governments. The ironic result of these different patterns of center/local conflict was that in the United States, which de Tocqueville saw as the true home of voluntarism and participatory democracy, the government felt compelled to stimulate participation. But in Japan, where the historical rule was for governments to lead and ordinary people to practice the art of acquiescent followership, the government was forced to accommodate unfamiliar demands from below for citizen participation.

Whatever the real success of the American civil rights movement and the Japanese environmental movement in enhancing participatory

64. *Studies in Comparative Local Government* 5:2 (Winter 1971, special issue on citizen participation), 94.

democracy in their respective societies, their historical significance is similar. Both were interpreted as political turning points, and both stimulated debate, not just over a few specific issues and policies but over fundamental political questions concerning the fulfillment of the democratic ideal.

Nonetheless, citizens' movements are still decentralized and have shown only tentative signs of an effort to form nationwide coalitions—for wildlife preservation, consumer protection, and opposition to nuclear power. Thus their impact on Japan's achievements in environmental cleanup was only indirect, in that the government adopted stringent antipollution policies in order to preempt further growth of citizens' movements rather than in response to any concerted lobbying effort on their part. Similarly, the greatest significance of citizens' movements for Japanese politics may be their indirect influence, from the bottom up, on electoral trends and patterns of political competition and conflict. As the effort to assess the consequences of citizens' movements for Japanese politics as a whole takes us beyond the local level, interpretations necessarily become increasingly tentative. The concluding comments which follow are offered as speculations, which can be firmly accepted or rejected only with the passage of time and extensive further research.

Speculation on the Long-term Significance of Citizens' Movements

Although they are too commonplace now to be as newsworthy as they once were, citizens' movements continue to monitor environmental conditions in Japan, as well as a host of new problems, whenever the government cannot take the initiative quickly enough to nip new problems in the bud. Whereas the Big Four pollution diseases were the focal point of media attention in the late 1960s and antidevelopment struggles received emphasis in the early 1970s, the environmental consequences of the energy crisis are the chief concerns of the late 1970s. The Japanese government is trying to construct new petroleum complexes in yet undeveloped ports (new supertankers simply do not fit anymore into Japan's sludge-filled bays and clogged harbors), inciting further controversy.[65] Similarly, the government wants to construct nuclear power plants in order to reduce Japan's dependence on imported oil, and the

---

65. The crowding of Japanese ports and anticipated difficulties with local citizens are two reasons that the Japanese government is anxiously pursuing a joint venture with the United States to build a transshipment superport for oil tankers in Palao in the South Pacific, where supertankers would divert their cargo onto smaller ships, which could fit more smoothly into Japanese harbors, and reduce the likelihood of any one particular shipping accident releasing vast tonnage of oil into Japanese coastal waters. See "International Opposition to Oil Port Pacific," *Japan Quarterly* 23:4 (October–December 1976), 331–335.

disputes over plant siting have already reduced the scope of government plans and led to the most important environmental lawsuits of the decade.[66]

• Electoral Trends and Partisan Realignment

Many writers argue that pollution and citizens' movements are related to the steady decline of the LDP over the past decade and the emergence of a floating vote in the general electorate.[67] It is difficult to identify the beneficiaries of this floating because the combined left vote (DSP-JSP-JCP) seems to have stabilized in percentage terms, and the rise of any one leftist party seems to occur only at the expense of one of the others.[68] Arima and Imazu suggest that much of the recent increase in support for the JCP consists of an antipollution floating vote which could just as easily seek other outlets.[69] We see the same developments in microcosm in individual election districts where there have been powerful citizens' movements.[70] Similarly, our survey of individual activists revealed plenty of disillusioned switching toward the left, but also indicated that unhappiness with the LDP was more responsible for this switching than any

66. Margaret A. McKean, "Japan's Beleaguered Ruling Party," *Current History* 75:441 (November 1978), 158–163.

67. See Hajime Shinohara, "Postwar Parties and Politics in Japan," pp. 393–409, and Takeshi Ishida, "Emerging or Eclipsing Citizenship? A Study of Changes in Political Attitudes in Postwar Japan," pp. 410–424, both in *Developing Economies* 6:4 (December 1968). More recently, see Taketsugu Tsurutani, "A New Era of Japanese Politics: Tokyo's Gubernatorial Election," *Asian Survey* 12:5 (May 1972), 429–443; and Tosh Lee, "A Tenuous Victory: The General Election of 1972," *Japan Interpreter* 8:1 (Winter 1973), 5–15. See also Tsurutani, *Political Change in Japan*, pp. 175–258; Sumisato Arima and Hiroshi Imazu, "The Opposition Parties: Organization and Policies," *Japan Quarterly* 24:2 (April–June 1977), 158–160; and Hans H. Baerwald and Nobuo Tomita, "Japan's 34th General Elections: Cautious Change Amidst Incremental Instability," *Asian Survey* 17:3 (March 1977), 236.

The 1979 House of Representatives election was an unexpected departure from this trend. For the first time the LDP actually increased its share of the popular vote, though it continued to lose Diet seats. This may mean that the floating vote can occasionally drift back into the LDP fold, but that it is beyond the reach of LDP support organizations, which are so important in managing the party's distribution of votes. Though the LDP has halted its decline in popularity, it is now the party's organizational structure which seems to be dissolving.

68. Richard J. Brynildsen, "A Decade of Japanese Diet Elections, 1967–1976: Conservatism and Radicalism Reevaluated," *Asian Survey* 17:10 (October 1977), 975–977.

69. Arima and Imazu, "The Opposition Parties," pp. 158–160.

70. Bradley M. Richardson, "Stability and Change in Japanese Voting Behavior, 1958–1972," *Journal of Asian Studies* 36:4 (August 1977), 675–694. On conservative decline and the *datsu-seitō* phenomenon in Kagoshima Third District after the rise of the citizens' movement in Shibushi, see chapter III.

firm loyalty toward the left. Moreover, most of those who identified with and voted for the left explained their behavior as protest voting for the reformist opposition.

There is also a fundamental similarity between disillusioned switchers among activists and *datsu-seitō*, or unaffiliated voters in the general population, who with about 30 percent of the electorate now outnumber LDP partisans.[71] Whether they switched or not, most activists voted at least in local elections on the basis of issue-oriented utilitarianism and autonomous judgments rather than simply absorbing the appropriate partisan identity from the social networks they belonged to. Similarly, it is usually said that *datsu-seitō* voters consciously sense their dissatisfaction with the existing range of parties and demand constructive alternatives, unlike the apathetic American independents who tend to withdraw from politics.

Certainly citizens' movements have closely touched the lives of millions of Japanese, but they cannot possibly have produced every single unaffiliated voter and new reformist identifier in the general electorate. But perhaps we can extrapolate from their effects on individual members that citizens' movements may have an *indirect* relationship with the *datsu-seitō* phenomenon and realignment of the parties from conservative dominance to greater balance between the conservatives and the opposition. First, citizens' movements, along with the growth of government and the increasing complexity of industrial (or postindustrial) society, diverted attention from the polemical exchanges between the polarized right and left elites to more practical issues.[72] Shinohara Hajime notes that the bimodal distribution of left/right opinion in Japan is being transformed into a distribution with a single mode located in the center.[73] However, analysis of public opinion over the last three decades indicates that polarization of opinion was generally limited to the well-educated elite, and that the majority of the general public has held moderate views all along.[74] In essence citizens' movements provided a voice and a forum to the dormant center (the "silent majority"?) so that it could become politically significant and push the quibbles of the elite off center stage.

71. Allinson, "Japan's Independent Voters"; Richardson, "Stability and Change in Japanese Voting Behavior"; and Tsurutani, *Political Change in Japan*, pp. 188–191. On the *datsu-seitō* phenomenon, see Hashimoto Akikazu, *Shiji seitō nashi: kuzureyuku 'seitō' shinwa* [Nonsupport of Political Parties: The Crumbling Myth of 'Political Parties'] (Tokyo: Nihon Keizai Shimbunsha, 1975).

72. Muramatsu, "Gyōsei katei to seiji sanka," pp. 56–62. Tsurutani regards the displacement of ideology by issues as a major characteristic of postindustrial society and gives citizens' movements substantial credit for accelerating this transformation. See *Political Change in Japan*.

73. Hajime Shinohara, "The Opposition Party System," *Japan Quarterly* 24:2 (April–June 1977), 177–178.

74. See chapter I, n. 3, for public opinion studies on this point.

As a source of arguments in favor of independent votes and as a successful model of how flexible and independent voting could elicit concrete results, citizens' movements have at a minimum symbolized, and quite probably contributed in a small way to, these gradual shifts in the electorate.

The electorate is "more and more dissatisfied with the political process while at the same time becoming somewhat more active and involved in that process," resulting in a "more volatile" and "mobilized" electorate, but with "weaker institutional ties."[75] Although they are describing the changing American voter, Nie, Verba, and Petrocik could just as easily be describing citizens' movement activists or reporting the indirect effects of citizens' movements on the Japanese voter. The authors go on to argue that these changes will lead to decay and decomposition of political parties, but that a realigned party system is unlikely to replace it. Rather, Americans may be headed for a "post-partisan" era of issue-based politics in which the organizations linking voters to political institutions will be single-issue interest groups rather than parties with an integrated platform on many issues. Some observers have gone so far as to assert in a similar way that citizens' movements in Japan are replacing political parties.[76]

I would offer a less drastic interpretation. Just as there are parallels between voting behavior in citizens' movement activists and in the general electorate, there are parallels between the behavior of citizens' movements as a social protest movement and that of the opposition parties, which have moderated their stance considerably in the last decade. Although the opposition parties certainly appreciated the fact that the steady LDP decline in elections created a vacuum into which they could move, this objective fact on its own provided no incentive for any of the opposition parties to alter their approach to gathering votes. Citizens' movements could have contributed to the gradual moderation within the opposition parties by providing the missing motive for this change. First, the rapid proliferation of citizens' movements constituted evidence not just to voters but also to attentive political parties that contemporary political institutions neglected certain issues and forced people to create their own channels to put these issues on the local and national agenda. Citizens' movements thus demonstrated that there did now exist a political task for the opposition to fulfill by accommodating the rising interest in these issues. Second, the nationwide eruption of citizens' movements constituted proof positive that the Japanese public could indeed be

75. Norman H. Nie, Sidney Verba, and John R. Petrocik, *The Changing American Voter* (Cambridge: Harvard University Press, 1976), p. 348.

76. "Citizens' Movements," *Japan Quarterly* 20:4 (October–December 1973), 370–371.

moved (something about which many observers long had doubts), and therefore that there might be some advantage to be reaped in appealing to it. In this sense, citizens' movements gave the opposition parties—and the LDP when it was looking—a much needed push in a direction set not by party officials but by the public itself.

Citizens' movements have affected existing parties in another way, by challenging their ability to serve their supporters and thus stimulating the existing parties to cultivate the mass base that they had never developed. Citizens' movements arose during a period when only the JCP had an effective mass organization capable of serving as a channel for demands to flow upward. The JCP's resulting sensitivity to popular concern about pollution may be the reason that it was the only party that activists regarded favorably. Had the other parties already succeeded in creating a mass base independent of formal institutions, citizens' movements might never have arisen. Yet prior to the rise of citizens' movements, the parties had little reason to bother building grass-roots organizations. Now they are belatedly trying to create the missing mass base. The LDP adopted new rules to democratize the election of the party president. Whereas the LDP's 500-odd members of the two houses of the Diet used to monopolize the entire process, 1,500,000 newly recruited party members were eligible to vote in the LDP's first primary in late 1978, which chose Ōhira Masayoshi as party president and prime minister. The JSP also announced plans in 1978 to expand membership from 44,000 to 1,000,000.[77]

The evidence does not indicate that citizens' movements are replacing political parties or that Japan is entering a post-partisan era. The failure of the Social Democratic League (formerly the Socialist Citizens' League) and the United Progressive Liberals to win many votes in the 1977 House of Councillors election or the 1979 House of Representatives election indicates that citizens' movements cannot replace existing parties. But they may still have a constructive role to play. Environmental publicists have called upon the reformist parties to cultivate a new issue-oriented constituency from citizens' movements, by modifying internal party structure (especially the rigid dependence on organized labor) and policy goals.[78] Similarly, citizens' movements might become lower-level organizational vehicles for reconstruction and regrouping

77. Nathaniel Thayer, "The Current Status of the Liberal Democratic Party in Japan," paper presented to the Association of Asian Studies in Chicago, March 1978. See also *JTW*, 14 January, 4 March, and 18 March, in 1978. On the JSP plans to build a mass base, see *JTW*, 4 March 1978.

78. *Kōgai: yosoku to taisaku*, pp. 257–258, 289–290. See also Yokoyama Keiji, "Jichitai kaikaku to kakushin seitō no kadai" [Issues in Local Government Reform and Reformist Political Parties], *Kōmei* 152 (January 1975), 60–65.

among existing parties (as in Mishima), or they might produce a new generation of grass-roots politicians to compete with those recruited through more conventional channels.

• Participation and Conflict

All good democrats agree that participation by individuals with high information, high political efficacy, high support for democratic and libertarian norms, and high propensity to compromise is healthy for a democratic system. But whenever increased participation is accompanied by conflict and confrontation, debate over the desirability of different types of participation ensues. Contemporary pluralism (called elitism by its critics) grows in part out of alarm at the behaviorists' discovery that most citizens in "democratic" nations fall far short of the ideal democratic character posited by classical theory. It warns that too much participation by *undemocratic* characters and those who are alienated, disenchanted, or inclined to engage in expressive and possibly violent protest could undermine democratic norms and practices. Similarly, high participation by ideologues or single-issue activists with mutually exclusive demands would overload the system. Thus the pluralists agree with Schumpeter, Sartori, and Dahl that democracy should properly be viewed as a method rather than as a utopian state, guaranteed by processes (free elections and the rotation of elites) and institutions (legislatures and courts). Nonparticipation by a portion of the populace is a rational choice based on satisfaction with the status quo, rather than an indictment of the system, and is in any case better for the survival of democracy-as-method than high participation would be.[79]

The opposing populist view articulated by Bachrach and Pateman argues that political systems serve only the insiders who do participate, that nonparticipants lack protection whether they recognize their disadvantage or not, and therefore that a democracy cannot live up to the

79. The work that stimulated much of the recent skepticism about the relationship between participation and democracy and about classical theory was Joseph A. Schumpeter, *Capitalism, Socialism, and Democracy* (New York: Harper, 1942). Other milestones in what is called contemporary pluralist theory, which warn about the hazards of too much participation, are Bernard R. Berelson, Paul F. Lazarsfeld, and William N. McPhee, *Voting: A Study of Opinion Formation in a Presidential Campaign* (Chicago: University of Chicago Press, 1954), pp. 305–323; Robert A. Dahl, *A Preface to Democratic Theory* (Chicago: University of Chicago Press, 1956), especially the appendix to chap. 3; Lipset, *Political Man*, pp. 14, 226–229; Dahl, *Who Governs: Democracy and Power in an American City* (New Haven: Yale University Press, 1961), pp. 311–325; Giovanni Sartori, *Democratic Theory* (Detroit: Wayne State University Press, 1962); Almond and Verba, *The Civic Culture*, pp. 337–374; Harry Eckstein, *Division and Cohesion in Democracy: A Study of Norway* (Princeton: Princeton University Press, 1966), Appendix B, "A Theory of Stable Democracy," pp. 225–288.

name without high levels of participation. Participation is valuable not only in itself but in the cultivation of the traits of the classical democratic character. Far from being a threat, mass participation protects the system by teaching democratic values and practices to those who were formerly nonparticipants. Whereas the pluralists see contemporary protest as a potential danger, the populists regard it as an expansion of participation in fulfillment of the lost democratic ideal, as an opportunity for society to resolve conflicts that fester under the surface and no doubt harm nonparticipants the most, and as an opportunity for the disenchanted and alienated to acquire influence, alleviate their grievances, and become citizens supportive of democracy.[80]

We may use this debate to inspire questions about what citizens' movements mean for the ability of Japanese society to handle the expression of conflict and increased participation. First, we must note that serious objective problems caused the conflicts which sought expression in citizens' movements. To imagine that citizens' movements somehow caused the conflict would confuse cause with effect. Citizens' movements did not cause environmental pollution, shoddy products, or inadequate housing; the conflicts of interest over these issues are very real and would exist anyway. Rather, what citizens' movements have done is to encourage the expression of sectional- and self-interest, as opposed to deference to some collective or national interest however it might be defined, and to legitimize dissent. What is at issue then is whether citizens' movements will overburden the system with conflicting demands, or instead will enlarge the system's capacity for conflict resolution.[81]

The mechanisms that predated citizens' movements were clearly inadequate for handling the conflicts that environmental problems produced. If citizens' movements channel and resolve these conflicts, then they can help Japan weather the crises that are bound to recur as the resource/environment dilemma grows more serious. Citizens' movements may actually be a force for compromise rather than conflict in that they

80. Peter Bachrach, *The Theory of Democratic Elitism: A Critique* (Boston: Little, Brown, 1967); Carole Pateman, *Participation and Democratic Theory* (Cambridge: At the University Press, 1970). For discussion of the controversy over full participation set in terms of civil rights and local control in America, see James V. Cunningham, "Citizen Participation in Public Affairs," pp. 589–602, and David K. Hart, "Theories of Government Related to Decentralization and Citizen Participation," pp. 603–621, and John H. Strange, "Citizen Participation in Community Action and Model Cities Programs," pp. 655–669, all in *Public Administration Review* 32 (special issue, October 1972); and John H. Strange, "Impact of Citizen Participation on Public Administration," *Public Administration Review* 32 (special issue, September 1972).

81. Satō Atsushi, *Tenkanki no chihō jichi*, p. 110; Abe Hitoshi, "Gyōsei no sekinin to jūmin sanka," p. 56; Katō Tomiko, "Jūmin sanka to gyōsei no taiō" [Residents' Participation and Administrative Response], also in Jichi Daigakkō kenkyūbu, *Jūmin sanka to gyōsei*, pp. 125–148.

seem to be dissolving barriers between conservative and progressive camps and creating new opportunities for broad horizontal forms of collaboration among formerly irreconcilable poles. Citizens' movements may signify that the Japanese are coming to accept the inevitability of some conflict in a complex society of 115 million people, so that what we are seeing is an increased tolerance for conflict rather than a dangerous amount of it.

On the other hand, citizens' movements may also represent a decline in the ability to handle conflict, in that they obviously signify the replacement of polite consensus politics by open confrontation. Whether they overload the system with incompatible demands (for example, simultaneous demands to build more nuclear power plants and to build none) depends on whether citizens' movements concentrate on policy or process in the future. If local "ego" prevails, as their critics charge, making each movement incapable of compromising on policy objectives, then citizens' movements may add to Japan's problems. But if they instead emphasize procedure—democratization of local politics to ensure that decisions are made in consultation with local wishes and ordinary citizens—and are willing to compromise with other forces on actual policies, then they will be part of the solution. If performance since the oil crisis of 1973 is any indication of how well Japan preserved national consensus and contained conflict within manageable limits, then its successful recovery, relative to both pessimistic forecasts and the experience of the other democracies, suggests that citizens' movements have not damaged Japan's governability. But it is simply too early to be sure.

The evidence we have collected on the characteristics of individual citizens' movement members makes it easier to determine whether the quality of participation occurring in citizens' movements enhances or endangers Japanese democracy. Citizens' movements verify the expectations of the populists but should also cause the pluralists to relax, because they go beyond mobilizing political innocents into an active public. They also transmit democratic values to some extent and instruct their new members in the channeling of anger into useful and legal modes of participation. Citizens' movements demonstrate that there is potential for parochials and isolates to internalize democratic norms through participation, and thus that the politically attentive public can in this instance be enlarged without damage to the system.

Their message is home-grown, not imported, indicating that Japanese political culture had an indigenous potential for democratic "evolution." To the Japanese who have become active in citizens' movements, the idea they have something called "rights" which have been "unjustly" trampled upon, that the system itself owes them some recourse, that democratic procedures are actually devices that exist precisely for the situation in which they find themselves, is attractive and satisfying. It helps them to interpret their situation and it gives them guidance in responding to it. Or, in the words of an elderly fisherman:

In this kind of situation, we used to just put up with it and cry ourselves to sleep [*nakineiri suru*]. But this time it affected our economic circumstances and our health. So we just had to rise up and protest against it! Why, it went against the idea of democratic politics! . . . The way things are now, the government tells the people what to do, but it's supposed to be the other way around, you know. (K4)

Appendix

Sampling Procedures

The first challenge was to obtain a representative sample of movements and activists from a virtually unknown population of anonymous, informally organized citizens' movements for which there was no master list or registry. Strict random sampling could not be used to reach individual participants, because it was impossible to identify every movement (many of which existed only temporarily), and impossible to identify all of the participants in any given movement (almost no group kept membership records). The only way of obtaining a pure probability sample would have been to locate citizens' movement activists through a nationwide poll. If at any given time 5 percent of the adult population is active in citizens' movements, a national sample of 2,000 persons would yield only 100 activists, and one could not obtain a random sample of 1,000 activists without a national sample of 20,000, a quantity almost unheard of in survey research. Many polls on national samples, done *since* 1972 after funding sources began to appreciate the importance of citizens' movements, have asked respondents if they were citizens' movement activists (I have used these polls to construct my estimates of total citizens' movement population) and thus could have yielded a supposedly random sample of perhaps 50 to 100 activists. However, these polls do not go on to ask other questions related to participation in citizens' movements, so they do not yield data on the issues this inquiry is concerned with. Within my limited means, and in essence the limited means available to anyone investigating citizens' movements in their formative period, these expensive techniques for procuring a pure probability sample were beyond reach. Therefore I was forced to use a three-stage method of cluster-stratified-judgment sampling, in which the first stage was to select a nearly random sample of clusters (a representative list of movements, discussed below), the second stage was to select a stratified sample among the clusters (the movements) to assure variety in the groups eventually selected, and the third stage was to use judgment sampling to select individual respondents from within the groups.[1]

The first step in this task was to locate as many movements as possible. Although several national organizations and news services compiled lists of citizens' movements all over Japan, these were still incomplete, probably biased in several ways, and contained only the name and address of each group. Fortunately, a new periodical called *Shimin* (*Citizen*) conducted its own survey to produce an elaborate list of movements, supplying not only names but descriptions of each group. *Shimin* drew up a roster of 350 groups by combining all the above-mentioned lists along with its own independent sources, thus compensating somewhat for bias that may have existed in these separate lists, and asked each group to send in an outline of its history, goals, membership, activities, external contacts, and special problems. One hundred twenty-five groups responded in time for publication (only 10 more sent in late replies, and many of the other groups were defunct by the time of the questionnaire mailing).[2] The *Shimin* survey revealed the range and variety among different antipollution groups, along several dimensions relevant to a study of political participation and interest-group behavior.

Therefore, assuming the *Shimin* list to be the most representative one available, I went on to classify the groups in that survey according to several variables concerning movement goals, tactics, the nature of the membership, and the local political and economic setting. These were (1) group size, (2) occupation of the members, (3) whether the participants were direct victims of damage, (4) whether it was a compensation or prevention group, (5) whether the group was concerned primarily about one specific local problem or was instead a study group or one concerned about a general issue, (6) the variety of pollution that concerned the group, (7) whether the group had any interest in general ecological issues, (8) the group's political tactics, (9) whether the group described itself in a righteous or a humble tone, (10) the age and experience of the group itself, (11) the group's prognosis for eventual success, (12) any political affiliations mentioned, (13) the nature of opposition *to* the group (the strength of the "pro" pollution forces in the area), (14) the existence of formal ties to a political party, (15) whether the local government was conservative or reformist, (16) the level of industrial development in the area, and (17) whether the city or town was totally dependent on one industry or even one firm.

Fifteen target groups which reproduced the variation on these traits shown in the larger list were selected. Because many of these had disbanded by the time

---

1. Alternatives to random and pure probability sampling methods, including judgment sampling, are discussed in Russell L. Ackoff, *The Design of Social Research* (Chicago: University of Chicago Press, 1953), pp. 83–131.
2. "Zenkoku no shimin undō" [Citizens' Movements across the Nation], *Shimin* 1 (March 1971), supplement, 1–82.

of my own survey, I asked knowledgeable persons familiar with my objectives to suggest equivalent alternative groups that would represent the appropriate characteristics. The assistance I received from the chief member of the *Shimin* staff, Mr. Chikushi Tatehiko, was invaluable. Mr. Chikushi understood the necessity of obtaining a balanced, representative sample, and why an objective study would also sample establishment-linked, conservative groups as well as radical movements. In addition, he had traveled all over Japan to talk to antipollution activists, so his knowledge was thorough and up-to-date. With his understanding of my purposes and his complete information about many groups not on the *Shimin* list of March 1971 which nonetheless might meet my requirements, Mr. Chikushi was able to provide many suggestions and descriptions of these groups, which I most gratefully employed to complete the sample.

In addition to assuring variety on the traits itemized earlier, I also used additional criteria to fill out the sample. Two problems which attracted a great deal of attention in the American environmental movement but which were less conspicuous in Japan were concern for the integrity of the natural environment for its own sake and the recycling of waste products. At the risk of oversampling Japanese groups with these concerns, I wanted to make sure that the final sample contained at least one group concerned about general ecological principles and at least one group devoted to recycling solid waste, in order to learn why these issues are relatively minor in the Japanese environmental movement. Although the final sample included four groups with some interest in waste disposal, this probably did not overrepresent the "garbage lobby," for several reasons. First, two of the groups yielded only two interviews each. Moreover, two of the groups were concerned with keeping garbage out of their neighborhood (and thus with the environmental implications of urban planning and development), rather than with recycling it. In fact, only two of the groups, quite different from each other in other respects and yielding only eight interviews, were expressly concerned with recycling waste materials.

A final criterion that governed the selection of groups in the sample was the inevitable limitation on time and money available. Five of the groups were selected from predominantly rural areas (in Toyama, Oita, Kagoshima, and a still-rural section of Kanagawa), but the remaining urban groups were all located in four prefectures in the Greater Tokyo area, to the exclusion of other urban zones, largely to permit the scheduling of interviews at times convenient to respondents. I felt it was legitimate to select the urban groups from this large zone as long as variety on other characteristics was strictly preserved.

Thus the target groups were selected, and the remaining task was to reach individual activists within them. I established contact with group leaders, explained the project to them, and asked them to introduce me to approximately five members of their group to be interviewed. The leader of one group refused to cooperate, so the final sample consisted of sixty-four coded interviews with respondents in fourteen movements, all conducted from September to December 1972. In most cases I also had extensive conversations with several informants other than the actual respondents—family members, movement leaders, or community residents—whose comments were helpful in providing additional detail about the movements and in placing respondents' remarks into proper perspective.

Questionnaire Design and Interview Format

The exploratory nature of this study influenced the interview format. There was no ready-made set of questions that would be useful, so an original questionnaire had to be devised. Similarly, the range of possible responses could not be predicted with confidence at this stage, so I relied for the most part on open-ended questions rather than highly structured ones. Five Japanese, including three political scientists, edited my Japanese version of the questionnaire, and as a validity check the resulting Japanese version was translated back into English. Each question was written on a card, permitting respondents to read lengthy questions for themselves and to refer to the original question as they replied.

Because of the nature of the open-ended inquiry planned, the questionnaire was designed for use in flexible face-to-face interviews lasting two to three hours each. This permitted probing for more complete answers, especially on sensitive topics, and also permitted pursuit of subjects of special interest with certain respondents. The personal interview also permitted the evaluation of factors not anticipated by the questionnaire, adding depth to the interpretation of responses. The scholars who advised me on the questionnaire also suggested that as a foreigner I would have many advantages as an interviewer, which would be lost if I employed a native interpreter, so I conducted the interviews myself in Japanese. Most important, respondents would be more frank and revealing with a foreigner, a "safe" outlet for their opinions (this actually turned out to be the case, and some respondents explicitly requested that I promise not to tell other Japanese what they had said).

For this same reason, interviews were conducted in the respondent's home or place of work without the presence of friends or family members whenever possible. Naturally, in order to elicit candid, frank responses, I tried to maintain good rapport with respondents without abandoning my own neutrality as an interviewer. Although it is impossible to devote space here to a detailed discussion on the problems involved in questionnaire design and cross-cultural interviewing, these were surmountable ones. All respondents went through with the interview agreeably and never engaged in the evasiveness or hostility to which handbooks on interviewing in the United States devote so much attention.[3]

Statistical Analysis

Although the questionnaire consisted almost entirely of open-ended questions, there was sufficient uniformity in styles of response to permit coding of most responses gleaned from interviews into ordinal-level variables which could be subjected to statistical analysis. Many people have doubts about the utility of

---

3. Aaron V. Cicourel, *Method and Measurement in Sociology* (New York: Free Press, 1964), p. 83; and Herbert H. Hyman et al., *Interviewing in Social Research* (Chicago: University of Chicago Press, 1954). American literature on interviewing techniques contains many quotations from American survey respondents who are quite rude and hostile toward their interviewers. See also Robert F. Kahn and Charles F. Cannell, *The Dynamics of Interviewing: Theory, Technique, and Cases* (New York: Wiley, 1957); and Robert K. Merton, Marjorie Fiske, and Patricia L. Kendall, *The Focused Interview: A Manual of Problems and Procedures* (Glencoe: Free Press, 1956).

conclusions based on small samples, but the judicious use of suitable statistical methods permits us to draw reliable conclusions from small samples.[4] Samples of N < 100 are usually considered small, and there is almost no difference between the power of a particular test as N increases from 50 to 100. Experimental psychologists, who frequently use samples of 20 or 30, consider N ≥ 40 to be "large" (as it is for the Kolmogorov-Smirnov test).

In view of the small sample size of N = 64, I was conservative in the choice of statistical methods, confining myself to nonparametric statistics, which are highly suitable for small samples, require only ordinal data, and are distribution free, in contrast to parametric measures, which require interval-level data and uniform normal distribution. Among these, Kendall's Tau, also known as the Tau-beta or Tau-b measure of association, was used because it is both powerful and conservative. Along with the Spearman rank-order correlation coefficient, Tau-b is one of the two most powerful nonparametric measures of association, having 91 percent of the efficiency of the Pearson product-moment correlation coefficient (which is, in turn, the most powerful parametric measure of correlation).[5] At the same time, Tau-b avoids inflating relationships between variables because it accounts for ties in the ranks.[6]

I allowed myself the luxury of regarding my ordinal-level measures as adequate surrogates for otherwise unobtainable interval-level measures in only two situations: in adding scores on different variables together to create comprehensive indices, and in calculating mean scores rather than medians as a measure of central tendency on indices where the range of possible scores was too small for medians, the nonparametric analog of the mean, to be meaningful. There are of course techniques for establishing interval-level scores for the categories of an ordinal variable, involving construction of dummy variables for each score or rank within an ordinal variable. However, these have restricted meanings and usefulness, are elaborate and expensive to construct, and are used very sparingly in survey research.

Instead, most social scientists simply fly in the face of theoretical limitations and use interval-level techniques like parametric statistics, including correlation, factor, regression, and path analyses, on their ordinal-level attitude and opinion scales and measures of education, socioeconomic status, party identification, and so on. Most scholars who do this do not bother to acknowledge the apparent incompatibility between data and approach, but as a result of the increasing prevalence of the usage, some methodologists have explored the problem. They conclude that ordinal data can be considered a surrogate for interval-level data, and that interval-level operations up to and including factor and regression anal-

4. Sidney Siegel, *Non-Parametric Statistics for the Behavioral Sciences* (New York: McGraw-Hill, 1956), pp. vii–34.

5. Siegel, *Non-Parametric Statistics*, pp. 195–204, discusses the power efficiency of several non-parametric measures.

6. Nie et al., recommend using Tau-c for rectangular tables, but Anderson and Zelditch recommend using Tau-b because it corrects for ties. See Norman H. Nie et al., *Statistical Package for the Social Sciences*, 2d ed. (New York: McGraw-Hill, 1975), p. 228; and Theodore R. Anderson and Morris Zelditch, Jr., *A Basic Course in Statistics with Sociological Applications*, 2d ed. (New York: Holt, Rinehart, and Winston, 1968), 153.

yses yield acceptable results.[7] Thus the use of addition to construct scales and of division to calculate means is well within the range of established practice.

Accompanying all Tau-b figures shown in the text are the associated p values, or levels of significance for the N used to calculate the given value of Tau-b. In fact, it is not legitimate to indulge in statistical inference or to perform tests of significance with data that is not based on a pure probability sample. The methodological slipperiness that is becoming more common in social sciences might allow one to make the case that the efforts to ensure representativeness in this nonprobability sample permits us to pretend that it is a surrogate for the hypothetical one that would have resulted from systematic probability sampling. Without going this far, I have simply decided to provide p levels as a rough indicator of how significant or reliable a particular relationship for a small N would be *if* inference were appropriate, to assuage skepticism of readers who are troubled by the use of small samples. The tests of confidence for small samples simply require that statistical relationships be a good deal stronger than for large samples before they can be interpreted as reliable, that is, as statistically significant. Many of the relationships highlighted in the text would be statistically significant, in spite of the small sample size, at p values much lower than the .05 or even .01 which are generally regarded as acceptable.

7. On the use of factor analysis with ordinal data, see C. A. Moser and G. Katlin, *Survey Methods in Social Investigation* (London:Heinemann Educational Books, 1971), pp. 361–366; on the use of regression analysis in the same situation, see Bohrnsted and Carter, "Robustness in Regression Analysis," in H. D. Costner, ed., *Sociological Methodology 1971* (San Francisco: Jossey-Bass, 1971), pp. 118–146; and H. M. Blalock, *Measurement in the Social Sciences* (Chicago: Aldine, 1974), pp. 325–457.

Bibliographic Note

Specific references are listed where appropriate in notes accompanying the text; a list of selected sources on citizens' movements is provided here. Articles that are available in English include Jun Ui, "The Singularities of Japanese Pollution," *Japan Quarterly* 19:3 (July–September 1972), 281–291; Yasumasa Kuroda, "Protest Movements in Japan: A New Politics," *Asian Survey* 12:11 (November 1972), 947–952; Bradford L. Simcock, "Environmental Pollution and Citizens' Movements: The Social Sources and Significance of Anti-Pollution Protest in Japan," *Area Development in Japan* 5 (1972), 13–22; "Peasant Uprisings and Citizens' Revolts," *Japan Interpreter* 8:3 (Autumn 1973), 279–284; "Citizens' Movements," *Japan Quarterly* 20:4 (October–December 1973), 368–373; Keiichi Matsushita, "Politics of Citizen Participation," *Japan Interpreter* 9:4 (Spring 1975), 451–464; Michitoshi Takabatake, "Citizens' Movements: Organizing the Spontaneous," *Japan Interpreter* 9:3 (Winter 1975), 315–323; Michael Reich and Norie Huddle, "Pollution and Social Response," *Area Development in Japan* 7 (1973), 34–47. The Matsushita and Takabatake articles have been reprinted in a volume that discusses citizens' movements in the context of a broader historical view of citizen protest in Japan: J. Victor Koschmann, ed., *Authority and the Individual in Japan: Citizen Protest in Historical Perspective* (Tokyo: University of Tokyo Press, 1978). A well-written book with thorough descriptions of environmental disruption in Yokkaichi, Minamata, and other cases, is Norie Huddle and Michael Reich, with Nahum Stiskin, *Island of Dreams: Environmental Crisis in Japan* (Tokyo: Autumn Press, 1975). For a thorough chronology, see Nobuko Iijima, ed., *Pollution Japan: Historical Chronology* (Tokyo: Asahi Evening News, 1979).

Naturally, most of the material on citizens' movements is in Japanese. In the early 1970s, almost all serious periodicals and magazines in Japan published articles and special issues on citizens' movements. The periodical with the greatest interest in citizens' movements was *Shimin* [*Citizen*], published from 1971 to 1973 and then again briefly in 1976. For a sample of essays by most of the scholars, journalists, and activists who wrote about citizens' movements during the early 1970s, see in particular the following specials in *Shimin*: "Shimin undō no tenkai" [The Development of Citizens' Movements], 1 (March 1971); "Kankyōken no kakuritsu to shimin sanka" [Citizen Participation and the Establishment of Environmental Rights], 5 (November 1971); "Jichitai kaikaku to jichi keisei no kokoromi" [Reform of Local Government and the Attempt to Build Self-Government], 8 (May 1972); "Komyūnitei kyōdō shakai no fukken" [The Recovery of Community and Cooperative Society], 13 (May 1973).

Three central early works on citizens' movements and pollution from the scholarly community are Miyamoto Ken'ichi, ed., *Kōgai to jūmin undō* [Pollution and Residents' Movements] (Tokyo: Jichitai Kenkyūsha, November 1970); Miyamoto Ken'ichi and Endō Akira, eds., *Toshi mondai to jūmin undō* [Urban Problems and Residents' Movements], vol. 8 in the series Gendai Nihon no toshi mondai [Urban Problems in Contemporary Japan] (Kyoto: Sekibunsha, July 1971); Matsubara Haruo, *Kōgai to chiiki shakai: seikatsu to jūmin undō no shakaigaku* [Pollution and Regional Society: The Sociology of Livelihood and Residents' Movements] (Tokyo: Nihon Keizai Shimbunsha, October 1971). See also Tsuro Shigeto, *Gendai shihonshugi to kōgai* [Contemporary Capitalism and Pollution] (Tokyo: Iwanami Shoten, March 1968); his later *Kōgai no seiji keizaigaku* [The Political Economy of Pollution] (Tokyo: Iwanami Shoten, April 1972); Kainō Michitaka, *Kankyō hakai* [Destruction of the Environment] vol. 5 in the series Gendai ni ikiru [To Live in the Present] (Tokyo: Tōyō Keizai Shimbunsha, November 1971).

Japan's best-known environmental scientist and activist is Ui Jun, whose early works include *Kōgai no seijigaku: Minamata byo wo megutte* [The Politics of Pollution: On Minamata Disease] (Tokyo: Ushio Shuppansha, November 1971); *Kōgai genron* [Lectures on Pollution], 3 vols., (Tokyo: Aki Shobō, March, May, and July 1971); *Kōgai rettō: 70 nendai* [Polluted Islands: The 1970s] (Tokyo: Aki Shobō, June 1972). A second set of 4 volumes in the Kōgai genron series was issued by Keisō Shobō from August 1972 to April 1973 under the titles *Gendai shakai to kōgai* [Contemporary Society and Pollution], *Gendai kagaku to kōgai* [Contemporary Science and Pollution], *(Toku) Gendai kagaku to kōgai* [Special: Contemporary Science and Pollution], and *Higaisha no ronri* [The Logic of the Victims]. Still another 3-volume set in the series was issued by Aki Shobō from August to November 1974, titled *Kōgai to gyōsei* [Pollution and Administration], *Kōgai jūmin undō* [Residents' Movements Concerned with Pollution], and *Kōgai jishu kōza undō* [The Independent Forum Movement Concerned with Pollution].

A few of the works by journalists and free-lance commentators who share optimistic views of citizens' movements are the following: Igarashi Fumio, *Niigata Minamata byō* [Niigata Minamata Disease] (Tokyo: Gōdō Shuppan, April 1971); Hayashi Eidai, *Yahata no kōgai* [Pollution in Yahata] (Tokyo: Asahi Shimbunsha, May 1971); Yomiuri Shimbun shakaibu, eds., *Tōkyo wo dō suru:*

hametsu ka saisei ka [What to Do about Tokyo: Destroy It or Revive It?] (Tokyo: Toshima Shobō, July 1972); Fujiwara Kunitatsu, *Shokuhin kōgai to shimin undō* [Citizens' Movements and the Pollution of Foodstuffs] (Tokyo: Shinjidaisha, November 1970); and the very useful Kaji Kōji, *Kōgai gyōsei no sotenken: kaiketsu no michi wa?* [A General Examination of Pollution Administration: A Road to Solutions?] (Tokyo: Gōdō Shuppan, May 1971).

Finally, for the better-known works by participant-observers in citizens' movements, see Ishimure Michiko, ed., *Waga shimin: Minamata byō tōsō* [Our Dead: The Struggle with Minamata Disease] (Tokyo: Gendai Hyōronsha, April 1972); the surprisingly sophisticated Jūmin ni yoru Keiji baipasu kōgai kenkyū guruupu [Residents' Pollution Research Group on the Kyōto-Shiga Bypass], *Kōgai: yosoku to taisaku* [Pollution: Forecasts and Countermeasures] (Tokyo: Asahi Shimbunsha, March 1971); Saitō Kōji and Sawa Keitarō, *Jūmin pawā nyūmon: kayowaki shomin ga jiei suru tame ni* [Introduction to Residents' Power: So That the Helpless Common People May Defend Themselves] (Tokyo: Shufu to Seikatsusha, April 1972), on the sunshine-rights movement; Maruya Hiroshi, *Kōgai ni idomu: Mizushima kombinaato aru ishi no tatakai* [In Defiance of Pollution: A Doctor's Struggle against the Mizushima Kombinat] (Tokyo: Shin Nihon Shuppansha, August 1970); Yokokawa Yoshio and Onogi Yoshiyuki, *Kōgai hasseigen rōdōsha no kokuhatsu: Zeneraru sekiyū seisei rōsō no tōsō* [An Indictment by Workers at the Source of Pollution: The Struggle of the Labor Union at General Petroleum Refinery] (Tokyo: San'ichi Shobō, April 1971); Kondō Shutarō, *Kōgai Yokkaichi no kiroku: aozora wo kaese* [A Record of Polluted Yokkaichi: Give Back Our Blue Skies] (Nagoya: Fūbaisha, October 1967); Ono Eiji, *Genten: Yokkaichi kōgai 10 nen no kiroku* [From the Beginning: A Record of Ten Years of Yokkaichi Pollution] (Tokyo: Keisō Shobō, February 1971); Kōda Toshihiko, *Waga sonzai no teiten kara: Fuji kōgai to watakushi* [From the Depth of My Existence: Fuji Pollution and Me] (Tokyo: Yamato Shobō, July 1972); Iwata Tomokazu, *Shokuhin kōgai e no chōsen* [A Challenge to Pollution in Foodstuffs] (Tokyo: Bijinesusha, November 1970); San guruupu [Sun Group], *Kōgai zensen wo saguru: shufu no gomi hakusho* [To the Battlefront: The Housewives' White Paper on Garbage] (Tokyo: Jichi Nippōsha, August 1972).

Finally, there is a growing body of recent scholarly literature on citizens' movements and local government which attempts to analyze rather than to describe or prescribe. Much of this is published by Gakuyō Shobō. The most important items in this category are Akimoto Ritsuo, *Chiiki seiji to jūmin: shimin sanka no tame ni* [Regional Politics and Residents: For Citizen Participation] (Tokyo: Ushio Shuppan, March 1972); Ishida Takeshi, ed., *Nempō seijigaku 1974: Seiji sanka no riron to genjitsu* [Annual of the Japanese Political Science Association 1974: The Theory and Practice of Political Participation] (Tokyo: Iwanami Shoten, March 1975), especially articles by Muramatsu, Nishio, Yokoyama, Sogame, Mizoguchi, and Satake; Matsubara Haruo, ed., *Jūmin sanka to jichi no kakushin* [Residents' Participation and Reform of Self-Government], and Satō Atsushi, ed., *Chiiki kaihatsu, kōgai e no taiō* [The Response to Regional Development and Pollution], vols. 2 and 3 in the series Asu no chihō jichi wo saguru [Toward Local Self-Government for the Future] (Tokyo: Gakuyō Shobō, February and April 1974); Satō Atsushi and Watanabe Yasuo, *Jūmin sanka no jissen: jūmin shutai no gyōsei wa dō kokoromirareteiru ka* [The Practice of Residents' Participation: How Is Administration by the Residents Themselves Being Conducted?] (Tokyo: Gakuyō Shobō, March 1975). Possibly the best work in this group is Matsubara Haruo and Nitagai Kamon, *Jūmin undō no ronri: undō no tenkai katei, kadai to tembō* [The Logic of Residents' Movements: Developmental Process, Issues, and Prospects] (Tokyo: Gakuyō Shobō, January 1976). A more discursive work is Nakamura Kiichi, ed., *Jūmin undō "watakushi" ron* [The Theory of "Self" in Residents' Movements] (Tokyo: Gakuyō Shobō, August 1976). See also Nitagai Kamon, Ōmori Wataru, and Nagai Susumu, *Chiiki kaihatsu to jūmin undō* [Regional Development and Residents' Movements] (Tokyo: Fuji tekuno shisutemu, 1976). Finally, an article-length work is Kanagae Haruhike et al., "Jūmin undō no jisshōteki kenkyū: undō sankasha no bunseki wo chūshin to shite" [A Concrete Study of Residents' Movements: Through an Analysis of Participants in the Movements], *Tōkyō Daigaku Kyōiku gakubu: Kiyō* 15 (1975), 69–85, with a sequel in 16 (1976).

Three important works on the administrative response to citizens' movements are Satō Atsushi, *Tenkanki no chihō jichi: atarashii shimin to gyōsei no hōkō* [Local Self-Government in a Time of Transformation: New Directions in Citizens and Administration] (Tokyo: Gakuyō Shobō, April 1976); Takayose Shōzō, *Shimin jichi no toshi seisaku* [Urban Policy for Citizen Self-Government] (Tokyo: Gakuyō Shobō, July 1976); and Jichi Daigakkō Kenkyūbu, eds., *Jūmin sanka to gyōsei* [Residents' Participation and Administration] (Tokyo: Daiichi Hōki Shuppan, March 1976).

Two particularly useful periodicals whose recent issues have included excellent pieces on citizens' movements are *Chiiki kaihatsu* (the Japanese-language counterpart of *Area Development in Japan*), particularly issues 135 (1975), 136 (1976), and 154 (1977), the last of which is a special issue, "Chiiki kaihatsu to shakaiteki kinchō: sono riron" [A Theory of Regional Development and Social Strain], with articles by Yamamoto, Ōmori, Nakamura, Yasuhara, Satō, and Abe on *jūmin undō*; and *Local Government Review* (in English).

Index

Abortion, 135

Activists in citizens' movements, 126–162; age of, 128–129, 235; attitudes of, toward decision-making, 144–145; clusters of, 172–177, 186–187; education of, 127, 129, 235; knowledge and commitment of, to environmental issues, 138–142, 200; leaders of, 142–144, 146, 208–211; male and female roles of, 127–128; motivations of, 129–131, 138, 160, 162, 173, 186, 201–202; previous political experience of, 168–169, 172, 176, 187–188, 206–207, 209–210, 220, 229; recruitment of, 126–131, 228; socioeconomic status of, 129–130, 140, 141, 160, 161, 206; views of, on environmental problems, 131–142. *See also* Citizens' movements; Political attitudes of activists; Political participation by activists

Adachi, Yoshio, Mayor of Usuki, 83, 84; recall and reelection of, 86

Adult socialization, 232, 235. *See also* Socialization

AF-2 chemical agent, 70

Agano River, 54, 55

Age of environmental activists, 128–129, 235

Agriculture, 252; vs. industry, 93–94. *See also* Farmers

Aichi prefecture, 38, 39

Air pollution, 36, 92; asthma caused by, 60–61; and automatic compensation of pollution victims, 71; by automobiles, 116–117; causes of, 63; by cement factories, 85; by incineration of sludge, 118; standards for, 60

Airports, noise pollution caused by, 69

Almond, Gabriel A., 15, 175n

American environmental protection, compared to Japanese system, 33, 131, 135, 136–138, 141–142, 143, 255–260; and compensation of pollution victims, 73–74; and consumer demand, 133; litigation, 70–79; and regulation of economic activity, 256; size and scope of, 255–260; tactics, 257; and wilderness, 122–123

Anglo-American legal system, 44

Antifactory movement, 98–101

Designer: Al Burkhardt
Compositor: G&S Typesetters, Inc.
Printer: Thomson-Shore, Inc.
Binder: Thomson-Shore, Inc.
Text: Linotron 202 Sabon
Display: VIP Friz Quadrata
Cloth: Joanna Oxford 64450
Paper: 50 lb P&S Vellum B 32